RETRIEVING THE NATURAL LAW

A CRITICAL ISSUES IN BIOETHICS SERIES BOOK FROM

THE CENTER FOR
BI🌐ETHICS
AND HUMAN DIGNITY

This volume continues the Center's second series of bioethics books. Whereas every book in the Center's well-established Horizons in Bioethics Series brings together an array of insightful writers to address important bioethical issues from a forward-looking Christian perspective, volumes in the Critical Issues in Bioethics Series have a different purpose. Each of these volumes features one or two authors bringing Christian perspectives into dialogue with other perspectives that are particularly influential today. The first volume addresses the field of bioethics broadly, while subsequent books focus on particular topics such as end-of-life issues.

Both series are projects of The Center for Bioethics and Human Dignity, an international center located just north of Chicago, Illinois, in the United States of America. The Center endeavors to bring Christian perspectives to bear on today's many pressing bioethical challenges. It pursues this task by developing two book series, nine audio series, nine video series, numerous conferences in different parts of the world, and a variety of other printed and computer-based resources. Through its membership/support program, the Center networks and provides resources for people interested in bioethical matters all over the world. Members/supporters receive the Center's international journal, *Ethics and Medicine,* the Center's newsletter, *Dignity,* special Center communications, an Internet News Service, and discounts on all Center resources and events.

For more information on membership in the Center or its various resources, including present or future books in the Critical Issues in Bioethics Series, contact the Center at:

The Center for Bioethics and Human Dignity
2065 Half Day Road
Bannockburn, IL 60015 USA
Phone: (847) 317-8180
Fax: (847) 317-8101
E-mail: cbhd@cbhd.org

Information and ordering are also available through the Center's World Wide Web site on the Internet: www.cbhd.org

RETRIEVING THE NATURAL LAW

A Return to Moral First Things

J. Daryl Charles

WILLIAM B. EERDMANS PUBLISHING COMPANY

GRAND RAPIDS, MICHIGAN / CAMBRIDGE, U.K.

Published 2008 by
Wm. B. Eerdmans Publishing Co.
2140 Oak Industrial Drive N.E., Grand Rapids, Michigan 49505 /
P.O. Box 163, Cambridge CB3 9PU U.K.
www.eerdmans.com

Printed in the United States of America

12 11 10 09 08   7 6 5 4 3 2 1

Library of Congress Cataloging-in-Publication Data

Charles, J. Daryl, 1950-
Retrieving the natural law: a return to moral first things /
J. Daryl Charles.
p.   cm. — (Critical issues in bioethics series)
Includes bibliographical references.
ISBN 978-0-8028-2594-0 (pbk.: alk. paper)
1. Natural law. 2. Ethics.   I. Title.

K420.C33   2008
340′.112 — dc22

2007044579

Used in this book is the epilogue taken from *The Unformed Conscience of Evangelism* by J. Daryl Charles. © 2002 by J. Daryl Charles. Used with permission of InterVarsity Press, PO Box 1400, Downers Grove, IL 60515. www.ivpress.com

To Jesse and Ian,
beloved sons,
who helped make this volume possible

and

To Carl Braaten
whose theological reflections on the natural law
prompted me to rethink my theology of creation

Contents

Series Editors' Foreword

We live in an age when scientific knowledge has provided human beings with an unprecedented ability to manipulate life and death. In the West there has been a cultural shift from a so-called Judeo-Christian consensus to fragmented secular assumptions about the nature of human life, community, and "reproduction" as well as the practice of medicine and scientific research. There is little doubt that these changes in science and culture have fueled the controversies surrounding abortion, physician-assisted suicide, genetic engineering, the patient-doctor relationship, reproductive technologies, cloning, and the allocation of health-care resources, to name just a few.

Bioethics is the interdisciplinary study of these and other issues of life and health. It involves an attempt to discover normative guidelines built on sound moral foundations.

The purpose of this series is to bring thoughtful and biblically informed Christian voices in bioethics into dialogue with other voices that are influential today. As Christians we believe that human persons are made in the image of God and for that reason their lives are sacred. We also believe that God's entire creation was made for a purpose, and we discover this purpose from the Holy Scripture as well as philosophical reflections on the nature of things. Because we live in a pluralist society, we believe that it is our responsibility to explain why all people should take Christian perspectives into account. Such is the case not least because these perspectives have shaped so much of Western culture, especially its assumptions about human dignity. Accordingly, the books in this series will be useful to those who do not share our theological commitments. They can be read side by side with books espousing secular or other perspectives and are ideal for bioethics courses in nontheological as well as theological settings.

Because bioethics is theoretical as well as practical, the authors in this series are committed to providing a principled case for their perspectives as well as suggestions and insights on how scientists and/or health-care practitioners may employ these principles in a laboratory and/or clinical setting. In addition, we believe that pastors, students, professors, and others will profit from these books. C. S. Lewis warned of a future in which "Man's final conquest has proved to be the abolition of Man." The purpose of this series is to help forestall or even prevent such a future.

DENNIS HOLLINGER
President and Professor of Christian Ethics
Evangelical School of Theology

FRANCIS J. BECKWITH
Associate Professor of Philosophy and
Church-State Studies
Baylor University

CHAPTER ONE

Introduction

We all know lots of people; we all know lots of persons. Normally we use the term "persons" as a synonym for "human beings," people like us. However, we are also familiar with the idea that there are nonhuman persons, and humans who are not, or may not be[,] persons or full persons. . . . Human nonpersons or humans who are not fully fledged persons may include zygotes and embryos, or individuals who are "brain-dead," anencephalic infants, or individuals in a persistent vegetative state.

JOHN HARRIS[1]

If nonhumans turn out to possess significantly more advanced capacities than customarily envisioned, their moral standing would be upgraded to a more human level. However, this possibility remains speculative and may be less important than the thesis that because many humans lack properties of personhood or are less than full persons, they are thereby rendered equal or inferior in moral standing to some nonhumans. If this conclusion is defensible, we will need to rethink our traditional view that these unlucky humans cannot be treated in the ways we treat relevantly

1. John Harris, "The Concept of the Person and the Value of Life," *Kennedy Institute of Ethics Journal* 9, no. 4 (1999): 293.

similar nonhumans. For example, they might be aggressively used as human research subjects and sources of organs.

Том Beauchamp[2]

Taken in itself . . . membership of the human species is not morally relevant. . . . [W]hatever criteria [for personhood] we choose . . . we will have to admit that they do not follow precisely the boundary of our own species. . . . There will surely be some nonhuman animals whose lives, by any standard, are more valuable than the lives of some humans. A chimpanzee, a dog, or pig, for instance, will have a higher degree of self-awareness and a greater capacity for meaningful relations with others than a severely retarded infant or someone in a state of advanced senility.

Peter Singer[3]

Nonhuman persons. Unlucky humans. Not fully fledged persons. Nonhuman animals with greater worth than some humans. What does it mean to be a "person"? To be a "human being"? Correlatively, what does it mean to be a "nonhuman person"? What are "humans who are not . . . persons or full persons"? More importantly, *who decides? By what criteria?* And what are the implications of these distinctions for human civilization, civil society, and individual lives?

Related questions press upon us. What does it mean to have "moral standing"? What indeed is "moral standing"? Who receives it? By what measure and by what criteria is it conveyed? What are basic moral intuitions? Are all people endowed with these basic intuitions, with a basic

2. Tom L. Beauchamp, "The Failure of Theories of Personhood," *Kennedy Institute of Ethics Journal* 9, no. 4 (1999): 320.

3. Peter Singer, "Ethics and the New Animal Liberation Movement," in *Defence of Animals,* ed. Peter Singer (Oxford: Blackwell, 1985), 4, 19. Elsewhere, in *Practical Ethics* (London: Cambridge University Press, 1981), Singer writes: "Now it must be admitted that these arguments [in favor of abortion and infanticide] apply to the newborn animals whose rationality, self-consciousness, awareness, capacity to feel (sentience), and so on, exceed that of a human being a week, a month, or even a year old. If the fetus does not have the same claim to life as a person, it appears that the newborn baby is of less value than the life of a pig, a dog, or a chimpanzee" (118).

moral sense? Does a consensus about "moral standing" and about being "human" change with time and social location? Is "moral standing" fluid, different today than it was decades ago? Centuries ago? Does it vary with different cultures, societies, and people groups?

Such are by no means academic questions, even when celebrated academics are weighing in on these matters in rather breathtaking ways. Rather, they lie at the heart of civilized culture and are foundational in nature. And they confront us anew as we navigate the entrance to the twenty-first century. Without question, the last three decades have been witness to the breakup of any ethical consensus that heretofore may have existed in Western societies. Nowhere has this dissipation been more clearly on display than in the realm of bioethics.

Consider, for example, the viewpoint advanced by some 150 scientists, philosophers, and engineers at an August 2004 conference at the University of Toronto organized by the World Transhumanist Association (WTA). The WTA, birthed in 1998, consists of nearly three thousand members, most of them engineers, computer scientists, philosophers, and research scientists who seek to advance "a new paradigm for thinking about humankind's future." Transhumanists argue that we can and should attempt to "overcome all our biological limitations by means of reason, science and technology." Such technological freedom will be thought to "augment human intelligence, increase human strength and beauty, bring about sustainable mood enhancements, prolong life greatly and make it possible to leave the earth and explore and inhabit space."[4] At bottom, if science and technology are left unfettered, humankind can achieve an enhanced, "transhuman" future that can free us from the chains of pain, death, and being "human."[5]

In the past, people tended to speak of developments in the life sciences in terms of "medical ethics," based on the fact that there existed in our cultural context an ethical consensus regarding physical nature and

4. Bernard M. Daly, "Transhumanism: Toward a Brave New World?" *America*, October 25, 2004, 18.

5. While some of the sessions at the Toronto conference bordered on absurd — e.g., topics included "quantum miracles and immortality," "a kinematic cellular automata approach to building self-replicating nanomachines," and "posthuman prototypes debating their own design" — an announcement followed the conference that a team of researchers from Newcastle University had been issued a license in England to clone human embryos for therapeutic research purposes (Daly, "Transhumanism," 19).

human nature. The entrenchment of ideological or philosophical pluralism in our own day has given rise to moral pluralism, whereby it is now broadly assumed that there are no objective, fixed moral norms, no transcendent ethical standards, by which to judge situations and human behavior. Truth, a term typically placed in quotation marks, and ethics are understood to be multiple, perspectival, and relative to the society, situation, or context in which one finds oneself.

Merely on the basis of broader interest in ethical issues at the popular level and our cultural fascination with bioethical developments, it would be mistaken to conclude that a moral consensus in our own society is reemerging. Much to the contrary. This interest, it can be fairly said, is fueled in large part by advances in science and technology and, in not a few cases, economics. And while advances in behavioral science, medical science, and technology are by no means unique to our day, what *is* unique is the rapidity with which those advances are progressing. Our ability to forge ahead into previously unknown realms of knowledge and experimentation outstrips our ability to reflect ethically on those developments. Are these advances "humane"? "Natural"? In accordance with human nature?

For some, however, pausing to engage in ethical reflection, to ponder what it means to be authentically "human," is to ruin the party, as it were. Arthur Caplan, director of the Center for Bioethics at the University of Pennsylvania and founding president of the American Association of Bioethics, asks, "Will the degree of *philosophical angst* be such that we ought to rein in the speed at which medicine, and especially gene therapy, proceeds?" But the question appears to be rhetorical. "Hardly," is his confident reply. "If being human means using intelligence to improve the quality of life, *there is little basis for ethical ambivalence or doubt* about eliminating genetic scourges. . . . Changing our biological blueprints in pursuit of longer, healthier lives should ideally pose *no more of a threat than does taking impurities out of the water supply* to protect human health."[6]

A committed metaphysical materialist, Caplan is clearly put off by the intrusion of moral considerations that slow down human progress. Like the cannibalistic chief, he is convinced that Christianity spoils our feasts. "Despite these rosy prospects [stemming from gene therapy in the

6. Arthur Caplan, "An Improved Future?" *Scientific American*, September 1995, 143, emphasis added.

womb and genetic manipulation] for increasing a person's chance of being born healthy and living longer, many in the ethics guild — which is inclined to hand-wringing — wear frowns today," he laments.[7] How might medical or bioethical advance look in Caplan's amoral society? "Treatment with designer drugs made to order for these problems [chronic schizophrenia, severe depression, or extreme substance abuse], with microchip implants that release chemicals into the body or perhaps with virtual-reality therapy, in which patients find relief from their condition in a computer-generated fantasy world, may well prove far less costly [yet productive]." The logic of changing our biological blueprint would also extend "to the most awe-inspiring option that will ultimately be available: the genetic modification of reproductive, or germ, cells. . . . Germ-cell therapy permanently changes the human gene pool, but the benefits of forever eliminating diseases such as spina bifida, anencephaly, hemophilia and muscular dystrophy would seem to make germ-cell gene therapy a *moral obligation*."[8]

Note the language of "moral obligation" used here. We are not told what moral values require "obligation" on our part, nor are we informed that both promise *and* peril attend modifying the human genetic blueprint. But we can be certain of one thing, namely, that anyone who resists these brave new technological advances is surely a Luddite. And we can reasonably wonder if, in time, it will be our *moral obligation* to design our own babies.

To attempt to bring ethical reflection to bear on the breathtaking technological advances of our day, and the ethical dilemmas they present, is to incur the wrath of many in our society. It is to reveal, at bottom, a fundamental clash between worldviews, between competing visions of *moral reality and human nature*. Caplan's perspective on life has a Promethean quality; it views moral considerations and restraints as impediments to advancement and progress. Any moral considerations remain nebulous and unspecified, if in fact they exist at all. The view of human nature that is genuinely annoying to Caplan and others is that which understands life to be an *endowment*. Because human beings are endowed by "nature and nature's God," because it is "natural" for human beings to act in accordance with their nature as created beings, life has a profoundly sa-

---

7. Caplan, "An Improved Future?" 142.
8. Caplan, "An Improved Future?" 143, emphasis added.

cred cast and therefore must be treated with reverence and a sense of stewardship.

Precisely on this account of human nature as an endowment, the abiding question confronting us on a continual basis in a cultural climate that disdains making moral judgments is not so much "*Can* something be done?" as "*Should* it be done, and *on what basis?*"

In his important 1993 book *The Moral Sense,* James Q. Wilson describes with considerable insight the enormous resistance from contemporary society that we encounter in our attempts at moral formation and pursuing what is virtuous. Surely Wilson does not overstate the matter in describing the extent of resistance culturally that characterizes our current moral state of affairs. Science has told us that morality is the realm of opinion or the emotions, since reality is material. Anthropologists have told us that morality is entirely the product of society; thus, a human being has no "nature" apart from his culture. Philosophers tell us — with increasing certitude, mind you — that there is no epistemological foundation for making moral judgments. And legal theorists tell us that law has no moral foundation in a widely shared sense of what is just and unjust; it is rather only arbitrary enactment of political power. Consequently, in present-day culture one must speak the wider cultural code of "values" rather than risk offending others by utilizing categories of "right and wrong," "good and evil," or virtue and vice. To do otherwise is to bear the mark of Cain, as it were, by committing the cardinal sin of "judgmentalism" — secularism's equivalent of blasphemy.[9]

But what precisely do we mean by "values"? Wilson captures the tentativeness with which Americans approach the subject, since the word "values" finesses all the tough questions. For most people, their fear of appearing "intolerant" makes them "shun any appearance of imposing their philosophical orientation or religious convictions upon others. But beneath that tolerance there lurks among many of us a worrisome uncertainty — some of us doubt that we have a defensible philosophy or credible conviction that we would want to impose."[10]

To insist on making moral judgments, then, is to be profoundly out of step with the spirit of the age. But we discover, alas, that *we all* do in fact

---

9. See Wilson's very lucid depiction in his introduction to James Q. Wilson, *The Moral Sense* (New York: Free Press, 1993).

10. James Q. Wilson, *The Moral Sense,* xi.

make judgments that are moral in nature. That is, all of us make moral discriminations as to what we will tolerate and what we will not. All people, at all times and in all places, make moral judgments; they simply draw the line between acceptable and unacceptable at different places and use different criteria.

On Making Moral Judgments:
The Disappearance of Good and Evil

Given the prevailing cultural climate, how does society tend to approach the pressing ethical issues of our day, whether euthanasia, human embryo research, cloning, stem cell research, in vitro fertilization, or genetic enhancement, to say nothing of crime, poverty, war, divorce, and human sexuality? Typically, contemporary discussions of ethics — where they are tolerated — and bioethical debates, in particular, aim at "balancing" the social and medical benefits over against any perceived ethical considerations. However, as Richard Doerflinger, associate director of the Secretariat for Pro-Life Activities of the U.S. Catholic Conference of Bishops, has warned, it is unwise to attempt to "balance" ethics and medical-scientific advance, for this would mean that one can pursue even research and practice that are known to be unethical *if in practice the potential medical or economic benefit were deemed great enough.*[11]

While society's — and the Christian community's — obligation to work to alleviate suffering is important and must be acknowledged, this "obligation" has no inherent moral limitations. Rather, it is a generic good, subject to no specific moral restraints or markers, and therefore needs to be qualified. By contrast, the negative obligation not to harm, not to demean human life, based on human beings' inherent dignity, not only is equally valid as the goal of alleviating suffering but also guides us in ways that are specific, tangible, and inviolable. Respecting this obligation requires that we draw the line in specific ways as to what may *not* be done to human beings.[12]

11. Richard M. Doerflinger, "Confronting Technology at the Beginning of Life," in *Human Dignity in the Biotech Century: A Christian Vision for Public Policy,* ed. Charles W. Colson and Nigel M. de S. Cameron (Downers Grove, Ill.: InterVarsity, 2004), 221-39.

12. Not surprisingly, preserving human dignity has been a resounding and abiding

How *does* society regulate what is ethical and unethical, acceptable versus unacceptable, enhancing of rather than harmful to human life? If we are to believe most academic and behavioral theorists, there are no fixed norms by which to "judge" behavior. Morality, as it turns out, is a social construction, a cultural-geographical coincidence, dependent on and reflective of those values emanating from a particular society or people group. Because we must think and speak in the plural, i.e., in terms of multiple "moralities" rather than a fixed, binding morality that governs all people, to "judge" people and their behavior is deemed altogether unfashionable — indeed, intolerable. Thus, we are admonished ad nauseam to tolerate all things — even the intolerable — in the name of tolerance, of course.

Given the hegemony of "tolerance" in contemporary life, Americans are accustomed to adopting any number of mind-bogglingly creative strategies in order to avoid naming good and evil, and therefore, confronting the latter. Creativity and ingenuity, after all, are hallmarks of American life. As Americans we are truly awash in victimhood, exoneration, plea bargaining, and immunity from wrongdoing. In the end, *no one* — at least, no one *alive!* — in our culture can be found guilty.

One common method of exculpation, of course, is to deny that evil exists.[13] Such is not merely the province of Eastern pantheistic religion; it is also the domain of metaphysical materialists, agnostics, and nihilists. If life is no more than the reorganization and shuffling of molecules, then there is no need to account for the "spiritual-psychological" dimension of human experience. Free will, depraved intention, catastrophic evil, and egregious human rights violations — all are to be explained away in a universe that subsists only of matter. Evil, alas, *cannot be permitted* to exist. As is vividly dramatized in Albert Camus's intriguing novel *The Plague,* an allegorical tale depicting the psychology of emergent tyranny, evil as a concept is not allowed to inhabit the minds of men.[14] Notwithstanding the fact that rats are overrunning the city of Oran, its citizens have convinced

---

theme in the encyclicals of John Paul II. See especially *Veritatis Splendor (The Splendor of Truth)* and *Evangelium Vitae (The Gospel of Life).*

13. I am indebted to the very helpful taxonomy of cultural denial that is set forth by social critic Dennis Prager in "Why Aren't People Preoccupied with Good and Evil?" *Ultimate Issues* 7, no. 2 (1991): 6-9.

14. Camus writes, "A novel is never anything but a philosophy expressed in images" (*Albert Camus: Lyrical and Critical Essays,* ed. Philip Thody [New York: Vintage, 1970], 199).

themselves that these vermin in fact do not exist. Why? Because they *may not* exist. Just as Western intellectuals and journalists in the 1930s and 1940s praised Joseph Stalin as "progressive" and denied that his reign was one of terror (and indeed denied that a famine in the Ukraine was taking the lives of five to ten million people), there are those today who would deny that a Jewish Holocaust took place, that genocide has occurred in several parts of the world between 1995 and 2005, that Christians (read: non-Muslims) in parts of Muslim Africa are being led into forced slavery, that the unborn possess personhood, and that crime is a moral decision.

At the intellectual level, a "scientific" justification, of course, for the view that evil does not exist lies in biology and Darwinian assumptions about life. That is, the "moral sense" — to use James Q. Wilson's vocabulary — evolves over time within human beings and possesses a foremost adaptive trait. Unlike Wilson, however, most neo-Darwinians find it difficult to explain the presence in human beings of moral sentiments such as empathy, kindness, generosity, and magnanimity.[15] Darwinians would fol-

---

15. James Q. Wilson, *The Moral Sense*, xi-xiii. Perhaps the most helpful part of this volume is the cultural critique found in the book's introduction. Wilson's thesis is not without its problems, however. One is the starting point for "the moral sense," i.e., evolutionary theory, which fails to lead the way out of the contemporary crisis in ethics. In 1985 Wilson coauthored, with Richard Herrnstein, *Crime and Human Nature* (New York: Simon and Schuster, 1985). In this vein, readers might also remember the controversial 1994 book *The Bell Curve* (New York: Free Press), coauthored by Herrnstein and Charles Murray, which examined the relationship between crime, various social pathologies, unemployment, family status, and IQ. At bottom, Wilson is unable to ground "the moral sense" in something that transcends mere intuitions, which he calls "feelings." These intuitions, he argues, begin developing "at an early age" about "how one ought to act when one is free to act voluntarily." For Wilson, the "moral sense" expresses itself in four characteristic feelings or ways: sympathy, fairness, self-control, and duty (*The Moral Sense*, 40-45, 70, 82, 100-101). Paul Knepper, professor of criminal justice at East Carolina University, believes that Wilson's argument, based on its assumptions that are indebted to evolutionary psychology and biology, is "hopelessly tautological." To say that moral intuitions reflect biological processes at work, as Wilson does, is "to say that there is a certain inevitability about human nature" from within based on biology, an assumption Knepper rejects. In pursuing a biological basis for moral judgment, Wilson mistakenly reduces qualities of human behavior to animalistic tendencies and "blind forces" (Paul Knepper, *Explaining Criminal Conduct: Theories and Systems in Criminology* [Durham, N.C.: Carolina Academic Press, 2001], 93-97). Also critical of Wilson's presuppositions is J. Budziszewski, *Written on the Heart: The Case for Natural Law* (Downers Grove, Ill.: InterVarsity, 1997), 212-18. Rightly, in my view, Budziszewski takes Wilson to task for employing the language of "feelings" and sentiment over against moral rules

9

low suit. The most that one might be able to argue is that our genetic "nature" prepares us as humans, through endless adaptation, to live civilly, morally, and empathetically. But why some people are civil, moral, and empathetic and others are not is not so readily explained. Merely to posit that some individuals have the corresponding genes for that predilection and some do not is hardly sufficient. That seems like a theory in search of a justification as opposed to a legitimate explanation that fits the evidence. Criminologist Paul Knepper well expresses the dilemma for the biological determinist: "To say that moral ideas reflect biological processes at work in the natural world is to say that there is a certain inevitability about human nature. If moral judgments are inborn within the human species, they simply *are*. There is [therefore] *no need to convince a person programmed genetically with a moral sense to pursue moral judgment*."[16] In fact, if biological determinism solely or best explains human "nature," then "there is no point in trying to bring about [much less, refine] other political systems because they would be unsuited for people."[17]

Writing over fifty years ago, C. S. Lewis fully expected that someday society would abolish punishment per se while at the same time viewing religion as neurotic. Both crime and religious conviction would be treated as a mental health disorder. Treatment, of course, would be "humanitarian" and therapeutic in nature. With the ascendancy of determinism and scientific technique in his own day, Lewis foresaw the eclipse of rationality and moral agency. (What he did *not* yet see in his day was the "triumph of the therapeutic" that has come to fruition in the last forty years.)[18] Lewis, it should be recalled, was writing precisely at the time B. F. Skinner was trumpeting, "If man is free, then a technology of behavior is

or "laws." Indeed, there is no *ought*, no obligatory behavior, *without* the existence of some rule or "law."

Criticisms of Wilson's book notwithstanding (criticisms that are exceedingly warranted), few people have contributed as much to national debates over crime, criminology, and civil society as Wilson, who, after chairing the White House Task Force on Crime in 1966, taught political science at Harvard for almost three decades before receiving an appointment at UCLA as James Collins Professor of Management and Public Policy. Wilson currently serves as the Ronald Reagan Professor of Public Policy at Pepperdine University.

16. Knepper, *Explaining Criminal Conduct*, 94.

17. Knepper, *Explaining Criminal Conduct*, 95.

18. See Philip Rieff, *The Triumph of the Therapeutic: Uses of Faith after Freud* (New York: Harper and Row, 1966), and Paul C. Vitz, *Psychology as Religion: The Cult of Self-Worship* (Grand Rapids: Eerdmans, 1977 [1995]).

impossible. . . . I deny that freedom exists at all. I must deny it — or my program would be absurd."[19]

In the end, for the metaphysical naturalist "evil" is no longer a *moral* entity if in fact human behavior is biologically determined.[20] For if behavior is established in a person's genetic makeup, there is, effectively, nothing that can be done about it. The naturalist can say only, at best, that moral sentiments that are present are unintended, arbitrary, and meaningless expressions of blind, genetic forces, and at worst, that evil does not exist, since behavior is (biologically) inevitable. Good and evil — and the tragedy that accompanies evil — are meaningful only against the backdrop of a moral standard (a "law") that transcends biology. And no one (really) can make moral judgments, be virtuous, or distinguish between "better" and "worse," since there is no such thing as a "moral judgment" or "moral standard" that exists independently, by which meaningful and enduring comparison can be made.[21]

Another strategy, short of denying evil, is to regulate it, that is, to reduce it to manageable proportions. A critique of this tendency was offered by the late senator Daniel Patrick Moynihan (New York) in a much-ballyhooed essay in the *American Scholar*. Moynihan sought to expose in the American mind-set the moral calculus he called "defining deviancy down."[22] Social evil and aberrant behavior, Moynihan observed, dare not be found to reach outlandish proportions and thereby cause a cultural stigma. But, what to do, should things reach epidemic levels? The answer is to redefine what constitutes normal and abnormal, acceptable and unacceptable. Thus, for example, rather than suffer the embarrassment of acknowledging staggering levels of criminal deviancy and hold people ac-

---

19. B. F. Skinner, *Walden Two* (New York: Macmillan, 1948), 213, 242.

20. On the ascendancy of biology in our day and the implications for moral accountability, see further discussion in chapter 5.

21. This is the dilemma of sociobiology, notwithstanding the grand assertions of E. O. Wilson — so, for example, his brimming confidence in *Sociobiology: The New Synthesis* (Cambridge: Harvard University Press, 2000), 129: "A science of sociobiology, if coupled with neurophysiology, might transform the insights of ancient religions into a precise account of the evolutionary origin of ethics and hence explain the reasons why we make certain moral choices."

22. See Daniel Patrick Moynihan, "Defining Deviancy Down," *American Scholar,* Winter 1993, 17-30. The flip side of this moral phenomenon was shortly thereafter articulated by Charles Krauthammer; see his essay "Defining Deviancy Up," *New Republic* 209, no. 21 (November 22, 1993): 20-25.

countable for their behavior, as a society we simply redefine, through psychosociological and economic analyses, what we deem "aberrant" behavior. In this way we conveniently — and painlessly — make society "safer" and criminal behavior less frequent.[23]

This sort of adjusting of numbers or redefining terms that minimize evil need not however be the exclusive domain of those in the social sciences. A notable example was supplied some years ago by the Anglican archbishop Desmond Tutu. Upon visiting Yad Vashem, the Israeli memorial dedicated to the six million Jews who were murdered in the Holocaust, Tutu declared that what he saw reminded him of the black experience in South Africa.[24] Did any in his audience pause? Unjust as apartheid was, it is no overstatement to say with one Jewish social commentator that "any one of the six million Jews would have prayed to be a victim of apartheid rather than of the Nazi genocide."[25]

Where denying evil or minimizing it is not employed, an effective exculpatory device is that of moral equivalence. So, for example, Hiroshima and the Jewish Holocaust bleed into one another and become morally indistinguishable. As do both former superpowers — the Soviet Union and the United States — who were thought to be equal threats to the world's peace. As do both militant jihadic Islam and American "imperialism," the latter being particularly noxious for its attempts to create stability in a historically unstable and nondemocratic cultural context characterized by egregious human rights violations. This tactic, it goes without saying, can be applied at any level to all types of action and has the benefit of being extremely elastic and elusive. For when nothing is ethically better than anything else, good and evil blend into one another.

Yet another ploy is perhaps, in a post-consensus culture, the strata-

23. Of course, another way of reducing evil to manageable proportions is to limit evil to a few select cases in history — e.g., to Mao, Stalin, Hitler, Idi Amin, Pol Pot, Jeffrey Dahmer, etc. — thereby removing the scourge of human depravity from the human heart to an outrageous few instances in human history.

24. Similar comments by Tutu were issued publicly again in the *Guardian*, Monday, April 29, 2002, in a column titled "Apartheid in the Holy Land," wherein Tutu makes comparisons between the Holocaust and the present-day plight of Palestinians. Tutu laments that Jews have a "monopoly" on the Holocaust. See www.guardian.co.uk/israel/comment/0,10551,706901,00.html. It will perhaps be remembered as well that Tutu urged Israelis "to forgive the Nazis for the Holocaust" — comments that appeared in the *Jerusalem Post*, December 31, 1989.

25. Prager, "Why?" 7.

gem of choice. Given the ascendancy of tolerance as the cardinal virtue of our time, an extremely effective maneuver by which to silence the public expression of religious or moral conviction is to accuse people of judgmentalism. This tool, though more subtle than related totalitarian tactics, has a powerful psychological effect on the populace, since it plays on people's self-perception, in the end paralyzing them in the face of genuine moral evil. While religious and nonreligious people find recourse in this method, particularly effective is the citing of Jesus' words from Matthew 7:1, "Do not judge, or you too will be judged" (NIV).

To be accused of judgmentalism in American culture these days is worse than to be branded a murderer. After all, suspected manslayers at least can find exculpation in a tragic childhood, high blood-sugar levels, or the cruel biological joke of a "violent gene." But let us pause to reflect just for a moment. Is judging indeed *not* to be tolerated? Is "judging" inherently unjust? Is moral judgment impermissible? Or is it perhaps just possible (God forbid) that human beings are actually capable of doing such in a correct and just manner? Or, are we consigned always and eternally to be "open-minded" and "tolerant," careful to offend no one as we live out our lives?

An important, though rudimentary, distinction to be made, as political ethicist Jean Elshtain reminds us, is the difference between prejudice and judgment. Judgment, rightly construed, is to "call things by their real names."[26] Thus, moral judgment is predicated on our ability to discern between good and evil, just and unjust, hypocritical and authentic — and to call them each accordingly. In the end, empathy and "open-mindedness" — healthy attitudes when qualified but prostituted by a "therapeutic culture" that refuses to assume or inculcate moral self-responsibility — are not enough. Feeling good, having a bloated self-esteem, and wallowing in pseudovictimhood utterly negate a culture's ability to do good, be morally accountable, and come to the aid of real victims. Jesus' anger, lest we miss the lesson of the biblical text, is aimed at hypocritical religion and vindictiveness; the Son of Man is not calling for the elimination of moral judgment, even when Psychological Man does.[27]

26. Jean Bethke Elshtain, "Judge Not?" in *The Moral Life: An Introductory Reader in Ethics and Literature*, ed. Louis J. Pojman (New York and Oxford: Oxford University Press, 2004), 195.

27. Sociologist Philip Rieff used the descriptors "moral man" and "psychological man" to describe American culture before and since the "triumph of the therapeutic" (*The Triumph of the Therapeutic*).

The Law Written on the Heart

But we must return to the previous question: How *is* society to regulate what is morally acceptable and unacceptable? What in fact constitutes "civil society," wherein people work for the common good and seek to preserve the moral-social order, based on the conviction of "permanent things"? Historic Christian theology affirms a very distinct view of the universe and the place of moral reasoning. Saint Paul, in Romans 1 and 2, uses the language of the created order — the *cosmos* — and human *conscience*. External *and* interior witnesses work together in harmony as those instruments by which all people intuit what is good and evil, just and unjust. Deep within human consciousness people discover a "law" — a "law written on the heart" (Rom. 2:15) — they have not created themselves yet are constrained to obey, even when, in theory, they reject it. The essential character of the Creator expresses itself through this consciousness in human beings, who as moral agents mirror the image or likeness of the Creator (Gen. 1:26-27; 9:6). That all people possess a basic knowledge is affirmed by Saint Paul insofar as God's invisible attributes "have been clearly seen" and "understood," whereby the apostle can maintain that all "know God" (Rom 1:20-21). This voice summons them to avoid evil, to respect the good, and to esteem their neighbor. While awareness of this moral "law" comes to full expression through Christian faith, it is not relegated purely to the realm of religious faith; all people, notes Saint Paul, are morally "without excuse" insofar as they possess a basic knowledge about themselves, about their Creator, and about moral accountability. The "moral law," then, is intuited by all, just as wisdom is universal and accessible to all, regardless of location in human history. The nature and substance of this moral law — this "law of nature" or "law of oughtness"[28] — will be treated in the chapters to come.

When we speak of "natural law," most Americans think immediately of the early 1990s and one of the more entertaining political dramas of our time. Peter Steinfels, writing in the *New York Times*, expressed the bafflement of so many of our contemporaries: "One of the more curious displays of cultural illiteracy has been the consternation . . . created by Judge Clarence Thomas's expression of esteem for 'natural law.' For some of the critics of the nominee to the Supreme Court, it was as though the man had let slip

---

28. These expressions are used by C. S. Lewis in chapter 1 of *Mere Christianity*, rev. ed. (New York: Macmillan, 1960), 15-39.

a reference to torture by thumbscrews. Others squinted as though Judge Thomas disclosed an obscure and probably sinister belief in alchemy."[29]

And so it was. Who could forget the Clarence Thomas hearings, with their vividly packaged double drama of Anita Hill, on the one hand, seeking to present Judge Thomas in an unfavorable light, and more substantively on the other hand, the reaction by the Senate Judiciary Committee, Joseph Biden presiding, to Judge Thomas's affirmation of "natural law"? Doubtless, Christian exponents of natural-law theory — from the early Christian fathers to Thomas Aquinas to Luther and Calvin to John Courtney Murray — rolled over in their graves.

Whether Hill or Biden provided the greater entertainment we will leave for historians — or television critics — to decide. Nevertheless, Senator Biden's grilling of Thomas was supremely instructive for several reasons, not least of which was his mirroring of a secularized — and thus, prostituted — understanding of natural law. The fact that Judge Thomas was indebted to a more classical understanding of natural law, an understanding that assumes and seeks to respect the moral foundations of law and politics, was supremely vexing — and in the end, unacceptable — to Senator Biden. The result was the senator from Delaware, a Catholic, waxing rather self-righteous as he proceeded to lecture both Thomas and the American public that natural law is a "dangerous doctrine."

Not a little distortion surfaced in Biden's either/or formulation before the Senate Judiciary Committee — i.e., natural law is either a "moral code" (to be eschewed) or a protector of individual freedoms (read, "choice,"[30] which is to be venerated). As Russell Hittinger aptly stated in the aftermath of the hearings, Christians in search of a public moral discourse quickly realized that they no longer lived in the age of Jefferson or Lincoln. Something indeed had degraded "natural law" discussions in the public arena.[31] The either/or sleight of hand on display in Senator Biden's performance was not lost on one social commentator, who pointed out somewhat wryly that it is convenient for naysayers to see "common morality" as the surreptitious smuggling of dogma into the political debate, where it is exceedingly un-

29. Peter Steinfels, "Natural Law Collides with the Laws of Politics in the Squabble over a Supreme Court Nominee," *New York Times*, August 17, 1991, A8.

30. The freedom to "choose," for Biden, was restricted to two critically important issues in the political arena: abortion and sexuality.

31. Russell Hittinger, *The First Grace: Rediscovering the Natural Law in a Post-Christian World* (Wilmington, Del.: ISI Books, 2003), 36, 65-66.

welcome.[32] As James Skillen, director of the Center for Public Justice, rightly noted at the time of the Thomas hearings, the either/or dualism presented by Senator Biden was simply a false dichotomy, for

> if the issue at stake in appealing to natural law is to find a standard by which to judge what is just or unjust, then natural law cannot be reduced to individual freedom and still be natural law. For Sen. Biden to prefer a standard that essentially leaves "matters to individual choice" is to drain all meaning from the very idea of natural law. If one holds that the "higher law" for government is simply individual freedom, then the appropriate word for that "philosophy" is "anarchy" [and] not "natural" or another kind of law.[33]

What Senator Biden was reacting against was Judge Thomas's insinuation that there are "moral predicates"[34] — viz., good and evil, justice and injustice — that undergird all law. However, Biden was simply mirroring what theorists for the last one hundred years, in the form of legal positivism, have understood and imported into their understanding of legal theory and "natural law." The positivist position holds that the state, as a collection of equally autonomous wills, establishes law qua law.[35] Since there is no accountability to a "higher" law or authority, the positivist approach to legal theory is bleached of any metaphysical or moral analysis.[36]

---

32. Ralph McInerny, "Commonsense Ethics" (an online review of *What We Can't Not Know,* by J. Budziszewski), published by the Claremont Institute at www.claremont.org/writings/crb/spring2004/mcinerny.html.

33. James W. Skillen, "Natural Law and the Foundations of Government," *Public Justice Report* (November 1991), also available at www.cpjustice.org/stories/storyReader$1012.

34. This expression is from Russell Hittinger's introduction to *The Natural Law: A Study in Legal and Social History and Philosophy,* by Heinrich A. Rommen, trans. T. R. Hanley (Indianapolis: Liberty Fund, 1998), xiii.

35. Representative of the legal positivist position are H. L. A. Hart, "Positivism and the Separation of Law and Morals," *Harvard Law Review* 71 (1958): 593-629; Hart, *The Concept of Law* (Oxford: Clarendon, 1961); Ronald Dworkin, "The Illusive Morality of Law," *Villanova Law Review* 10 (1965): 631-39; Dworkin, "Philosophy, Morality, and Laws," *University of Pennsylvania Law Review,* 1965, 668-90; Lon Fuller, "Positivism: Fidelity to Law," *Harvard Law Review* 71 (1958): 630-72; and Fuller, *The Morality of Law,* rev. ed. (New Haven and London: Yale University Press, 1969).

36. By way of illustration, recall Laurence Tribe's warning, at the time of the Clarence Thomas hearings, in 1991, against "moralistic intrusions on personal choice" ("'Natural Law' and the Nominee," *New York Times,* July 15, 1991, A15). The positivist, historicist, cultural rel-

It assumes that law is *constructed* rather than *discovered* or *preserved*. Legal positivists, because they deny a transcendent source of law, place justification for law in the social-political realm. Because there is no authority beyond human experience and outside of human willpower that informs and guides human morality, human "rights" are subjectively identified and culturally based, since there is no universally determinate "human nature."[37] The implication, though not explicit among positivists, is that human rights cannot exist where society does not acknowledge them. Thus, for the positivist, law and rights are always and everywhere contingent, dependent upon context and "the will of the people."[38]

Notwithstanding the historical fact that the notions of natural law and natural rights — as "self-evident truths" in accord with "the Laws of Nature and Nature's God"[39] — were foundational to the thinking of our nation's founders (and arguably, in its "refounding" in the 1860s),[40] American legal theorists in the twentieth century have been more concerned to understand and interpret law in the light of sociological and political considerations.[41] Simply stated, for the positivist, law is made, not discovered. Law so conceived becomes a tool for social and political "transformation" (or, more bluntly, revolution) rather than the vehicle by which to (a) preserve the common good, (b) serve our fellow human be-

---

ativist, and deconstructionist all share a denial or rejection of universal moral standards, and thus of natural-law assumptions. The world therefore is to be understood in terms of ideological pluralism; there can be no claims to truth in an objective sense.

37. Of course, the argument based on autonomy and "choice" was critical to preserving abortion rights, as Senate Majority Leader George Mitchell, who gave the closing speech prior to Thomas's confirmation vote, made perfectly clear. His comments appeared in the *New York Times,* October 16, 1991, A12.

38. Robert P. George has stated the contradiction of the positivist position quite lucidly, of which Senator Biden was merely, and dimly, representative: "Any serious student of civil rights must inquire into moral ground and epistemic status of civil rights. Is the mode of existence of civil rights *simply* historically contingent and conventional? That is, do civil rights come into being merely at some specific time and place, and then possibly disappear as 'history' or experience unfolds?" (*The Clash of Orthodoxies: Law, Religion, and Morality in Crisis* [Wilmington, Del.: ISI Books, 2001], 154).

39. Paragraph 1 of *The Declaration of Independence.*

40. So Hittinger, introduction, xv.

41. A critical figure in this recent history is Supreme Court Justice Oliver Wendell Holmes, whose intent was to call into question, through "enlightened skepticism," the objective basis of law as well as the link between law and morality. See, notably, his essay "The Path of the Law," *Harvard Law Review* 10 (1897): 359-469.

ings, and (c) mirror transcendent moral norms that explain "the way things are."

Retrieving Natural Law and Preserving Civil Society

Not long after the Clarence Thomas hearings, another perspective on natural law came forth, from a very different source. While in its presentation it lacked the theatrics of Senator Biden, it represented the consensus of mainstream moral thinking through the ages and did so with utmost moral clarity. John Paul II sought to emphasize, our protestations notwithstanding, that there are absolute (i.e., unchanging) truths that allow us, regardless of our placement in human history, to identify evil and good. During his pontificate, and particularly in his papal encyclicals that spanned the 1990s, John Paul continually reminded us that individual liberty is only meaningful in the context of an ordered society, and that political liberty — that rare and delicate treasure sought the world over — is rendered impossible when moral and social order collapses. This emphasis comes notably to the fore in John Paul's 1993 encyclical *Veritatis Splendor (The Splendor of Truth)*. Therein he observed that a denial of objective moral truth reduces law to the function of raw, totalitarian power. The former pope's cultural commentary is all the more significant and lucid, given that in his own lifetime he was intimately acquainted with totalitarian society.

In his important social encyclical *Centesimus Annus*, John Paul pointed out a present-day tendency that should give us pause: it is the assumption

> that agnosticism and skeptical relativism are the philosophy and . . . basic attitude which correspond to democratic forms of political rule. Those who are convinced that they know the truth and firmly adhere to it are considered unreliable from a democratic point of view, since they do not accept that truth is determined by the majority, or that it is subjected to variation according to different political trends. It must be observed in this regard that if there is no ultimate truth to guide and direct political activity, then ideas and convictions can easily be manipulated for reasons of power.[42]

42. *Centesimus Annus,* no. 34.

What precisely is it in the democratic context, he asks, that lies at the heart of this contemporary social-political transformation? The great idolatry of our time, as he sees it, is the prostitution of contemporary notions of "freedom" and the attempt to set freedom in opposition to truth, indeed to separate the two radically.[43] Thus, "giving himself over to relativism and skepticism . . . [man] goes off in search of an illusory freedom apart from truth itself."[44] In John Paul's thought, political philosophy is dependent on moral philosophy insofar as it draws upon a particular view of human nature. If there is nothing universal in the moral nature of humankind, if there is no natural law, then, to recall Thomas Aquinas's argument, "whatever the prince wills *is* the law."[45] At which point politics truly becomes "war by other means," *all things* become permissible, and we are confronted with the problem posed by C. S. Lewis in *The Abolition of Man*. In his own day Lewis perceived what Christian moral thinkers through the ages have enunciated, namely, that natural law and human civilization are closely connected. When the human soul is disordered, virtue collapses. And when human communities and cultures are disordered, they collapse. At the most rudimentary level, soulcraft and statecraft correspond.

But we digress. Let us return to the burden of *Veritatis Splendor*. The encyclical was not intended to be a jeremiad, projecting apocalyptic doom and gloom. Therein John Paul reminds us that the natural law corresponds to a way of living, a quest to live virtuously and with the good of the community in mind. To honor the natural law is to live according to rightly ordered reason and in accordance with "self-evident" truths. These realities express the "higher political philosophy of the Founding Fathers" that Clarence Thomas had acknowledged even prior to his confirmation hearings. Natural-law philosophy, as Thomas saw it, represented "the best defense" of liberty, limited government, and judicial process.[46]

While for much of Christian history "natural law" has been affirmed as a central component of general revelation accessible to all people (and thus bridges Christian faith and surrounding culture), in more recent times natural law has been almost exclusively the province of Roman

---

43. *Centesimus Annus*, no. 88.

44. *Centesimus Annus*, no. 1.

45. *Summa Theologiae* I-II Q. 90, a. 1 (objection 3).

46. Clarence Thomas, "The Higher Law Background of the Privileges or Immunities Clause of the Fourteenth Amendment," *Harvard Journal of Law and Public Policy* 63 (1989): 63-64.

Catholic moral theology. Protestants have been generally averse to acknowledge any form of "natural theology" or philosophical grounding of the natural-law tradition. Why is this? Several reasons might be cited — reasons that shall need further unpacking in a subsequent chapter.

One is the general philosophical approach to moral reasoning in the nineteenth and twentieth centuries that is peculiarly (though by no means exclusively) Protestant in nature. This Protestant rationalism, which drinks deeply from the assumptions of Enlightenment thinking, has rendered Protestant social ethics particularly susceptible to moral relativism and theological pluralism. Authoritative Roman Catholic moral theology,[47] by contrast, can be understood in terms of its interaction with and indebtedness to classical theology and philosophy — primarily in the Augustinian and Thomist tradition — that together have informed the broader Western cultural tradition in unmistakable ways.[48] While the Protestant reformers did not negate this tradition, their emphasis was to correct perceived late-medieval theological and ecclesiastical deficiencies.

Protestant thought of the last two hundred years might be best understood against the backdrop of several theological and philosophical tendencies. On the one hand, existentialism and historicism have undermined attempts to posit — and develop the implications of — any universally binding principles of morality that might guide theological ethics.[49] Each of these tendencies radically calls into question the very possibility of rational knowledge of a universal moral order. The lingering effects of historicist and existentialist thinking are such that one is at a loss to identify Protestant theologians or ethicists who have developed or defended the philosophical basis for natural law.[50] A residue of this sort of bias —

47. This is by no means to suggest that all "moral theology" that goes by the name "Catholic" is orthodox.

48. That this debt is greatly diminished and less and less acknowledged in our day does not negate this basic cultural fact.

49. James M. Gustafson, *Protestant and Roman Catholic Ethics* (Chicago and London: University of Chicago Press, 1978), chapter 3, has offered a helpful critique of these two tendencies in Protestant thinking.

50. At the theoretical level, exceptions to this are thinkers within the Reformed and Lutheran theological tradition. See more recently, for example, James W. Skillen and Rockne M. McCarthy, eds., *Political Order and the Plural Structure of Society*, Emory University Studies in Law and Religion (Atlantic: Scholars, 1991), especially parts 2 and 4, and Carl E. Braaten, "Natural Law in Theology and Ethics," in *The Two Cities of God: The Church's Responsibility for the Earthly City*, ed. Carl E. Braaten and Robert W. Jenson (Grand Rapids and

and notably existential thinking — can still be detected today among Protestant social ethicists. Roman Catholic social ethics, by comparison, given the debt to classical philosophical presuppositions, tends to be grounded in natural-law thinking, thus remaining more or less in continuity with mainstream Christian moral thinking throughout the ages.

In addition to the historicist and existentialist tendencies, pietism within the Protestant tradition — notably, within modern American evangelicalism — has contributed substantially to an absence of natural-law thinking. While at the theological level evangelicals stand in opposition to historicist thinking due to their affirmation of moral absolutes and a confessional position that is theologically orthodox, they nevertheless retain the Protestant bias against "thinking with the church" through the ages and imbibing the rich philosophical tradition of classical Christian thought. The effects of this bias — against history and against thinking philosophically — are not benign. Chiefly, this has meant a relative inability to develop a *robust public theology*, given the priority of the devotional life that is a hallmark of pietistic faith. Because evangelical thought-life tends to be strongly devotional and interior, evangelical *public witness* in the main has suffered to the extent that it lacks the theological-philosophical arsenal of Catholic social thought to enter and contend responsibly in the marketplace.[51] And despite evangelicals' entrance into the political realm in the 1970s and the seeming visibility of their political activity to the present, one is justified in wondering why their influence, at least ethically, is disproportionate to their considerable numbers.

By removing ethical intuition from universal knowledge and reason or denying that ethical norms are rooted in the order of creation, Protestants have eliminated the theological basis for natural law. And in so doing, they have lost any basis for a common moral grammar with which to enter moral discourse with non-Christians in a pluralistic social context.

Cambridge, U.K.: Eerdmans, 1997), 42-58. A generation removed, Princeton University ethicist Paul Ramsey, a Methodist, argued that "the rejection of natural law and 'middle axioms' in favor of contextualism and the study of decision-making" was a contributing factor to the moral malaise among Protestants ("The Problem of Protestant Ethics Today," in Ramsey, *War and the Christian Conscience* [Durham, N.C.: Duke University Press, 1961], reproduced in Wayne G. Boulton et al., eds., *From Christ, to the World: Introductory Readings in Christian Ethics* [Grand Rapids: Eerdmans, 1994], 212-14).

51. Where evangelicals do "discover" the social dimensions of Christian faith, not infrequently they tend toward social activism and downplay any sort of accountability to theological orthodoxy.

In some respects the theological component of the Protestant bias against natural law is understandable, given the primacy of faith and grace and the place of Scripture that the tradition accords. If ethics is based wholly (and narrowly) on the "Word of God," then theological ethics, in the words of Karl Barth, prostitutes itself to "natural theology" and becomes a "disastrous" and "traitorous" enterprise.[52] Such a fear, one must concede, is legitimate insofar as it is concerned to avoid the idolatry of human autonomy. It is misguided, however, to the extent that it construes "natural law" as being *outside* the realm of inscripturated revelation and divine grace.[53]

Because of Protestant pessimism toward human nature and the capacity of reason (over against its Catholic counterpart), there exists little or no room for natural-law thinking in Protestant social ethics. The result is not a happy one. We have consequently cut ourselves off at the knees in terms of developing a "public philosophy," at the heart of which lie natural law and "common grace." How *does* one then enter public moral discourse with people who do not share Christian faith? The apologetic bridge is thereby lost. Where there is no affirmation of natural law, the Christian community finds itself in relative isolation and withdrawal from the culture to which it has been called for redemptive purposes. And gone is any common ground on which Christians and non-Christians in a pluralistic society might engage in meaningful ethical conversation or debate.[54]

52. Karl Barth, *Church Dogmatics* II/2, ed. and trans. Geoffrey W. Bromiley (Edinburgh: T. & T. Clark, 1961), 523.

53. In fairness, we must acknowledge the context of Barth's reaction to "natural law." Barth, like many Catholic theologians of his day who watched with alarm the rise of National Socialism, observed that German legal theorists, who had been trained in positive law, were unable to resist Hitler's co-opting of the German legal and democratic process. The revitalization of natural-law thinking during the 1940s and 1950s, against the backdrop of and in reaction to totalitarianism, is noteworthy. Perhaps best representative of this revitalization is Heinrich Rommen, who had been imprisoned by the Nazis but subsequently fled Germany in 1938. The reason for his imprisonment was chiefly his views on law and morality that had appeared in *Der Staat in der katholischen Gedankenheit* (ET: *The State in Catholic Thought* [St. Louis: Herder, 1945]) and *Die ewige Wiederkehr des Naturrechts* (ET: *The Natural Law: A Study in Legal and Social History and Philosophy* [St. Louis: Herder, 1947]), published in 1935 and 1936 respectively. Interestingly, the second of these works translates literally "The Eternal Return of Natural Law," which suggests the enduring nature of natural law for an ordered society. The strength of this volume is twofold: it rehearses (1) the history of natural law as a concept, both within the pagan and Christian moral tradition, as well as (2) the content of natural law as the moral fabric of the universe.

54. The theological character of natural law's neglect is explored further in chapter 4.

Ultimately, the extent to which the Christian community and Christian intellectuals in particular affirm natural-law thinking will determine our ability to relate to and address surrounding culture. Not only does natural law endow all people with a minimum knowledge of themselves as moral agents and of their Creator, but, as we have argued, it furnishes common ground by which Christians and non-Christians can engage in moral conversation. In this way it allows people of faith to develop and articulate a public philosophy as they work toward preserving civil society. Natural-law thinking facilitates responsible engagement with their secular contemporaries in common moral categories.

Undergirding the argument of this book is the conviction that people of goodwill — and those of Christian faith, in particular — must not only come to terms with the cultural climate but also reacquaint themselves with those ethical resources that contribute to redemptive work in society — a society that, ethically speaking, is post-consensus. In the third millennium, the ethical issues confronting us not only force us to engage in serious ethical reflection but also force us to do so in conversation with generations past rather than in isolation. The present volume represents an attempt to focus on human moral intuitions that, like wisdom, are universal, and thus are part of what theologians call "general revelation" and "common grace." These intuitions inform us of what might be called "necessary truths" or moral "first principles." They are "necessary" insofar as certain human actions, arising from human beings as relatively autonomous moral agents, are of necessity morally right or wrong *by nature*.[55] While not explained solely by Christian religion, these intuitions, rooted in an abiding "natural moral law," are confirmed — and informed — by the Christian moral tradition. Any constructive attempt to (a) take one's faith into the public domain, (b) work for the good of the community and society, and (c) contend for what is true and ethical alongside people who do

---

55. Hadley Arkes puts the matter in proper focus: "Anyone who makes it his vocation these days to teach in the 'moral sciences' will soon encounter a primate who protests that, after all, 'there is no truth.' The stock response of the philosopher, of course, is to ask whether *that* proposition is itself true. . . . If it is, then people will no doubt be pleased to discover that there *is* truth after all" (*First Things: An Inquiry into the First Principles of Morals and Justice* [Princeton: Princeton University Press, 1986], 51; see in particular chapter 4 of Arkes's important volume "On Necessary Truths and the Existence of Morals"). The logic of moral "laws" is simply that, given moral agency and moral freedom among humans, they are made necessary in order to have access to any moral understanding.

not confess Christian faith will depend on whether we affirm the "permanent things," i.e., those values and priorities that are enduring and to which all people have access.[56]

Contending on the basis of the "permanent things" will necessarily inform how we address the contentious bioethical issues that confront us. For example, abortion, physician-assisted suicide, and suicide compel us to justify taking the life of a human being. Whence comes such justification? Are private citizens, over against the state, authorized to kill? At what point or points along the life spectrum does human life achieve or lose its humanness, its personhood? How does this accord with the human consensus that has remained constant throughout human history? On the basis of universal norms of justice, does the victim deserve the harm inflicted? Is lethal force in private cases justified? On what moral authority?

The practical challenge of Christians operating in the public square, not to mention Christian participation in the political process, is not how to create or preserve a "Christian society." Rather, it is how to coexist, in a pluralistic society, with unbelievers in a responsible manner that simultaneously avoids the twin idolatries of the triumphalist or theocratic heresy, on the one hand, which conflates faith and politics, and the opposite idolatry, separationist in character, which views faith as having little or nothing to do with politics, political considerations, and the ordering of society.[57]

56. For some of us, this will mean working alongside people of different religious or philosophical backgrounds to develop responsible public-policy recommendations.

57. Apart from appropriating natural-law thinking, believers are inclined toward several alternatives. In the American context, one is triumphalist in character, by which Christians seek to "restore Christian America" or impose "biblical standards of morality" upon surrounding culture. Such is the idolatry of conflating faith and the political-social order. Two alternative visions, rooted in an opposite form of idolatry, tend to be radically interior in nature, though in different ways. Both fail to see a meaningful connection between faith and the political-social order. And both, wittingly or unwittingly, call us away from the cultural mainstream rather than to faithful involvement therein. One of these two versions uses the grammar of "community," "radical discipleship," and "the kingdom of God" and not infrequently assumes the mantle of "prophetic" authority as it denounces both the church and society from the communities it seeks to build away from mainstream culture. More often than not it will have decidedly left-leaning political tendencies, in strong reaction to a perceived hegemony of "religious rightism" that is thought to dominate the political landscape and many congregations. In the end, this version, consciously separatist in character and self-righteous in its own way, will be deficient in its ability both to address the complexities of responsible civic engagement and to offer a viable public theology that emerges from "thinking with the church" consensually through the ages. The other separatist distortion

Introduction

Because much has been made of the "post-everything" cultural climate that presently characterizes our society, it is precisely there that we must begin. A brief critique of the culture is in order before an attempt is made, whether theologically or ethically, to reconstruct any sort of enduring ethical agenda.

---

promotes a foremost apocalyptic, future-oriented vision of culture and the church. This orientation issues out of a truncated view of the kingdom of God that is a by-product of a flawed, heavily future-oriented hermeneutic and reading of Scripture. Because culture is thought to be "going to hell in a handbasket," the spiritual dimension of Christian faith, narrowly construed, is all that is to be preserved. This negative way of thinking about culture, possessing an utmost narrow vision of redemption, is chiefly constrained by the need to "save souls," in anticipation of the "soon return of our Lord," rather than understanding *all* of creation — material and immaterial (cf. Col. 1:15-20) — as the scope of God's redemptive purposes, corresponding with the "incarnational humanism" of John Courtney Murray (*We Hold These Truths* [New York: Sheed and Ward, 1960], chapter 8), and more recently advanced by John Paul II. This particularly Protestant form of apocalypticism understands redemption foremost as "a rescue operation after intruding disaster" (so Robert W. Jenson, "The Church's Responsibility for the World," in *The Two Cities of God*, 3).

CHAPTER TWO

Contending for Moral First Things:
Christian Social Ethics and Postconsensus Culture

Assessing the Cultural Climate

With the unrelenting assault on truths previously held to be "self-evident" and universal, we find ourselves disoriented by philosophical pluralism that inexorably fades into moral pluralism. Concomitantly, we have grown increasingly accustomed in recent years to hearing that we've entered a post-Christian era. Not long ago Christian ethicist Vigen Guroian posed the rather intriguing question, "Is Christian ethics any longer possible?" in a volume with the equally intriguing title *Ethics after Christendom*.[1] Is it an overstatement to argue or suggest that Christian ethics is no longer possible? In what ways is it not "any longer possible"? How might the Christian community react to Guroian's question? To what extent does it matter?

Thoughtful cultural criticism suggests an answer to his question that differs more in degree than in kind. While Curtis Chang speaks of our post-consensus cultural climate in terms of the "epochal challenge" that it presents us,[2] Francis Fukuyama can speak of "the great disruption" in order to depict the disintegration of social bonds and moral values characterizing

---

1. Vigen Guroian, *Ethics after Christendom: Toward an Ecclesial Christian Ethics* (Grand Rapids: Eerdmans, 1994). Elsewhere I have attempted to access the cultural climate in similar fashion in *The Unformed Conscience of Evangelicalism: Recovering the Church's Moral Vision* (Downers Grove, Ill.: InterVarsity, 2002), 21-54.

2. Curtis Chang, *Engaging Unbelief: A Captivating Strategy from Augustine and Aquinas* (Downers Grove, Ill.: InterVarsity, 2000), 18-20.

contemporary culture.[3] This disintegration, as Michael Novak sees it, has not occurred in a cultural vacuum. Rather, our society's gatekeepers have been passionately disseminating a "vulgar relativism," what for Novak amounts to a "nihilism with a happy face."[4] Russell Hittinger is even prepared to speak of the "postmodern state," which, by his account, is "prepared to be the guarantor" of the rights and autonomy of the individual.[5]

Well-known is the supremely pessimistic view offered by moral philosopher Alasdair MacIntyre, who compares the present cultural climate with the period of decline in the Dark Ages. By his account, we are moral cave-dwellers who have undergone a catastrophic shift in our understanding that has warped our ability to engage in moral reasoning at all. He imaginatively likens the moral condition in which we find ourselves to a revolutionary antiscientific coup. Left remaining are only bits and pieces of evidence pointing to a prior state of affairs, as those wishing to revive science possess fragmentary knowledge of the past.[6] MacIntyre suggests that the survival of civilization as we know it requires an equivalent of the Benedictine order.[7]

Sociologist James Davison Hunter's assessment of our moral landscape is grim as well, and bears some resemblance to that of MacIntyre. In his postmortem examination of our moral character, Hunter concludes: "The social and cultural conditions that make character possible are no longer present."[8] James Q. Wilson would seem to agree, although he is less

---

3. Francis Fukuyama, *The Great Disruption: Human Nature and the Reconstitution of Social Order* (New York: Free Press, 1999), 3-26.

4. See his address "Awakening from Nihilism" as the twenty-fourth recipient of the Templeton Prize for Progress in Religion, subsequently published in *First Things* 45 (1994): 18-22.

5. Russell Hittinger, *The First Grace: Rediscovering the Natural Law in a Post-Christian World* (Wilmington, Del.: ISI Books, 2003), 137.

6. Alasdair MacIntyre, *After Virtue: A Study in Moral Theory,* 2nd ed. (Notre Dame, Ind.: University of Notre Dame Press, 1984), 1-3, 263. "What is the point of constructing this imaginary world inhabited by fictitious pseudo-scientists and real, genuine philosophy?" MacIntyre asks the reader. As he sees it, "in the actual world which we inhabit the language of morality is in the same state of grave disorder as the language of natural science in the imaginary world which I described" (2).

7. But in this regard Robert Jenson gently chastises MacIntyre: "Many who read this [book] wondered how there could be Benedictines without St. Benedict. . . . MacIntyre appears to have read his own book and wondered the same things, whereupon he reconverted to the faith" ("On the Renewing of the Mind," in Jenson, *Essays in Theology of Culture* [Grand Rapids: Eerdmans, 1995], 165).

8. James Davison Hunter, *The Death of Character* (New York: Basic Books, 2000), xiii.

despairing than Hunter. Wilson believes that to engage in moral reasoning and make moral judgments today is to be a veritable stranger in a strange land, for the Zeitgeist is one of extreme moral skepticism. When people speak of virtue, he notes, they must do so privately, in whispers, lest they be charged with the grievous crime of being "unsophisticated" or, if they press the matter, "fanatics."[9] Though for slightly different reasons, cultural historian Morris Berman shares the pessimism of MacIntyre and Hunter. In a lament not unlike that of the late critic Neil Postman, whose *Amusing Ourselves to Death* critiqued Americans' preference for and acquiescence to "entertainment" over "exposition,"[10] Berman mourns the rape of our intellectual and moral life and identifies parallels between the United States as it entered the third millennium and Rome as it began to collapse. With MacIntyre, he, too, speaks of an impending new "dark age" and calls for a "monastic option" that will serve as a conservator of our cultural heritage.[11]

The position of social critic Herbert Schlossberg would appear to mediate between hesitation and the despair of MacIntyre — we are not yet fully established as moral cave dwellers but well on the way. Schlossberg writes: "After biblical faith wanes, a people can maintain habits of thought and of self-restraint. The ethic remains after the faith that bore it departs. But eventually a generation arises that no longer has the habit, and that is when the behavior changes radically."[12] Ethicist Gilbert Meilaender, acknowledging a good measure of truth in the bleak diagnosis of our cultural predicament, nevertheless confesses: "I am not myself persuaded that ours is as fully post-Christian a culture as these diagnoses suggest."[13] Around us Meilaender sees "at least partial bits of

9. James Q. Wilson, *The Moral Sense* (New York: Free Press, 1993), x.

10. Neil Postman, *Amusing Ourselves to Death* (New York: Viking Press, 1985).

11. Morris Berman, *The Twilight of American Culture* (New York: Norton, 2000). In Berman's view, the sheer volume of data and information in our present age is drowning out knowledge and our ability "to think, analyze, compare and contextualize." This ravaging of the mind and morals, in his view, is facilitated in large part by "the emergence of an imagistic society," which quashes our ability to think (Morris Berman, "On the Verge of a Dark Age?" interview by Dale Krieger, in *Johns Hopkins Magazine,* September 2001, 22).

12. Herbert Schlossberg, *Idols for Destruction: The Conflict of Christian Faith and American Culture,* rev. ed. (Wheaton, Ill.: Crossway, 1990), 296. In the penultimate chapter of his book, Schlossberg does speak of "ethics in a post-Christian society" (287).

13. Gilbert C. Meilaender, *Faith and Faithfulness: Basic Themes in Christian Ethics* (Notre Dame, Ind., and London: University of Notre Dame Press, 1991), 8-9.

evidence for a resurgent ability of Christians to shape the moral life of our society."[14]

The prevailing mood, then, at least among many thoughtful social observers, may be thought of as disjunctive — and one might even say terminal. Quite accurately, I think, Richard John Neuhaus captures the mental disposition of the present cultural moment: "Whether in melancholia, in panic or in religious-revolutionary ecstasy, many experience our time as a sense of ending."[15] For Joseph Cardinal Ratzinger (Benedict XVI), as for his predecessor,[16] the sense of mental and spiritual disorientation that characterizes contemporary culture is the by-product of "the darkening of truth."[17]

Regardless of where we might place ourselves on this spectrum of cultural critique and how we might disagree, one observation remains uncontroversial. Our intellectual culture, by and large, has left ordinary men and women unassisted in making moral judgments. Intuiting the need to take stands on ethical issues of the day, people often feel like refugees living in a land captured by hostile forces.[18] Indeed, today we have grown rather accustomed to hearing our contemporaries deny even the *possibility* that moral judgments can be made. And most curiously, professional ethicists and moral philosophers seem to be resolutely leading the charge rather than sounding the alarm. The depiction of the moral landscape by T. S. Eliot in his day could well be a description of our own; Eliot frames the professional dilemma in this way: "The number of people in possession of any criteria for discriminating between good and evil is very small; the number of the half-alive hungry for any form of spiritual experience, or what offers itself as spiritual experience, high or low, good or bad, is considerable. My own generation has not served them very well. Never has the printing press been so busy, and never have such varieties of buncombe and false doctrine come from it."[19]

Once upon a time, as J. Budziszewski has recently reminded us, it was

---

14. Meilaender, *Faith and Faithfulness*, 8.

15. Remarkably, this statement was made already a generation ago. See Richard John Neuhaus, *Time toward Home: The American Experiment as Revelation* (New York: Seabury Press, 1975), 1.

16. See especially John Paul II's encyclical *Veritatis Splendor (The Splendor of Truth)*, published in 1993.

17. Joseph Cardinal Ratzinger, *Truth and Tolerance* (San Francisco: Ignatius, 2004), 66, 72.

18. In the introduction to his book *The Moral Sense*, James Q. Wilson describes with considerable poignancy the present state of affairs.

19. T. S. Eliot, *After Strange Gods* (London: Faber and Faber, 1933), 61.

possible for a philosopher to write that the foundational moral principles are "the same for all, both as to rectitude and as to knowledge"[20] — and to expect that most everyone would agree.[21] Different people and different cultures use different means to describe what we call "the natural law." What the Chinese call the Tao, what has been described in Plato and Jesus as the Golden Rule, what is embodied in the Ten Commandments, what Saint Paul refers to as the "law written on the heart," what the founders of the American republic refer to as the "laws of nature" (mirroring "nature's God") and "self-evident truths," and what moral and political philosophers call natural law or moral intuition — one could identify a *consensus* among human beings, notwithstanding our eternal excuse making, on what constitutes good and evil, right and wrong. Indeed, once upon a time.

But such consensus, spanning literally millennia, is difficult to find these days. In fact, what may have been assumed even a generation ago may no longer be assumed at all.[22] Rather, we must be prepared to hear a new story line, namely, that foundational moral principles are *not* the same for all. Thus, as the prophets of pragmatism and preference utilitarianism would have it, personhood is increasingly a matter of utility, function, and degree; human beings may *not* after all possess an inherent dignity, sanctity, and worth; and any attempts to engage in serious ethical reflection in our day are to be regarded as a public nuisance. Not only relatively obscure (to the average layperson) academics like John Harris and Tom Beauchamp, cited in the introduction of this volume, but also scholar-activists such as Peter Singer agitate and carry enormous influence and prestige in our culture. What is noteworthy about Singer's appointment several years ago to an endowed chair of ethics at Princeton University is not so much the appointment itself as the relative lack of controversy generated at the university by the appointment.[23] Neither abortion nor infanticide nor self-killing nor even bestiality,[24] we are

---

20. Thomas Aquinas, *Summa Theologiae* (hereafter *ST*) I-II Q. 94, a. 4.

21. J. Budziszewski, *What We Can't Not Know: A Guide* (Dallas: Spence, 2003). See also his prior work on natural law, *Written on the Heart: The Case for Natural Law* (Downers Grove, Ill.: InterVarsity, 1997).

22. The remarkable evaporation of this consensus is the story line of Budziszewski's book, which is written lucidly yet with an at-times-despairing tone.

23. The only volume I am aware of that offers a serious examination of Peter Singer's moral philosophy from a distinctly Christian perspective is *Rethinking Peter Singer: A Christian Critique* (Downers Grove, Ill.: InterVarsity, 2002), by Gordon Robert Preece, a fellow Australian.

24. As an "animal-rights activist," Singer went public in 2001 with his views on bestiality,

discovering, is intrinsically wrong. And murder? Well, blame it on the knife, if not a defective gene or traumatic childhood. Such characterizes the moral obtuseness of the present cultural moment.

It goes without saying, then, that the ethical challenges presently confronting the Christian community and broader culture are enormous. Not surprisingly, a recurring philosophical theme in the writings of John Paul II, particularly during the 1990s, was the *crisis of truth* in contemporary culture. This theme is especially pronounced in his 1993 encyclical *Veritatis Splendor,* and again in the 1998 encyclical *Fides et Ratio,* in which the pontiff observed a profound confusion between good and evil resulting from the corruption of conscience.

Having experienced totalitarian evil firsthand, John Paul in his lifetime was acutely aware of the toll on human life that resulted from a "corruption of conscience" in recent nondemocratic regimes, even when his writings have focused primarily on the moral-cultural climate of Western societies. While the century just concluded yielded more declarations of human rights than any other, it also produced the most notorious violations of human rights. What might we learn from this? The most basic lesson is that the denial of objective truth ultimately reduces law to a function of raw, totalitarian power.[25] Consider the words of John Paul in *Veritatis Splendor:* "Totalitarianism arises out of a denial of truth in the objective sense. If there is no transcendent truth, in obedience to which man achieves his full identity, then there is no sure principle for guaranteeing just relations between people. Their self-interest . . . would inevitably set them in opposition to one another. If one does not acknowledge transcen-

---

the final sexual taboo. He did so in a review of the book *Dearest Pet: On Bestiality* (London: Verso, 2000), written by Dutch biologist and naturalist Midas Dekker and appearing in the on-line magazine nerve.com. Much of Singer's review is simply unfit for eyes, and therefore caution is advised. Singer's conclusion, the product of his "preference utilitarianism" (which he learned from his mentors Jonathan Glover and R. M. Hare), is that "sex across species barriers" in fact "ceases to be an offence to our status and dignity as human beings" (www.nerve.com/Opinions/Singer/heavyPetting/main.asp). For a recent critique of Singer's preference utilitarianism, see Dianne N. Irving, "Reading Singer on 'Bestiality,'" found online at www.lifeissues.net/writers/irv/irv_23singerglobalethics.html. Singer, it will be recalled, was appointed to the DeCamp Chair of Human Values by (former) Princeton University president Harold Shapiro, who also chaired President Clinton's National Bioethics Advisory Commission.

25. For helpful commentary on the sobering implications hereof, see Charles E. Rice, "Natural Law in the Twenty-First Century," in *Common Truths: New Perspectives on Natural Law,* ed. Edward B. McClean (Wilmington, Del.: ISI Books, 2000), 312.

dent truth, then the force of power takes over."[26] As John Paul understands it, the root of modern totalitarianism is "the denial of the transcendent dignity of the human person" that inheres in natural law.

Consider, for the moment, the mind-boggling statistics that serve to illustrate the disappearance of evil and good in twentieth-century regimes. In his introduction to *The Black Book of Communism*, published in 1999 and causing an uproar in France at the time, French historian Stéphane Courtois breaks down according to individual nation-states the total number of victims sacrificed to Communist ideology. The estimate given by Courtois is in the neighborhood of 100 million. By contrast, the estimate of military historian Robert Conquest is in the 170 million range.[27] Truly, the stench of death surrounding Marxist-Leninist ideology is extraordinary, whichever estimate we accept, dwarfing Nazism's remarkable achievement within a shorter span of years of approximately 25 million deaths, based on our current reckoning. We find ourselves powerless to grasp the significance of 100 million *or* 25 million deaths. Such numbers are dizzying to the mind. And yet we *dare not* grow numb to their reality, much of which has occurred *within our lifetime.* They remain before us and exist for our benefit, to teach us and to humble us. The "natural lawyer" (not to mention the "just warrior") understands this, however imperfectly, and reckons accordingly. Surely, all these human lives matter, a fact for which pacifists and separatists, who reject natural-law thinking as well as just use of force, lack any legitimate answer.[28]

Notwithstanding the horrors of twentieth-century totalitarian regimes, John Paul in his encyclicals has sought chiefly to address the insidious conflation of good and evil in Western culture. In particular, he warns against an alliance of democratic pluralism and ethical relativism, which effectively removes any sure reference point from the political and social life of a people. A democracy without values, he reiterates, readily turns into *open or thinly disguised* totalitarianism.[29] And while some would soften the blow by describing the social climate as a "gentle," even "debonair," form of nihilism,[30] John Paul

---

26. *Veritatis Splendor* (hereafter *VS*), no. 99.

27. Stéphane Courtois et al., *The Black Book of Communism: Crimes, Terror, Repression,* trans. J. Murphy and M. Kramer (Cambridge, Mass., and London: Harvard University Press, 1999), and Robert Conquest, *Reflections on a Ravaged Century* (New York: Norton, 2000).

28. My point here is only that separatists and pacifists fail (or refuse) to see any *meaningful* linkage between the metaphysical and the political.

29. *Centesimus Annus*, no. 34. Cf. also *VS*, no. 101.

30. Thus Michael Gillespie, "Martin Heidegger," in *History of Political Philosophy,*

is more frank, calling it a "culture of death" — a culture that, in the view of some, is becoming "repaganized."[31] The nihilism of Western culture corresponds to the "vulgar relativism" so deftly critiqued by social commentator Michael Novak in his Templeton Prize address of 1994. As with John Paul, for Novak truth matters, and at the heart of truth lies a concern for human dignity. Only a commitment to the truth about truth will allow us as a society to turn nihilism "inside out" and remain civil. "Truth is not 'merely subjective,' not something we make up, or choose, or cut to today's fashions or the morrow's pragmatism — we obey truth. We do not 'have' the truth, truth owns us, truth possesses us. Truth is far larger and deeper than we are. Truth leads us where it will. It is not ours for mastering."[32]

Already a half-century ago, John Courtney Murray implied the presence of an incipient "barbarism" that was to be detected in American culture. His description could well be of our own day. Characteristic of this barbarism, Murray observed, was "the lack of reasonable conversation according to reasonable laws." Society becomes barbarous when "economic interests assume primacy over higher values," when "technology assumes an autonomous existence and embarks on a course of unlimited self-exploitation without purposeful guidance from the higher disciplines of politics and morals," and when "the ways of men come under the sway of the instinctual, the impulsive, the compulsive."[33]

The broader — and more basic — question suggested by Murray is not whether we as a free society are really "free"; it is whether American society is

---

ed. Leo Strauss and Joseph Cropsey, 3rd ed. (Chicago: University of Chicago Press, 1987), 889.

31. In addition to the social commentary of Berman (see n. 11), Guroian (see n. 1), and MacIntyre (see n. 6), others who underscore the pagan character of American culture include Schlossberg, *Idols for Destruction,* 268-73; Michael Novak, "Awakening from Nihilism," *First Things,* August/September 1994, 18-22; Carl E. Braaten, "The Gospel for a Neopagan Culture," in *Either/Or: The Gospel or Neopaganism,* ed. Carl E. Braaten and Robert W. Jenson (Grand Rapids: Eerdmans, 1995), 7-21; Benjamin D. Wiker, "The Repaganization of the West," *New Oxford Review,* May 1996, 19-22; as well as this writer, in "Engaging the (Neo)Pagan Mind," *Trinity Journal,* n.s., 16 (1995): 47-62. Already in 1976, Willem A. Visser 't Hooft, former general secretary of the World Council of Churches, warned, "It is high time that Christians recognize that they are [presently] confronted with a new paganism" ("Evangelism in the Neo-Pagan Situation," *International Review of Mission* 65 [1976]: 83).

32. Novak, "Awakening from Nihilism," 19.

33. John Courtney Murray, *We Hold These Truths: Catholic Reflections on the American Proposition* (New York: Sheed and Ward, 1960), 13-14.

in fact *civil*. Recall his somewhat arresting definition of barbarism: "the lack of reasonable conversation according to reasonable laws." Murray's understanding of the barbaric should give us pause. Barbarism threatens society "when men cease to live together according to reason, embodied in law and custom, and incorporated in a web of institutions that sufficiently reveal rational influence, even though they are not, and cannot be, wholly rational."[34] Characteristic of the work of the barbarian is "to undermine rational standards of judgment, to corrupt the inherited intuitive wisdom by which the people have always lived, and to do this not by spreading new beliefs but by creating a climate of doubt and bewilderment in which clarity about the larger aims of life is dimmed and the self-confidence of the people is destroyed, so that finally what you have is . . . impotent nihilism."[35] Such, without question, seems a depiction of our own day, forcing us to confess with George Orwell, "We have now sunk to a depth at which re-statement of the obvious is the first duty of intelligent men." Morally speaking, it is reasonable to ask, do we perhaps stand at such a cultural moment? What is our response to both academic and popular culture, mired in metaphysical murk (and stubbornly so)? Are Christians fully prepared to stand alongside all people of good will to counter the moral barbarism that presently surrounds us? And how will we contend against it?

This volume, it should be emphasized, is not an apocalyptic exercise in hand-wringing over the potential wreck of Western culture. Indeed, I think Whittaker Chambers was right: it is already a wreck from within. Rather, the following chapters represent a modest attempt not only to restate the morally obvious but also to emphasize in the Christian moral-philosophical tradition what is of enduring value, particularly with the daunting ethical and bioethical challenges before us. Perhaps for the Catholic reader a discussion of the importance of natural law may seem more familiar; for those of Protestant persuasion, such may be more difficult.

Contending for What Is Permanent

Writers such as G. K. Chesterton, T. S. Eliot, Evelyn Waugh, Dorothy Sayers, and C. S. Lewis, despite being generations removed, retain immense popularity among American Christians, due to their extraordinarily fecund

34. Murray, *We Hold These Truths*, 13.
35. Murray, *We Hold These Truths*, 12.

imagination and lucid defense of Christian basics. But they also have in common a metaphysical realism and the knack for stressing the "permanent things" — what has been called the *philosophia perennis*. While many of their contemporaries, in ways familiar to us, measured intellectual sophistication by *how much moral reality they could deny,* these literary apologists were devoted to seeing *how much they might affirm or recover.* While the cognoscenti of their day operated out of a spirit of deconstruction, they were committed to a project of reconstruction. And while their contemporaries were obsessed with the politics of power, they were concerned to uphold principle, supremely sensitive to the need to align themselves with the eternal and the unchanging.[36]

These individuals were profoundly unsympathetic to and out of step with the spirit of their age. Lewis states his commitment to the permanent things thusly: "For the wise men of old the cardinal problem had been how to conform the soul to reality, and the solution had been knowledge, self-discipline, and virtue. For magic and applied science alike the problem is how to subdue reality to the wishes of men."[37] Of these writers, literary critic Ian Crowther has well remarked: "it was never enough simply to capture the spiritual aridity of modern life," which they did splendidly. "It was also necessary to speak of a moral order which, although only perhaps surviving in scattered remnants in contemporary society, may yet be restored by the expressive power and beauty of the written word."[38] Thus, to be committed to the permanent is to live life in accordance with reason, sanity, and sanctity. It is to wrestle in earnest with Pilate's question "What is truth?" rather than twist it subversively or cynically only to advance doubt and indeterminacy.

Central to guardians of the "permanent things" who marshaled their wisdom and wit against the errors, vices, and novelties[39] of their era is the

36. See also chapter 5 of *The Unformed Conscience of Evangelism,* in which I reflect in a similar manner on the relationship between ethics, the permanent, and the natural law.

37. "Applied science," for Lewis, was of the sort that used technology to accomplish the "disgusting and impious," and hence humankind's self-annihilation (*The Abolition of Man* [New York: Macmillan, 1947], 88). Lewis did not oppose science in its pursuit of knowledge; he opposed its potential for enslaving humans. The problem is not with knowledge itself; rather, it is how that knowledge is used.

38. Ian Crowther, introduction to *Permanent Things: Toward the Recovery of a More Human Scale at the End of the Twentieth Century,* ed. Andrew A. Tadie and Michael H. Macdonald (Grand Rapids and Cambridge, U.K.: Eerdmans, 1995), xvi.

39. In the words of one cultural critic, "Unscrupulous originality thus terminates in a universal boring nihilism — or, yet more catastrophic than the pose of nihilism, the com-

permanent question, "Wherein lies the foundation of the moral order?" Or, framed differently, "What is the basis for human behavior?"

In numerous of his works Lewis mirrors a concern for moral first things. Consider, for example, how it finds multiple expressions in the Chronicles of Narnia. A common thread running through the series is that Narnians are to remain loyal to Aslan and to what they "know." Battles are a constant feature of Narnia, illustrating the stakes between what is "natural" and what is "unnatural." Edmund is ransomed from the powers of the White Witch precisely how? By means of the deeper wisdom. The final judgment of Narnia even has implications for the animals: the Talking Beasts, who had been given a privileged status by Aslan over against the Dumb Beasts, lose their privileged status. Instructively, in *The Screwtape Letters* we encounter Lewis's basic belief in the words of Screwtape, with the hortatory remark that the great moralists, ever a nuisance, "are sent by the Enemy, not to inform men, but to *remind* them, to *restate the primeval moral platitudes* against our continual concealment of them."[40]

In *Mere Christianity* and *The Abolition of Man* Lewis speaks of the Tao[41] to denote a universal moral code rooted in individual conscience. In the first of the essays composing *Mere Christianity*, "Right and Wrong as a Clue to the Meaning of the Universe," Lewis, in presenting evidence for the existence of God,[42] contends that every person is born with a moral sense

---

mon collapse of all standards, of all authority visible and invisible, the ruin of culture, the ruin of life" (Russell Kirk, "The Great Mysterious Incorporation of the Human Life," in *Permanent Things*, 10).

40. C. S. Lewis, *The Screwtape Letters* (New York: Macmillan, 1961), 107, emphasis added.

41. Perhaps it is unfortunate that Lewis chose this expression, to the extent that as a life view it implies more than he wished to summarize through it. To the Chinese, moral reality is the *Tao Te Ching* (variously translated as the "Way," the "Source," or the moral status quo); to Indians it is *dharma;* to Westerners it is "nature"; and to the apostle Paul it is "the law . . . written on their hearts."

42. "One is sometimes (not often) glad not to be a great theologian. One might easily confuse it with being a good Christian," wrote Lewis in *Reflections on the Psalms* (New York: Harcourt, Brace and World, 1958), 57, reminding his readers of his acute awareness that he himself was not a theologian. One is tempted to wonder, however, if this disclaimer was more a statement about the elitism that he sensed among most professional theologians. If so, then we can lament with Lewis that very often the language of academic theologians obscures rather than mediates theological truth to the layperson. See in this regard Gilbert C. Meilaender, "C. S. Lewis and a Theology of the Everyday," in *Things That Count: Essays Moral and Theological* (Wilmington, Del.: Intercollegiate Studies Institute, 2000), 123-44.

to distinguish between right and wrong. Lewis, in his time, was troubled by those who were committed to debunking traditional morality (i.e., the natural law) and arguing that basic human values change with time, culture, and location.[43] If there is no such thing as a fixed notion of right and wrong, no "law of nature," then what, he asks, is the difference between fair and unfair treatment? Why is an individual life valuable? A society? On what basis, aside from brute will to power, should life — any life — be deemed valuable? If nothing is self-evident, he argued, then nothing can be proven. In the end, then, nothing in life is morally obligatory, and *all* values disintegrate.

But no values, insisted Lewis, are free-floating and independent of the natural law. Even revolutionary moral reformers are parasitic on a coherent moral system outside of themselves, drawing from categories of natural law in order to tunnel under it and destroy it. Reacting to Darwinians who spoke of the "preservation of the species," he retorted, "But why should the species be preserved?"[44] As he saw it, no moral revisionists were able to give an adequate answer.

The normal person, Lewis believed, will recognize the natural law's existence. We refer to it as the "law of nature" precisely because "people thought that everyone knew it by nature and did not need to be taught it. They did not mean, of course, that you might not find an odd individual here and there who did not know it, just as you find a few people who are colour-blind or have no ear for a tune. But taking the race as a whole, they thought that the human idea of decent behaviour was obvious to every one."[45] Notably in *The Abolition of Man*, Lewis presses the argument of objective moral truths: "This thing which I have called for convenience the Tao, and which others may call Natural Law . . . is not one among a series of possible systems of value. It is the sole source of all value judgment. If it is rejected, all value is rejected. If any value is retained, it is retained. The effort to refute it and raise a new system of

---

43. Ethicist Gilbert Meilaender, *The Taste for the Other: The Social and Ethical Thought of C. S. Lewis* (1978; reprint, Grand Rapids and Cambridge, U.K.: Eerdmans, 1998), 199, believes that a moral universe and moral formation constitute "the strongest and most permanent theme" in Lewis. By the evidence, it is difficult to argue with Meilaender. See especially Meilaender's very insightful chapter "The Primeval Moral Platitudes" (179-234), which crystallizes the ethical in Lewis's writings.

44. Lewis, *The Abolition of Man*, 40.

45. C. S. Lewis, *Mere Christianity* (New York: Macmillan, 1960), 4.

value in its place is self-contradictory."[46] Thus, it would seem for Lewis, we are "forced" to believe in a concept of right and wrong. For despite our intellectual justifications to the contrary, we *expect unfailingly* to be treated with human decency, so much so that one is justified in calling this expectation a moral "law." What Lewis refers to as the "law of nature" or the "law of oughtness" — i.e., the awareness and expectation within all people to be treated fairly, justly, and decently — is to be distinguished from individual conscience, which is fickle and can be violated, hardened, seared, or ignored. Lewis is struck by the remarkable consistency — indeed, the perfect predictability — of the natural moral law. Why is it, he asks, that *all* people at *all* times react to injustice at the hands of others? There must be, he concludes, a moral "law" at work, independent of our knowledge or intentions.

Natural law, then, has to do with foundational principles of morality — the permanent things that govern both private and public life. It prompts us to ask whether human beings function in a distinct way. Is there a characteristic human conduct? Are there distinctly human behavioral ideals? What are they and where do they come from? What does it mean to be distinctly human? What are the criteria for functioning well as human beings? At the most rudimentary level, however, natural law prompts us to confront — and answer honestly, I think — the basic moral-philosophical question posed by Camus: Should I or should I not commit suicide? And, secondly, why or why not?

The notion of a fixed human nature and universal moral truths, of course, is as old as philosophy, extending as far back as Heraclitus, Socrates, and Aristotle. Thus, for example, Heraclitus observes: "Wisdom is the foremost virtue, and wisdom consists in speaking the truth, and in lending an ear to nature and acting according to her. . . . [A]ll human laws are fed by one divine law."[47] Aristotle distinguishes between two types of justice — one "natural" and one conventional. "What is by nature just," he writes of the former, "has the same force everywhere, and does not depend on what we regard or do not regard as just." A "law of nature" is "immutable," he argues, "and has the same validity everywhere."[48] In fact, Aristotle believes in

46. Lewis, *The Abolition of Man*, 56.

47. Heraclitus, *Fragments* 112-114, reproduced in Charles M. Bakewell, *Source Book in Ancient Philosophy* (New York: Scribner, 1907), 34.

48. Aristotle, *Nichomachean Ethics* 5.7 (1134b). What is "conventional" may be settled one way or another indifferently, he observes.

— and defends — the "legislating" of morality. That is, laws (whether written or unwritten) help shape character, since men are not born virtuous.[49]

Upon reflecting in *Nichomachean Ethics* on what is peculiar to being human, Aristotle responds that human beings are deliberative, rational, and purposeful. To be uniquely human, he believes, is to strive for the good; to live and act well is *aretē*, moral excellence. It is in this context that Aristotle describes the "cardinal virtues," without which a "good" society cannot exist. Justice, therefore, is that virtue that causes us to treat others with dignity; to receive one's due is to be treated as a moral agent and to honor nonfluid standards of judgment. Since it sustains social relationships by means of principled reason, justice is that moral tissue that holds together the community. The virtue of temperance, as well, serves the common good insofar as it rationally and willingly places a restraint on human appetites and passions. Not all appetites are to be indulged; not all are to be sanctioned. Civil society depends on the ordering and prioritizing of human wants and needs, and for the good of the community. Some of these wants and needs are best *not* expressed. Likewise, courage will inevitably lead us to deny ourselves certain privileges, luxuries, or benefits, for the sake of a greater good. It will choose the honorable path of self-sacrifice, where that sacrifice has the well-being of others in mind. And wisdom, or prudence, causes human beings to evaluate and discriminate regarding their behavior. Wisdom asks what it means to be truly human and why particular behaviors decorate or destroy human dignity. By its character it aids human beings in making moral discriminations.

Such rational reflection, then, is peculiar to human beings. This method of thinking about moral excellence, the virtues, along with corresponding vices, while not original to Stoic moral philosophy, is nevertheless subsequently systematized by the Stoics, into whose moral lexicon the Christian fathers were able to pour their conception of divine revelation.[50] Sadly, for those of us living in the twenty-first century, the language and logic of virtue seem utterly quaint, if not wholly irrelevant.

But defenders of the "permanent things," whatever age they represent, are much occupied by virtue and vice and the fact that we are moral creatures. This awareness of a moral universe is inescapable and accessible

49. Aristotle, *Nichomachean Ethics* 10.9 (1179b-1180b).
50. See chapter 3.

to all people, independent of social upbringing, cultural background, or private experience. "Natural law," then, may be understood as a moral consensus[51] about notions of right and wrong that arises — and is reaffirmed — throughout history.[52] Human beings, wherever they may be found, are capable through reason, their sinful inclinations notwithstanding, of discerning what is good and what is evil. People who do not necessarily ascribe to Judeo-Christian belief nevertheless do that which is right "by nature," a belief shared by Christians and Stoics alike, as C. S. Lewis readily pointed out.[53] For this reason Lewis rejected a narrow "Christian morality," arguing for the existence of a natural moral law *accessible to all via rational perception.*[54] As such, he stands in the Pauline and Thomist tradition. The New Testament presupposes, rather than negates, natural law — a natural law that expressed itself in the Ten Commandments: "Ever since the creation of the world his invisible nature, namely, his eternal power and deity, has been clearly perceived in the things that have been made. So they [human beings] are without excuse" (Rom. 1:20 RSV). This, for Saint Paul, is the law "written on their hearts" (Rom. 2:15), corresponding to what the church variously has referred to as "common grace" and general revelation.

In several of his encyclical letters, John Paul II reaffirms the place of natural law and rationality in light of the deeply irrational and morally skeptical age of which we are a part. Man is able, he observes in *Veritatis*

---

51. We follow Murray (*We Hold These Truths,* 97-123, "The Origins and Authority of the Public Consensus"), who follows Aquinas (*ST* I-II Q. 100, a. 1) in his understanding of "consensus."

52. Christians historically have been united in the belief that all people everywhere and at all times possess a basic knowledge. *How* they know is another matter; on epistemological questions there is room for great disagreement. This, of course, is the critical distinction between Thomas Aquinas and John Locke.

53. C. S. Lewis, *The Discarded Image: An Introduction to Medieval and Renaissance Literature* (New York: Cambridge University Press, 1964), 160.

54. Stoicism, as Lewis saw it, prepared the way of a Christian construction of natural law to the extent of its understanding — true in and of itself — that virtue is rightly ordered reason, which keeps human passions and appetites in check. Such is not to deny the fundamental difference between Stoic and Christian metaphysics, since the former denies any place for divine intervention and grace as Christianity understands it, while the latter "sanctifies" reason and knowledge (note, for example, that faith predicates knowledge in the catalogue of virtues in 2 Pet. 1:5-7). Nevertheless, the points of contact are worth noting.

Splendor, "to recognize good and evil thanks to that discernment of good from evil which he himself carries out by his reason, and particularly by his reason enlightened by Divine Revelation and by faith, through the law which God gave to the Chosen People, beginning with the commandments on Sinai."[55]

The twin notions of fixed moral truth and human rationality are perhaps most fully developed in his 1998 encyclical *Fides et Ratio.* In it John Paul emphasizes that "reason is by its nature oriented to truth and is equipped moreover with the means necessary to arrive at truth."[56] He thereby challenges us: Do we hold certain truths because they are universally so, or are they true because we hold them?[57] For John Paul truth is universal: "if something is true, then it must be true for all people and at all times" (*FR,* no. 27). "Truth can never be confined to time and culture; in history it is known, but it also reaches beyond history" (no. 95).

The pope-philosopher's thoughts on the place of reason in discerning moral truth are not random. Rather, they are a response to the "lack of faith" in reason itself that typifies the postmodern Zeitgeist. Reason, John Paul believes, has been effectively relativized by the pervasiveness of a "hard perspectivialism."[58] Whether in its secular or religious form, fideism joins skepticism and relativism in the contemporary context to undermine our belief in the truth-oriented capacity of our cognitive powers. There now prevails a widespread mistrust in human cognitive ability as such, much less that it can apprehend truth and thus fulfill the deepest of human longings. John Paul's purpose in *Fides et Ratio* is to restore a confidence in the truth-attaining powers of reason — a confidence that has been all but shattered. As a defender of the "permanent things," John Paul understands that truth liberates, exposing autonomy masquerading as "freedom" to be self-induced imprisonment. His emphasis in the encyclical on "nature" and "seeking the truth" allows several themes to emerge:

55. *VS,* no. 44.

56. *Fides et Ratio* (hereafter *FR*), no. 49. References to this encyclical have been placed in the text.

57. Eduardo J. Echeverria helpfully explores the theme of truth in John Paul's recent encyclicals in "The Splendor of Truth in Fides et Ratio: Alethic Realism and Dominus Jesus," *Revista Portuguesa de Filosofia* 58 (2002): 17-42.

58. This term is used by Eduardo J. Echeverria, "FIDES ET RATIO — the Catholic and the Calvinist: Prospects for Rapprochement," *Philosophia Reformata* 65 (2000): 76.

- Reason is by its nature oriented to truth and is equipped moreover with the means necessary to arrive at truth (no. 49).
- Humans are by nature truth-seekers, pausing to ask why things are as they are (no. 3).
- Humans seek to know the truth about personal existence, about life, and about the Creator, for man has been created as the one who seeks after truth (nos. 5 and 28).

But the Protestant reader surely is apt to ask: Is John Paul not overly optimistic with regard to human rationality? Has not sin altered — indeed, permanently marred — humans' ability to comprehend the truth through reason? What about the radical effects of sin's distortion? The reader of *Fides* discovers, however, that John Paul is under no illusion about the effects of sin's devastation: original sin has "wounded," "impaired," and "alienated" reason, causing us to view ourselves as "autonomous" and "sovereign" (nos. 22, 80, and 107). The former pontiff stands squarely within the mainstream of historic Christian theology in acknowledging the natural limitations of human reason due to the problem of sin. Nevertheless, he also agrees with historic Christian teaching in maintaining that reason's limitations are *not* grounds for *abandoning* reason.[59] Neither do we conclude that natural theology serves no purpose, or that the unregenerate person is incapable of recognizing truth. Indeed, the church has always understood natural "proofs" for the Creator as preparing the way for faith, as leading to an ever fuller apprehension of divine truth.[60]

In response to those who contend that we are at "the end of metaphysics," John Paul cautions: the abandonment of metaphysics further alienates and fragments us, forcing us into "an ever deepening introversion, locked within the confines of its own immanence without reference of any kind to the transcendent" (*FR*, no. 55; also, no. 81). For this reason he calls for "a philosophy of genuinely metaphysical range, capable, that is, of transcending empirical data in order to attain something absolute, ultimate and foundational in its search for truth" (no. 83). Philosophy, then,

---

59. Right use of reason, which apprehends the natural law, is to be properly rational, not rationalist. Human reason is not autonomous, but neither is it obliterated.

60. Here we discover a certain irony among theologically conservative Protestants. On the one hand, they have advocated the necessity of apologetics, to their credit; on the other hand, they reject or ignore the significance of the natural law as general revelation.

properly understood, reminds our contemporaries "that men and women are always called to direct their steps toward a truth which transcends them" (no. 5).[61] Christian revelation therefore is "the true point of encounter and engagement between philosophical and theological thinking in their reciprocal relationship" (no. 79).

It is clear that John Paul stands within the Thomist tradition, particularly as he understands human nature. Aquinas identifies three essential human tendencies — inclinations of reason and nature — that constitute being human and distinguish human beings as a species: procreation,[62] self-preservation, and rationality. These inclinations lie at the very foundation of the moral life. The "natural" aspect of natural law reminds us that evidence exists all around us, universally so, as to *how nature operates,* both in the cosmos and among humans. The "law" aspect reminds us of the consistency and uniformity of things as they should be. Both elements together remind us that human constitution is relatively unchanging, despite differences in time, culture, and perception of the divine.[63] Thus the essence of natural law: the foundations of the moral life are unchanging. Deep within the human conscience we discover a "law" — a law we did not create and yet are obliged to obey. To be distinctively human is therefore to act as a moral agent, to act reasonably and to act accountably.[64]

The existence of natural law, it must be emphasized, is independent of salvific faith, even when it is an intricate part of divine revelation. That is, regenerate as well as unregenerate people establish abiding moral-social norms that condemn child molesters, murderers, thieves, adulterers, and the like. Christians and non-Christians draw the same conclusions about behavior that is acceptable and unacceptable, mirrored in the "criminal justice" system. They do this for the common social good, and this "public philosophy" rests on universal and timeless principles that are rooted in

---

61. For John Paul, the wholesale retreat from metaphysics, resulting in nihilism — the denial of all metaphysical foundations and negation of objective truth — is the root of our current cultural crisis.

62. Although sexual congress is not peculiar to human beings, viewing it as a shared good and ordering it responsibly is.

63. Aquinas, *ST* I-II, Q. 94, a. 2.

64. See the very lucid and engaging account of natural law's role in Ralph McInerny, "The Case for Natural Law," *Modern Age,* Spring 1982, 168-74, which attempts to underscore Thomistic assumptions about human nature.

natural law. Both unregenerate and regenerate are held accountable to the temporal judgment that those laws and sanctions express. Natural-law thinking thus provides a common grammar for moral discourse and a common basis for moral judgments in a pluralistic environment.[65] These impulses reveal personal and social goods that are "givens"; we do not "choose" them. We are born into society, into the human community, and we do not choose this particular context. Natural law, then, provides metaphysical, moral, and (by implication) political starting points by which humans, by nature, order their lives and communities. For this reason natural law is not one among many value systems; it is the sole source of all value judgments. To rebel against this "law of nature," this "law of oughtness," is, metaphorically speaking, like branches rebelling against the tree. This rebellion, left uninterrupted, results in the self-annihilation of the branches.[66]

Protestant theology in the main, because of its emphasis on total depravity and its Christocentrism, has had greater difficulty than its Catholic counterpart in affirming the natural moral law and the place of reason in apprehending revelation. But sin, while it devastates and mars, cannot tear up nature at its roots, as Reinhold Niebuhr was quick to point out.[67] Injustice has meaning only against the background of a sense of justice that is universally intuited and universally on display. Natural-law thinking presupposes a realist epistemology; it proceeds under the conviction that humans can grasp the nature of things as they really are. Discerning basic good and evil is part of this knowledge.

The fear among many well-meaning Christians that natural-law thinking is insufficiently christological, and therefore undermines the gospel of grace, is quite mistaken. In no sense is natural law a substitute for divine revelation and salvific grace; to the contrary, it is part of divine revelation and points in the direction of grace, since natural-law philosophy, rightly construed, exposes the devices of the human heart through which we suppress the truth. Nor does it undermine or eliminate the uniqueness of the Christian ethic, even when the Christian begins interacting with unregenerate people at the level of "general" revelation before

65. Thus, in theory it is possible for a society to be *relatively* "just" without necessarily having an established religion and without being "Christian."

66. Such is the argument developed by Lewis in *The Abolition of Man*, 95-97.

67. See *Love and Justice: Selections from the Shorter Writings of Reinhold Niebuhr*, ed. D. B. Robertson (Philadelphia: Westminster, 1957), 50-51.

introducing "special" revelation, which culminates in the person and work of Christ.

Saint Paul and the Permanent:
The Apostle's Work among "Cultured Pagans" at Athens

A basic premise of our argument up to this point is that "general revelation," as evidenced by the internal witness of the "law written on the heart" (Rom. 2:14-15; cf. 1:21) and predicated on creation in the image of God (Gen. 1:26-27), serves as common ground between the Christian and unbeliever and thus serves a necessary apologetic function. Christians, therefore, can appeal to unbelievers on the basis of the "natural law," which is necessarily conditioned by certain metaphysical and political assumptions about reality.[68]

Let us, for the moment, leave aside the political implications of natural-law thinking. At the most fundamental level, *how* we as a society seek to order ourselves politically is best reserved for another context. *That* natural law grounds common moral discourse between Christians and non-Christians remains our present focus and requires further exploration.

The New Testament affords us a glimpse into the utility of natural-law thinking, which is implicit in statements by the Apostle to the Gentiles in his first letter to the Christians at Corinth: "To the Jews I became as a Jew, in order to win Jews.... To those outside the law I became as one outside the law — *not being without law toward God* . . . — that I might win those outside the law" (1 Cor. 9:20-21 RSV, emphasis added). Theory becomes practice as the Spirit of God leads the apostle into the heart of Hellenistic culture (Acts 16:6-10).

Three of Paul's speeches are recorded in the book of Acts — one to a Jewish audience (13:16-41), one to a Christian audience (20:17-35), and one to a pagan audience (17:22-34). This distribution surely is not by chance. Rather, from this the reader might reasonably assume that Luke, as narrator, has some sort of pedagogical aim in mind. This distribution, moreover, illustrates *in practice* what the apostle reveals to be his personal philosophy of ministry (1 Cor. 9:19-23). If Luke's intent is pedagogical, Paul's

---

68. One needs no particular faith commitment to acknowledge that people should do good, avoid evil, respect others, and do justly.

work in Athens (Acts 17:16-34) might provide useful insights into how the Christian community engages philosophical pluralism.

Nothing in Acts 17:16-34 suggests that Paul's strategy in Athens is misguided, contrary to some biblical commentary.[69] In fact, Luke presents Paul in a way that depicts the apostle as being in line with other noted philosophers of the past who came and "disputed" (*dialegomai:* 17:17) in the marketplace — among these, Anaxagoras and Protagoras (both mid–fifth century B.C.), Socrates, and more recently the renowned Stoic Chrysippus (first century B.C.). Luke may well have in mind the tradition surrounding Socrates, who was also accused in Athens of introducing "foreign deities," when he writes of Paul's interaction with Stoic and Epicurean philosophers in the agora: "Others said, 'He seems to be a proclaimer of foreign deities'" (17:18).[70] Indeed, not only Socrates but also Anaxagoras and Protagoras were accused of this very "crime."

From the vantage point of the twenty-first century, Acts 17 engenders important questions concerning not only Christian proclamation but also the church's relationship to culture, and specifically educated pagan culture.[71] Some of what confronted Paul and the subsequent Christian com-

---

69. Writing a century ago, William Ramsay gave credence to the view that Paul became "disillusioned" by his experience in Athens; hence we hear nothing more about the church in this city hereafter (*St. Paul the Traveller and the Roman Citizen,* rev. and ed. Mark Wilson [Grand Rapids: Kregel, 2001], 194). Others deem Paul's Areopagus speech "ineffective" and an "unrealistic experiment," since it falls outside the normal "evangelical" pattern of preaching usually used by the apostles (so, e.g., Claus Munsinger, *Paulus in Korinth* [Heidelberg: Knecht, 1908], 5; Jean Dupont, *Les Actes des Apôtres* [Paris: Duculot, 1953], 157; and Martin Dibelius, *Studies in the Acts of the Apostles* [New York: Scribner, 1956], 63). A negative view of Paul's work in Athens has even found its way into the notes of the *New Jerusalem Bible* ([New York: Doubleday, 1985], 1829). The negative appraisal of Paul's ministry in Athens, not shared by all, nevertheless raises important questions. Do Paul's work and his preaching involve compromise with contemporary pagan religious notions? Is Paul "sidetracked" by a "natural theology" that obscures the distinctives of the Christian message? Ultimately, is Acts 17:16-34 evidence of Paul's "failure" in Athens? And in Luke's mind, does this account serve as a model or as a foil for the reader?

70. For this we are dependent on the testimony of Xenophon: "Socrates does wrongly, for he does not acknowledge the gods which the state acknowledges; rather, he introduces other new-fashioned gods" (*Memorabilia* 1.1.1).

71. Not only Acts 17 but also Acts 16 serves to demonstrate Paul's dictum of being "all things to all men." The apostle's ministry in the region of southern Galatia, where there existed a large Jewish population (cf. 16:3), resulted in a decision to have Timothy circumcised. Luke's intent is to mirror Christian "accommodation" to the culture of which Christians are a part.

munity in Athens — the little we know of it — confronts Christians in the Western cultural context as well. What lessons might be drawn from Paul's encounter with "cultured paganism"?[72]

By Paul's day the city had lost much of the preeminence that it once possessed.[73] Nevertheless, Cicero, writing one hundred years earlier, could observe that despite its decline in political power, Athens still enjoyed "such renown that the now shattered and weakened name of Greece is supported by the reputation of this city."[74] People generally came to Athens, Alexandria, or Tarsus to study philosophy or rhetoric, or to get a general education. In the writings of Strabo and Ovid Athens is depicted as a tourist center and the site of great festivals, while attracting itinerant philosophers and mystics. One such traveling teacher-mystic, Apollonius of Tyana, is described by Philostratus in the early third century as having arrived at Athens about the same time as the apostle Paul.[75] Interestingly, the account mentions that Apollonius was struck by the altars "to unknown gods," corroborating Luke's narrative.[76]

It is to the cradle of pagan culture that the apostle is led for divine purposes (cf. Acts 16:6-10), adapting himself to the dialectical habits of its inhabitants. Historians of antiquity record the intellectual atmosphere of first-century Athens as mildly promiscuous and idolatrous (cf. 17:16-21), in

72. Elsewhere I have similarly explored the Pauline strategy that was adapted to Athenian pluralism in "Paul before the Areopagus: Reflections on the Apostle's Encounter with Cultured Paganism," *Philosophia Christi* 7, no. 1 (2005): 123-38, and more briefly, *The Unformed Conscience of Evangelicalism: Recovering the Church's Moral Vision* (Downers Grove, Ill.: InterVarsity, 2002), 144-57.

73. Although thirty years of exhaustive strife with Sparta as a result of the Peloponnesian Wars (431-403 B.C.) left Athens politically weakened, the rich cultural heritage of the city remained unsurpassed. Its contributions to sculpture, literature, philosophy, and oratory from the fifth and fourth centuries were unparalleled in the ancient world. In addition to being the native city of Socrates and Plato, it became the adopted home of Aristotle, Epicurus, and Zeno. Demosthenes, an "unsuccessful Churchill" of the mid–fourth century B.C., strove in vain to rouse his fellow Athenians once more to political independence and greatness. Athens was home to the poet Menander (quoted by Paul in 1 Cor. 15:33: "Bad company ruins good morals"), whose New Comedy as a form of entertainment eclipsed the classical Greek tragedy in the late fourth and early third century B.C.

74. Cicero, *Pro Flacco* 26.62.

75. See Eduard Mayer, "Apollonius von Tyana und die Biographie des Philostratos," *Hermes* 52 (1917): 371-424.

76. Acts 17:23. His allusion is in the plural ("unknown gods"), contrasted with Luke's reference in the singular.

both a religious and a nonreligious sense. Even while a growing percentage of the city's population had been initiated into mystery cults, Athenians appear to have had little knowledge of Old Testament revelation.[77] Despite the city's past intellectual reputation, by Paul's day Athens exhibited a somewhat indiscriminate, almost casual, approach to life issues. Several of the church fathers allude to Athens as a city of talkers, a people obsessed with curiosity (cf. 17:18, 21). According to one ancient source, Athenians were a particularly litigious lot.[78] With hermaphrodites commonplace sights at house doors and symbols of phallic worship and sexual obsession on public display throughout the city, one can envisage the dislocation in the apostle's spirit (17:16) as he encounters a culture in moderate to excessive decline.

Luke spends no time prefacing the speech to the Council of the Areopagus, but this is not because it is a casual or insignificant encounter. Much to the contrary, the council was an elite and prestigious body that deliberated over educational, legal, and social issues. The contemporary reader would have understood the import of Paul's invitation to address this esteemed body. It is supremely unfortunate that virtually all of this is lost on the modern reader. It is *not*, however, lost on Luke Timothy Johnson, who writes: "What impresses every reader with even the slightest knowledge of Hellenistic culture is how cunningly Luke has . . . everything right."[79] Indeed, the closer one looks, the more apparent it becomes that Paul's encounter with Athens is significant, at the cultural and philosophical level.

With the passing of the centuries a canonical twelve gods were thought to hold power on Mount Olympus. Athens was the site of an altar dedicated to this twelve-member pantheon, which included Athena, daughter to Zeus. Religion and politics appear to have been inextricably combined in Athenian society, as evidenced by the surviving literature. One such example is a somewhat turgid speech dated A.D. 155 by Aelius Aristides at the Panathenaic Festival. In it the author recounts a legal battle of the gods that is significant for an understanding of Athenian history —

77. This is in spite of Luke's statement that there was a Jewish synagogue in the city (Acts 17:17).

78. *Charito* 1.2.6 (cited in Hans Conzelmann, *Acts of the Apostles*, Hermeneia [Philadelphia: Fortress, 1987], 139).

79. Luke Timothy Johnson, *The Acts of the Apostles* (Collegeville, Minn.: Liturgical Press, 1992), 218.

and for the reader's appreciation of the momentous opportunity that permits Paul to address the Council of the Areopagus. In his pursuit of justice, Poseidon sued Ares over the murder of his son, ultimately winning his case in the presence of all the gods.[80] As a record of the event, the purported site of disputation took on Ares' name. Hence, throughout Athens's rich cultural history the Areopagus (literally, "Ares' hill") constituted for many the pinnacle of authority and respect. It was here that justice was to be eternally manifest. Thus it was that Athenians looked to the Areopagus as a source of knowledge, wisdom, reason, and justice.

Since the mid–third century B.C. the Council of the Areopagus functioned as an authoritative body in civil-legal and educational matters.[81] The council consisted of thirty members and was presided over by a "ruling elder" who was charged with conducting official business. In the Roman era the Areopagus was comprised of several committees, one of which was educational and on which Cicero, one hundred years before Paul, is said to have served.[82] Acts 17:22-33 may well be Luke's report of Paul being led before this elite committee for an informal inquiry, where the Apostle to the Gentiles engages in moral and religious discourse with the cultural elite of his day.[83] As mirrored by Luke, the apostle shows an ability to clothe revelation in relevant arguments that are intelligible to his pagan contemporaries.

An examination of Paul's Areopagus speech allows us to observe his *method* at work. We might summarize his goals or aims as follows:

---

80. Aelius Aristides 1.40-48.

81. Cicero himself, a century before Paul arrived at Athens, had been a member of the Areopagus Council.

82. We learn this from Plutarch (late first and early second century). Cicero (*De natura deorum* 2.29.74) informs us that in the Roman period the Areopagus had jurisdiction over criminal matters.

83. Perhaps the best English-language resource on the background of the Areopagus Council is Bertil Gaertner, *The Areopagus Speech and Natural Revelation*, Acta seminarii neotestamentici upsaliensis 21 (Uppsala: Almquist, 1955). On Paul's actual speech to the council, see Pascal P. Parente, "St. Paul's Address before the Areopagus," *Catholic Biblical Quarterly* 11 (1949): 144ff.; Hans Conzelmann, "The Address of Paul on the Areopagus," in *Studies in Luke-Acts*, ed. Leander E. Keck and J. Louis Martyn (Nashville and New York: Abingdon, 1966), 218ff.; L. Legrand, "The Areopagus Speech: Its Theological Kerygma and Its Missionary Significance," in *La Notion de Dieu*, ed. J. Coppens (Louvain: Gembloux, 1974), 338ff.; and J. Daryl Charles, "Engaging the (Neo)Pagan Mind," *Trinity Journal*, n.s., 16 (1995): 47-62.

- to communicate truth in the language of his audience;
- to build upon pagan concepts and utilize pagan illustrations — whether philosophical, literary, or religious — for the purposes of expressing the reality of divine revelation;
- to adjust pagan assumptions about nature, the cosmos, the Creator, and creation;
- to give credence to the Creator's self-disclosure (the cosmos and the resurrection); and
- to move his audience in the direction of repentance with rhetorically heightened moral persuasion.[84]

We can clarify Paul's intention with his audience by considering the specific rhetorical tactics he employs in his address. Several are conspicuous:

- He addresses core philosophical assumptions of both Stoics and Epicureans (cf. 17:18) that need adjustment — for example, (a) what can be "known" (17:23, 30);[85] (b) the cosmos as independent or contingent (17:24-25); (c) the universe as solely material (17:24, 25, 31); (d) the "divine" as impersonal reason; and (e) kinship with the "divine."
- He employs rhetorical devices that are thoroughly Hellenistic, personable yet formal — for example, the very opening of his speech, whereby he addresses his audience with "Men" (ἄνδρες) followed by the designation "Athenians" (Ἀθηναῖοι), and his commendation that his listeners are very "religiously minded."[86]
- He exploits an element of irony — for example, in developing the important subtheme in his address of "ignorance" (17:23, 30) over against Athenians' (and particularly Stoics') great learning and erudition.
- He extracts, with the skill of a surgeon, quotations from Epimenides and Aratus of Soli (17:28-29) — two poet-philosophers held in high

---

84. These goals are explored more fully in Parente, "St. Paul's Address," 144ff.; Legrand, "The Areopagus Speech," 338ff.; and Charles, "Engaging the (Neo)Pagan Mind," 54-60.

85. The occurrence of the verb "to know" and cognate forms in the Greek text — e.g., "unknown" (ἄγνωστος) in v. 23 and "ignorance" (ἄγνοια) in v. 30, from which forms the English "agnostic" derives — gives the appearance of a wordplay.

86. Thus C. F. Evans, "Speeches in Acts," in *Mélanges bibliques,* ed. A. R. Charne (Paris: Duculot, 1969), 291-92.

esteem by Athenians — and employs them selectively in the service of his argument.[87]

- He uses his knowledge of the city's cultural background and history to engage his audience — for example, utilizing a public monument (17:23) as a springboard for his argument based on creation.[88]
- He appeals to "general revelation" for the purposes of establishing a bridge with the audience, in order to introduce "special revelation."
- He exposes the fallacy of metaphysical naturalism (i.e., materialism) (17:24-25, 29).[89]
- He contrasts pagan inclusivity with Christian exclusivity.
- He dismantles the Stoic view of universal continuum, which denies that history as we know it will terminate and that an afterlife,[90] which follows a moral day of reckoning, exists (17:31).[91]

---

87. The statement "in him we live, move, and have our being" (17:28a) is a near-verbatim citation and adaptation of a poem attributed to the sixth century B.C. poet Epimenides of Crete, who was considered one of the seven sages of Greece (so Diogenes Laertius, *Lives of the Philosophers* 1.109-115). It expresses the Stoic belief in closeness to and kinship with the divine. Any Stoic worth his salt readily conceded that God "fills" the universe, and that a union exists. The second citation, "we are his offspring" (17:28b), according to Clement of Alexandria (*Stromata* 1.19.91), stems from the third century B.C. Stoic philosopher Aratus of Soli, who, significantly, hailed from Paul's native city of Tarsus. Aratus had penned these words in a poem in honor of Zeus. Titled *Phaenomena*, the poem is an interpretation of constellations and weather signs. The particular citation reads: "in all things each of us needs Zeus, for we are also his offspring" (*Phaenomena* 5).

88. That there were altars to many "unknown gods" in Athens is established by several ancient writers. Pausanius (*Description of Greece* 1.1.4) and Philostratus (*Vita Apollonii* 6.3) describe Athens as the scene of innumerable gods, heroes, and corresponding altars. Tertullian (*Ad nationes* 2.9) writes that Paul chose the singular description, "unknown god," over the plural even though the latter is understood. On the identity of the altar referred to by Paul, it is impossible to be conclusive, although one ancient commentator believes that it traces to an Athenian legend, according to which a demon appeared following defeat in battle. Out of fear, not wishing to exclude any deity, the Athenians erected an altar "to an unknown god."

89. The materialist and pantheist stamp of the Areopagus address is a clear reflection of Luke's intent to show how the apostolic message engages the pagan mind-set.

90. The doctrine of the resurrection is strategic in its validation of the Christian message. But at Athens it is even more strategic because of the city's patron goddess Athena, who proclaims, "Once a man dies and the earth drinks up his blood, there is no resurrection" (ἀνάστασις) (so Aeschylus, *Eumenides* 647).

91. As evidence that epistemological ignorance is not bliss, the one true God has ordained "a day" on which "the man" Jesus "will judge the world in righteousness." In this way

- He alters the Stoic understanding of reason, since, for the Stoic, the divine essence is *logos*, reason.

The last of these aims is extremely important, especially with unbelievers who pride themselves in being sophisticated, virtuous, and "reasonable." Stoic thinking maintains that in the structure of the universe itself lie the seeds of knowledge, the *logos spermatikos*,[92] which give rise to the universe. Reason, then, is understood as the highest expression of nature.[93] Paul bridges the chasm between Stoic and Christian thought by appropriating common philosophical ground, asserting that the use of reason can lead to the knowledge of God, even when he dismantles the Stoic idol of self-sufficiency that denies the fundamental notion of grace.[94]

Although Acts 17:16-34 follows a somewhat different rhetorical pattern than Romans 1, which is thought by many to be a primary New Testament text supporting general revelation, in both texts Paul identifies a common apologetic bridge to the pagan mind: *nature* itself. In Pauline thinking there exists an inseparable connection between creation, the moral order, and human accountability. This link, articulated before the Areopagus Council in the idiom of his day, is the core of Paul's speech. Pagans "know" because of creation as well as conscience; in the end, their "ignorance" is "without excuse." That Paul ends with "radical discontinuity," based on his presentation of special revelation, is not to deny the unmistakable role that ethical continuity plays in his discourse. *All* are morally accountable, and this is precisely how natural law functions.

This connection, rooted in the awareness by all people in every place of a "law of nature," has an important function in Paul's strategy, since the Athenians — and particularly the members of the council — have no the-

---

for Paul the Judeo-Christian understanding of history, begun by and ending with divine fiat, marks a radical discontinuity with the worldview of his audience.

92. Note in Acts 17:18 the derogatory language being used by Epicureans and Stoics of Paul: the Greek term translated "babbler" is *spermologos*. Luke may be appropriating irony here.

93. "Right reason" *(logos orthos)*, as taught by the Stoic philosopher Zeno, "is the same as Zeus" *(Frag.* 162, cited in C. K. Barrett, ed., *The New Testament Background: Selected Documents* [New York and Evanston: Harper and Row, 1961], 62). On this aspect of Stoic thought, see Eduard Zeller, *The Stoics, Epicureans, and Skeptics* (New York: Russell and Russell, 1962), 126-66.

94. Paul does not remain, however, at the level of human reason, even though he will go as far as Greek assumptions will allow him. Creation ex nihilo and divine self-disclosure require more from the philosopher.

istic or christological understanding. The apostle's discourse on creation and the cosmos, then, serves as a necessary "pedagogical-missionary preamble."[95] In both Romans 1 and Acts 17 the phenomena of creation are said to be accessible to all;[96] in Romans 1:20 "all things" are visible for all to see. For Paul, this knowledge of the Creator God is innate and rational. Even pagans without knowledge of Christ have a fundamental awareness of moral accountability; "by nature" they do the moral law, even though they do not have the law (Rom. 2:14). This is why the apostle can assume and speak of universal norms — norms that are rationally perceived. Whether he is writing to Christians living in the imperial seat of Rome or addressing academics sitting on the Council of the Areopagus, Paul's purpose is to stress that *all people* are morally accountable. To be sure, the fact *that* pagans *possess* the moral law does not mean they *attain* it. Nevertheless, moral norms are known to all.

Paul's model in Athens is instructive in important ways. Not least of these is the manner in which Christian faith engages pre-Christian pagan society. Both his method, which skillfully draws on subtleties of style and fitting technique, and his message,[97] which presumes and builds upon general revelation, are appropriate and adapted to his audience. The modus operandi of the street preacher and the policy analyst, both of whom serve Christ, requires that different strategies be employed; neither, it must be emphasized, capitulates in using the *appropriate* method of service to others.

Paul's address to the Areopagites reminds us that we must be conversant both with culture and with the Creator; we must be students as well as disciples. And although Paul's ministry in Athens predates Tertullian's famous question, "What does Athens have to do with Jerusalem?" a fresh re-

95. This expression has been used by German commentator Philip Vielhauer, "Zum 'Paulinismus' der Apostelgeschichte," in *Aufsätze zum Neuen Testament* (Munich: Chr. Kaiser, 1956), 13.

96. See H. P. Owen, "The Scope of Natural Revelation in Romans i and Acts xvii," *New Testament Studies* 5 (1958/59): 142-43.

97. While our present focus is on *method,* and specifically Paul's use of general revelation, the Areopagus address has much to teach us. What can we derive from the *message?* Inter alia, that monism must yield to monotheism, that the Divine is personal and not impersonal, and that immanence must be wed to transcendence. Sovereignty, providence, and purpose trump chaos, process, and determinism. Moral accountability replaces self-sufficiency and moral relativism. History is marked by a beginning and a terminus rather than being cyclical and eternal. Finally, death, resurrection, and judgment undermine any illusions about reincarnation on the one hand or annihilation and cessation on the other.

reading of Acts 17 sheds light on the perennial question he raised. Significantly, it answers Tertullian's resolute "Nothing" with an even more resolute "Something indeed!"[98]

The ability to "be all things to all men," and to do so in the language of his audience, is praiseworthy and commends itself as an example to the contemporary reader. Alas, we discover that the first and twenty-first centuries show notable affinities. Both are pagan (one being pre-Christian, the other "post-Christian"), both are biblically-theologically illiterate,[99] and both require adaptation of the gospel in ways that are culturally sensitive yet theologically faithful.[100] Both necessitate an emphasis on moral "first things."[101]

Natural Law, Christian Social Ethics, and Civil Society

Natural law is by no means the sole resource that undergirds an account of Christian ethics. It is, however, a necessary starting point in understanding

98. It is precisely the Athens-Jerusalem question that is addressed by John Paul II in his 1998 encyclical *Fides et Ratio,* in which the former pontiff appeals to philosophers, theologians, teachers, scientists, and concerned laypeople to take their respective places in helping work toward what he calls the "reevangelization" of our culture. It is not incidental that philosophy has pride of place in *Fides;* as a moral philosopher, John Paul aimed much of his cultural criticism during the 1990s at renegade philosophers, given their influence in legitimizing nihilism and a pagan view of reality. John Paul believed that Christian philosophers carried a special burden into the third millennium. And for this task we have an important resource in Acts 17.

99. Note that, unlike elsewhere, Paul does not cite the Hebrew Scriptures in his appeal to the Athenians.

100. In many respects Western culture — and North American culture in particular — resembles Athens in Paul's day. It is a culture, intellectually and morally, in relative decline. Like first-century Athenians, to whom belonged an illustrious past, ours is what Aleksander Solzhenitsyn has called a "culture of novelty." In our obsession with that which is novel, truth and its consequences are of little value. For this reason Paul's model in Athens beckons us. William Abraham writes that "we are back in the position of the church of the first three centuries. Christians live in a world that is radically pluralistic and fragmented. For the most part, the age of Christendom is gone, and we must now happily acknowledge our marginal, minority, and even sectarian status in the conflict of ideas and ideologies" ("C. S. Lewis and the Conversion of the West," in *Permanent Things,* 272). I am inclined to agree.

101. In the end, Paul's "accommodation" in Athens should in no way be misconstrued as syncretism. Paul accommodates himself, not the message, to the assumptions of those in his midst. Antithesis, where it arises, should be the product of our *message,* not our *method.*

— and advancing — moral goodness and social norms. As Thomas Aquinas argues with remarkable precision, the natural moral law is the expression of divine wisdom by which all participate in the eternal law.[102] This does not suggest a dual conception of the moral universe — one track for the regenerate and one for the unregenerate. Rather, it assumes the ontological priority of nature as a prerequisite for the reception of divine grace. Grace does not eliminate nature; rather, it *fulfills* and *perfects* it.[103] Seen in this manner, natural law is foundational for both the belief in human dignity[104] and a public theology that *works toward the common good* of society.[105] On these two counts, namely, affirming human sanctity and promoting the common social good, we have much to glean from the Christian moral tradition — and from thinkers like Thomas Aquinas, in particular, who concern themselves with the commonweal — as we wrestle with the conundrum of public-versus-private morality and seek to advance a responsible public philosophy.

The necessity of translating Christian faith into responsible social and public policy — policy that works for the common social good — was the burden of Roman Catholic theologian John Courtney Murray in *We Hold These Truths*, penned nearly five decades ago. From the standpoint of Christian faith's relationship to surrounding culture, Murray's book is arguably one of the most significant works of the twentieth century. As a theologian, Murray was at the center of many policy discussions, given his

102. Aquinas, *ST* I-II Q. 91, a. 2 and 4.

103. Fittingly, the "law of nature" *(lex naturalis)* is understood in patristic theology as "the first grace of God" *(per primam Dei gratiam)*. See more recently, in this vein, the important book by Russell Hittinger, *The First Grace*, whose title draws inspiration from patristic usage.

104. In the thinking of Aquinas, the great champion of natural law for whom natural law was "natural" insofar as it mirrored the order of creation, a corrective to a distorted view of total depravity is necessary. Aquinas counters that the *imago Dei*, though marred, is still intact. Natural law also assists us in countering a secularized preference utilitarianism on the other hand. Both errors — the religious and the secular — negate human dignity.

105. Working toward the common good of society is an important theme for Aquinas. Coupled with the emphasis on natural law, this forms the backbone of any credible "public theology." On the element of the common good in Thomistic thought, see Jacques Maritain, *The Person and the Common Good*, trans. J. J. Fitzgerald (New York: Scribner, 1947); Ralph McInerny, "The Golden Rule and Natural Law," *Modern Schoolman* 69 (1992): 421-30; and McInerny, *Ethica Thomistica* (Notre Dame, Ind.: University of Notre Dame Press, 1997).

belief in truths that were self-evident, which in turn ground a civil society and principled pluralism. Murray insisted that religious freedom — inclusive of those ancillary civil freedoms it engenders — is rooted in human dignity, which for him is anchored in the natural moral law. German legal theorist Heinrich Rommen, imprisoned by the Nazis before emigrating to the United States in the mid-1930s, concurs. Human rights, he insists, can have no foundation other than natural law. And because they are rooted in "nature," they are inalienable and morally inviolable, to be removed only by the Creator.[106]

Religious freedom, issuing out of human dignity, benefits *all* members and segments of society — private and familial, public and social — and not merely those of religious conviction. Natural law, for Murray, is foundational to the establishment of basic freedoms as well as to the very ordering of society. It informs private and public policy, soulcraft as well as statecraft.[107]

Viewed historically, the language of natural law and the common good is by no means restricted to Catholic social ethics. Despite its relative neglect in recent Protestant thought, it was widely assumed by the Protestant Reformers — notably, by Luther, Calvin, and Bullinger. It undergirds the foundations of international law and civil society as developed by the influential Dutch legal theorist Hugo Grotius (1583-1645). And it retains an esteemed place in writings of Puritan thinkers such as Richard Hooker (1553-1600) and William Ames (1576-1633). In our own day, against much resistance, it has survived — when not universally — in some Lutheran and Reformed theological circles.[108] In Protestant Reformed — and notably Kuyperian — theological terms, the goals of pursuing common ground in a pluralistic society will be "civic virtue," "domesticity," "human

---

106. Heinrich Rommen, *The Natural Law: A Study in Legal and Social History and Philosophy*, trans. T. R. Hanley (Indianapolis: Liberty Fund, 1998), 216 n. 50.

107. In addition to *We Hold These Truths*, see also his essay "Religious Freedom," in *Freedom and Man*, ed. John Courtney Murray (New York: P. J. Kenedy, 1965), 131-40.

108. Thus, e.g., Emil Brunner, *Justice and the Social Order* (New York: Harper and Row, 1945), and more recently, Carl E. Braaten, "Natural Law in Theology and Ethics," in *The Two Cities of God: The Church's Responsibility for the Earthly City*, ed. Carl E. Braaten and Robert W. Jenson (Grand Rapids and Cambridge, U.K.: Eerdmans, 1997), 42-58, and Braaten, "Protestants and Natural Law," *First Things*, May 1992, 20-26. Lutheran theologian Robert Jenson's essay "Is There an Ordering Principle?" in Jenson, *Essays in Theology of Culture* (Grand Rapids: Eerdmans, 1995), 67-75, assumes natural-law thinking, even when the author refrains from using the term "natural law" explicitly.

virtue," "natural love," an "improvement of the public conscience," "loyalty among people," and an increased sense of "piety" among the citizenry.[109] Apart from common-ground moral discourse that is rooted in natural-law thinking, such goals are inconceivable. Whether or not Protestants believe they should work toward these goals is of course another matter.

One of the reasons present-day Protestants are uncomfortable with talk of "common ground" discourse is a tendency toward dualisms. Consider, for example, the characteristic Protestant bifurcation between sacred and secular, between public and private, and between grace and works. The result, in much recent Protestant thought, is a strong emphasis on personal piety (where it is not riddled with secularism) coupled with a weak "public theology" and corresponding (relative) absence from the public square. Where Protestants *are* active in the political sphere, it is frequently in the form of social-political activism (and not infrequently motivated by a loathing of "fundamentalism" or the dreaded "religious right" bogeyman). But our political preferences aside, ecumenically minded Protestants, whose interests extend beyond "evangelism" narrowly construed, on the one hand, and mere social activism, on the other, will need to confront the wider implications of Christian faith — for example, working for standards of justice and the preservation of civil society. As such, they will need to join hands with like-minded Roman Catholic believers in working for the common good. This, of course, may necessitate a reordering of spiritual priorities, and it may, at the most basic level, require rethinking their theology.

To begin, for example: What *is* the common good in society? *How* is it discerned/known? And what role does the Christian community have in its maintenance? Stated otherwise, what responsibility does the church have for the world?

In a provocative essay titled "The Church's Responsibility for the World," Lutheran theologian Robert Jenson argues that in the most elementary sense, the church is responsible for and to the world in that "were it not for the church there would be no world."[110] Therefore, the church is first and foremost *morally* responsible for society based on creation and

---

109. Abraham Kuyper, "Common Grace," in *Abraham Kuyper: A Centennial Reader*, ed. James D. Bratt (Grand Rapids: Eerdmans, 1998), 181.

110. Jenson, "The Church's Responsibility for the World," in *Essays in Theology of Culture*, 1. Page numbers referring to this essay have been placed in parentheses in the text.

redemption. Moral "tending of the garden" is implicit in the language of Saint Paul to the Christians in Colossae: "All things were created through him [Christ] and for him [Christ]" (1:16). This theological declaration, which is both instrumental and teleological in stating Christ's relationship to creation, at the very least suggests the place of the church with regard to stewardship of "all things."

Jenson is quick to remind us, in order to counter any apocalyptic or fideistic understanding of "tending," that stewardship and redemption do not amount to "a rescue operation after intruding disaster" (3). That is, they are not reactive but rather proactive in their trajectory. Thus, the church's role is not to be passively awaiting the eschaton while nurturing contempt for the world.

A second and opposite error, in answer to the question of the church's responsibility to the world, also needs to be avoided. As Jenson sees it, this is the fallacy of Protestant mainline churches over the last sixty years — namely, allowing the world to set the church's agenda (4-5). This mind-set fails to comprehend both the nature and the mission of the church as it is placed in this world by Providence. Rather than look to the world, the church instead should be continually rethinking its priorities in light of its divine calling; it is the world's agenda and not vice versa. By this we do not have in mind some sort of religious triumphalism. We merely mean to argue that human civilization, in the divine scheme of things, has flourished only because of the church's existence. The idea that the world might be able to exist apart from the church is biblically-theologically untenable.

If these erroneous positions indicate what the church is not to do, what then is the church's responsibility to the world? It is, according to Jenson, quite simply "to preserve the being of the world" (5). More to the point: through its lifestyle and its message, the church is "to combat the world's decline toward nothingness" (6). Such is foremost an ethical assignment. The church does this not in a vacuum, nor is its moral arsenal any different than that of covenantal Israel. Through the Ten Commandments, which give expression to the natural moral law (i.e., what Adam, Abraham, and Melchizedek knew), the church as a community addresses the human community. These moral guidelines provide for and protect the human community.[111] For this very reason, it is "the church's re-

111. The New Testament maintains full ethical continuity with the Old Testament in

sponsibility to address the Ten Commandments, in their minimal, boundary-setting sense, to the world, in the hope that thereby the world-community can be restrained from undoing itself" (7). In addition, Jenson admonishes us, we can "first and last . . . pray that God will, by our instrumentality and by other means, not permit our worldly community to collapse" (8).

This, of course, brings us back to the question of the common good. *That* there exists a common good in society presupposes that people — all people, not just some — can discern the good and that the good is knowable. Thus, it would seem, two spheres — the metaphysical and the political — are inextricably linked in the notion of the common good.[112] If we as a society must make political judgments about what is good and bad, acceptable and unacceptable, then the good is somehow knowable. Moreover, this good, as Jenson emphasizes, is not merely *willed;* it is *discovered.* While such an assumption flies in the face of modern and postmodern epistemological thinking, it can nevertheless stand on its own, for a "common good" is by nature a common, shared territory and not private. Political judgments and the political process become impossible where there is no shared repository of values and priorities. Ethically speaking, society collapses due to the sheer velocity and weight of atomizing and alienating centripetal forces, based on private wants and "needs," that pull people away from the moral center. But are all wants and needs to be satisfied? Are all legitimate to a self-governing people? The "good" can exist only where society is willing to evaluate and debate those wants and needs.[113]

We hold — and indeed strive to preserve — a consensus about the common good for important reasons. This enterprise is necessary because it is an *inherited* moral consensus; that is to say, we affirm basic moral truth because it is the moral thread that unites generation with generation, civilization with civilization. It is foundational to our vast cultural heritage. Moreover, we reaffirm this moral tradition because it is true in and of itself, independent of our beliefs and biases; it is not true because we believe it; rather the reverse: we believe it because it corre-

---

affirming the Ten Commandments as the core of the moral life. Thus, e.g., Matt. 5:19; 15:3-4; 19:16-22; Mark 7:8-9; 12:28-31; Luke 18:18-30; Rom. 7:12; 13:8-9; 1 Cor. 7:19; Eph. 6:2; James 2:8-11; 1 John 2:3-4; 3:22-24; Rev. 12:17; 14:12.

112. This linkage Thomas Aquinas well understood.

113. This necessity has been argued forcefully by John Courtney Murray, *We Hold These Truths,* 73-75.

sponds with reality. Because of the character of pluralism and the need to pass on to the next generation what we have inherited, this moral tradition must *not* be taken for granted; the consensus needs preservation, argument, debate, and dialogue. But if the very idea of the "good" is fluid and open to question, even denied, the challenge of striving for civil society becomes much more difficult.[114]

If the Christian community is to participate in this ongoing debate and work for the common good in society, that is, if in biblical terms we are to have the preserving effect of "salt" (Matt. 5:13; cf. Num. 18:19), there must exist some shared moral grammar between Christians and culture.[115] For example, public policy work becomes impossible for the Christian if there is no shared language of moral discourse with surrounding society. Indeed, those theologians and moral philosophers who reject the place of natural law in Christian social ethics fail to give an adequate account of *how to bridge the chasm* between the church and pluralistic society. And they are powerless, without any resources, to help cultivate any sort of public consensus about what is good, what is acceptable, what is just; they can only talk among themselves.

Let us consider the idea of justice. If "justice" is not rooted in a firm notion about *the way things are,* whether or not one embraces religious faith, how can a society determine what is *just?* If there is no "higher" law, then there is no justification at all for declaring *any* law — or behavior, for that matter — to be just or unjust. At best, it can only argue matters of *legality* and concede that *force alone* justifies what is "law." "Criminal justice" thus becomes utterly impossible. For "criminal justice" as a concept to be workable, people operating in the public square must proceed from a fixed, nonfluid, shared notion of what is "just." Common-ground moral discourse that is rooted in an understanding of natural law will prevent "Christian ethics" from being reduced to an all-too-common type of Protestant existentialism, whereby meaning is to be found only in one's personal experience or one's "narrative." Given its rejection of natural law, one doubts *whether* — and precisely *how* — the narrative approach to Christian ethics can inform and mold civic discourse.[116] This is especially true when

---

114. On the idea of cultivating a moral consensus, see Murray, *We Hold These Truths,* especially chapters 1 and 2.

115. What isolationist "fundamentalists" and radical Anabaptists have in common is a relative disavowal of the public square.

116. See further discussion in chapter 4.

Christian narrative-ethicists, who tend to be separatist (in some cases "radical separatists") anyway, presuppose that we *not* engage the cultural mainstream *at the level of public policy.* Gilbert Meilaender offers the needed corrective in this regard: "Even if Christian moral knowledge is built upon no foundation other than the biblical narrative of God's dealings with his world, that story itself authorizes us to seek and expect some common moral ground with those whose vision is not shaped by Christian belief."[117] But how is this to be done? Those who reject natural-law thinking are powerless to engage surrounding culture in meaningful terms.

It is here — viz., working for the common good and contributing to civil society — that recent Protestant theology has shown itself to be generally impotent in the public square. Either, with apocalyptic foreboding, we have withdrawn from it (to await the eschaton), or we have deliberately and "radically" separated ourselves from it (content to build our "prophetic" communities on the side), or we simply don't care about it (enough said). None of these postures is commendable, even though each in its own way tends to wax somewhat self-righteous. More importantly, none accords with the mainstream teaching of the Christian church historically; none finds sufficient biblical-theological warrant.

If Robert Jenson is correct, that the church is morally responsible for the world (and I think he is), we need not give up our burden for "evangelism" as it is popularly understood; but we must broaden the scope of our vision to the "reevangelization" of the entire culture, as John Paul II has described it in several important encyclicals of the 1990s. That is, we must "reseed" society, and this will necessitate beginning with cultural and moral foundations that support "civil society."[118] We shall need to stress the "permanent things" that have been forgotten, denied, or eclipsed. What are those permanent things that need enunciation? Again, with John Courtney Murray, we confess, against the spirit of the age:

---

117. Meilaender, *Faith and Faithfulness*, 19-20. Vigen Guroian, *Ethics after Christendom*, chapters 1 and 2, also offers wisdom in his judicious critique of "narrative" ethics. In addition, Jean Porter, *Natural and Divine Law: Reclaiming the Tradition for Christian Ethics* (Grand Rapids and Cambridge, U.K.: Eerdmans, 1999), hints at the weaknesses of the strictly "narrative" approach to Christian ethics in chapters 2, 3, and 5 of her important book, observing the deficiency in public policy that an absolute precommitment to "nonviolence," which frequently attends construals of "narrative" ethics, engenders.

118. Recall the prior distinction we made between "free" and civil society.

- that there are truths (i.e., nonfluid principles and standards of moral judgment that are everywhere and at all times applicable);
- that we as citizens of two kingdoms affirm these truths, in continuity with past generations, since this is what wisdom requires;
- that these truths order the moral, political, social, and economic life of our society — for the good of *all* citizens, whether or not they confess religious faith; and
- that these truths, these permanent things, must be sustained rationally through persuasion as well as through positive example.[119]

We need to accentuate and clarify the role of natural law in this reconstructive project. First, "natural law" is no mere "Roman Catholic" domain; rather, natural law corresponds, quite simply, to moral reality. Protestants beware. The first principle of the moral world is that reason apprehends certain foundational moral truths, namely, that good is to be done and evil to be eschewed. The starting point of discerning good and evil gives rise to guidelines for how to live our lives, how to conduct ourselves in particular situations. These guidelines we call the Ten Commandments, "the basic moral laws of human life, sanctioned by reason and also sanctioned by their inclusion in the Jewish and Christian codes."[120] At yet another level, moral reasoning gives rise to wisdom, moral-political prudence, that guides humans in community to establish just laws by which to order the community. The fundamental structure of human nature, as Thomas Aquinas emphasized, does not change with altered circumstances. Nor is it altered by history. Therefore, neither history nor culture alters the natural law, since it is constituted by the ethical a priori, i.e., by first principles of moral reason.

For this reason it can be properly argued that only the natural law is able to mold a public moral consensus. And in what ways? It bridges the gap between Christians and non-Christians; it assumes the acknowledgment of and distinction between good and evil; it expresses itself in the recognition of basic moral guidelines for society; and it is the source of political-legal and moral wisdom by which civil society governs itself.

Thus, to work for a "civil society," to take seriously the church's mandate to contribute toward a moral "consensus" within society, Chris-

---

119. Murray, *We Hold These Truths*, 106-7.
120. Murray, *We Hold These Truths*, 110.

tians will need to engage, in the marketplace, their non-Christian contemporaries. Apart from natural law, which expresses general — that is to say, indirect — revelation to which all are held accountable, fulfilling this mandate is impossible. General revelation furnishes the basis on which Christians and non-Christians relate to one another.[121] Natural-law thinking does not aspire or pretend to do more than it can or should, which is "to give a philosophical account of the moral experience of humanity and to lay down a charter of essential humanism."[122] While general revelation is insufficient to *justify* humans before their Creator, it does give *all* people a *minimal knowledge* of the Creator as well as of the moral standard to which *all will be held accountable*. Thus, natural law possesses an important "apologetic" function. While natural law is not all there is to say about ethics, it is the necessary starting point to address the moral life.

Theologically conservative Protestants, in their recent history, have tended to view the apologetic task solely in terms of antithesis. While at one level there is an oppositional element in Christians' relationship to the world that is not to be denied, neither should it be overemphasized to the exclusion of moral discourse with surrounding culture. If the Son of God "so loved the world," his disciples must follow in his steps; this will mean caring for people — particularly those among whom we have been placed — as well as participating responsibly in those cultural institutions of which they are a part. Salt has "lost its savor" if it is content to flee society while it awaits the eschaton.

If Christians approach public dialogue and civil discourse with only the vocabulary of "culture wars,"[123] they will find that their efforts are severely diminished and counterproductive. Rather, people of strong Christian conviction must learn, difficult as it may be, to dialogue with non-Christians and those who are ideological opposites, and they must do so in creative and more irenic ways. While the *message* that Christians bear will ultimately offend because of the lordship of Christ over all things, never

---

121. J. Budziszewski's *What We Can't Not Know* makes this case with supreme moral clarity, taking on the many objections to natural-law thinking marshaled by both the religious and the secular.

122. Murray, *We Hold These Truths*, 297.

123. I in no way wish to deny the reality of ideological battles that are raging, with their considerable ethical implications, on many cultural fronts. Indeed, much is at stake in Western and American culture.

should our *method,* i.e., the mode of our discourse or living, offend; it is important that we make this critical distinction. This, I think, is part of the weakness described by H. Richard Niebuhr in *Christ and Culture* of the "Christ against culture" model. And it is an abiding weakness of fundamentalists, radical Anabaptists, and other separatists — a weakness for which influential theologians and ethicists have nevertheless attempted to marshal theological and philosophical justification.

Richard Mouw and Sander Griffioen speak of this posture of more irenically engaging the culture as "learning from idolatries," by which they do *not* mean spineless accommodation or polite capitulation. Rather, they wish to describe a humble recognition that dialogue with nonbelievers can help us in refining our own understanding of reality.[124] This posture of humility need *not* be construed as *compromise.* It is only to acknowledge that Christians don't possess the totality of truth that exists in the universe; wisdom, after all, is accessible to all who seek it. Thankfully, over the last decade some Protestant conservatives have begun dialoguing — philosophically, theologically, and ethically — both with those outside of the faith as well as with those outside of their own confessional tradition, and as a result they have grown the richer.

Ecumenical dialogue on the place of natural law in Christian ethics is both necessary and timely given the social climate that Americans presently encounter. It is precisely this burden — Christian unity in the service of cultural witness — that lies at the heart of John Paul II's encyclical letter *Ut Unum Sint (That They May Be One),* published in 1995. The lack of unity among Christians, insists the former pontiff, contradicts the truth Christians have, thereby undermining our service to the culture in which we have been placed. In fact, some have argued with considerable erudition, as does David Novak, that Jews and Christians, given their common beliefs regarding the revelatory and creative "word of God" and the Hebrew Bible, must be able to talk to one another *before* they can talk authoritatively to secular culture.[125] After all, a broadly "Judeo-Christian" value system emerged from both groups to inform the founding of the American republic. The wholesale deconstruction of the classical moral and po-

124. Richard Mouw and Sander Griffioen, *Pluralisms and Horizons: An Essay in Public Philosophy* (Grand Rapids: Eerdmans, 1993), 107.

125. See Novak's essay "John Courtney Murray, S.J.: A Jewish Appraisal," in *John Courtney Murray and the American Civil Conversation,* ed. Robert P. Hunt and Kenneth L. Grasso (Grand Rapids: Eerdmans, 1992), 44-63.

litical foundations upon which our society rests hastens the need for such dialogue. Lutheran theologian Carl Braaten well summarizes the exigencies of the moment: "Moral relativism joins political activism [in the academy] to sabotage the rules and standards needed to implement a societal system ordered by the principles of justice and truth. When the normlessness and the nihilistic effects of the deconstructionist mindset are no longer confined to academia, but invade the wider public, the way is prepared for the moral collapse of social institutions and the enthronement of the totalitarian state."[126]

It is highly instructive that a revival of natural-law thinking occurred between 1930 and the mid-1950s among European intellectuals who emigrated to the United States — for example, among thinkers such as Leo Strauss, Yves Simon, Heinrich Rommen, Jacques Maritain, and Eric Voegelin. It is also telling that these "natural lawyers" tended to be Catholic, in time taking up influential teaching posts in the United States following their emigration. Why was this rediscovery of natural law not found among Protestant thinkers? Were they co-opted by the totalitarian forces of their respective regimes? Were they riddled with secularism and pragmatism beyond recognition? Did Protestant thinkers simply lack the intellectual apparatus, or the moral-philosophical grounding, to resist the encroachment of social-political evil?

Surely, the experience in Europe of these and other "natural lawyers" with totalitarianism and moral collapse during the early to mid–twentieth century was not lost on them or their students. All shared a commitment to reflect seriously on the ethos of epistemological nihilism that characterized their day. It is entirely possible that the current renewal of natural law — chiefly among Catholic intellectuals — represents a reaction to the epistemological nihilism and moral destitution of our own time.[127]

Perhaps, as Braaten suggests, it is time to expose relativist/nihilist theory, even when it dons a religious cloak, as the handmaiden of totalitarian ideology and political authoritarianism. Perhaps it is time as well to critique Protestant existentialism that has plagued several generations of Christians — liberal and conservative — and rendered them ineffective in

126. Braaten, "Protestants and Natural Law," 25.

127. Charles E. Rice, *50 Questions on the Natural Law: What It Is and Why We Need It*, rev. ed. (San Francisco: Ignatius, 1999), 26, rightly observes that two striking revivals of natural-law thinking occurred in the twentieth century in opposition to National Socialism and racial segregation.

(if not removed from) the public square. A revival of natural law can be of use in that project. This is particularly needful amidst the wider and deep-rooted disintegration in American culture of any sort of binding public philosophy, wherein neither a moral consensus nor a common language of discourse by which to debate public issues exists. Without such, civility — and with it, civil society — dies.[128]

Law of Nature or Abolition of Man?

John Paul II reminded us continually during his pontificate that individual liberty is meaningful only in the context of an ordered society, and that political liberty — that rare treasure sought the world over — is rendered impossible when moral-social order collapses.[129] "The attempt to set freedom in opposition to truth, and indeed to separate them radically, is the consequence, manifestation and consummation of another more serious and destructive dichotomy, that which separates faith from morality."[130] Thus, "giving himself over to relativism and skepticism . . . he goes off in search of an illusory freedom apart from truth itself."[131] The implications of this illusory freedom are by no means benign: "Once the idea of a universal truth about the good knowable by human reasons is lost, inevitably the notion of conscience also changes. . . . Instead, there is a tendency to grant to the individual conscience the prerogative of independently determining the criteria of good and evil and then acting accordingly."[132] For John Paul, political philosophy is dependent on moral philosophy insofar as it draws upon a particular view of human nature. If there is nothing universal in the moral nature of humankind, then politics truly becomes "war by other means," culture wars are no mere metaphor, and we are confronted with the problem posed by Lewis in *The Abolition of Man*.[133]

128. This was the concern articulated by Murray, *We Hold These Truths*, chapters 1 and 2, and reiterated more recently by Kenneth L. Grasso, "We Hold These Truths: The Transformation of American Pluralism and the Future of American Democracy," in *John Courtney Murray and the American Civil Conversation*, 100-115.

129. This emphasis is most notable in his 1993 encyclical *Veritatis Splendor*.

130. *VS*, no. 88.

131. *VS*, no. 1.

132. *FR*, no. 98.

133. Lewis speaks in this regard of the Controllers ("Conditioners") over against the controlled ("conditioned"). "Man's conquest over nature" can only mean inhumanity in the

Ultimately, the extent to which the Christian community and Christian intellectuals in particular affirm natural-law thinking will determine our ability to relate to and address surrounding culture. Those Christians who oppose (or ignore) natural-law thinking convey the belief that creation possesses no intrinsic moral order. If Christian believers have no understanding — or reject the notion — of natural law, then there remain two alternatives, both of which are fideistic and existentialist. One is a version of Christian faith that is radically separatist and interior — a version that very intentionally calls us *away* from the cultural mainstream rather than to faithful involvement therein. While this version employs the grammar of "community," "radical discipleship," and "the kingdom of God," it is deficient in its ability to address the complexities of responsible civil engagement and to offer a viable public theology that is done by "thinking with the church" consensually through the ages. The other alternative, also radically interior, is to promote a foremost *apocalyptic*, future-oriented, and thus truncated, understanding of the kingdom of God. This vision, as well, eschews cultural involvement, though for somewhat different reasons, and has little or no regard for moral education and the long-term, multigenerational project of reseeding or reevangelizing culture in the sense that John Paul II has advocated.

About the time that the noted "ethicist"/animal-rights activist Peter Singer — an open advocate of infanticide and euthanasia — was appointed as Ira W. DeCamp Professor of Human Values at Princeton University, the university's then-president, Harold Shapiro, was delivering a lecture at Cornell University on the university's role in moral education (subsequently published in the January 27, 1999, *Princeton Alumni Weekly*).[134] Asked the nagging question of how to morally educate the coming generation of cultural gatekeepers, Shapiro attempted to underscore three elements that are thought to anchor liberal education: The university's role, he argued, is to (1) "provide an understanding of the great traditions of thoughts"; (2) "prepare us for an independent and responsible life of choice"; and (3) "free our minds from unexamined commitments and unquestioned allegiances." Shapiro further qualified the third

---

guise of "innovation." Only when we acknowledge the permanent — i.e., "the law written on the heart," the Tao — can we escape enslavement to lower animal instincts.

134. Shapiro, it will be remembered, was chairman of President Clinton's National Bioethics Advisory Commission.

of these points by offering the rather remarkable statement that such freedom is "especially important in a world where we increasingly depend on individual responsibility and internal control to replace . . . the *rigid kinship rules, strict religious precepts,* and *other aspects of totalitarian rule* that have traditionally imposed order on societies" (emphasis added).

One wonders whether Shapiro's comments caused any stir in his audience. The suggestion that "kinship rules" are "rigid" and that "religious precepts" belong to the category of "totalitarian rule" should strike us as rather frightening and certainly give us pause. Nonetheless, Shapiro's commentary on moral education well illustrates the present moral state of affairs and helps explain why a prestigious university can endow a chair, with relatively little protest, for an animal-rights activist who denies those very same rights to the handicapped neonate and the elderly in our midst and who, more recently, has argued for the permissibility of bestiality. *There is no consensus*[135] in the present cultural climate as to fundamentals of right and wrong behavior. *We do not hold these truths,* to borrow John Courtney Murray's words, and to contend for such is deemed "rigid" and "totalitarian."

But contend we must, which is why the insight of Lewis strikes us as all the more prescient: without the Tao, without an acknowledgment of a universal moral law, we are inevitably and irrevocably consigned to the abolition of man. "Ethical, intellectual, or aesthetic democracy is death."[136] Apart from natural law, what argument and protection do we have against evil when it manifests itself? Apart from natural-law thinking, the Nuremberg Trials were arbitrary and wrongheaded, and the Nazis, to their great misfortune, ended up on the wrong side of a postwar power grab. Apart from natural law, there are no human rights that are due every living creature. Indeed, apart from natural-law thinking, it is simply impossible, if not disingenuous, to decry injustice, inhumanity, oppression, and moral atrocity, since one man's mugging or extermination is another man's good time.

To be sure, our discussion of natural law is no mere academic exercise, though it must begin there.[137] Nor is it merely the concern of philoso-

135. "Consensus" should not be construed merely as "majority opinion"; properly understood, it depends on evidence of "first principles," the "ethical a priori" (so Murray, *We Hold These Truths,* 97-123).

136. *Present Concerns: Essays by C. S. Lewis,* ed. Walter Hooper (New York: Harcourt Brace Jovanovich, 1986), 34.

137. Four volumes that are winsomely written and commend themselves to a non-

phers, lawyers, theologians, or political theorists, though of all people it must be their concern. For as John Courtney Murray noted, it is the "clerks" and gatekeepers of our culture — academics, professional philosophers, ethicists, politicians, economists, lawyers, writers, journalists, and clergy — who "are supposed to be in conscious possession" of a public philosophy rooted in natural-law thinking. The very sign of a vacuum, especially at the intellectual level, is the futility of arguing over *whether or not* there is in fact a public philosophy.[138] Surely it is reasonable to suggest that entrenched moral skepticism and postmodern nihilism are the cultural effects of disordered philosophy, and that a more classical orientation in law, political philosophy, and moral philosophy is needed to address (at the ac-

---

technical audience are Budziszewski, *What We Can't Not Know;* Budziszewski, *Written on the Heart: The Case for Natural Law* (Downers Grove, Ill.: InterVarsity, 1997); Cromartie, *A Preserving Grace;* and Rice, *50 Questions on the Natural Law. What We Can't Not Know* in particular is to be highly commended for several reasons. In this, his second book on natural law, Budziszewski does not assume, as he appears to have in *Written on the Heart,* that the reader may share his theistic or baseline moral assumptions (remarkably, only six years stand between publication of the two books). He argues logically, in a commonsense manner, in order to lead the reader to a point of moral conviction. Thus, Budziszewski does not wish to obliterate his ideological adversaries so much as to help them concede that their arguments against a transcendent or common standard of social morality, in the end, are illusory and cannot stand. After all, as the title indicates, *all people* have access to knowledge that we all simply can't *not* know. Slightly more technical but equally important is Hittinger, *The First Grace.* For treatments of natural law that are oriented toward a technical audience, see Jean Porter, *Nature as Reason: A Thomistic Theory of the Natural Law* (Grand Rapids: Eerdmans, 2005); Porter, *Natural and Divine Law;* Hittinger, *A Critique of the New Natural Law Theory* (Notre Dame, Ind.: University of Notre Dame Press, 1987); Yves R. Simon, *The Tradition of Natural Law: A Philosopher's Reflections,* ed. Vukan Kuic, rev. ed. (New York: Fordham University Press, 1992); Robert P. George, *The Clash of Orthodoxies: Law, Religion, and Morality in Crisis* (Wilmington, Del.: ISI Books, 2001); George, ed., *Natural Law Theory: Contemporary Essays,* rev. ed. (Oxford: Clarendon, 1996); Robert P. George and Christopher Wolfe, eds., *Natural Law and Public Reason* (Washington, D.C.: Georgetown University Press, 2000); Edward B. McLean, ed., *Common Truths: New Perspectives on Natural Law* (Wilmington, Del.: ISI Books, 2000); Thomas Hibbs and John O'Callaghan, eds., *Recovering Nature: Essays in Natural Philosophy, Ethics, and Metaphysics in Honor of Ralph McInerny* (Notre Dame, Ind.: University of Notre Dame Press, 1999); Rommen, *The Natural Law;* and Jacques Maritain, *The Rights of Man and the Natural Law* (San Francisco: Ignatius, 1986). On the implications of natural law for public policy, see David F. Forte, ed., *Natural Law and Contemporary Public Policy* (Washington, D.C.: Georgetown University Press, 1998).

138. Murray, *We Hold These Truths,* 85-86.

ademic level) this deficiency. A traditional metaphysics of natural law lies at the heart of that reconstructive project.[139]

At the most fundamental level, natural law forms the *basis* for moral formation and cultivating the virtuous life, since it encourages us to ask: Do humans possess inherent dignity — a constitution that is inviolable? What are the implications of this moral constitution for pressing bioethical dilemmas that confront us? How *ought* one live? What standards of behavior are acceptable and unacceptable for society? By what standard do we measure what is unacceptable? Can people be held accountable for their actions? On what basis? What is the basis for justice? For the criminal justice system? For entering into armed conflict and justified use of force? For dealing with crimes against humanity and mass murder? For cutting-edge bioethical developments?

The natural law both constitutes a consensus, enduring over time, about moral first principles and serves as a bridge between Christian and non-Christian morality. In civil society, religious and nonreligious people conform to the same ethical standard in order to be governable.[140] A revival in natural-law thinking, therefore, must be the highest priority for the Christian community as we contend in, rather than abdicate, the pub-

---

139. The "new natural law" theory as articulated by John Finnis and Germain Grisez twenty years ago understands itself to derive from the operation of pure reason and not metaphysical premises. In this way it distinguishes itself from the "old" notion of natural law, which derives conclusions concerning morality from our observations about human anthropology. For Finnis and Grisez, morality is a self-evidently human good. See John Finnis, *Natural Law and Natural Rights* (Oxford: Clarendon, 1980); Finnis, *Aquinas: Moral, Political, and Legal Theory* (Oxford: Oxford University Press, 1998); Germain Grisez, *The Way of the Lord Jesus*, vol. 1, *Christian Moral Principles* (Chicago: Franciscan Herald, 1983); and Grisez, "The First Principle of Practical Reason: A Commentary on the Summa Theologiae 94.2," *Natural Law Forum* 10 (1965): 168-201. Robert P. George, *In Defense of Natural Law* (Oxford: Clarendon, 1999), offers a theoretical defense of the "new natural law" theory of Finnis and Grisez while also considering policy implications of natural law. Offering a more critical assessment are Keith Pavlischek, "Questioning the New Natural Law Theory: The Case of Religious Liberty as Defended by Robert P. George in *Making Men Moral*," in *A Moral Enterprise: Politics, Reason, and the Human Good*, ed. Kenneth L. Grasso and Robert P. Hunt (Wilmington, Del.: ISI Books, 2002), 127-42; Hittinger, *A Critique of the New Natural Law Theory*; and Budziszewski, *Written on the Heart*, 196-202.

140. The Christian understanding of the natural law is that divine revelation reveals to us moral truths that are not grasped solely by reason as well as moral truths discernible through the natural law. For this reason, the Christian church speaks of *interpreting* or *guarding* the natural law and not *inventing* it, since the natural law mirrors the divine will.

lic square.[141] Indeed, public institutions, if they truly prize the freedom they advertise, must in their workings be governed from within and made to serve the ends of virtue: "Political freedom is endangered in its foundations as soon as the universal moral values, upon whose shattered possession the self-discipline of a free society depends, are no longer vigorous enough to restrain the passions and shatter the selfish inertia of men."[142] Those universal moral values are embedded in none other than the natural law. If there is no natural law, or if we do not acknowledge it, the alternative is moral, social, and political anarchy, leading in time to softer or harder forms of political totalitarianism. We invite what Lewis, with prophetic insight in *The Abolition of Man,* sought to forestall.[143]

Abolition concludes with the moral possibilities when natural law is denied and the "Controllers" revolt against nature. The scenarios offered by Lewis are rather bleak. "The final stage is come when man, by eugenics, by pre-natal conditioning, and by an education and propaganda based on a perfect applied psychology, has obtained full control over himself. Hu-

---

141. Natural-law thinking presently seems to be staging something of a comeback. One "natural lawyer" and cultural critic observed that in 1998 and 1999 alone at least twenty-six books with the words "natural law" in their title had been published in the United States (J. Budziszewski, "Natural Born Lawyers," *Weekly Standard,* December 20, 1999, 31). One of these volumes deserves mention. In 1998 Heinrich Rommen's classic work *The Natural Law: A Study in Legal and Social History and Philosophy* (already noted) was reissued; this volume was originally published in 1936 under the German title *Die ewige Wiederkehr des Naturrechts* (The eternal validity of natural law). The inspiration for this volume came from Rommen's deep concerns that both law and politics were being co-opted by Nazi ideology during the 1930s. Rommen watched with alarm as National Socialism attempted a legal grasp of power, under which crimes against humanity in time were justified. (In chapter 8 I examine several decades of German academic thinking that prepared the soil, as it were, for National Socialist attitudes toward life-and-death issues. This has been reproduced with permission from the epilogue of *The Unformed Conscience of Evangelicalism: Recovering the Church's Moral Vision* [Downers Grove, Ill.: InterVarsity, 2002], 246-62, a modified version of which appears in the essay *"Lebensunwertes Leben:* The Devolution of Personhood in the Weimar and Pre-Weimar Era," *Ethics and Medicine* 21, no. 1 [2005]: 41-54.) For an extensive bibliography on natural law prior to 1995, see James V. Schall, "The Natural Law Bibliography," *American Journal of Jurisprudence* 40 (1995): 157-98.

142. Murray, *We Hold These Truths,* 37.

143. In *That Hideous Strength,* Lewis also depicts the totalitarian spirit of secularized social science. He does this imaginatively in his depiction of the National Institute for Coordinated Experiments (NICE), whose operators correspond to the "controllers" in *The Abolition of Man.*

man nature will be the last part of Nature to surrender to Man. The battle will then be won. We shall . . . be henceforth free to make our species whatever we wish it to be."[144] Just as John Courtney Murray speaks of "barbarians" wearing suits and carrying briefcases, Lewis perceives the possibility of sophisticated "savages." Contrasting the civil or civilized person with the "savage," Lewis describes the latter as the person who "either has not learned or who has forgotten what the rest of the human race know."[145] By abdicating the Tao, the natural law, humans cease being humane. Nevertheless, he maintains, as long as we recognize the "law of nature," we participate in what it means to be "truly human" and preserve the "beauty" and "dignity" that are ours.[146]

Recall from chapter 1 the understanding of personhood advanced by bioethicist Tom Beauchamp, namely, that we will need to rethink our traditional view that "unlucky humans," who "lack properties of personhood," cannot "be treated in the ways we treat relevantly similar nonhumans." They might, for example, be "aggressively used as human research subjects and sources of organs." In Beauchamp's view, "[a]lthough nonhuman animals are not plausible candidates for moral personhood, humans too fail to qualify as moral persons if they lack one or more of the conditions of moral personhood."[147]

Recall, too, the subtitle of this volume: "A Return to Moral First Things." An urgent defense of the natural law acquires new meaning in our own day, particularly among Protestants who have not been greatly inclined to "think with the church." Regardless of confessional commitments, Christians will need to contend in the public square that human beings are sacred in the *biological processes* no less than they are sacred in the human *social* or *political* order. This dignity does not originate with humans; rather, as Paul Ramsey has persuasively argued, it has been conferred upon them by divine decree.[148] If nature cannot guide us and instruct us about humane or inhumane treatment, if our traditional under-

144. Lewis, *The Abolition of Man*, 72.

145. C. S. Lewis, "On Ethics," in *Christian Reflections*, ed. Walter Hooper (Grand Rapids: Eerdmans, 1967), 56.

146. Lewis, *The Abolition of Man*, 86.

147. Tom L. Beauchamp, "The Failure of Theories of Personhood," *Kennedy Institute of Ethics Journal* 9, no. 4 (1999): 309.

148. Paul Ramsey, "The Morality of Abortion," in *Moral Problems*, ed. James Rachels (New York: Harper and Row, 1971), 13.

standing of human fulfillment cannot be culturally sustained, what shall serve as our ethical guide? In the words of Leon Kass, "how, in a world morally neutered by the effects of objectified science, will we know which genetic or functional or behavioral alterations of human nature we should welcome as improvements?"[149]

It has been said that being merely worldly on the one hand and merely otherworldly on the other hand are both moral failures of the Christian community. A robust and faithful "public theology" will be necessary, despite the ever-present danger of conflating Christ and culture. Natural-law thinking is an indispensable part of that public theology, since it is part of divine revelation. In the words of one public philosopher, "As a metaphysical idea, the idea of natural law is timeless, and for that reason timely"[150] — especially for such a time as this.

149. Leon R. Kass, *The Hungry Soul: Eating and the Perfecting of Our Nature* (New York: Free Press, 1994), 6.
150. Murray, *We Hold These Truths*, 320.

CHAPTER THREE

Natural Law and the Christian Tradition

All moral truth, like "Lady Wisdom" as depicted in the book of Proverbs, derives from the Creator and the created order, and thus is accessible to all people. As evidence, one need only contemplate the role that proverbial wisdom plays in the diverse cultures of human civilization. There exist certain moral, social, and physical realities in life that apply to all people at all times and in all places; these are intuited regardless of one's social or cultural location. Consider, even from the perspective of the Western cultural context, the wisdom encapsulated in these aphorisms and wisdom sayings drawn from African life:

- No polecat ever smelled his own stink.
- When it rains, it always drips in the same place.
- You don't need to teach the sons of a king about power.
- The strength of a crocodile is in the water.
- All the villagers throw their concerns on a huge ashheap before the chief.
- He who marries a beautiful woman marries problems.[1]

Even people living in Western societies will readily grasp and appreciate the wisdom that can be mined from these sayings that find their provenance in African culture. In fact, the truth lodged in these observa-

---

1. These examples are drawn from the appendix of Claus Westermann's *Roots of Wisdom: The Oldest Proverbs of Israel and Other Peoples*, trans. J. D. Charles (Louisville: Westminster John Knox, 1995), 140-48.

tions doubtless would be grasped in ancient Near Eastern culture, contemporary Middle Eastern culture, Asian culture, European culture, indeed all cultures. In the same way, people living in Western societies will readily appreciate the wisdom from the following ancient Near Eastern sayings:

- Better is a dry morsel with quiet than a house full of feasting and strife.
- When you sit down to eat with a ruler, observe carefully what is before you and put a knife to your throat if you are given to appetite.
- The lips of a forbidden woman drip honey and her speech is smoother than oil, but in the end she is bitter as wormwood.
- A little sleep, a little slumber, a little folding of the hands to rest, and poverty will come upon you like a robber and want like an armed man.
- Even in laughter the heart may ache, and the end of joy may be grief.
- Whoever is slow to anger is better than the mighty, and he who rules his spirit than he who takes a city.
- A good name is to be chosen rather than great riches, and favor is better than silver or gold.[2]

And the following proverbial riddle, which consists of multiple parts, nevertheless rings true to the reader/listener regardless of social or geographical location:

> Four things on earth are small,
> Yet they are exceedingly wise:
> The ants are a people not strong,
> Yet they provide their food in the summer;
> The rock badgers are a people not mighty,
> Yet they make their homes in the rocks;
> The locusts have no king,
> Yet all of them march in ranks;
> The gecko you can take in your hands,
> Yet it is found in kings' palaces.
>
> (Prov. 30:24-28, my translation)

2. These are taken from the Old Testament book of Proverbs.

What all these aphorisms have in common is that they communicate basic truths that are universally knowable and observable regardless of one's location. Proverbial wisdom is gleaned by observation and deduction and is not the reserve of religious people or any particular life view. All people may grow wise; all individuals have the capacity for perception, insight, and prudence. Why? Because of inherent capacities that accord with human nature. Thus, we are justified in describing the acquisition of wisdom as "living according to nature," that is, living according to what is "natural" for all human beings.

Historically, Christian belief has understood human essence, with its unique features, in terms of the *imago Dei*. Every individual bears the imprint of the divine image. Significantly, the notion of humans stamped with the divine image or seal is not exclusive to Christian religion, even when Christian faith expresses the fullness of divine revelation. That humans express the divine is a prominent feature in pagan thought from earliest antiquity. It is altogether possible, for example, that 2 Peter 1:3-4, expressing the apostle's wish that Christians might "share in the divine nature," is borrowing a common metaphysical assumption found in pagan or mystery religion about the divine and infusing it with christological meaning.

The notion, then, of a "natural moral law," by which humans intuit that in their essence and in their behavior they mirror a certain transcendence and thereby live in accord with their true nature, is as old as the study of philosophy and religion itself. And because it is "natural" for human creatures to act in accordance with their true nature, morality is properly a subset of religion, philosophy, and the social sciences.[3]

At the most basic level, the concept of a "natural law" is rooted in the awareness that within human nature and within human society there exist certain elements of the moral and social life that are unchanging, not subject to amendment by human customs, regulations, and ordinances. This awareness is heightened when one considers, in historical perspective, how varied cultures, customs, and social institutions are. For despite such mind-boggling cultural diversity, certain time-honored moral values and

---

3. That the social sciences "exclude" morality due to secular assumptions does not negate the fact that every worldview, including that of secularists, has a particular understanding of how humans *ought* to behave; secularists are not morally "neutral." Few have addressed the myth of moral neutrality with greater precision or clarity than Brendan Sweetman in his recent volume *Why Politics Needs Religion: The Place of Religious Arguments in the Public Square* (Downers Grove, Ill.: InterVarsity, 2006).

principles surface and remain in force for all peoples.[4] Human nature (and not merely formal religion per se) obliges all people, in a remarkably predictable fashion, to honor particular moral principles — for example, not to murder, not to steal, not to harm one's neighbor, not to violate sacred oaths and covenants, not to defraud others, etc.

Why is it, one may reasonably ask, that all people and all societies, past and present, Christian *and* non-Christian, intuit that genocide, bestiality, child abuse, adultery, theft, and defrauding one's neighbor are forbidden? Surely the reason does not lie in various "town meetings" that over time yielded a consensus in the community that these practices were deemed unacceptable. Moreover, what forbids these behaviors particularly in cultural or social climates in which some individuals feel "free" to do them? Although many laws are arbitrary — for example, driving on the right side of the road or paying taxes on one's income at roughly 30 percent — and many moral principles have exceptions — for example, not keeping one's promise due to illness — some moral principles have no exceptions and are universally and uniformly valid. Thus they cannot merely be ascribed to consensus, custom, or social contract; they are right and valid whether or not the majority prefers to honor them. We must never kill an innocent person nor commit adultery nor molest children nor steal another's belongings. These rules or "laws" we call "moral absolutes."

A nagging question arises: Why is it that although an individual's conscience as an internal moral guide can be ignored, hardened, or seared, all people at all times and in all places, regardless of social location and placement in history, react to injustice *when it visits them,* and they do so without fail? Indeed, how are we to account for this constancy even in a radically pluralistic and relativistic culture, wherein we are regularly bombarded by alternative moral theories that deny moral "law" and erode our intellectual and moral defenses? That which philosophers and theologians variously call *judicial sentiment,* namely, the unwillingness in myself to let *others* off the hook in the face of injustice — over against *conscience,* which refuses to let *myself* off the hook — demands of human beings a reasonable accounting. Why is this moral predilection so constant, in fact, unfailing, with 100 percent predictability? Why does it appear to be a moral "law"?

---

4. During the previous half-century it has been the inclination of cultural anthropologists to focus on what is exotic, peculiar, and unique to particular societies under examination rather than give an account of similarities that bind diverse human cultures together.

The historic Christian tradition has affirmed that this moral "law" is inscribed within the human soul of every person. This moral inclination, in the language of Saint Paul, accords with the "law written on the heart" (Rom. 2:15). Possession of this intuition does not mean that humans are infallible or possess all moral knowledge. Rather, it means that every person is capable of knowing the first principles of moral reasoning, i.e., the "permanent things." It is from these moral "first things" that people derive a rudimentary awareness of who they are, how they relate to fellow human beings,[5] and what role they fill in the cosmos.

While justice cannot be done in this volume to a history and philosophy of law, the philosophical tradition that informs theory and practice of law in the Western cultural tradition shows remarkable consistency in distinguishing between two types of "natural law." One is anchored in a particular view of the state, and to a lesser extent in social contract, and is arbitrary and utilitarian in its character. It is not indebted to or issuing out of moral or metaphysical duty. The other, by contrast, is rooted in certain metaphysical convictions.

Pre-Christian Development of Natural-Law Thinking

Despite the observation that all things change, Heraclitus (ca. 536-470 B.C.) believed that wisdom points to a wider "law" of the universe, a transcending *logos,* or reason, to which human nature and human ethical striving are ordered. All human laws are informed by and issue from one "divine" law. Such, Heraclitus taught, was intuited through wisdom: "Wisdom is the foremost virtue, and wisdom consists in speaking the truth, and in lending an ear to nature and acting according to her. Wisdom is common to all."[6] Heraclitus's attempt to understand a "natural moral

---

5. Indeed, grappling with how moral "law" binds the conscience of every individual over against one's neighbor — or, in the language of the Golden Rule, "Do to others as you would have them do to you" — leads to the broader question of how to order society. As Arthur J. Dyck reminds us, all human beings are held responsible, without excuse, for living in accord with the Golden Rule, since this derives from being created in the divine image (*Life's Worth: The Case against Assisted Suicide,* Critical Issues in Bioethics [Grand Rapids and Cambridge, U.K.: Eerdmans, 2002], 86).

6. Heraclitus, *Fragments* 112-114, reproduced in Charles M. Bakewell, *Source Book in Ancient Philosophy* (New York: Scribner, 1907), 34.

law" as unchangeable stands in noted contrast both to the demagoguery of the Sophists and to the capriciousness of the population. The Sophists of Heraclitus's day, as the sophists of any era, refused to venerate the "natural moral law," since they viewed laws as artificial constructs that merely served the interests of those in power. It is in this light that we perhaps understand Socrates' and Plato's veneration of the νόμοι, the "laws"; so, legal historian Heinrich Rommen: "The philosophers spoke of the . . . laws with great respect: the peoples who had no polis were to them barbarians. Hence, it happened, too, that Socrates, despite his distinction between what is naturally right and legally right, pronounced the laws of Athens to be 'right' without qualification."[7] Something in the classical philosophers' observations about human nature was enduring, for Heraclitus's understanding of the "natural law" would serve as a precursor to the Stoic notion of the *Logos* that pervades and unifies all the cosmos while placing upon all humans certain ethical obligations.

Natural-law thinking in Plato and Aristotle is characterized by a high regard for the polis. All of life, for them, is therefore "political" insofar as the city-state subsists in rightly ordered relationships. Our natural inclinations and abilities should order the ideal society. Both Plato and Aristotle reject a subjectivism about what is "good." The good, for Plato, consists, for example, in knowledge and beauty and is self-evident, independent of a human reference point. Aristotle differs on one point. He holds the good to be understood in terms of human nature, for which an analogy is helpful. An acorn derives from the genus oak *by nature,* from which all oaks, regardless of their maturation point or variety, are identified. Yet despite their differences on what constitutes the "good," we observe in both Plato and Aristotle a care to preserve the social order. As a result, both place strong emphasis on ethics, what is just and how human laws might reflect transcending moral norms. And both recognize that what is *legally* just may or may not be what is *naturally* just.

Plato acknowledges that laws might protect the narrower interest of a particular class and not all of society. Bona fide justice, by contrast, is thought to inform proper laws, since justice will seek to provide for and protect the common good.[8] While positive laws are arbitrary and subject

---

7. Heinrich A. Rommen, *The Natural Law: A Study in Legal and Social History and Philosophy,* trans. T. R. Hanley (Indianapolis: Liberty Fund, 1998), 7.

8. This is a recurring theme in *Laws,* especially book 4.

to change, the demands and obligations of justice remain unchanging. In this way they mirror a higher moral standard. In the end, then, the polis or state exists as a teaching mechanism to test the moral character of its citizens. Its function is to make human beings virtuous to the extent that they embody justice. In this way humans accord with the "law of nature." In a "naturally" ordered society, each person utilizes those abilities with which "nature" has endowed him.[9]

Even when direct appeals to nature as the foundation of unchanging ethical norms are not developed very explicitly in Plato, the basic argument found in his *Republic* is that there exists an order both in physical nature and in human nature that is objective and universal. The proper use of reason, coupled with the ordering of impulses, becomes the source of human moral obligation. To violate this is to create disorder and unhappiness.[10]

In Aristotle we find perhaps the high point of the development of pagan ethical theory,[11] and certainly one that furnishes a stepping-stone toward natural-law thinking, even when it is incomplete. Aristotle believes that everything occurring in life has a purpose or proper place (τέλος), resulting in a "natural" order of all things.[12] The intrinsic nature (φύσις) of anything can be known by identifying its end, its τέλος. Given this order, we may determine what is "good" in its essence. Nature, then, serves as a guide for citizens, for politicians, and for statesmen.[13]

Transferred to social-political life, the aim of each member of the polis is to pursue what is virtuous and just and thereby embody good citizenship. Human beings are free to act in accordance with reason, that is, to do what *ought* to be done. Ethics, therefore, as Aristotle makes clear, is to act in accordance with our fundamental nature. Nature, consequently,

9. This is a distinctive feature of Plato's *Republic*.

10. Cf. also *Laws* 889-890, wherein Plato argues that proper laws are to be derived from and find parallels in physical nature. Paul E. Sigmund, *Natural Law in Political Thought* (Cambridge: Winthrop, 1971), 8-9, summarizes the presence of "natural law" theory in Plato: "To the extent . . . that Plato believed that there were universal principles inherent in nature which imposed a moral obligation on all men, he was enunciating a natural-law theory. Insofar as he viewed any given law as an inadequate representation of the eternal principles of justice, he was asserting a theory of natural (i.e., ideal) justice rather than one of natural law."

11. Hence, the attention in Thomas Aquinas's own work to Aristotelian categories.

12. Aristotle, of course, is a naturalist and not a theist; the cosmos is to be understood as self-existing.

13. It should be noted, however, that Aristotle used "nature" to justify the inferiority of women, children, and slaves (*Politics* 1254-1255).

where it is illumined by right reason, guides human beings in distinguishing between virtue and vice. The implication, in social-political life, is that laws can be legally justified yet morally unjust. "Natural law" therefore describes both how things *are* in their essence and how they *ought to be*. By analogy, morality can be compared to gravity to the extent that it is grounded in "natural-law" thinking. That is, there are moral "first principles" that are self-evident and needing no explanation.[14]

In *Nichomachean Ethics* Aristotle acknowledges some human behaviors to be intrinsically wrong — for example, murder, theft, and adultery.[15] Moreover, a distinction between "conventional" justice, by which constant change is to be expected, and unchanging "natural" justice surfaces later in the work.[16] Also found in *Nichomachean Ethics* is a clear distinction between natural law and positive or conventional law. What is legal is not inevitably moral; Aristotle is not inattentive to the difference.[17]

In Aristotle, as in Plato, justice is not the domain of private individuals. Freedom is legitimate only to the extent that one acts in accordance with nature. Justice expresses itself corporately in the city-state among the citizens; hence, the veneration of the polis.[18]

It can be reasonably argued, as Paul Sigmund has done, that Plato's and Aristotle's understanding and discussion of "nature," "natural justice," and "common law according to nature" laid the foundations for a theory of metaphysical natural law, although the formalizing of such theory remains for Stoic moral philosophers. Nature was to be viewed as harmonious and purposeful, while human nature was thought to exhibit an intelligible order from which ethical norms might be extracted.[19]

As a moral-philosophical outlook, Stoicism emerged at a time when the city-state had been eclipsed by a world empire, and that empire subsisted largely of two classes, the aristocracy and the masses. The Stoic view of reality emphasizes the seriousness of life. Surrounded by a world of war,

---

14. From a Christian standpoint, Aristotle intuits properly; as a nontheist, however, he simply cannot make sense of first cause and guilt.

15. Book 2.

16. Book 5.

17. Aristotle, *Nichomachean Ethics* 5.7 (1097a-1135a).

18. For this reason both are thought by political philosophers to be state socialists, and this denomination is not inaccurate. Nonetheless, much in their ethical thought coincides with Christian revelation, even when the state, potentially, can be deified.

19. Sigmund, *Natural Law*, 12.

corruption, disease, sorrow, and natural disaster, Stoics believed that happiness was attainable not by the appetites or the pursuit of gain but by virtue and right reason. Wisdom, they believed, was clouded by human passions. Through knowledge one attains understanding as to human nature; proper use of reason and "nature" are one. To achieve happiness is to live rationally, and thus to live in accordance with nature.

Stoic ethics is to be understood against the backdrop of Stoicism's view of nature, the cosmos, and humankind's place therein. To conform to the good is to live in conformity with reason and "nature." In contradistinction to Epicurean thought, Stoics believed that the virtuous life is grounded not in pleasure, but rather in one's pursuit of what is good, of which pleasure is merely a by-product. Passion and human appetites are perceived as irrational, and therefore "unnatural." In late antiquity Stoicism affected broader cultural attitudes through its emphasis on individual moral attainment irrespective of class distinctions.[20]

Writing in the first century B.C., Cicero is considered the primary interpreter and transmitter of the Stoic understanding of natural law.[21] He speaks of the *lex nata*, the law within, which he regards as the foundation of law in general. This law of right and wrong, he observes, is universally valid and unbending. It is born within us, not learned or received by tradition, but imbibed from nature itself. Accordingly,

> True law is right reason in agreement with nature; it is of universal application, unchanging and everlasting; it summons to duty by its commands, and averts from wrongdoing by its prohibitions. . . . It is a sin to try to alter this law, nor is it allowable to attempt to repeal any part of it, and it is impossible to abolish it entirely. We cannot be freed from its obligations by senate or people, and . . . there will not be different laws at Rome and at Athens, or different laws now and in the future, but one eternal and unchangeable law will be valid for all nations and all times.[22]

---

20. While not all Stoic philosophers were thus minded, Seneca (first century) and Epictetus (late first and second century) opposed slavery and the laws that upheld it, based on the natural-law implications of human dignity and equality that presupposed freedom. See, in this regard, Vincent Cauchy and Michel Spanneut, "Stoicism," in *New Catholic Encyclopedia*, vol. 13, 2nd ed. (Detroit: Gale, 2003), 534-39.

21. So Rommen, *The Natural Law*, 20.

22. *On the Republic* 3.22, trans. C. W. Keyes, Loeb Classical Library (Cambridge: Harvard University Press, 1928), 79.

For Cicero, the inner law allows human beings to distinguish between good and bad human ordinances, between just and unjust laws, between what is honorable and what is dishonorable. Only a madman "would conclude that these judgments are matters of opinion, and not fixed by Nature."[23] "The civil law," he contends, "is not necessarily also the universal law."[24] Ruinous consequences were for him proof positive that the "Laws of nature" had been violated. Therefore, civil laws *must* find their roots in the deeper principles of enduring moral judgment. Cicero was able to look past legal *forms* to the moral *substance* of legislation. There is a marked difference between expediency and moral rectitude.[25]

Although by the time of the Christian advent Stoic thought had been in existence for three centuries, it was in the first century — the period of the Caesars — that Stoic ethical *Massenpropaganda* blossomed.[26] This was spawned in no small measure by the excesses, despotism, and moral bankruptcy that attended this era; social conditions served to create fertile soil in which both Stoic and Christian ethics emerged. It is thus not coincidental that Stoic themes and categories surface in the writings of the New Testament, where one finds evidence of interaction between Christian and Stoic life views. Both groups were active in the marketplace (cf. Acts 17:18), propagating their views for consumption by broader audiences. Both used similar techniques — e.g., diatribe, parenesis, epistles, and ethical catalogues — as well as a common moral vocabulary in advancing their message.

Perhaps our most lucid demonstration of early Christian interaction with that Stoic worldview is Saint Luke's brief but tantalizing portrait of the apostle Paul in Athens (Acts 17:16-34) — a narrative examined in the previous chapter. Here, in the Socratic mold, Paul is seen "dialoguing" with the philosophers in the agora, the marketplace, prior to addressing the Council of the Areopagus. Significantly, in the Areopagus address Paul appeals to "nature" in contending for the God who has made himself known, while exploiting important Stoic themes — among these, cosmic unity, di-

---

23. Cicero, *On the Laws* 1.16, trans. C. W. Keyes, Loeb Classical Library.

24. Cicero, *De officiis* 341.

25. Cicero, *De officiis* 401. Rather creatively, Hadley Arkes has pondered the implications of Cicero's "natural law" thinking for our time. See his essay "That 'Nature Herself Has Placed in Our Ears a Power of Judging': Some Reflections on the 'Naturalism' of Cicero," in *Natural Law Theory: Contemporary Essays,* ed. Robert P. George (Oxford: Clarendon, 1992), 245-77.

26. By the first century, Stoics and Cynics were viewed as the popularizers of ethics.

vine kinship, and divine offspring. As noted previously, Paul also utilizes wordplay on "knowledge," not incidental in light of the Stoic primacy of knowledge and knowing as the foundation of the moral life (see especially 17:22-31; cf. 17:18). To observe that Paul is "accommodating" himself by employing moral categories that Stoics and Christians have in common is not to deny the radical difference between the two. It is only to point out that the Christian message will look for common ground in building bridges to the pagan mind. In the Areopagus speech, general revelation and "natural law" give way — that is, they serve as an introduction to — special revelation in Christ the "God-man" (17:31). The truth of the gospel is disclosed by the "Apostle to the pagans": God has made himself known to all, and all are called to repentance, in anticipation of the great day of moral reckoning, on which the God-man, who was raised from the dead, will judge all (vv. 30-31). Herewith Paul exposes deficiencies in the Stoic worldview — for example, the Stoic understanding of divine *logos* as reason and knowledge rather than transcendence embodied in the "god-man"; Stoic rejection of the notion of a bodily resurrection; and Stoic absence of eschatological perspective, wherewith it rejects any notion of an afterlife as well as a climactic future day of moral accountability.

Two further transparent uses of Stoic categories by New Testament writers for expressly Christian purposes are the prologue to the Fourth Gospel and the catalogue of virtues found in 2 Peter 1. In the former the writer presents Jesus as the eternal, preexistent *Logos,* through which all things were made and are constituted and in which all things inhere (cf. Col. 1:15-20; Heb. 1:3) — consistent with Stoic cosmology. The *logos,* however, is not pure reason; rather, it is personal and preexistent, incarnated as flesh and blood within the constraints of the temporal world. The use in 2 Peter of a catalogue of virtues (1:5-7) shows a debt to the technique of Stoic moralists who dominated ethical discourse at the popular level in the first century.[27]

---

27. On the convergence of Stoic and Christian moral categories, see J. Daryl Charles, *Virtue amidst Vice: The Catalog of Virtues in 2 Peter 1,* Journal for the Study of the New Testament: Supplement Series 150 (Sheffield: Sheffield Academic Press, 1997). The use of ethical catalogues in the New Testament is frequent and varied; hereon see B. S. Easton, "New Testament Ethical Lists," *Journal of Biblical Literature* 51 (1932): 1-12, and more recently, J. Daryl Charles, "Vice and Virtue Lists," in *Dictionary of New Testament Background,* ed. Craig A. Evans and Stanley E. Porter (Downers Grove, Ill.: InterVarsity, 2000), 1252-57. Several definitive works on ethical lists in the New Testament and in intertestamental Judaism remain untranslated from the German.

It is a standard feature that "knowledge" begins or ends pagan ethical lists. Thus, because in the Stoic scheme all virtues are corollaries of knowledge (γνῶσις), philosophy can be viewed as both a means and an end. By this moral calculus, vice is to be equated with ignorance. It may well be that in 2 Peter 1:5-7 the writer is exploiting this common epistemological assumption in his moral exhortation; hence, his strategic use of the catchwords "knowledge" and "knowing" throughout the epistle in addition to its inclusion in the catalogue of virtues (1:5-7).[28] In the 2 Peter catalogue, moral progression occurs by adding γνῶσις to ἀρετή, virtue or moral excellence, which is rooted in the foundation of πίστις, faith. Christian ethics differs from its Stoic counterpart in that it strips knowledge of its technical nuance so that it is not a goal or end in itself. Knowledge in the Christian ethical scheme is necessary to the extent that reason, part of the image of God in human creation, is subordinated and conjoined to divine grace.

Ethicist Gilbert Meilaender has made the observation that Stoic ethics strikes us as far too sane and austere, albeit heroic.[29] And indeed it is neither theocentric nor christocentric; it is rather an ethic based wholly on willpower and devoid of grace. Nevertheless, in the period of its blossoming at the time of the Christian advent, it preserves, in the words of Heinrich Rommen, the "seeds of the Logos" and provides the literary forms and linguistic vessels into which Christian writers would pour their own theological ideas. Out of this mixture there emerged in time a new, yet not unrelated, doctrine of natural law.

Early Christian and Patristic Development of Natural-Law Thinking

Given the decomposition of ancient culture, sectarian thinking within parts of the early Christian community, and the eschatological element inherent in the Christian prophetic message, it should not be surprising that many in the early church were eschatologically minded to the point of

---

28. That Paul appears to be utilizing a wordplay on "knowledge" and "knowing" in his Areopagus speech (Acts 17:22-31) is also striking evidence that the apostle is engaging Stoic assumptions at the level of his audience, making important adjustments.

29. Gilbert Meilaender, "Stoic or Christian?" in *Things That Count: Essays Moral and Theological* (Wilmington, Del.: ISI Books, 2000), 298. In this essay Meilaender is reflecting specifically on the writings of the late-second-century emperor and Stoic Marcus Aurelius.

viewing the end of the world as imminent. Indeed, the need to exercise vigilance in the light of Christ's unexpected return is a strand of teaching that can be readily extracted from Jesus' teaching in the Gospel accounts. What's more, every generation since the first disciples has wrestled with the eschatological element.

At the same time, the authors of the New Testament and early Christian writers assume and build upon the theological and ethical foundations of the Hebrew Scriptures. These foundations contain elements that are critically important to human society anywhere it is found — for example, the Creator as lawgiver, law as the basis of civil society, justice as the moral tissue that holds society together, and love of neighbor as the means and preservation of social bonds. All these components together, mirroring the reality of the natural law, create the underpinnings upon which civil society rests.[30] We observed earlier that Saint Paul's tactic when working among Jews — for example, strategic citation of the Hebrew Scriptures (Acts 13) — was quite different from that which characterized his work among Gentiles, as in Athens (Acts 17). Three centuries later John Chrysostom testified to operating in similar fashion when he remarked, "We use not only Scripture but also reason in arguing against the pagans." What is John's rationale? "They [John's opponents] say they have no law of conscience, and that there is no Law implanted by God in nature. My answer is to question them about their laws concerning marriage, homicide . . . [and] injuries to others, enacted by their legislators. . . . From whom did he learn? Was it not by his own conscience and conviction?"[31] "Neither Adam, nor anybody else, can be shown ever to have lived without the law of nature," John insists. And even when fuller revelation of God's purposes is expressed in the New Covenant, the natural law is not abrogated by Christ, since the manner in which the entire created order is governed by God has not changed.[32] The pagans cannot have "heard Moses and the prophets, for Gentiles could not have heard them. It is evident [rather] that they derived their laws from the law which God engrafted in man from the beginning."[33]

John Chrysostom is by no means alone in his understanding of

---

30. Rommen, *The Natural Law*, 30-31, expresses well this interrelationship.

31. John Chrysostom, *Homiliae in epistulam ad Romanos* 7 (Migne, Patrologia Graeca 60:502).

32. John Chrysostom, *Homiliae in epistulam ad Romanos* 7.

33. John Chrysostom, *Ad populum Antiochenum de statuis* 12.4 (Migne, Patrologia Graeca 132).

moral reasoning. Nor is he under any illusions about the ravages of sin. The Christian fathers who preceded and followed him are one in their acknowledgment that sin wounds and weakens human nature. As such they give a full reckoning of human depravity; reason, because of the fall, has been impaired. Nevertheless, the same Christian fathers — even the more sectarian among them like Tertullian — are one in the belief that while reason has been altered, *it has not been obliterated.*

Justin, while he believes that pagan understanding of truth is partial, nonetheless affirms that all truth is one. Christian morality was previously known only in part but now has been disclosed fully through Christ. At the same time, the pagan philosopher "spoke well in proportion to the share he had of the spermatic Word [i.e., the Logos that was disseminated among human beings]. . . . Whatever things were rightly said among all men . . . are the property of us Christians. . . . All the [pagan] writers were able to see realities darkly."[34]

Despite his sectarian tendencies, Tertullian, in the second century, understood aspects of Old Testament law to be obsolete, and yet he believed that one fixed morality unites "the law of nature" with Mosaic law, the teaching of Christ, and the leading of the Holy Spirit as he works in the life of the church. "Why should God, the Founder of the Universe, the Governor of the whole world . . . be believed to have given a law through Moses to one people, and not to all nations?"[35] Behind this question is his pondering of how God governed the world prior to Sinai and the Mosaic law. Tertullian understands this governance to have occurred through the natural law — a law "given to Adam" and inferred in Genesis 2:17. This "law unwritten, which was habitually understood naturally, and which the fathers kept," is the "embryo of all [moral] precepts" (*Adversus Judaeos* 2).

Significantly, Tertullian quotes Paul's first letter to the Corinthians, inquiring "Does not nature itself teach you?" (cf. 1 Cor. 11:2-16), to stress that some moral matters are intuited by *all.* "We first of all, indeed, know

---

34. Justin, *1 Apology* 13.

35. Tertullian, *Adversus Judaeos* 2 (in Migne, Patrologia Latina 2.2.599-600); *Adversus Praxean* 31. However, Tertullian, unlike Clement of Alexandria and Origen, was impatient with pagan learning, as mirrored in his rhetorical question, "What indeed has Athens to do with Jerusalem?" "Away with all attempts to produce a mottled Christianity of Stoic, Platonic, and dialectic composition," he insists. Heresies, in fact, are the product of philosophy itself, he believes (*De praescriptione haereticorum* 7). For this reason Saint Paul, in Tertullian's view, warns against human wisdom (1 Cor. 1 and 2).

God Himself by the teaching of nature." Nature's laws can stand on their own: "the appeal for Christian practices becomes all the stronger when also nature, which is the first rule of all, supports them. . . . Ours is the God of nature," he asserts, and "everything which is against nature deserves to be branded as monstrous among all men . . . to be condemned also as sacrilege against God, the Lord and Creator of nature" (*Adversus Judaeos* 2).

Truth is one for Clement of Alexandria as well, who seeks to show that the Christian ethic is the fulfillment of pagan ideals and aspirations. Thus, "the barbarians and Hellenic philosophy has [*sic*] torn off a fragment of eternal truth . . . from the theology of the ever-living Word." If Hellenistic philosophy does not comprehend the whole extent of truth as God has revealed it, nevertheless it prepares the way for the truly royal teaching. What shall we then make of natural moral law that even unbelievers intuit? "There is then in philosophy a trace of wisdom and an impulse from God."[36]

Clement sees it as part of his calling to demonstrate that Christian understanding of moral truth is the fulfillment of pagan aspirations: "Before the advent of the Lord," he notes, "philosophy was necessary to the Greeks. . . . And now it becomes conducive to piety, being a kind of preparatory training for the Gentile" (*Stromata* 1.5). Clement understands philosophy as a "schoolmaster" to the Hellenistic mind that paved the way for completion in Christ. Because truth is one, Clement believes that all people are "illuminated by the dawn of light" (1.13). In this way, Hellenic philosophy "has torn off a fragment of eternal truth" (1.16). And if it has not comprehended the whole extent of the truth, it nevertheless prepares the way. There is then in philosophy "a trace of wisdom and an impulse from God" (1.17).[37]

Irenaeus, too, sees one standard of morality extending from "the law of nature" through Mosaic legislation to Christian ethics. For him, proof of this moral unity lies in the words of the Lord Jesus himself[38] — "This is the first and greatest commandment. And the second is like it: 'Love your neighbor as yourself.' All the law and the prophets hang on these two commandments (Matt. 22:38-40)." Thus, Irenaeus understands the ethical life to be unchanging: "The precepts of an absolutely perfect life . . . are the

---

36. Clement of Alexandria, *Stromata* 1.5, 13, 16, 17; 6:17.

37. Clement, however, is emphatic that knowledge of God comes by faith. See 2.2-6, 11-12; 5.1, 2.

38. Irenaeus, *Adversus haereses* 4.12.2-3; 13.1-4; 16.5.

same in each Testament" (*Adversus haereses* 4.12.2). And even when the moral life finds its growth and completion in Christ, the moral "laws" are "natural, noble and common to all" (4.16.5).

With Irenaeus and Tertullian, Origen sees one moral code uniting the Old and New Testaments. In remarks that are part of his argument against Celsus, he reasons from the fact of punishment — a concept that all men accept — that the same Spirit of God who today reveals Christ also formerly made known truths to humankind. "Unless all men had naturally impressed upon their minds sound ideas of morality, the punishment of sinners would have been excluded." Therefore, he reasons, "[i]t is not a matter of surprise that the same God should set in the hearts of all men those truths He taught by the prophets and the Savior."[39]

Similarly, Gregory of Nyssa writes that the "unwritten characters of the law" were to be understood as resident "in our nature in turning us away from evil and in honoring the divine."[40]

Ambrose, spiritual mentor to Augustine, waxes thoroughly philosophic in his major work on ethics, *On the Duties of the Clergy*.[41] His appeal in this volume is regularly an appeal to nature. "Nature arranges for us both character and appearance, and we ought to observe her directions." "It is seemly to live in accordance with nature," he writes, and "whatever is contrary to nature is shameful" (1.28; cf. 3.3). What does nature teach us? We learn that nature "has poured forth all things for all men for common use" (1.27). Further, it teaches us to avoid excessive grief, that reincarnation is unthinkable, to care for others, to be modest, and to be thankful (1.28). Justice, as well, is "in accordance with nature" inasmuch as it is "ingrained in all creatures to preserve their own safety" (1.46). "There is one law of nature for all," he insists, "and we are bound by the law of nature to act for the good of all." Because nature "arranges for us both character and appearance," therefore "we ought to observe her directions" (1.46).

What is further striking about Ambrose's ethic is his assimilation of pagan moral philosophy in his extensive treatment of virtue and vice, and the cardinal virtues in particular. As a bishop in the church, Ambrose stresses the importance of the cardinal virtues, which are given full expres-

---

39. Origen, *Contra Celsum* 1.4 and 7.2.

40. Gregory of Nyssa, *The Life of Moses*, ed. A. J. Malherbe and Everett Ferguson (New York: Paulist, 1978), 2:215-16.

41. The fathers do not write programmatically on "Christian ethics"; rather, such discussions are part of their theology and apology proper.

sion in the Christian virtues of faith, hope, and charity. For Ambrose, both Scripture and nature teach us to be virtuous. Justice, for example, shows itself to be a cardinal virtue to the extent that it is the moral tissue that — coupled with goodwill — holds society together (1.14-15). Ambrose's burden appears to have been expressing Christian ideals in philosophical categories. While the Christian ethic was to him distinct, indeed superior, it nevertheless remained intelligible and accessible to the unbeliever.[42] The bridge between the two, he believed, was the natural law.

Does Ambrose compromise by viewing pagan virtue as consonant with Christian ethics? By no means. The Christian ethic, he acknowledges, is superior. At the same time that he understands Christian revelation as the fullest expression of the virtuous life, he acknowledges the need to make Christian faith intelligible to unbelievers around him. One legitimate concern of his is that, ethically speaking, Christians might isolate themselves from society and become separatist, waiting for the return of the Lord instead of occupying themselves responsibly in the cultural context to which they are called.

Augustine confesses that God, through his providence and eternal law, governs all things. Nothing can alter this fact. All may collapse around us, as was literally the case of Roman culture at the time Augustine penned *The City of God,* yet the divine order remains the same. The natural law, an expression of divine law, makes possible that human beings work for justice in the earth, however imperfectly. Evil disturbs the natural order, and consequently laws and lawmakers are instituted by the wisdom of providence to restrain and punish. Nevertheless, Augustine can speak of the eternal law being impressed in the soul.[43] Moreover, he maintains that temporal law is just only to the extent that it derives from the eternal law (*De libero arbitrio* 1).

Natural-Law Thinking in Aquinas

Although Christendom today exhibits a bewildering diversity of approaches to ethics, orthodox Catholics and Protestants alike look to

---

42. To argue that Christian ideals are "accessible" to the unbeliever does not deny the role that repentance and faith play. It is only to acknowledge that the spark of the *imago Dei* resides in the heart of every human being.

43. Augustine, *De libero arbitrio* 16.

Thomas Aquinas as a source of moral authority. In most discussions of the natural law it is assumed that Aquinas best represents the tradition both in its theological grounding and in its application to virtuous character and Christian social ethics. Aquinas concerns himself with the perennial questions that affect the moral life. For this reason, in his last major encyclical, *Fides et Ratio* (1998), John Paul II concedes that in Aquinas the church "has seen and recognized the passion for truth." Moreover, "precisely because it stays consistently within the horizon of universal, objective and transcendent truth, his thought scales 'heights unthinkable to human intelligence.'"[44] John Paul thinks Aquinas provides an authentic model for all who seek the truth, since in his integrated thinking the demands of reason and the power of faith "find the most elevated synthesis ever attained by human thought" without demeaning the distinctiveness of either.[45] Therefore, a Christian understanding of the natural law must be conversant with Thomist thought.

Aquinas's work can be understood inter alia as a response to challenges to the faith arising both from Aristotelian thought as it reemerged in the thirteenth century and from pagan and Muslim influences.[46] Most commentators tend to view Aquinas's system as a fusion or synthesis of Aristotelian, Stoic, and Christian thought. While this is not inaccurate, it needs qualification: Thomas does not wish merely to view reason as some vague source of "natural law"; rather, he attempts to identify and underscore the manner in which human "nature" fulfills the *divinely intended* purpose for which it was created. In contemporary parlance, he understood that "all truth is God's truth."

Aquinas's account of the natural law is far more extensive than that of Augustine, yet it builds upon the assumption that "all things subject to divine providence are ruled and measured by the eternal law."[47] It begins

44. *Fides et Ratio*, no. 44.

45. *Fides et Ratio*, no. 98.

46. Perhaps the best account of the medieval development of natural-law thinking is found in the careful historical scholarship of Jean Porter, *Natural and Divine Law: Reclaiming the Tradition for Christian Ethics* (Grand Rapids and Cambridge, U.K.: Eerdmans, 1999), especially chapters 1-3. Whereas her 1999 volume has a foremost historical trajectory, in *Nature as Reason: A Thomistic Theory of Natural Law* (Grand Rapids and Cambridge, U.K.: Eerdmans, 2005), Porter adopts a more philosophical orientation by engaging contemporary debates over the distinctiveness and universality of Christian ethics.

47. Aquinas, *Summa Theologiae* (hereafter *ST*) I-II Q. 91.2.

with the assumption that human nature is a reflection of the divine nature, notably in moral agency and the capacity to reason, which separate humans from all other species of creation. For Thomas the natural law is that component of eternal law, i.e., God's plan for the universe, in which human beings participate through proper use of reason. It is evident that all things participate in this eternal law on the basis of "their respective inclinations to their proper acts and ends."[48] This participation is what we call the natural law.

Consistent with historic Christian theology, Aquinas believes that God's divine law constitutes his *direct* revelation via Christ and the Scriptures. And because grace, properly understood, does not contradict nature, but rather completes or perfects it, natural law is the foundation on which Christian ethics — in its ethical completeness through faith, hope, and love — stands. By way of "natural reason" human beings "discern what is good and what is evil,"[49] which is a self-evident premise and "habit" to all people; this is "nothing else than an imprint on us of the divine light." "It is evident," Thomas concludes, "that the natural law is nothing else than the rational creature's participation" in the eternal law.[50] Natural law may be expressed in the following manner: "Act in conformity with your rational nature. For rational nature, known through self-consciousness, or reflex thinking, constitutes the ontological criterion of man's oughtness. Through its free realization he becomes a man, a free rational being. God's wisdom and knowledge as well as His will stand revealed in the essential idea of man."[51]

Human law, then, is to accord as much as possible with the natural law. The function of laws thus amounts to "a rational ordering of things for the common good, promulgated by the one in charge of the community." Where humans depart from or reject right use of reason, "it has the quality not of a law but of an act of violence."[52]

---

48. Aquinas, *ST* I-II Q. 91.2.

49. The "good" that is to be manifest by human beings is mirrored in the way in which the Creator designed them. God has placed within them "natural inclinations" to guide their moral intuitions.

50. Aquinas, *ST* I-II Q. 91.2.

51. Rommen, *The Natural Law*, 41.

52. For this reason Aquinas departs from Aristotle and the ancients regarding slavery: slavery is a by-product of sin, since "in the state of innocence" before the fall all people were equal as predicated by the natural law (*ST* II-II Q. 57.3). Moreover, the slave still retains the basic "rights" that inhere in the natural law — self-preservation and procreation (Q. 104.5).

What is interesting is that Thomas does not insist that our awareness of the natural law is dependent on religion per se, even when he acknowledges Christ to be the fullest expression of divine revelation. "We cannot know the things that are of God as they are in themselves." Rather, he believes, these things are revealed to us, based on the teaching of Romans 1.[53] In the words of Russell Hittinger, "That the moral order bespeaks a higher cause is derived, by most people, from philosophically untutored inferences from the things that are, from tradition, and also, for Christians, from infused faith."[54] Significantly, then, the rediscovery of Aristotle in Thomas's day, with its renewed interest in the natural world and the function of "law" within the natural order, places Aquinas in conversation with pagan philosophy. While pagan and Christian ideals are ultimately distinct due to the reality of divine grace, there is common ground that needs exploiting. This common ground is a teleological view of human nature that presupposes that authentically human behavior is directed toward a good end, and that the human by the light of natural reason is able to discern what is good and what is evil.[55] "All desire the final end, because all desire their perfection, which is what the final end signifies," even when all "do not agree about the concrete nature of that final end."[56] Human rationality is *by nature* directed toward the good of man and the good of *society*. Thus, every human act is to be measured as right or wrong, morally acceptable or unacceptable, to the extent that it fulfills or undermines human nature and the divine intention.

Reason is the chief means by which we determine the moral quality of an action.[57] Thus, for Aquinas, a "law" is to be observed operating in human nature. What is this law? That good be done and evil avoided. All other moral principles issue out of this basic "law." And what is law in its essence, according to Aquinas? It is a derivative of reason that is advanced *for the commonweal.* Not that it is biologically or physically induced, since not all human appetites and passions are legitimate; rather, it is a moral

53. Aquinas, *ST* I-II Q. 93.2.

54. Russell Hittinger, *The First Grace: Rediscovering the Natural Law in a Post-Christian World* (Wilmington, Del.: ISI Books, 2003), xxi.

55. Aquinas notes: "All inclinations of human nature, to whatever part they belong . . . , all come under natural law so far as they can be charged with intelligence" (*ST* I-II Q. 94.2).

56. Aquinas, *ST* I-II Q. 1.17.

57. Hereon see Porter, *Nature as Reason*, 231-324, and *Natural and Divine Law*, 63-119.

necessity that accords with the *imago Dei* as an intellectual creature. When human beings direct themselves toward objective moral good, they are functioning according to right reason. Aquinas understood the eternal law to reveal the distinction between good and evil, and reason operates to apply this moral standard for the common good of all.[58] At the same time, Aquinas is careful to distinguish between the general principles of natural law — discerning between basic good and evil — and its specific applications in particular situations.

Natural Law in Early Modern Christian Thought

In our brief survey of natural-law thinking that locates itself in the mainstream of the historic Christian tradition, several further names deserve inclusion, even when discussion of one of these — John Calvin — is reserved for the following chapter. An important contribution to natural-law thinking during the early modern period is found in the work of theorists Francisco de Vitoria (1480-1546), Francisco Suárez (1548-1617), and Hugo Grotius (1583-1645).[59] Their appeal to natural law comes at a time of New World discovery and social-political upheaval in Europe. Spanish and Portuguese discoveries in the Indies and the Americas brought to light the necessity of renewed reflections on the fundamental character of justice. These reflections were to proceed on the basis of the doctrine of natural law. Justice has a deeper basis than mere religious confession. It is known through nature and intuited universally as binding on all people everywhere. Thus the law of nature becomes a law to the nations *(ius gentium)*, holding them accountable to the unchanging demands of justice.

By the time of Luther's revolt against the church in Germany, disquieting reports were already reaching Spain from the New World — reports that native Americans were being denied basic liberty and property. The immediate challenge that confronted theologians and philosophers was the Spanish vision to colonize the discovered peoples of the Americas. Spain was prepared to justify war and expansion with indigenous American peoples in the hopes of possessing their land.

---

58. Aquinas, *ST* I-II Q. 90.

59. Elsewhere I discuss the role of Vitoria, Suárez, and Grotius as it pertains to early modern just-war thinking in *Between Pacifism and Jihad: Just War and Christian Tradition* (Downers Grove, Ill.: InterVarsity, 2005), 56-66.

Francisco de Vitoria was a professor of theology at Spain's leading university, the University of Salamanca, during this period of conquest of the New World. The struggle between expansionists and missionaries was protracted and bitter. Spanish treatment of indigenous people, in war and peace, instigated necessary discussions about justice. Vitoria's task was to challenge the Spanish throne because of the unjust treatment of the American Indians: the king has no right, even if he were lord over the whole earth — which he is not — to claim ownership of the land of the native Americans. Looking back five centuries, we fail to appreciate how revolutionary Vitoria's work was at the time. The words of one fourteenth-century Spanish lawyer tell us much about the religious and political environment of the time: "If anyone asserted that the Emperor is not the monarch of the entire world, he would be a heretic; for he would make a pronouncement contrary to the decision of the Church and contrary to the text of the Gospel which says: 'A decree went forth from Caesar Augustus that a census should be taken of all the world,' as St. Luke has it, and so Christ, too, recognized him as emperor and master."[60]

Against conventional thinking, Vitoria argued that the emperor was *not* the ruler of the world: *Imperator non est dominus orbis*. In fact, Vitoria maintained, *the church* is not subject to him, *nor are other nations*. Neither the king nor the pope, for that matter, could authorize war against the Indians in the Americas. Neither religious nor economic nor political reasons alone justify coercion. Therefore, war with the Indians to acquire their land is unjust, he argues in *Reflections on the Indians and the Law of War;* Indians and Spaniards have equal rights. The only just cause for war is a wrong that is intuited through natural moral law, a wrong that is discernible to all people everywhere through reason. Conflict with the American Indians based on religious differences or "the spirit of discovery" is not justifiable. And even were the Indians to attack the Spanish, a just response would be only a defensive response that sought to minimize loss.[61]

Vitoria's criticisms of Spanish expansion strike us as all the more radical given the existence of slavery as practiced by Spain and Portugal.[62] What the professor from Salamanca was willing to maintain was exceed-

---

60. Cited in the introduction to Francisco de Vitoria, *De Indis et de Iure Belli Reflectiones*, ed. Ernest Nys, trans. J. P. Bate (reprint, New York: Wiley; London: Oceana, 1964), p. 76.

61. Vitoria, *De Indis et de Iure Belli Reflectiones* 1, 2, and 10.

62. In Vitoria's day, Spanish slaves consisted of blacks, whites, Moors, and Jews.

ingly unpopular, for Spain had been "guilty of numerous scandals, crimes, and impieties" against the Indians.[63]

Like Vitoria before him, Francisco Suárez taught theology at a leading university of his day.[64] Trained both as a lawyer and theologian, Suárez addressed the subject of war and human rights not unlike Augustine and Aquinas — as a duty of love. This, along with his belief that the natural law is binding on all nations, forms the main argument of his most important work, *The Three Theological Virtues*, published posthumously in 1621. In this work Suárez asks whether war itself is evil. It is both inevitable and not always evil, he responds, even when it is utterly susceptible to abuse. Suárez follows Vitoria and previous thinkers in the just-war tradition: war is permitted by natural law and by the gospel, "which in no way derogates from the natural law."[65]

Suárez is careful in his qualification of legitimate authority. While kings exercise sovereignty, that sovereignty is limited and does not extend to all parts of the world. Neither God nor reason grants that sort of power to an individual, whether in war or in peace. Any authority that enacts laws in conflict with the natural law ceases to have legitimate authority in the rightful sense and thereby becomes tyrannical. The exercise of brute power neither qualifies nor justifies authority.

The overriding concern in Suárez's work is natural law and how states are to conduct themselves in that light. Whereas civil or municipal law is alterable, based on customs and usage, the law of nature is universal and unchanging, governing how human beings as well as nations deal with one another. All aspects of justice flow from this reality.[66]

The Dutch legal theorist Hugo Grotius, roughly contemporary to Suárez, is considered the father of modern international law. Grotius confronts the dilemma of national sovereignty and just limits to war in much

---

63. Vitoria, *De Indis et de Iure Belli Reflectiones* 1.

64. Suárez taught at the University of Portugal at Coimbra. Portugal, at this time, was in the shadow of Spain.

65. Suárez, *The Three Theological Virtues* 3.8.1.

66. A further contribution of Suárez — as with Vitoria — is extending the moral qualifications and limitations of just-war thinking to additional criteria. Aquinas had identified three — just cause, right intention, and sovereign authority. Vitoria and Suárez add three further conditions: proportionality, last resort, and reasonable chance of success. The latter two are best understood as prudential tests that assist the application of moral principles in particular situations.

the same way as Vitoria and Suárez. The results of his work would be foundational for international relations in the modern era. Insofar as he serves — with Vitoria and Suárez — to bridge the scholastic and modern eras, it would be wrong to assume that Grotius advocated an autonomy of human reason as the source of natural law. To the contrary. As a Christian theist, he acknowledges God as Creator, the source of reason and thus the source of the natural law. In the same way, he acknowledges the authority of Scripture and assumes no conflict between human reason and the authority of Scripture as divine revelation. Hence, the *ius naturale* for Grotius is

> a dictate of right reason which points out that an act, according as it is or is not in conformity with rational nature, has in it a quality of moral baseness or moral necessity; and that, in consequence, such an act is either forbidden or enjoined by the author of nature, God. . . .
>
> The law of nature, again, is unchangeable — even in the sense that it cannot be changed by God. Measureless as is the power of God, nevertheless it can be said that there are certain things over which that power does not extend. . . . Just as even God, then, cannot cause that two times two should not make four, so He cannot cause that that which is intrinsically evil be not evil.[67]

In his important work *The Law of War and Peace* (1625), Grotius argues that how nations relate to one another is governed by universally binding moral principles. These principles are "binding on all kings" and "known through reason."[68] This argument has important implications for both the church and the state, for it places limitations on both. It also places limitations on whether nations may go to war justly and how warfare is to be conducted. Given the divinely instituted natural law, such rules of military engagement are valid for all people.

Grotius is remarkable both for his insight into the human condition and for his in-depth application of biblical and general revelation to the problem of peace that was so fleeting in his day.[69] He lived and wrote in the

---

67. Grotius, *The Law of War and Peace* 1.1. I rely here on the translation found in Hugo Grotius, *De Jure Belli ac Pacis Libri Tres*, trans. F. W. Kelsey (Oxford: Clarendon, 1925), 38-39.

68. Grotius, *The Law of War and Peace* 1.1.

69. He is remarkable as well in that he matriculated at the University of Leiden at the ripe age of eleven.

context of the Thirty Years' War that had ravaged much of Europe prior to the Peace of Westphalia in 1648. It was the bitterness of this strife, rending church and state and leaving no international authority, that caused him to pick up the pen and write. Grotius brooded much over the horrors of war and the ways of peace. For this reason, he reflected deeply on the social nature of human beings and the social dimension of civil society. What principles did Grotius believe informed our understanding of a civilized order? Among those that inhere in the natural law are respect of another person's property and belongings, restitution in the event of loss, the binding nature of keeping one's word, and proportionate punishment for injustices.[70]

Yet, committed as he was to peace, Grotius did not exclude the possibility of war. Rather, the ravages of war led him to refine just-war thinking in such a way as to become the handmaiden of authentic justice, in the end securing an enduring social peace. In *The Law of War and Peace* he probes when, how, and by whom war might justly be conducted. To his great credit he sought systematically to understand international law as anchored in the time-honored foundation of the natural law, consistent with the historic Christian tradition.

Grotius was well aware that an impartial and wholly objective understanding of justice is impossible; all efforts to apply justice are subjective. And given his abhorrence of the ravages of war, his chief objective was to prevent such in the first place. Nevertheless, in those situations where we are unable to prevent war, we must aim to minimize its devastation. Grotius self-consciously placed himself between what he called two "extreme" positions — militarism and pacifism. He exhorts: "For both extremes a remedy must be found, [in order] that men may not believe either that nothing is allowable, or that everything is."[71] Human reason and social necessity do not prohibit all force, only that which is morally repugnant, such as human oppression.

In considering the contribution of Grotius to natural-law thinking, we are justified in observing that Grotius "separates" natural law from the strictly *theological* arena to the extent that he makes "secular" application of the natural law in the political-legal realm as it affected international relations. Yet, this is not to say that he developed natural-law theory inde-

70. Grotius, *The Law of War and Peace* 1.1.
71. Grotius, *The Law of War and Peace* 1.1.10 and 1.3.16.

pendent of theological assumptions. His application of the natural law to international politics following the Thirty Years' War united Catholics and Protestants at a time when religion was utterly incapable of bringing about any unity between them. Given the religious fracture of much of Europe, the use of the natural law to regulate states achieved a new importance. The "higher" law of nature, thus, in the words of Paul Sigmund, was used "to criticize the inadequacies of human law in secular affairs, and to regulate the relations of non-Christians who did not recognize the Christian law of love."[72] While it could not be codified in a legal sense, the natural law could be *known through reason,* even when human beings tend to suppress the truth that they intuit. Grotius proceeded from certain truths that he believed to be self-evident — among these, the social nature of human beings and the social-moral obligations that foster civil society such as respect of property, the keeping of promises, and the legitimacy of self-defense.

The significance of Grotius's placement in Western cultural history is not to be underestimated. Bridging two eras, Grotius wrestles with the dimensions of justice as they affect nations' sovereignty and at the same time guard against egregious human rights violations. His application of the natural law furnishes the underpinnings for the emergence of international law.

The Encyclical Teaching of John Paul II
and the Catholic Catechism

The death of John Paul II has caused Christians everywhere, irrespective of their theological vantage point, to reflect with gratitude on the contributions of the former pontiff. Over the last quarter-century — but particularly during the 1990s — this reader has expressed sheer wonder at the profundity, the ecumenical breadth, and the timely cultural commentary that have characterized John Paul's encyclicals.[73] The "crisis of truth" has been a recurring theme in these encyclicals, none more so than *Veritatis Splen*

72. Sigmund, *Natural Law,* 62.

73. Remarkably, after his accession in 1978, John Paul produced thirteen major encyclicals (excluding apostolic letters). Especially helpful to this reader, both inside and outside the classroom, have been *Ut Unum Sint, Veritatis Splendor, Evangelium Vitae,* and *Fides et Ratio.*

dor (The Splendor of Truth), which opens with an allusion to Jesus' dialogue with the rich young man (Matt. 19:16-22). John Paul understood the question posed to our Lord — "What good must I do in order to have eternal life?" — as containing the rudiments of the ethical life. The encounter with Jesus, then, is worthy of John Paul's examination. Throughout the encyclical the former pope analyzes different facets of morality, at the heart of which are lodged the natural law and the Ten Commandments. Divine revelation, he argues, comes initially through the natural law, illuminating the human heart at the most fundamental level. The Ten Commandments are said to embody the contours of the natural law, while the covenants ratify human participation in this moral life. Christ, the eternal Logos and Light, represents in the divine economy the final and fullest expression of divine illumination.

What is fascinating to the reader of *Veritatis* is that from the very beginning John Paul understands the moral order to be Christoform in nature. That is, in the words of Russell Hittinger, the call to Christian discipleship and to moral perfection is not "an addendum to an already complete this-worldly order"; nor is specially revealed truth foreign to us and to be viewed as "externally imposed" upon that which we know from general human experience.[74] Rather, there is full continuity, morally speaking, between the natural law and the "ethics of Jesus." The purpose of Jesus' encounter with the rich young man is to reinforce the harmonious relationship that exists between the natural law, the law as given to Israel, and the gospel. To separate these and place them in antithesis to one another, or to view one of these as "autonomous" (even heteronomous), is to erect a false dichotomy, since freedom and nature, when we understand "freedom" properly in the context of divine revelation, are not opposed to one another. John Paul senses that even among theologians there has been a widespread tendency to set nature and freedom, law and grace, in opposition. This false deduction arises from a false dichotomy in our own thinking.[75]

74. Russell Hittinger, "The Pope and the Theorists," *Crisis*, December 1993, 32.

75. In *Fides et Ratio* (1998) John Paul builds further on the assumption of the natural law by emphasizing that while there are natural limitations on human reason due to the fall, we must not therefore conclude that natural theology should be abandoned. The natural light of reason, rather, does possess a basic knowledge of the Creator and of moral first things. Thus we must be vigorous in affirming the symbiotic relationship between faith and reason. To separate the two is to fall into the errors of either fideism or rationalism, undermining or denying the reciprocal relationship between philosophical and theological think-

The connections in *Veritatis Splendor* — with its emphasis on moral reasoning, the crisis of truth, and pastorally sensitive admonitions — to part 3, sections 1 and 2 of the Catholic *Catechism* are readily identifiable and worthy of note. As with *Veritatis,* the *Catechism's* articulation of the moral life, at the heart of which stands the natural law, is characterized by clarity — clarity in its expression and in its implications.

Section 1 of part 3 in the *Catechism* begins with a full-orbed description of human beings as created in the image of God.[76] Because of the *imago Dei,* human beings by nature pursue "happiness" (= blessedness) as qualified by Jesus' teaching. The Beatitudes "respond to the natural desire for happiness. This desire is of divine origin: God has placed it in the human heart in order to draw man to the One who alone can fulfill it. . . . The Beatitudes reveal the goal of human existence, the ultimate end of human acts" (nos. 1718-19).

God has created humans as rational beings; in this way they are like God. However, to the extent that human freedom is not tethered to God, the source of ultimate good, there is the possibility of choosing between good and evil. The more one does the good, the freer one becomes. The more one chooses to do evil, the more enslaved one becomes. From the outset, human history has been witness to the abuse of freedom and violation of the moral law of God. Through the working of grace of the Holy Spirit, human beings are liberated and educated in authentic freedom (nos. 1730-42).

Following a discussion of the morality of human acts and human passions that distinguishes between object of choice, intention, and circumstances, the *Catechism* highlights the role of conscience, human moral reasoning, and the cultivation of human virtues (nos. 1750-1869). This serves, along with a useful discussion of Christian responsibility to civil society, as a necessary prelude to the *Catechism's* explication of "the Moral Law." The natural law, accordingly, expresses the original moral sense that "enables man to discern by reason the good and the evil, the truth and the lie"; as an internal witness to moral reality, it "would not have the force of

---

ing. Hence, John Paul's passionate plea for the integrity of a wide-ranging metaphysics in *Fides.* One of the finest commentaries on John Paul's thinking from the standpoint of the harmony of faith and reason is Eduardo J. Echeverria's "FIDES ET RATIO — the Catholic and the Calvinist: Prospects for Rapprochement," *Philosophia Reformata* 65 (2000): 72-104.

76. *Catechism of the Catholic Church* (Washington, D.C.: U.S. Catholic Conference, 1994), 424 (nos. 1700ff.). References to the *Catechism* have been placed in the text.

law if it were not the voice and interpreter of a higher reason to which our spirit and our freedom must be submitted" (no. 1954). The natural law "states the first and essential precepts which govern the moral life. Its principal precepts are expressed in the Decalogue. This law is called 'natural,' not in reference to the nature of irrational beings, but because reason which decrees it properly belongs to human nature" (no. 1955). Citing Aquinas, the *Catechism* reiterates: "The natural law is nothing other than the light of understanding placed in us by God; through it we know what we must do and what we must avoid. God has given this light or law at the creation" (no. 1955).[77]

Because it is present in the heart of each person and established by reason, the natural law is therefore universal in its precepts, possessing an authority that extends to all men. It expresses the dignity of the person and determines the basis for his fundamental rights and duties (no. 1956). In its application it is "immutable and permanent throughout the variations of history. . . . Even when it is rejected in its very principles, it cannot be destroyed or removed from the heart of man" (no. 1958).

Although the practical application in particular situations of the natural law's precepts is not necessarily "clearly and immediately" perceived by everyone, the natural law nevertheless "provides revealed law and grace with a foundation prepared by God and in accordance with the work of the Spirit." As such, it furnishes "the solid foundation on which man can build the structure of moral rules to guide his choices." In addition, it also provides "the indispensable moral foundation for building the human community." Finally, it provides "the necessary basis for the civil law with which it is connected, whether by a reflection that draws conclusions from its principles, or by additions of a positive and juridical nature" (nos. 1959-60).

Moral First Things and the "First Grace"

The notions of self-governance and the common good are foremost in the thinking of America's founders, even when they are more deist than theist in their theological outlook. Because these moral necessities furnish the basis for a "civil" society, it should not be surprising to find in the charter documents the language of "self-evident truths" that reflect "Laws of Na-

---

77. Citing Thomas Aquinas, *Collationes de decem praeceptis* 1.

ture" and "Nature's God." That the commonweal, and not the expression of individual rights, is paramount is explicit in the thoughts of James Madison on what constitutes civil society: "It is the duty of every man to render to the Creator such homage and such only as he believes to be acceptable to him. This duty is precedent, both in order of time and in degree of obligation, to the claims of Civil Society. Before any man can be considered as a member of Civil Society, he must be considered as a subject of the Governor of the Universe."[78]

The founders understood that human law is legitimate only to the extent that it is anchored in natural moral law. In this sense a common moral thread unites Augustine, Aquinas, Calvin, Grotius, John Paul II, and the framers of our nation's charter documents. All ascribe to a common moral philosophy — that of natural law — which requires that we pursue the good and just for the sake of the commonweal of all members of society. To pursue the common good of society, in accordance with the natural-law tradition, is, in the words of Jesus, to "love your neighbor" and to "treat others as you would have them treat you." But this moral intuition, it should be emphasized, did not originate with Jesus,[79] even when he enunciated it for the sake of his audiences.

Because the human person is "by nature a social animal,"[80] the social order depends on humans' commitment to preserve the good and resist what is evil. To fail to do so is to pervert justice and breed moral anarchy.[81] Society's laws, then, out of necessity must deliberately seek to affirm and reinforce the natural law; the commonweal depends on it. Members of society are to advance and uphold human positive laws that embody and mirror the natural law. The Decalogue, properly understood, provides the ethical contours of the natural moral law — a "law" predicated on humans being rational and social moral agents. Those moral norms expressed through the Decalogue protect and sanctify critical social elements such as family and parental authority, human life, material property, and respect for others. As moral obligations they are self-evident and unchanging with time and culture. The Decalogue, then, expresses the *content* of the natural

78. James Madison, "Memorial and Remonstrance against Religious Assessments," in *Church and State in the Modern Age: A Documentary History*, ed. J. F. Maclear (New York: Oxford University Press, 1995), 60.

79. Nor does it originate with Saint Paul (Rom. 13:9). Plato also uses this formulation.

80. Thus Aquinas, *ST* I-II Q. 96.4.

81. Aquinas, *ST* I-II Q. 95.2.

law. Aquinas understands the Ten Commandments in this way: "Now the precepts of the Decalogue contain the very intention of the lawgiver, who is God. For the precepts of the first table, which directs us to God, contain the very order to the common and final good, which is God; while the precepts of the second table contain the order of justice to be observed among men, namely, that nothing undue be done to anyone, and that each one be given his due. . . . Consequently, the precepts of the Decalogue admit of no dispensation whatever."[82]

John Murray, in his work *Principles of Conduct,* enunciates the abiding character of the Decalogue in terms not unlike those of Aquinas. The commandments promulgated at Sinai "were but the concrete and practical form of enunciating principles which did not then for the first time come to have relevance but were relevant from the beginning." And as they "did not begin to have relevance at Sinai, so they did not cease to have relevance when the Sinaitic economy had passed away."[83] Rather, they "embody principles which belong to the order which God established for man at the beginning, as also to the order of redemption."[84]

So, for example, while not all killing is viewed as murder, premeditated killing of innocent human beings or terminating one's own life *is* — always and without equivocation. The same is true of theft or child molestation or adultery or sexual impurity or torturing human beings; all constitute violations of human sanctity. The natural law is therefore "a judgment of reason which presents actions as commanded or forbidden by the Author of reason, because the light of reason shows them to be in agreement or disagreement with man's essential nature."[85] The natural law, moreover, applies to Christian believer and unbeliever alike. Specific application of the abiding moral principles of the natural law requires prudence and insight; these principles do not come to us "prepackaged" or with specific instructions. Likewise, in the realm of positive law there is great room for disagreement and variance. For example, how debt is to be canceled, the extent of medical insurance provided, how taxes are to be levied, how education is to proceed, how municipalities order themselves, how food is to be processed, on what side of the road vehicles may drive,

---

82. Aquinas, *ST* I-II Q. 100.8.

83. John Murray, *Principles of Conduct: Aspects of Biblical Ethics* (1957; reprint, Grand Rapids: Eerdmans, 1991), 7.

84. John Murray, *Principles of Conduct,* 8.

85. Rommen, *The Natural Law,* 57.

and how fast those vehicles may travel are all subject to debate, disagreement, and varied interpretation. The application of such rules and regulations is culturally specific and will be subject to change and alteration. Nevertheless, while the natural law does not guide us in the construction and application of all law, all law must mirror and accord with the moral basis of the natural law.

The title of a recent — and exceedingly important — book by Roman Catholic philosopher Russell Hittinger, *The First Grace,* derives from the second council of Arles (A.D. 473), which was instrumental in affirming that human freedom, while weakened and distorted by the effects of sin, nonetheless is not totally eradicated. The natural law, consequently, is described as the "first grace of God" *(per primam Dei gratiam),* in accordance with the Pauline assertion in Romans 2:15 that the natural law is "written on the heart."[86] Taking his cue from patristic usage, Hittinger follows the notion of natural law as it laces its way through early and later patristic thought, through medieval and scholastic formulation, and through early modern and modern reinterpretation, down to the present in the encyclicals of John Paul II — particularly as articulated in *Veritatis Splendor.* Hittinger believes that in *Veritatis* the former pontiff properly summarizes the critical issues contained in natural-law thinking: viz., that (1) there is a moral order of human nature; (2) this moral order is perceived by reason; and (3) this moral intuition is ordained by divine providence.[87] While I am sympathetic to Hittinger's critique of *Veritatis,* my own reading of John Paul's final encyclical letter, *Fides et Ratio,* leads me to think that the theological and philosophical basis for natural-law thinking is perhaps best laid in this latter document. Over that small difference of opinion, however, there is no need to quibble, for *Veritatis* is a timely and eloquent reminder of the "permanent things."

What is in need of emphasis is this: the natural law is rightly understood as the "first grace." It is part of divine revelation and the created order. For this reason it forms the basis of — and is consonant with — a faithful construal of "Christian social ethics."

---

86. Hittinger observes that the Council sought to steer clear of Pelagian heresy on the one hand, which held human efforts to be sufficient for salvation, and an extreme form of predestination on the other hand, which obliterated moral agency.

87. Hittinger, *The First Grace,* 26.

Concluding Reflections

Scripture itself affirms the place of the natural law as a moral norm that is woven into the fabric of creation (e.g., Gen. 2:17; Ps. 19:1-6; Acts 14:17; 17:22-31; Rom. 1:18–2:16). This is in essence the message of Paul and Barnabas as they minister in the city of Lystra, a predominately Gentile city in southern Asia Minor and founded as a Roman colony by Caesar Augustus in 6 B.C.: the living God "has not left himself without testimony" among pagans (Acts 14:17) — testimony corroborated by Paul's work in Athens (17:16-34). Therefore, all people are "without excuse"; to be without excuse is to be morally culpable for what one knows and should do. All are said to be morally accountable, since all have a basic knowledge of the Creator and his moral designs (cf. 17:30-31).

Unbelievers, however, do not begin with Scripture and then reason to saving faith. Traditionally, Christian "apologetics" has assumed this process — correctly, I think — that as Christians we engage the unbeliever initially at the place of moral first things, in our attempts to introduce people to the faith; then we proceed from there. This is not to say that Scripture has no place in our witness. It is only to illustrate that we must engage people where they are located in terms of their underlying worldview assumptions. Every unbeliever has a guiding set of presuppositions about ultimate reality that must be properly interpreted and then exposed for that unbeliever to come to Christian faith.

The Christian must avoid two opposite, yet exceedingly common, attitudes toward the natural law. On the one hand, it is erroneous to think that the natural law is obliterated, and thus futile, because of the effects of sin. Indeed, sin's effects are pervasive; yet sin does not eradicate the *imago Dei*. Otherwise, we should simply give up our feeble attempts to work for criminal justice, to hold people accountable for their actions, or to preserve civil society. On the other hand, we must avoid seeking to demonstrate through mere philosophical method the fact of the natural law, since reason *and* faith are the wings that work harmoniously in the pursuit of truth. The proper posture lies somewhere in between these twin errors. We must therefore insist that the natural law is grounded both in nature and in Scripture.

Natural law, as it has thus far been presented, is by no means the sole account of Christian morality. Rather, we have attempted to argue that it is the necessary starting point for distinguishing between good and evil, for measuring and advancing the common good in a pluralistic society, as well as for requiring a basic level of moral accountability for all. Moral norms in broader society are impossible apart from a presumption of natural law.

Natural law presumes — and respects — individual autonomy and thus distinguishes itself from "divine command" ethical theory in that it does not deny secondary causality. Humans, as Thomas Aquinas insisted, *participate* in divine law, and they do so in two essential ways. First, human nature inclines us to act in particular ways — ways that are characteristically human. Second, human nature — and ordered human behavior — presupposes the existence of a transcendent moral order, which God in his wisdom has ordained and by which God orders human societies for a wider, eternal purpose. From the Christian standpoint, divine sovereignty and human moral freedom coexist. In this way, we can affirm what Aquinas emphasized: humans *participate* by means of volitional reason in eternal law.[88]

The most profound expression of human personhood and dignity is the manner in which we imitate the Creator. Therein we mirror the *imago Dei*. While it is true that Christ and Christ alone brings ethical fullness to human beings, which is to say that natural law does not serve as a substitute for salvation by grace, natural law nevertheless occupies a pivotal spot in Christian social ethics, since it presumes, rightly, that all human beings are capable of — and therefore responsible for — grasping basic principles of moral reasoning. This ability has basic spiritual, intellectual, biological, and psychological dimensions that set the human species apart from all of creation. Christian theology and moral philosophy, therefore, can promote the dignity of human personhood in its uniqueness, regardless of whether people are self-consciously religious.

To speak in terms of preserving the common good of society, as Aquinas does, Christians of every age must be able both to conceptualize and to articulate a "shared" or common nature that unites all people. Natural law does not pretend to offer an exhaustive account of ethics with a set of detailed prescriptions. Rather, it presupposes basic inclinations — that is, cognitive foundations of the moral life that must be cultivated in the direction of virtue. Moral theologian Jean Porter is surely correct to argue that by re-

---

88. Romanus Cessario, *Introduction to Moral Theology* (Washington, D.C.: Catholic University of America Press, 2001), 80, has argued that the key term in Aquinas's definition of natural law is "participation" — i.e., a sharing in the eternal law. John Paul II, similarly, speaks of a "participated theonomy" in his writings.

jecting the natural law as a source of moral reflection theologians neglect one of the richest resources in our tradition for developing a distinctively Christian account of the moral life.[89] Ethicists and theorists who reject natural-law thinking are wholly unable to give an account of morality in the public square. Inter alia, this has decided effects for the realm of bioethics.

Bioethics, medical research, and the arena of public health offer a useful illustration of the biological and moral "givens" of our common human nature and the need to promote the common good in society, against the prevailing spirit of the times and, tragically, against the dogged resistance of many Protestants. By way of illustration, one physician of note calls attention to several fundamentals that have been largely forgotten in our society's attitudes toward sexual promiscuity and AIDS. He reminds us that

> the biological purpose of the sexual act is not only to transmit a body fluid. That fluid must be capable of carrying living elements from one individual into a receptive environment in the other. The full weight of evolution bears down upon sexual union to make it maximally effective in so doing. Any living agent other than sperm gets a first-class free ride in a nutrient medium. There is a long list of venereal diseases that testifies to the efficiency of this [biological] mechanism. . . . The second element is that there is simply no historical precedent for so many individuals sharing body fluids. Even polygamous societies typically restricted the number of wives to that which the man could support economically, and those women had no additional sexual partners.[90]

These unhappy phenomena invite us to do a bit of much-needed ethical reflection: "The complex matrix of biological relationships set up by intravenous drug users and the multiplicity of sexual partners is the modern analog of a contaminated water supply. Anyone who dips into it is at risk of becoming infected. This huge reservoir of disease in so many individuals becomes a common source of infection for those who engage in the few behaviors known to transmit the disease. Biologically, humankind cannot safely sustain this kind of activity."[91]

---

89. Porter, *Natural and Divine Law*, 15.

90. J. D. Robinson, "Our Society Must Finally Start to Take AIDS Seriously," *Chicago Tribune*, August 3, 1988, 17.

91. Robinson, "Our Society," 17.

What is the lesson here? The analogy points us in the direction of the natural law, for it well illustrates, at the physical and anatomical level, the design for which humans are created to function properly as human beings. To contravene this design is to incur the wrath, as it were, of biology at the most fundamental level. And while it has been the inclination of humans to rationalize "unnatural" sexual behavior, even the most socially and politically biased research has not confirmed aberrant sexuality to be "normative."[92]

It is the position of classical Christian theology and moral philosophy that the natural law exists as an enduring and concrete expression of divine providence. As a common fund of moral knowledge, it is the basis on which all people, then, may be held morally accountable in the public square for their actions, regardless of their worldview or life orientation.[93] It represents moral realities that, in the words of J. Budziszewski, we "can't not know."[94] As a shared and public standard, it furnishes the basis for a common code of morality, for "criminal justice" and for "civil society." Natural law provides guidance in a world that mixes belief and unbelief, virtue and vice — in a world where all people, who *by nature* are moral agents, are accountable for their actions. Natural law allows us to praise or commend what is good and not merely what is religious. Also, it allows us to condemn what is evil, since this category of human behavior, like basic good, is unchanging. For this reason we can seek to promote "justice" in

92. That the American Psychological Association in 1972 removed homosexuality from the realm of "disorders" in its *Diagnostic and Statistical Manual of Mental Disorders* is best understood as a political act and not the product of careful scientific research. Three studies conducted in the 1990s that sought to provide legitimization for homosexuality and that received widespread media coverage deserve mention: Simon LeVay, "A Difference in Hypothalamic Structure between Heterosexual and Homosexual Men," *Science,* August 1991, 1034-37; John M. Bailey and Richard Pillard, "A Genetic Study of Male Sexual Orientation," *Archives of General Psychiatry,* December 1991, 1089-96; and Dean Hamer et al., "A Linkage between DNA Markers on the X Chromosome and Male Sexual Orientation," *Science,* July 1993, 3221-27. These studies were subsequently neither replicated nor confirmed in their findings. It is worth noting that the lead researchers in two of the three studies were self-professing homosexuals, which at the very least may be thought to call into question the integrity of their results.

93. In religious terms, this is the meaning of Saint Paul's argument in Rom. 1 and 2 that "all are without excuse"; all humans have the moral law "written on the heart."

94. J. Budziszewski, *What We Can't Not Know: A Guide* (Dallas: Spence, 2003). In this regard, see also Ralph McInerny, "Are There Moral Truths That Everyone Knows?" in *Common Truths: New Perspectives on Natural Law,* ed. Edward B. McLean (Wilmington, Del.: ISI Books, 2000), 1-15.

society, for justice is not a fluid concept; it remains immutable with the passage of time.

Society takes on an uncivilized cast, as John Courtney Murray observed, when people cease talking together according to reasonable argumentation and law. Argument ceases to be civil "when it is dominated by passion and prejudice" and when conversation "becomes merely quarrelsome and querulous." As a result, "[c]ivility dies with the death of dialogue."[95]

Indeed, not everyone will come to the same conclusion about what goals are necessary for "civil society." And most of our contemporaries, it goes without saying, have a phobia about the place of religious values in the public square. The question, then, is not whether moral values will be tolerated but rather *whose* values in the end will prevail. How will we people of faith enter the public square, and what will be our ethical resources? Assuming a commitment on the part of Christians to scriptural revelation, bioethical challenges such as cloning and artificial reproductive technology will necessitate that we argue on the basis of design and "respecting nature." Thus, for example, we shall need to maintain the critical difference between *repairing* the human reproductive system and *bypassing* it.[96] According to natural-law thinking in the Christian moral tradition, our nature indeed *is* our design, and human design respects *both legitimate ends and legitimate means.*

95. John Courtney Murray, *We Hold These Truths: Catholic Reflections on the American Proposition* (New York: Sheed and Ward, 1960), 14.
96. So Budziszewski, *What*, 110.

CHAPTER FOUR

Natural Law and the Protestant Prejudice

It is difficult — though by no means impossible — to make generalizations about Protestant theology, given the splintered nature of Protestantism as well as the multiplicity of theological fads to be found within its borders. Nevertheless, people who otherwise have very little in common theologically find common ground in their opposition to natural law. Such, of course, might be argued of both Protestants and Catholics, even when the latter are characterized by a greater degree of theological control than the former.[1] Generic opposition to natural law can be found among revisionist theologians and ethicists as well as among those who are confessionally orthodox.

Despite Protestantism's bewildering diversity, there exists across Protestantism a broad consensus that rejects the natural law as a metaphysical notion rooted in divine revelation.[2] This consensus is mirrored in the fact

---

1. Long-standing opposition to natural law, for example, has come from Catholic revisionist moral theologian Charles Curran. See inter alia, *Christian Morality Today* (Notre Dame, Ind.: University of Notre Dame Press, 1966), as well as his essay "Natural Law," in *Directions in Fundamental Moral Theology* (Notre Dame, Ind.: University of Notre Dame Press, 1985). Roman Catholic moral theologian Romanus Cessario, in his *Introduction to Moral Theology* (Washington, D.C.: Catholic University of America Press, 2001), 71, has wryly noted that it is actually "difficult to determine what constitutes a revisionist moral theologian," since the moniker is oxymoronic.

2. Elsewhere I address, in abbreviated form, the problem of Protestant bias against natural-law thinking. See "The Natural Law and Human Dignity," in *Life and Learning XVI: Proceedings of the Sixteenth University Faculty for Life Conference at Villanova University, 2006*, ed. Joseph W. Koterski (Washington, D.C.: University Faculty for Life, 2007), 323-34, and "Protestants and Natural Law," *First Things*, December 2006, 33-38. Copyrighted material is used with permission.

that one is hard-pressed to identify a single major figure in Protestant theological ethics who has developed and defended a theory of natural law.[3]

James Gustafson has classified Protestant opposition to natural law in the modern era according to two notable philosophical tendencies — historicism and existentialism.[4] Much in Gustafson's critique commends itself. It accurately gives an account of both rationalism and fideism as theological responses to the modernist spirit since Hume and Kant. While Catholic and Protestant theologians both have drunk deeply from the wells of modernism, the absence of theological authority, it goes without saying, has made Protestant thinkers much more susceptible to heterodox currents as well as to opposition to natural law.

Revisionist objections to natural law tend to be of two types. Either they proceed on the assumption that natural law is "prescientific" — and specifically a mirror of *medieval* social and cultural conditions — and therefore requires critical assessment by the modern mind, or they tend to conflate (and equate) the innate structure of human nature with a sort of metaphysical biology or inert physicalism. Both mind-sets, it should be reiterated, drink deeply from the waters of secularism and naturalism.[5]

In response to these general objections, it should be said that natural-law thinking certainly takes the physical and biological elements of human constitution seriously. Yet, as Romanus Cessario has rightly emphasized, the basic ground for natural law's legitimacy rests on more than mere accounting for biological or physical parts of human existence. It entails the basic discernment through reason of moral first principles.[6]

Equally common in our day, however, is rejection of natural-law thinking among nonrevisionist and confessionally more orthodox thinkers, for whom the chief objection takes several forms.[7] Natural law, it is

3. As an exception one might cite Lutheran theologian Carl Braaten.

4. James M. Gustafson, *Protestant and Roman Catholic Ethics: Prospects for Rapprochement* (Chicago and London: University of Chicago Press, 1978), 62-80.

5. Without question the influence of Hume and Kant has been notable in approaches to ethics, particularly on the Protestant side. J. Budziszewski, *What We Can't Not Know: A Guide* (Dallas: Spence, 2003), 161-81, observes a confluence of cultural factors that have helped undermine the natural law in our time — among these: the eclipse of tradition in general, the "cult of the expert" that disregards ancient wisdom and common sense, postmodern sophistry, the "infantile regression" of public discourse and reflection, the removal of shock and shame in our society's moral desensitization, and therapeutic culture.

6. Cessario, *Introduction to Moral Theology,* 72.

7. Natural-law opposition, as I wish to argue, is a foremost recent Protestant phe-

presumed, fails to take seriously the condition of human sin and places misguided trust in the powers of human reason, which has been debilitated by the fall. Correlatively, those nonrevisionist thinkers who emphasize human depravity typically argue that natural-law theory is insufficiently christocentric. "Christian social ethics," thus construed, is to be located solely and exclusively within a particular understanding of grace. As a consequence, natural-law theory is thought to engender a version of "works righteousness," since it is seen as detracting from the work of grace through Christ. These critics of natural law remain skeptical out of a concern that it is autonomous and somehow external to the center of theological ethics and God's providential care of the world.[8]

In response to this general concern, it is imperative to insist that nothing in natural-law thinking either implies or presupposes salvation by human works. The supposition that the natural law supplants grace or has a salvific function demonstrates a fundamental misunderstanding of the natural law and of the ethical relationship of the covenants. Many Protestants assume that because of the distinctiveness of the new covenant, there is therefore little or no ethical continuity between the precross and postcross era. The natural law, however, mirrors the moral order of creation, not salvation, and thus underscores the ethical *permanent things* — what applies to all people at all times and in all places. In the words of one public philosopher, it denotes what we all can't *not* know.[9] The belief among confessionally orthodox Protestants that natural law engenders a form of works righteousness and detracts from divine grace, because it is a widely held conviction, must be taken seriously, given the fact that it rests on mistaken theological premises. The false dichotomy between creation ordinances and redemptive grace that gives rise to the natural law's rejection is a relatively recent development in Protestant thought.[10] Nothing of

---

nomenon that issues out of a particular theological construal of the relationship between creation and redemption. It cries out for thoughtful theological and philosophical reflection that is consonant with and faithful to the Christian moral tradition. As such, this opposition might be said to mirror an inability to "think with the church."

8. This position unites theologians and ethicists as diverse as Karl Barth, Hans Urs von Balthasar, John Howard Yoder, and Stanley Hauerwas, several of whose views are examined in the present chapter.

9. Budziszewski, *What We Can't Not Know.*

10. In his important recent work that breaks fresh ground, Stephen J. Grabill identifies three factors that have contributed to Protestant rejection of natural-law thinking in the

the sort was believed by the early church fathers, the medieval fathers, or the Protestant Reformers, for whom the natural law was readily affirmed (even when it was not a strong emphasis in their teaching).

Natural-Law Thinking in the Protestant Reformers: Ethical Continuity

However deeply entrenched the neglect of — or opposition to — natural law is among Protestant thinkers, it cannot be attributed to the Reformers of the sixteenth century. While it is decidedly true that they championed a particular understanding of grace and faith, this was *not* to the exclusion of other vehicles of divine agency. Rather, they assumed the natural law as a moral-theological bedrock in their system and therein maintained continuity with their Catholic counterparts.[11] It is accurate to insist that the Reformation controversies with the Catholic Church were foremost theological and not ethical.

To the surprise of many, the notion of natural law is resolutely affirmed in the writings of Protestant Reformers. The conventional stereotype of Luther, Calvin, and company is that in their concern to address matters of faith, Scripture, and the sufficiency of Christ they cared little about — or were at best indifferent to — the natural-law emphasis of their Catholic counterparts. To the contrary. They remain in ethical continuity with the Christian moral tradition, even though they do not emphasize the natural law as much as faith, grace, and forensic justification.

---

preceding century — factors that indeed are overlapping: (1) influence of Karl Barth's epistemological criticism of natural theology, with its christocentric and logocentric premises, (2) the perception that Roman Catholic moral theology does not take seriously enough the effects of sin on human reason, and (3) the antimetaphysical trajectory of nineteenth-century German theology that left its mark on the Protestant mainstream (*Rediscovering the Natural Law in Reformed Theological Ethics*, Emory University Studies in Law and Religion [Grand Rapids and Cambridge, U.K.: Eerdmans, 2006], 3-5).

11. See the surprisingly strong argument to that effect in John T. McNeill, "Natural Law in the Teaching of the Reformers," *Journal of Religion* 26, no. 3 (July 1946): 168-82.

Luther

Natural-law thinking is firmly ensconced in Luther's thought. In his 1525 treatise *How Christians Should Regard Moses,* the Reformer distinguishes between the law of Moses, with its historically conditioned components, stipulations, and illustrations for theocratic Israel, and the natural law.[12] "If the Ten Commandments are to be regarded as Moses' law, then Moses came too late," Luther can quip somewhat wryly, for "Moses agrees exactly with nature"[13] and "what Moses commands is nothing new."[14] Moses "also addressed himself to far too few people, because the Ten Commandments had spread over the whole world not only before Moses but even before Abraham and all the patriarchs. For even if a Moses had never appeared and Abraham had never been born, the Ten Commandments would have had to rule in all men from the very beginning, *as they indeed did and still do.*"[15] The law that stands behind the Ten Commandments, Luther notes emphatically, was in force prior to Moses, from the beginning of the world, and also among all the Gentiles. So far as the Ten Commandments are concerned, "there is no difference between Jews and Gentiles."[16]

And in case he might still be misunderstood, Luther clarifies his position: "We will regard Moses as a teacher, but we will not regard him as our lawgiver — unless he agrees with both the New Testament and the natural law."[17] "Where . . . the Mosaic law and the natural law are one, there the law remains and is not abrogated externally."[18] Faith, says Luther, fulfills the law, to which assertion he adduces Romans 3:31. By contrast, those aspects of the Mosaic code that were temporal and confined to theocratic Israel are "null and void" and "not supported by the natural law."[19] Luther's position is unambiguous: the moral norms that apply to all people,

---

12. Luther joins Melanchthon and Calvin in making the threefold Pentateuchal distinction of ceremonial, judicial, and moral law.

13. *Luther's Works* (hereafter *LW*), vol. 47 ("Against the Sabbatarians"), ed. Franklin Sherman (Philadelphia: Fortress, 1971), 89.

14. *LW,* vol. 35 ("How Christians Should Regard Moses"), ed. E. Theodore Bachmann (Philadelphia: Muhlenberg, 1960), 168.

15. *LW* 47:89, emphasis added.

16. *LW* 47:54. Cf. Luther's comments in 35:166-69.

17. *LW* 35:165.

18. *LW,* vol. 40 ("Against the Heavenly Prophets"), ed. Conrad Bergendorff (Philadelphia: Fortress, 1958), 97.

19. *LW* 40:97.

Christians and non-Christians, are the same. There are no two ethical standards that exist within the realm of divine revelation.

Luther adopts the basic definition of natural law set forth in Philip Melanchthon's commentary on Romans 2:15: the natural law is "a common judgment to which all men alike assent, and therefore one which God has inscribed upon the soul of each man."[20] "Everyone," observes Luther, "must acknowledge that what the natural law says is right and true." There is no one, he insists, who does not sense the effects of the natural law.

Luther is well aware of a common misperception among religious-minded people, namely, that "natural law" is presupposed by — and therefore the common fund of — only "Christian" societies. To the contrary, insists Luther; it is born out by human experience that all nations, all cultures, and all people groups possess this rudimentary knowledge. The natural law "is written in the depth of the heart and cannot be erased."[21] In fact, people have this awareness, this natural moral sense, when they come into the world. Although this natural law was concretized through the Decalogue in a particular manner at a single time and place on Mount Sinai, nations knew of the moral realities behind these laws before the law formally was given to Israel.[22]

In his treatise on temporal authority, Luther deliberates over particular situations that require Christians to participate intelligibly with unbelievers in the public square. Two such situations that potentially involve believer and unbeliever are the unlawful seizure of private property and resolving financial debts. Luther exhorts his readers to use both "the law of love" and "the natural law." However, when love has no observable effect, the latter is to be our guide, since natural law is that "with which all reason is filled."[23] Societies, therefore, "should keep written laws subject to reason, from which they origi-

---

20. The "Loci Communes" of Philip Melanchthon, ed. and trans. Charles L. Hill (Boston: Meador, 1944), 112. Luther believes the Decalogue to be lodged in the human conscience.

21. LW 40:97. Luther adds, "The devil knows very well too that it is impossible to remove the [natural] law from the heart" (111). Moreover, even the demons themselves help illustrate the reality of the natural law's intuition. "The very reason for their condemnation," Luther writes, "is that they possess his [God's] commandment and yet do not keep it, but violate it constantly" ("On the Jews and Their Lies," 40:168).

22. LW 47:94-110.

23. LW, vol. 45 ("Temporal Authority: To What Extent It Should Be Obeyed"), ed. Walther I. Brandt (Philadelphia: Muhlenberg, 1962), 128.

nally welled forth as from the spring of justice."[24] If neither of the concerned parties is Christian, "then you may have them call in some other judge, and tell the obstinate one that they are acting contrary to God and natural law."[25]

It should be emphasized that Luther is perfectly content to allow the natural law and righteousness that comes by faith to stand side by side.[26] The Protestant Reformers as a whole did not perceive general revelation to be canceling out or undermining faith, as have many of their spiritual offspring down to the present day. Rather, the natural law was presumed to be at work within all people and thus to be lodged at the core of Christian social ethics. Were this not the case, "one would have to teach and practice the law for a long time before it became the concern of conscience. The heart must also find and feel the law in itself."[27] Otherwise, it would not become a matter of conscience for anyone.

Luther's theology of law has frequently been less than fully understood, and a significant reason for this has to do with the standard "law-versus-gospel" antinomy for which Luther is well known. But as much as this emphasis can be legitimately thought to derive from Luther, it is properly located within the context of *salvation,* not ethics. Despite conventional thinking about the Reformer, it is not an all-encompassing rubric in Luther's theological system that absorbs every other theological topic. And yet the Protestant tendency since Luther has been precisely that, namely, to amplify the law-versus-gospel presumption, as Bernd Wannenwetsch correctly points out:

> The narrow focus on this antinomy as the formal principle of modern Protestantism . . . has led to a variety of antinomian accounts of law's fundamental opposition to grace and gospel, in which law is either flatly rejected as altogether "heteronomous" or, by way of a second-order antinomy, reduced to its (formally) negative impact as a mirror of sin or a barrier against anarchy. . . . Apart from the soteriological language game, in which the most extreme contrast of law to gospel is required to convey the radical nature of grace, when it comes to *moral theology,* the law [in Luther] plays a more complex role.[28]

24. *LW* 45:129.

25. *LW* 45:127.

26. For Luther, as for the other Reformers, Scripture and the natural law in no way stood in opposition to one another.

27. *LW* 45:127.

28. Bernd Wannenwetsch, "Luther's Moral Theology," in *The Cambridge Companion*

The law for Luther is not, as many Protestants might assume, some "postlapsarian device, a makeshift repair provoked by the fall."[29] To the contrary, it belongs to Adam's original righteousness and as such accords with Paul's statement that the law is "good, righteous and holy" (Rom. 7:12).[30] Luther believed that, properly viewed, the law presupposes not sin but grace. And even the fall itself does not eliminate the law's original function and identity, as Luther clarifies in his writings.[31]

Calvin

Given the emphasis on divine sovereignty and human depravity in Calvin's theological system, one would think that the Reformer might have a dim view of the natural law, in contrast to his Catholic counterparts. Such is not the case.[32] Notwithstanding the ravages of sin, Calvin is keenly aware of Paul's argument in Romans, namely, that the Gentiles "show the work of the law written on their hearts" (Rom. 2:15). Calvin's uses of the law — ceremonial, judicial, and moral — presuppose his conviction that there are aspects of human law that are both binding and nonbinding.[33]

Calvin carries on the Thomist assumption that "by nature man is a social animal." Because of this anthropological reality, man is disposed, "from natural instinct, to preserve society," the result of which is that "human societies must be regulated by law," without which there would be no civil order.[34] The seeds of these just laws are "implanted in the breasts of all without a lawgiver." Moreover, they remain unaffected by the vicissitudes

---

to *Martin Luther,* ed. Donald K. McKim (Cambridge: Cambridge University Press, 2003), 124-25, emphasis added.

29. Wannenwetsch, "Luther's Moral Theology," 125.

30. Luther appears not to have deviated during his lifetime regarding his understanding of the natural law, which is affirmed in personal correspondence, theological treatises, as well as biblical commentary written by him.

31. This remains true even when the law assumes an "accusatory" function due to sin. Helpful correctives to the standard Protestant reading of Luther and law are to be found in Wannenwetsch, "Luther's Moral Theology," 123-35, and David Yeago, "Martin Luther on Grace, Law and Moral Life: Prolegomena to an Ecumenical Discussion of *Veritatis Splendor,*" *Thomist* 62 (1998): 163-91.

32. While it is sharply debated among Reformed scholars precisely how important in Calvin's writings the natural law is, *that* he affirmed it wholeheartedly is not in question.

33. Calvin, *Institutes of the Christian Religion* 2.7.6-13.

34. Calvin, *Institutes* 2.2.13.

of life; neither war nor catastrophe nor theft nor human disagreement can alter these moral intuitions since nothing can "destroy the primary idea of justice" that is implanted within.[35]

Two general themes form the heart of Calvin's theology: (1) that God is sovereign and incomparably majestic, and (2) that the divine will directs everything in the world. In addition, a twofold knowledge of God *(duplex cognitio Dei)* grounds for Calvin the natural law on a natural knowledge of the Creator, which is assumed by (rather than antithetical to) Scripture.[36] This universally imprinted knowledge of God is nonsalvific in nature yet affirms human culpability for actions that violate the moral law. How is it that the world is ordered? The divine law expresses itself in the natural law, thus forming the basis for all of morality.

> By nature a social animal, man is disposed, from natural instinct, to preserve society; the minds of all have impressions of civil order . . . every individual understands how human societies must be regulated by law . . . the seeds of them being implanted in the breasts of all without a lawgiver. . . . An apostle declares "the gentiles . . . show the work of the law written on their hearts." . . . We certainly cannot say that they [the gentiles] are altogether blind as to the rule of life. Nothing is more common than for men to be sufficiently instructed in right conduct by natural law.[37]

In her assessment of Calvin's theological system, Susan Schreiner believes that the presence of natural law in Calvin's thoughts might raise more questions than it solves. For her the main question is properly understanding Calvin's view of the effect of sin on the human mind.[38] Con-

---

35. Calvin, *Institutes* 2.2.13. I would take issue with Irena Backus, "Calvin's Concept of Natural and Roman Law," *Calvin Theological Journal* 38, no. 1 (April 2003): 7-26, who argues that despite similarities of terminology, "Aquinas' and Calvin's concepts of natural law turn out not to have a great deal in common" (12). On the contrary, Calvin stands in broad continuity with Aquinas, even when we allow particular theological and political concerns to color their outlook. See in this regard Grabill, *Rediscovering the Natural Law,* 70-97.

36. Grabill, *Rediscovering the Natural Law,* 70-71.

37. Calvin, *Institutes* 2.2.22 and 2.13.22.

38. She points out that natural law has been sharply debated in Calvin studies for the last century (Susan E. Schreiner, "Calvin's Use of Natural Law," in *A Preserving Grace: Protestants, Catholics, and Natural Law,* ed. Michael Cromartie [Washington, D.C.: Ethics and Public Policy Center; Grand Rapids: Eerdmans, 1997], 51-55). See also her previous mono-

sider, for a moment, this statement by Calvin on the human condition: "But man is so shrouded in the darkness of errors that he hardly begins to grasp through this natural law what worship is acceptable to God. Surely he is very far removed from a true estimate of it. Besides this, he is so puffed up with haughtiness and ambition and so blinded by self-love that he is yet unable to look upon himself and, as it were, to descend within himself, that he may humble and abase himself and confess his own miserable condition."[39]

How corrupt is the human heart? Thoroughly. Is there any realm of human experience that has gone untouched by sin? Emphatically not. But to acknowledge the pervasiveness of sin and human depravity, for Calvin, is not to obliterate the rudimentary moral sense in each person:

> When men grasp the conception of things with the mind and the understanding they are said "to know," from which the word "knowledge" is derived. Likewise, when men have an awareness of divine judgment adjoined to them as a witness which does not let them hide their sins but arraigns them as guilty before the judgment seat — this awareness is called "conscience." It is a certain mean between God and man, for it does not allow man to suppress within himself what he knows, but pursues him to the point of making him acknowledge his guilt.[40]

Notwithstanding the emphasis in his teachings on human depravity, Calvin cannot be interpreted as saying that humans are incapable of basic moral reasoning. Rather, he sides with the apostle Paul: "natural law is that apprehension of the conscience which distinguishes sufficiently between just and unjust, and which deprives men of the excuse of ignorance while it proves them guilty by their own testimony."[41] The Reformer acknowledges that despite "man's perverted and degenerate nature," the image of God is not "totally annihilated and destroyed"; rather, "some sparks still shine" in human creation.[42]

---

graph *The Theater of His Glory: Nature and the Natural Order in the Thought of John Calvin* (Durham, N.C.: Labyrinth Press, 1991), in which is found a fuller discussion of the natural law.

39. Calvin, *Institutes* 2.8.1.

40. Calvin, *Institutes* 4.10.3.

41. Calvin, *Institutes* 2.2.22.

42. Calvin, *Institutes* 1.15.4 and 2.2.12. The fact that the Ten Commandments are primarily framed in negative imperatives leaves no doubt that they presuppose human deprav-

Three general themes in Calvin that relate to his understanding of the natural law and moral reasoning have been identified by Schreiner and call for our understanding. First, Calvin believed that human beings are created as social animals, and thus are made for community. For this reason it is "natural" to care for the human race. Second, humans have a natural instinct for order in the context of family relations. For Calvin the moral impulse is mirrored in a desire for structured relationships, whether within the natural family or within the human family; hence, a third sphere in which the natural law is shown to be operative, namely, government. A frequent subtheme in Calvin's writings, the role of government is such that it safeguards justice, which constitutes the tissue holding together human society.[43] Divinely ordained by the Creator, government preserves an order and harmony among human beings, without which chaos would ensue.[44] While salvation is necessary to justify human beings before God, in the temporal order we rely on nature and reason.

Zwingli

The threefold use of the law, for which the Protestant Reformers are well known, finds a supplemental use — belonging to the judicial realm — in the Swiss Reformational emphasis on covenant. The use of the biblical concept of covenant as a sociopolitical idea emerges particularly in the writings and work of the Swiss Reformers. Covenant not only provides a theological basis for understanding divine work in history, but conjoined to the natural law it furnishes the basis for communal and civil (i.e., moral) obligations that are thought to be binding on all human beings and all societies.[45]

---

ity. Nevertheless, what is commanded can and should be done. For Calvin, the mind still mirrors a native love of truth; for this reason, he argues, a society can govern itself in an orderly fashion.

43. See in this regard the discussion of equity as the expression in civil society of the natural law in Guenther Haas, *The Concept of Equity in Calvin's Ethics* (Waterloo, Ont.: Wilfrid Laurier University Press, 1997).

44. See the helpful expanded treatment of these themes in Schreiner, "Calvin's Use," 69-73, and *The Theater of His Glory*.

45. Hereon see Leonard J. Trinterud, "The Origins of Puritanism," *Church History* 20 (1951): 37-57; Charles J. Butler, "Religious Liberty and Covenant Theology" (Ph.D. diss., Temple University, 1979); and more recently, Andries W. G. Raath and Simon de Freitas,

Covenant and the natural law function together in the political theology of Huldrych Zwingli (1484-1531) as a buttress against tyranny and as a safeguard of the natural-law rights of the citizenry. In Zwingli's thought, the natural law serves as a bulwark and primary vehicle by which to resist injustice and political oppression. With the other Reformers, Zwingli believes that all human laws should conform to the natural law, which has been implanted in the hearts of all men. But with even greater emphasis than Luther, Zwingli understands the natural law to be the equivalent of "true religion, to wit the knowledge, worship, and fear of the supreme deity."[46] The "law of nature," as Zwingli understands it, is implanted by God in the heart of man and is confirmed by the grace of God through Christ. This internal light is owing to the work of God's Spirit in every person, and is only strengthened after conversion to Christ.[47] Mirroring the Swiss Reformational distinctive, Zwingli believes that due to the imperfection of reason, only those rulers and magistrates who are God-fearers properly know the natural law.[48]

Law, as the Swiss Reformers understood it, has two primary functions. It mirrors grace to the extent that it is a gift from the Creator. And it has a pedagogical use in that the civil authorities protect the moral-social order, punishing evildoers and rewarding the good. Where law does not restrain evil, evildoers force their will upon society. Thus, the natural law mirrors both divine and human justice.[49] The commandments of the Creator, as Zwingli and his successor, Heinrich Bullinger, insist, are not merely spiritual in their essence; they are to be implemented in the human social context. For this reason they require civil-legal application.[50]

Because of the depravity of the human heart, Zwingli reasons, humans cannot do justly; hence the necessity of the "law of nature" as the divine imprint on the human heart, allowing even pagan unbelievers basic knowledge of good and evil.[51] This "restraining" influence upon humans

---

"Calling and Resistance: Huldrych Zwingli's Political Theology and His Legacy of Resistance to Tyranny" (unpublished manuscript, University of the Free State, 2001).

46. *Huldreich Zwinglis Werke* (Zürich: Schultess, 1828-42), 4:243.

47. *Huldreich Zwinglis Werke*, 4:243.

48. *Huldreich Zwinglis Sämmtliche Werke* (hereafter *SW*) (Berlin and Leipzig: Pustet, 1905-), 2:320-33.

49. *SW* 2:481-83.

50. *SW* 2:481-83.

51. Even the most unjust, according to Zwingli, possess a rudimentary knowledge of justice.

is owing to the natural law. Without this influence, society would descend into anarchy.

Bullinger

Zwingli's successor in Zürich, Heinrich Bullinger (1504-75), is perhaps best known for his role in drafting the Second Helvetic Confession of 1566. Like Zwingli, but in even more pronounced ways, he affirms the "law of nature" as "an instruction of the conscience, and as it were, a certain direction placed by God himself in the mind and hearts of men, to teach them what they have to do and what to eschew." This conscience is understood to be "the knowledge, judgment, and reason of a man, whereby every man in himself . . . either condemns or acquits himself" of what he has done. This ability to reason morally issues from the Creator, who "both prompteth and writeth his judgments in the hearts and minds of men."[52] Thereby even the Gentiles possess a basic discernment between good and evil, so that the natural law functions in the same way as the written law, teaching us "justice, equity, and goodness" and having as its source God himself.[53]

Like the other Reformers, Bullinger is not inattentive to the ravages of sin. He recognizes that the disposition of the human heart is "flatly corrupted," "blind," and "in all points evil." Nevertheless, God has left his imprint on the soul of every person, so that each person possesses *some* knowledge and retains a *basic awareness* of justice and goodness.[54]

Have moral norms — and thus the requirements of human societies — changed at all in the period of the new covenant? Bullinger answers emphatically in the negative. We are still to regard basic moral truth, respect parents, live out the Golden Rule, and keep the Ten Commandments, for the natural law reminds us that there exists an objective moral order in which human laws are said to inhere. "Among all men, at all times and of

---

52. The English translation is drawn from sermons of Bullinger collected and edited by Thomas Harding. See *The Decades of Heinrich Bullinger*, 4 vols. (Cambridge: The Parker Society, 1849), 2:194 (sermon 1). Moreover, Bullinger writes in the same context: "that which we call nature is the proper disposition or inclination of everything," and "God himself" is the one who "fasteneth in our nature" the moral law (2:194-95).

53. *Decades of Heinrich Bullinger*, 2:195.

54. *Decades of Heinrich Bullinger*, 2:194-95.

all ages," he writes, "the meaning and substances of the laws touching honesty, justice, and public peace, is kept inviolable."[55]

In the main, what distinguishes Bullinger from Zwingli, despite the affirmation by both of the "law of nature" as the means by which God restrains human beings, is his ability to avoid the theocratic tendency.[56] For Bullinger the ministry and oversight of the church are not to be conflated with the magistrate of Romans 13, which bespeaks all political office. The priest is not called "to sit in the judgment seat, and to give judgment against a murderer, or by pronouncing sentence to take up matters in strife," just as the calling of the magistrate is not to teach, baptize, and administer the sacraments.[57]

The interlocking themes of sovereignty, the natural law, and covenant retain a special place in Reformed theology, particularly in its Dutch Reformed version, which, like its Swiss counterpart, sought to embody a synthesis of the social, political, and theological. This would reach its apex in the "sphere sovereignty"[58] and political theology of Dutch Reformed theologian Abraham Kuyper, who was the Dutch prime minister at the turn of the twentieth century. While a discussion of Kuyperian thought and "common grace" takes us too far afield of our present discussion, Kuyper was convinced that no political scheme ever has become dominant that was not founded on religious and natural-law assumptions.[59] And why is this? For Kuyper the answer clearly lies in the fact that common grace and moral law constitute the best guarantee and safeguard of certain liberties.[60]

---

55. *Decades of Heinrich Bullinger*, 2:340.

56. Both Zwingli and Bullinger share a high view of the magistrate as ordained by God.

57. *Decades of Heinrich Bullinger*, 2:239.

58. That is, divine providence has seen to it that the spheres of the state, society, and the church possess a limited autonomy in their relationship one to the other.

59. Abraham Kuyper, *Lectures on Calvinism* (Grand Rapids: Eerdmans, 1931), 78.

60. Kuyper's thinking is noteworthy for another reason, not merely for the accent on common grace. Many Protestant "Reformed" today overlook the fact of Kuyper's ecumenical sensitivities. It is significant that at the level of cultural witness, he was able to prioritize his theological differences with Rome. Read his remarks from the lecture "Calvinism and the Future" (part of his 1898 Stone Lectures at Princeton and collected in *Lectures on Calvinism*): "Even confining ourselves to the Apostles' Creed, which for almost two thousand years substantially has been the common standard of all Christians, we find that the belief in God as the 'Creator of heaven and earth' has been abolished; for creation has been supplanted by evolution. Abolished also has been the belief in God the Son, as born of the Vir-

It is important to reiterate that the Protestant Reformers' disagreement with the church was fundamentally *theological* in nature. As to ethics, they maintained *full continuity* with their Catholic counterparts. Thus, the contention of Roman Catholic theologian Romanus Cessario that "the sixteenth-century Protestant Reform championed grace and faith to the practical exclusion of all other instruments of divine agency" needs moderation.[61] While the Reformers protested what they believed to be a neglect of grace and faith, they uniformly affirmed the role of general revelation and the natural law, even when the accent of their teaching was forensic justification. They were, however, one in their conviction that Christian ethics presupposes — and stands on the bedrock of — the natural law. They stand, then, in continuity with the fathers of the church, that it is not possible to alter or abrogate this law that corresponds to nature and right reason, even if the people themselves or the Senate would wish to do so,[62] and that even sin, with its drastic effects, cannot efface it.[63]

---

gin Mary. . . . Abolished further, with many, the belief in His resurrection and ascension and return to judgment. . . . It [this theology of the day] is a theology without hold upon the masses, a quasi-religion utterly powerless to restore our sadly tottering moral life to even a temporary footing. May more perhaps be expected from the marvelous energy displayed in the latter half of this century by Rome? Let us not too hastily dismiss this question. Though the history of the Reformation has established a fundamental antithesis between Rome and ourselves, it would nevertheless be narrow-minded and shortsighted to underestimate the real power which even now is manifest in Rome's warfare against Atheism and Pantheism. Only ignorance of the exhaustive studies of Romish philosophy and of Rome's successful efforts in social life, could account for such a superficial judgment. Calvin in his day already acknowledged that, as against a spirit from the Great Deep, he considered Romish believers his allies. A so-called orthodox Protestant need only mark in his confession and catechism such doctrines of religion and morals as are not subject to controversy between Rome and ourselves, to perceive immediately that what we have in common with Rome concerns precisely those fundamentals of our Christian creed now most fiercely assaulted by the modern spirit. . . . Calvin at least was accustomed to appeal to Thomas of Aquino. And I for my part am not ashamed to confess that on many points my views have been clarified through my study of the Romish theologians" (182-84).

61. Cessario, *Introduction to Moral Theology*, 69.

62. Thus Lactantius, *Institutes* 6.9.

63. Thus Augustine, *Confessions* 2.4.

Protestant Protestations to Natural Law in the Last Sixty Years: Ethical Discontinuity

Karl Barth

To his great credit, the teaching of this Swiss theologian in the decade before Hitler's rise to power paved the way for the resistance that took the form of the Confessing Church. This group, emergent within the official state (Lutheran) church, "confessed with fresh devotion historic Christian commitments in the light of their immediate political situation."[64] One year after Hitler's accession to power, a conference of confessional church leaders, meeting at Barmen, drew up the brief declaration consisting of six points that became the theological foundation for resistance to Nazi hegemony.

Barth played a key role in the Barmen Declaration, and, with others, confessed that "Jesus Christ, as He is witnessed to in the Scriptures, is the Word of God which we have to hear, which we have to trust and give heed to."[65] With their theological affirmation the participants at Barmen rejected the Nazification of German culture and affirmed that a Christian's ultimate allegiance could not be given to an earthly führer. For him, the lordship of Christ extends beyond the interior life and beyond the church to all of humanity, where it confronts the "principalities and powers of this world." The sole function of the church is to preach the Word of God and bear witness to Christ's lordship. This mandate does not occur in a cultural vacuum; rather, it must appear in concrete historical circumstances in which Christians are located. Not for nothing would Barth be removed from his university teaching post in the year following the Barmen synod.

Barth does not deny the function of the state in the divine economy. Its role is to maintain justice and order over against injustice and chaos. It fails in its duty to the extent that it does not protect what is right in the face of evil. Christians, therefore, are not absolved from their duty to help establish and maintain a just state. For precisely this reason National Socialism, Barth asserts unequivocally, constitutes a "fundamental dissolution of the just State."[66] Faith in the sovereignty of Jesus Christ and affirmation of

---

64. Karl Barth, *The Church and the War* (New York: Macmillan, 1944), v.
65. Barth, *Church and the War*, 7.
66. Barth, *Church and the War*, viii.

the sovereignty of National Socialism are mutually exclusive. Consequently, the Christian is doing the will of God in opposing the Nazi evil.[67]

Writing in *The Church and the War,* Barth argues that despite the ability of some to distinguish between the "Communion of Saints" and a community of "race, blood and soil," between "the might of brutality" and "the power of truth," Western civilization as a whole had failed to confront National Socialism firmly "because the realization of the Christian revelation among the civilized people of the West (not only among the Germans!) had become dim" (5). In the German context, this spiritual dullness was evident among many "educated or half-educated persons who were estranged from the Church but who still required a certain religiosity and religious ideology" (7). Barth speaks of the "artificial structure" of German Christianity that characterized the period preceding Hitler's ascendancy. Thus, the German church had little resistance to offer since German political parties, German jurisprudence, science, art, and philosophy had already capitulated (7-8). In offering resistance to the Nazi idolatry, Barth was convinced that "the far better equipped Roman Catholic Church has done no better" than the Protestant church. Both had drunk too deeply from the eighteenth and nineteenth centuries in order "to be equal to the [present] crisis" (8).

Barth's own examination of the eighteenth and nineteenth centuries leads him to conclude that "man, at least at the higher levels of society, had very close ties with nature," and that these ties were "far from being simply of the kind which lead man to study nature scientifically."[68] The "idealized" and "humanized" understanding of nature, as Barth viewed it, would have serious implications for German thought. Inter alia, it would mean "an attitude of detachment towards the view of history held in earlier times, which had been dictated by church dogma." In fact, echoing the words of Goethe, the whole history of the church might be described as a "hotchpotch of violence and error."[69] The increasing secularization of European culture, coupled with a romantic view of "nature," as Barth saw it, blended easily into the core assumptions of Enlightenment thinking and the new humanism of the eighteenth century.

67. Barth, *Church and the War,* ix. Page references to this work have been placed in the text.

68. Karl Barth, *Protestant Theology in the Nineteenth Century: Its Background and History,* rev. ed. (London: SCM, 2001), 41.

69. Barth, *Protestant Theology,* 45.

In his important work *Protestant Theology in the Nineteenth Century,* Barth considered how these assumptions were further mirrored in the theology and politics of the preceding century. What sort of Christianity needed to be fashioned? The great desire, notes Barth, was for a more "natural" and more "reasonable" religion, over against the dogma of a revealed or miraculous Christianity. The dominant spirit of the time understood "nature" as "the embodiment of what was at the disposal of [man] himself, his spirit, his understanding, his will and his feeling, what was left for him to shape, what could be reached by his will for form." And reason was "the embodiment of his capacity, his superiority over matter, his ability to comprehend it and appropriate it for himself. Thus *natural* Christianity simply means a Christianity that presents itself to man in a manner appropriate to his capacity, and *reasonable* Christianity means a Christianity that is understood and affirmed by man in accordance with his capacity."[70]

It is Barth's conviction that eighteenth- and nineteenth-century man inevitably "longed for a purification of the sphere of the Church from the elements which disturbed it."[71] This theological emptying of Christianity's theistic, christological, and anthropological core constituted for Barth the creation of an entirely different religion, and thus a departure from Christianity, which is revealed through Christ the living Word of God and Scripture as the mediator of the Word of God. The result is that authority, divine command, and the sacraments all are undermined by an emphasis on "nature" and "reason." The preoccupation with "nature" and "reason" in much pre-twentieth-century thinking, as Barth understands it, has pernicious consequences. It prepares the soil for a secularized humanism that empties Christian faith of its substance and undermines or denies the absolute lordship of Christ. Correlatively, it facilitates the emergence of a "natural religion" and "natural theology" that serve as a substitute for a "Word of God"–centered and christocentric faith.

Thus, Barth viewed any theological or philosophical concept that is rooted in "nature" as not merely deficient, but rather heretical, and therefore a radical departure from Christian — which is to say, Christ-centered — faith. Likewise, any moral theology that "tries to deny or obscure its derivation from God's command" and "set up independent principles in the face of autonomies and heteronomies," and aims "to undertake the re-

70. Barth, *Protestant Theology,* 91.
71. Barth, *Protestant Theology,* 92.

placement of the command of the grace of God by a sovereign humanism or even barbarism," is to be utterly rejected.[72] For "natural theology" functions as a Trojan horse inside the walls of Christendom, producing a sort of latent deism. The God of natural law cannot be the God of the Bible. Natural law theory, he worried, creates an autonomous locus of theological and moral reflection that is severed from God's revelation in Jesus Christ. It is overly optimistic about the human condition insofar as it fails to address seriously the matter of sin.[73]

On the surface this warning seems not only plausible but commendable. Given the character of political and cultural fascism of his day, Barth is to be commended in admonishing a "confessing church" that bears witness to the lordship of Christ over all things. Hence, we might not be surprised to find in the first article of the Barmen Declaration a categorical repudiation of natural theology: "Jesus Christ, as he has testified to us through the Holy Scripture, is the one Word of God, whom we are to hear, whom we are to trust and obey in life and in death. We repudiate the false teaching that the church can and must recognize yet other happenings and powers, images and truths as divine revelation along side this one Word of God, as a source of her preaching."[74]

But there is a problem here that Christians of any era must address. To be faithful to Christ's lordship is not to deny the challenge — or the necessity — of communicating truth to the nonbeliever, whose worldview and language are devoid of biblical and christological understanding. How do we as Christians communicate in a non-Christian world? How do we hold conversation with unbelievers? How does Christian faith clothe itself in pluralistic society, wherein few people, relatively speaking, know what "the Bible says" or have heard of "the Word of God"? Our point of contact with nonbelievers, as J. Budziszewski well reminds us, is established by God himself. That reference point, that place of entry into the thinking of nonbelievers, is general revelation, which,

---

72. Karl Barth, *Church Dogmatics* II/1, trans. G. W. Bromiley (Edinburgh: T. & T. Clark, 1961), 527.

73. In this regard, see Carl E. Braaten's critique of Barth's views, appearing in his response to Russell Hittinger, "Natural Law and Catholic Moral Theology," in *A Preserving Grace*, 31-40, as well as Stephen J. Grabill's trenchant assessment of Barth's displacement of the natural law in chapter 4 of *Rediscovering the Natural Law in Reformed Theological Ethics* (21-38).

74. Cited in John H. Leith, ed., *Creeds of the Churches* (Atlanta: John Knox, 1982), 520.

despite humanity's rebellion against the Creator, nevertheless penetrates the conscience of the unbeliever, so that all people are, in Pauline terms, "without excuse." Natural law is the moral aspect of the penetrating arrow of general revelation.[75] Without the natural law, there is no common ground, no point of connection, no meaningful engagement between Christians and nonbelievers.

Barth, it should be remembered, is not the only Christian mind at this time to have grappled with the dilemma of National Socialism and the totalitarian state. Heinrich Rommen, Jacques Maritain, Yves Simon, and Eric Voeglin were among European émigrés of note who arrived in the United States in the 1930s and early 1940s and contributed substantially to a renewal of natural-law thinking, notably among political and legal theorists. And not coincidentally, the leading thinkers who contributed to this renewal were Catholic. What these thinkers shared in common, in contrast to Barth, was the conviction that a traditional metaphysics of natural law, consistent with mainstream Christian political and moral thinking, might be advanced *without* capitulating to the modernist, secularist, positivist (or fascist) Zeitgeist.

One must note in this context the heated debate between Barth and Emil Brunner during the mid-1940s that centered around natural law. At the heart of this controversy lay the epistemological question of whether fallen humans possess a natural knowledge of God. Brunner represented the position that nature is normative insofar as "nature teaches" or "nature dictates." Implied therein is that a basic awareness of God is embedded in creation and that it can be recognized as such by all people. As Brunner saw it, the reality of sin does not eradicate reason and conscience as the constituents of the *imago Dei*. Rather, human beings *by nature* are inclined toward truth and have a capacity for recognizing truth, the effects of human sinfulness notwithstanding.

Barth's response to Brunner was adamant. Knowledge that is naturally intuited about God, he argued, is "a possibility in principle but not . . . in fact."[76] The reason for this is that sin has obliterated any possibility of natural theology, and therefore any utility of "natural law." No second or

---

75. J. Budziszewski, *Written on the Heart: The Case for Natural Law* (Downers Grove, Ill.: InterVarsity, 1997), 185.

76. See Emil Brunner and Karl Barth, *Natural Theology,* trans. P. Fraenkel (London: Geoffrey Bles/Centenary Press, 1946), 106.

"independent" category of knowledge, for Barth, could exist in the aftermath of the fall. Reason simply cannot regain its original powers that it had before humans sinned.[77]

The difference between Barth and Brunner is illustrative, for it captures the fundamental disagreement between Roman Catholics and Protestants over natural law to the present day.[78] The critical question is whether human reasoning and human apprehension of basic moral truth are universal, present, and operative within fallen human beings by nature, and thus, whether human beings can be held accountable for their actions. The historic Christian tradition, without equivocation, answers affirmatively to both questions. Ever since the Barth-Brunner controversy Protestant theology has been riddled with suspicion and skepticism vis-à-vis natural law. In this regard, it would appear that the influence of Barth has been dominant. With few exceptions, it is difficult to identify any Protestant theologian or ethicist of note to this day who has robustly championed the natural law.[79]

In times of cultural crisis, when social, legal, and political institutions are crumbling and rendered incapable of making basic moral judgments, it then becomes necessary to inquire anew into moral-philosophical first things.[80] The crisis of Nazi Germany rendered necessary a response by the Confessing Church, to which Karl Barth belonged. But because National Socialists deftly made use of German legislative, judicial, and political institutions in their grasp of power, what was also rendered necessary was a reexamination of the moral foundations of law and politics. These foundations are grounded in the natural law, what Karl Barth in the end, on the basis of a so-called "Word of God" and christological rubric, rejected. In the name of the radical sovereignty of God, Barth denied a rightful place to general revelation and thereby helped undermine the

---

77. Schreiner, "Calvin's Use," especially 52-55, attempts to place the Barth-Brunner debate in the context of faithfulness to Calvin's teaching.

78. Grabill's lucid account of the Barth-Brunner rift captures the sense in which Barthian thought, to the present day, has exerted its influence in predisposing Protestant theologians negatively toward natural-law thinking (*Rediscovering the Natural Law*, 21-29).

79. An exception is Lutheran theologian Carl Braaten. See, e.g., his essay "Protestants and Natural Law," *First Things*, January 1992, 20-26.

80. None has argued this more persuasively than Heinrich Rommen, *The Natural Law: A Study in Legal and Social History and Philosophy*, trans. T. R. Hanley (Indianapolis: Liberty Fund, 1998).

theological foundations of the natural law rather than prevent its secularization.[81]

The orders of creation, of which natural law is a part, are part of biblical theology. They do not exist apart from the order of salvation made known through Christ. Both the creational and the salvific belong to the divine economy; both are confessed by Christians creedally. They are simply, to use Luther's metaphor, the left and right hands of God.[82]

Jacques Ellul

While not particularly known for his theological writings, Jacques Ellul nonetheless warrants a brief critique, given his adamant and explicit rejection of natural law on expressly theological and christological grounds. In the brief but significant volume that initially appeared in 1946 and was subsequently translated under the English title *The Theological Foundation of Law,* the French social and legal critic concedes the renewal of natural-law thinking that was occurring in his day. Ellul grants that a response to the "disastrous consequences" of positivism is needed. However, the state of modern culture and the emergence of numerous and unprecedented domains of law — e.g., laws addressing liability, labor, and social legislation — constitute for him barriers that are insurmountable. The natural law, as he perceives it, cannot address these realms.

At the conceptual level, Ellul is suspicious of the constant attempt by theologians and natural lawyers to find common ground between Chris-

---

81. So, correctly in my view, William Edgar in his response to Daniel Westberg's essay "The Reformed Tradition and Natural Law," in *A Preserving Grace,* 124.

82. The orders of creation are the media through which God governs the cosmos. As Lutheran theologian Carl Braaten forcefully argues, God has placed human beings in particular structures of life such as nationality, race, religion, sexual identity, family, work, politics, and government — structures that signify and demarcate our creaturely existence. Christians of all ages affirm that God works through these vehicles, no less than that he mediates his grace through word and sacrament. While it is true that these orders of creation are not to be equated with the kingdom of God, neither are they to be divorced from or viewed as unrelated to God's reign. Any theological framework that is dismissive of these natural orders of life advances a view of both the church and the world that is deformed and heretical. The creational orders are central to a proper definition of the church's role in the world. See Carl E. Braaten, "God in Public Life: Rehabilitating the 'Orders of Creation,'" *First Things,* December 1990, 32-38.

tians and non-Christians. Such an aim, he believes, is misguided, since it reveals a wrongheaded wish to ignore or circumvent "the tragic separation created by revelation and grace."[83] The common humanity that we all share, Ellul insists, is not subject to modification by grace. Thus, to emphasize "nature" is to abandon grace and the "supranatural" and collapse any distinction between grace and what is merely human (10). Natural law, then, becomes part of a major humanist project to bring about reconciliation apart from grace. Even *the very desire* to create a universally binding law on the basis of the law of God, for Ellul, is "undeniably heretical," since it presupposes the possibility of non-Christians accepting the will of God (13).

But natural law is not the lone culprit: "It is just one aspect of this [misguided] effort," he notes, "along with natural theology and Gnosticism, natural morality, and the absolute value of reason." Each of these is "designed to permit man to escape from the radical necessity of receiving revelation." As Protestant Christians, Ellul believes we are "called upon to confront the fact of natural law with the teaching of the Scriptures, the rule of our faith" (11).

Ellul does not deny that in human civilizations law is necessary, or even that it has religious significance. What disturbs him is the inevitable evolution of law that takes place, so that an enormous separation occurs between law as a concept and the practice of law in juridical systems. Such was the case during the Enlightenment, whereby "natural law" was no longer *discovered* but rather became the product of autonomous reason, exalting itself against the Creator (25).

But Ellul's bias against natural law is rooted not merely in the fear of rationalist autonomy. At the most elementary level, Ellul insists that "[t]here is no place in biblical revelation" for "a legal concept, an idea, or law governing all human laws and measuring all human law" (25). And because all justice and judgment in Scripture are understood by Ellul within the context of redemption (61), we cannot therefore understand law without the cross of Christ at the center; only at the cross do we understand God's will (46-47). A christocentric view of justice "radically destroys the ideas of objective law and of eternal justice" (49).[84]

Ellul's christocentric rejection of the natural law is further buttressed

83. Jacques Ellul, *The Theological Foundation of Law,* trans. M. Wieser (New York: Seabury Press, 1969), 10. The page references in the succeeding paragraphs are to this work.

84. It should be noted that much of Ellul's critique is a reaction to Paul Ricoeur, and particularly Ricoeur's views as expressed in *The Symbolism of Evil* (New York: Harper and Row, 1967).

by his peculiar reading of the early chapters of Genesis. Through the fall, man loses any resemblance to Adam that he may have otherwise had. Man's perversion by sin is radical; hence, "we cannot admit the idea of the *imago Dei* being preserved in man as the foundation of natural law. . . . To identify natural law with the *imago Dei* means either to admit that man has not totally fallen, or to rob human law of all its value" (61). Remarkably, Ellul insists that prior to the fall "there is no moral conscience [in Adam]; there are [*sic*] no ethics."[85] Adam has knowledge of the good and of evil only *after* the fall: "before the alienation, Adam had no *knowledge* of the good."[86] Ellul is forced, then, to side with Barth on this theological point: "If one adopts a strictly biblical view, then it would seem that one could hardly do otherwise than to follow Karl Barth on the subject of the impossibility of the natural knowledge of God by man, which leads to the same impossibility for the knowledge of the good."[87]

And on this point Ellul is emphatic: "In scripture, there is no possible knowledge of the good apart from a living and personal relationship with Jesus Christ."[88] Ellul does not offer an account of how Noah or Abraham or Melchizedek knew right from wrong. For him there is no "normative ethics of the good," only an "ethics of grace."[89] Ellul is adamant in his contention that natural knowledge of the good does not derive from a knowledge of the will of God but rather is in competition with it, producing a "double standard of morality."[90] One is either wholly in obedience to the Word of God and Christ the Lord or one is wholly in disobedience. Thus, for Ellul, unregenerate man is incapable of doing what is authentically good; one can perform what is good only as a result of radical conversion. For him there is no innate preconversion "voice of conscience" that leads one to an awareness of the need for repentance and conversion.

In the end, Ellul is forced to reject the notion — what he believes to be a mistaken "medieval presupposition"[91] — that there exists a universal

85. Jacques Ellul, *To Will and to Do*, trans. C. E. Hopkin (Philadelphia and Boston: Pilgrim Press, 1969), 6.

86. Ellul, *To Will*, 14, emphasis Ellul's.

87. Ellul, *To Will*, 16. Similarly, Stephen J. Grabill traces the Barthian cast of Ellul's presuppositions in *Rediscovering the Natural Law*, 40-43.

88. Ellul, *To Will*, 16.

89. Ellul, *To Will*, 43.

90. See Ellul, *To Will*, 73-110 (chapter 5, "The Double Morality").

91. Ellul, *To Will*, 118.

morality. "There is a morality everywhere and in every society, but not necessarily the same morality. Morality has no permanent content. Murder is generally reproved, but that is not always true. . . . Morality only exists in particular species."[92] The boundless diversity of moralities existing within human societies obligates Ellul to conclude that man is not a moral animal: "Unfortunately, there is no more agreement among the theoretical moralities than among the lived moralities, which destroys the moralist's claim to universality."[93]

The difficulty with this view is that it presumes Adam, in his pristine condition, to have had no knowledge of the Creator in a moral sense prior to having sinned. This means that Adam was born without a moral sense, without the ability to engage in moral reasoning or reflection. The question naturally arises, however, about why he should be held accountable for sin and subsequently banished from the garden. Whence comes "disobedience" if there is no prior moral knowledge? By Ellul's account, Adam would have had to be an automaton, possessing no will and no rational powers. Ellul assumes a sort of crude "divine command" ethics that presupposes that human beings had no moral intuition of what would please the Creator prior to disobedience. Morality is born of disobedience, not the divine image, and "whatever it is of the *imago Dei* which survives [original sin], that cannot in any case be the moral sense."[94] What humans call the "moral conscience," Ellul contends, "cannot be a reflection of God, a remainder from man's initial integrity."[95] "Commandment is not based on the divine essence but on the sovereign will of God."[96] Human beings are *not* born with the divine essence within; rather, the "image of God" is to be understood in the sense of humans' ultimate destiny. In support of this contention, Ellul disputes both the standard translation of Genesis 1:27 — "man was created in the image of God" — and its inference. He believes that the "image of God" is intended to denote promise, future actualization, a future state of becoming, and not a sacred quality of divine essence at the moment of creation.[97]

To presuppose such with Ellul, however, is to deny that men and

92. Ellul, *To Will*, 124-25.
93. Ellul, *To Will*, 126.
94. Ellul, *To Will*, 42.
95. Ellul, *To Will*, 43.
96. Ellul, *To Will*, 268 n. 1.
97. Ellul, *To Will*, 277 n. 3.

women — that Adam and Eve — were created in the divine image. To require, as Ellul does, that human moral reasoning exists only after the fall, predicated solely on *disobedience,* is to collapse any theology of creation[98] and cut off Christian social ethics at the knees.[99] But this will not do.

Our interest in Ellul is due not to his broader influence but primarily to the extent that he typifies and amplifies the "Protestant error" of ethical discontinuity not only between the old and new covenants but also between creational and salvific orders. While he is partly correct to argue for "the impossibility of the Christian ethic" apart from divine grace,[100] he is mistaken to deny the *imago Dei* within all human beings and the "moral sense" that attends being created in the divine image. This view, it goes without saying, has profound theological and ethical implications. His commentary on Calvin's "error" well illustrates this misguided thinking on his part and deserves to be reproduced at length. Calvin, we learn,

> was under the powerful influence of his time. In the degree in which he was living within Christianity, or in which he shared the philosophic ideas of his age, especially concerning the nature of man, he was prevented from drawing from his theology the logical consequences in the field of natural morality and of natural law. But today, Christians who have based themselves on the existence of a permanent human nature which they used as a point of departure for the doctrine of a partial fall, of the possibility of a natural knowledge of the good on the part of man, etc., and who have imposed this interpretation on the biblical texts, should be embarrassed by the fact that scientific investigations tend to deny the existence of this "nature," unless it be in a sociological sense. In looking at the biblical texts, we are obliged to set

---

98. One cannot understate the tenacity with which Ellul holds to this position. He writes: "To claim to find any other origin than the fall for the phenomenon of natural morality is to run counter to all that the Bible can tell us" (*To Will,* 269 n. 4).

99. There are some similarities in the theological vantage point of Ellul and Karl Barth. See the latter's *Church Dogmatics* II/2 (Edinburgh: T. & T. Clark, 1957), 747-48.

100. See his chapter 12, pp. 201-24 ("The Impossibility of a Christian Ethic"). We give credit to Ellul, however, for his deep concern, partially justified, regarding "a renewed tendency in contemporary Protestant theology to minimize the seriousness of the fall" (*To Will,* 276 n. 1). Unfortunately, Ellul's antidote is as bad as the disease itself insofar as it robs us of the theological foundation, lodged at the core of the Christian moral tradition, upon which a viable Christian social ethics might be built as we engage post-Christian culture.

aside these natural premises, which in the present situation do not appear to be confirmed.[101]

In his appeal to modern "science" as disproof of the "natural morality" mistakenly affirmed by Calvin, Ellul does not tell us what error informed fellow Protestant Reformers Luther, Melanchthon, Zwingli, and Bullinger, all of whom, with Calvin, unequivocally affirmed the natural law.

John Howard Yoder

Another species of opposition to natural-law thinking grounds itself in what it believes to be "radical obedience" to the biblical witness to Jesus. Perhaps the most persuasive representative of this view is Anabaptist theologian John Howard Yoder, whose well-known work *The Politics of Jesus* sets forth the argument that the authentic Christian social ethic is rooted in a radical understanding of Jesus' teaching — and a particular reading of the so-called Sermon on the Mount.[102]

In seeking to understand the political order theologically, Yoder laments that two dominant interpretations have clouded our thinking. One rests on the "catholic" concept of natural law, which is questionable because it presumes an optimistic view of human nature and capacity for divine revelation.[103] But the other is even more regrettable, namely, the "Augustinian-reformed" version of "necessary compromise or order of preservation." Both of these, Yoder insists, are "unacceptable."[104]

A baseline assumption pervades all of Yoder's work. Yoder believes that the early church, in time, wrongly absorbed pagan philosophical influence — for example, the Stoic emphasis on reason and the law of nature — which played a significant role in permitting it, by Ambrose's and Augustine's day, to be "compromised" by the political powers. Christian ethics, according to Yoder, was developed in such a way as to justify Christian presence and participation in Roman imperium; hence, Yoder's unrelent-

---

101. Ellul, *To Will*, 269-70 n. 4.

102. John Howard Yoder, *The Politics of Jesus* (Grand Rapids: Eerdmans, 1972; rev. ed. 1994).

103. John Howard Yoder, *Karl Barth and the Problem of War* (Nashville and New York: Abingdon, 1970), 120.

104. Yoder, *Karl Barth*, 120.

ing "radical critique of Constantinianism." The history of the church is thus one long, unrelenting road of apostasy and cultural idolatry — that is, until the period of the "radical Reformation" in the sixteenth century. Christian ethics, as Yoder conceives it, is located neither in human "nature" nor in rational notions of justice or the common good. Rather, it subsists in our radical obedience to what Yoder understands as Jesus' ethics of nonviolent resistance to political and social oppression.

For Yoder the political powers are always and irrevocably fallen — inevitably opposed to the purposes of God. Revelation 13, not Romans 13, represents the state as normative for all time. In *Discipleship as Political Responsibility* he writes, "The divine mandate of the state consists in using evil means to keep evil from getting out of hand."[105] Because political power is inherently evil, according to Yoder's reading of the New Testament, any cooperation with or working through political power represents nothing less than compromise of the Christian. In fact, because the state is "a pagan institution in which Christians would not normally hold a position,"[106] it follows that participation by the Christian in the affairs of the state constitutes ethical compromise. Yoder believes that as Christians we have failed to understand the cross with its implications. If our understanding *was* properly formed, we would be ever vigilant to the triumphalist temptation and assume our place, with the crucified Lamb, in opposition to the powers in whatever form they might appear.[107] And, of course, we would be "nonviolent."

Commenting on "standard ethical discernment" of our time, Yoder advances what he understands as Jesus' prophetic stance over against other models of ethical decision making, which he believes have "distracted" us over the last several centuries. One "distraction" is that Roman Catholics keep reminding us that nature and grace do not stand in opposition.[108]

---

105. John Howard Yoder, *Discipleship as Political Responsibility* (Scottdale, Pa., and Waterloo, Ont.: Herald, 2003), 18. That political power is inherently evil is a recurring theme in Yoder's writings. See especially "The State in the New Testament," in *Discipleship as Political Responsibility*, 17-47, wherein Yoder's position finds perhaps its most highly concentrated form.

106. Yoder, *Discipleship as Political Responsibility*, 25.

107. While this is a constant theme in Yoder's writings, see in particular his essay "The Power Equation, the Place of Jesus, and the Politics of King," in *For the Nations: Essays Public and Evangelical* (Grand Rapids and Cambridge, U.K.: Eerdmans, 1997), 125-47.

108. Yoder is borrowing the language of "distraction" regarding the natural law from

The Catholic emphasis has "foreshortened" the vision of the kingdom of God by its focus on "the nature of things" in this fallen world. The result, he worries, is national idolatry and patriarchy.[109]

As a product of the radical Reformation, Yoder is supremely pessimistic about any moral education that predates "radical Anabaptism," to which he belongs. And given the genesis of Anabaptism in the sixteenth century, with persecution coming from both the Catholic and the Protestant side, this pessimism is certainly understandable. The tenor of Yoder's writings consistently reveals his belief that he stands within the prophetic tradition. And indeed, the minority status of Anabaptism would seem to confirm this presumption. Yoder is at his best when critiquing the Christian community's tendency toward cultural idolatry; this tendency, without question, is a recurring temptation. And here he is also at his worst, to the extent that Yoder is unwilling to submit his notion of moral formation — and Christian social ethics — to the collective wisdom of the historic Christian tradition.[110] Yoder is fluent in his critique of twentieth-century idolatries; he is simplistic, when he is not silent, in his understanding of Christian ethics as the cumulative wisdom of the fathers of the church — be they ancient, medieval, or modern. Given his overarching commitment to ideological pacifism, Yoder's rejection of natural law, then, might be viewed as a by-product, not a cause, of his pacifist ethics. And like Barth, Yoder believes that the natural law is "an addition" to the Word of God as divine revelation. In this regard, "[t]he warning of the Barmen confessor is still needed."[111]

Karl Barth, who insists, "The central task of the Protestant . . . polemic in relation to Roman Catholic theology is to recall it from this distraction to its proper business, the Christian theme. For in this distraction it is particularly incapable of establishing the concept of the divine command, and therefore of introducing serious theological ethics" (*Church Dogmatics* II/2, *The Doctrine of God*, ed. G. W. Bromiley and T. F. Torrance, trans. G. W. Bromiley [Edinburgh: T & T Clark, 1957], 532).

109. This critique is developed extensively in *For the Nations*.

110. Yoder's understanding — and illegitimate redefining — of natural law is perhaps most concisely on display in Donald E. Miller and John H. Yoder, "Does Natural Law Provide a Basis for a Christian Witness to the State? A Symposium," *Brethren Life and Thought* 7 (1962): 8-22, especially 18-22.

111. John Howard Yoder, "Discerning the Kingdom of God in the World," in *For the Nations*, 245. That a Barthian cast can be detected in Yoder's writings should not be surprising, since Yoder studied under Barth. He writes in the preface of his work *Karl Barth and the Problem of War*, "To Karl Barth, who taught me to rethink my faith in the light of the Word of God" (7).

While a fuller response to Yoder's ethics, with its rejection of the natural law, is incorporated in the next section, it is fair to question the preoccupation with "Constantinianism" on the basis of its fruit. It tends to promote — inevitably, one might argue, even when inadvertently — a sectarian approach to culture. While Yoder shares the fundamentally pacifist outlook of H. Richard Niebuhr, he is nevertheless quite critical of Niebuhr's *Christ and Culture*, and understandably so.[112] For Niebuhr, Anabaptists join other sectarian exemplars to illustrate the "Christ against culture" model, which Niebuhr believes is deficient when contrasted with the "Christ transforming culture" model. In this light it is understandable why Yoder is agitated by a fellow pacifist; in his writings Yoder is at pains to convince the reader that the Anabaptist, pacifist model is *the authentically Christian* model for Christian faith engaging culture. Yoder believes that the Christian community should speak to the "powers," and he is right to presuppose that the church has a prophetic mission. He is wrong, however, to insist that (1) the church had it fundamentally wrong for fifteen centuries, (2) Christians must abstain from public and military service, and (3) political power is *inherently* evil, thus requiring the church's constant and eternal denunciation.[113] And he is

112. At times this criticism of Niebuhr is more veiled, at times more adamant. It is more subdued, for example, in *The Politics of Jesus*, 15-19 and 157-59. By contrast, it assumes a more vehement tone in his essay "How H. Richard Niebuhr Reasons: A Critique of *Christ and Culture*," in *Authentic Transformation: A New Vision of Christ and Culture*, ed. Glen H. Stassen, D. M. Yeager, and John Howard Yoder (Nashville: Abingdon, 1994), 31-89. Yoder protests: "There is widespread agreement among historians of ethics, in the wake of Ernst Troeltsch, Max Weber, and H. Richard Niebuhr, that such a 'withdrawn' or 'purist' position is represented by . . . Tertullian, the Anabaptists, and Tolstoy. Niebuhr's description of what he calls the 'Christ against Culture' position, in his vastly influential *Christ and Culture*, is seriously distorted by his prior polemical stance. Whether or not such a characterization be fair to the persons and movements just named, it in any case does describe the position of the present study" (157-58 n. 15). Despite his disclaimer and protestations to the contrary, Yoder's radical Anabaptist separatism is properly located in the "Christ against culture" category. Niebuhr has done us a service in reminding us, in his "vastly influential" way, of this ethical reality.

113. Our present concern is with Yoder's rejection of the natural law, not his principled pacifism and commitment to nonviolent resistance of the "powers." However, at another level, both are inextricably related, rooted in the assumption of a radical ethical discontinuity between the Testaments — one ingredient of which is Jesus' reputed "radical" ethic of nonviolent love. Part of the confusion created by Yoder's "politics of Jesus" is his conflation of the personal and the political. That is, he fails to distinguish between the Pau-

wrong to maintain that the natural law has no place in the Christian ethical framework.

Stanley Hauerwas

In assorted writings, the Methodist theologian Stanley Hauerwas confesses his debt to Yoderian Anabaptism, wishing to advance Yoder's vision of Christian social ethics. That one newsmagazine in 2001, rightly or wrongly, described Prof. Hauerwas as the most influential theologian in America is some indication not only of his celebrity but also of his influence in molding Protestant ethical thought. A prolific writer and creative thinker, Hauerwas has been explicit in his rejection of the natural law — for example, in *The Peaceable Kingdom* and in *Truthfulness and Tragedy*. As with Yoder, Hauerwas's deep-seated distrust of natural-law thinking in ethics is related to the church's purported compromise with "Constantinianism." Thus, it is argued, "the alleged transparency of the natural law norms reflects more the consensus within the church than the universality of the natural law itself."[114] Natural-law thinking, Hauerwas believes, rather than indicating agreement between Christian and non-Christian, served to mediate agreements within a widely scattered and pluralistic Christian community. "This is substantiated by the fact that the power of natural law as a

---

line *proscription* in Rom. 12 of "vigilante justice" — taking justice into one's own hands — and the Pauline *prescription* in Rom. 13 of the sword in the hand of the powers to protect justice at the societal level. *Both* proscription *and* prescription are legitimated by New Testament teaching. This same theological and hermeneutical conflation informs Yoder's interpretation of the Sermon on the Mount. On the basis of Matt. 5–7 and his pacifist interpretation, Yoder requires nonviolence of all Christians while decrying use of the sword as a lesser "evil" — an evil that can be performed only by Gentiles (see especially chapters 7 and 10 of *The Politics of Jesus*). One of the reasons for his pessimistic interpretation of Rom. 13 is "the crisis of Nazism" that "struck into the heartland of Protestant German scholarship." This tragic part of our recent history, as Yoder perceives it, has forever skewed the way we read Rom. 13, confirming the tragedy of a "post-Constantinian" reading of Rom. 13 that has long characterized both Catholic and Protestant theology. The German situation of sixty years ago, for Yoder, is proof that the powers are evil, proof that Rev. 13 (not Rom. 13) is the normative New Testament teaching on government, and proof that Rom. 13 does *not* call for the Christian's obedience (see chapter 10 of *The Politics of Jesus*).

114. Stanley Hauerwas, *The Peaceable Kingdom: A Primer in Christian Ethics* (Notre Dame, Ind., and London: University of Notre Dame Press, 1983), 51.

systematic idea was developed in and for the Roman imperium and then for 'Christendom.' Thus, ironically, 'natural law' became the means of codifying a particular moral tradition."[115]

Consequently, the natural-law tradition, as interpreted by Hauerwas, rather than offering an account of moral principles that are "the same for all, both as to rectitude and as to knowledge" (Thomas Aquinas) and that we can't *not* know (Saint Paul in Rom. 1 and 2),[116] is a "culturally assimilationist" attempt at "Christian ethics" that mirrors the church's cultural captivity. Thus understood, "moral theology" gave expression to "an unquestioned ecclesial assumption" rather than to the practice of Christian virtue.[117]

Hauerwas believes that the "abstractions" of "nature and grace" have "distorted how ethics has been undertaken in the Catholic tradition."[118] His explanation of these "abstractions," however, contains no sustained interaction with mainstream voices in the Christian moral tradition that have explicated the natural-law tradition through the ages, making it difficult for the reader to understand how the emphasis on natural law indeed distorts Christian ethics. Hauerwas is reticent to look at human "nature" apart from Christian discipleship in the strictest sense: "While the way of life taught by Christ is meant to be an ethic for all people, it does not follow that we can know what such an ethic involves objectively by looking at the human."[119]

At this point it is fair to observe that the natural lawyer would not go so far as to prescribe "the way of life taught by Christ" for all people. That is to say, the Christian ethic is not known by all, but the presence of the natural law does attest to those basic moral realities in all that are "perfected" through grace. The natural law is not the end of ethics, to be sure; it is rather where we must begin. And while Hauerwas does acknowledge points of contact between Christian ethics and "other forms of the moral life," he believes that these "are not sufficient to provide a basis for a 'universal' ethic grounded in human nature per se."[120]

Anticipating objections to the absence of any natural-law and

---

115. Hauerwas, *The Peaceable Kingdom*, 51.
116. See in this regard, more recently, Budziszewski, *What We Can't Not Know*.
117. Hauerwas, *The Peaceable Kingdom*, 51, 52.
118. Hauerwas, *The Peaceable Kingdom*, 55-57.
119. Hauerwas, *The Peaceable Kingdom*, 58.
120. Hauerwas, *The Peaceable Kingdom*, 60-61.

creational considerations in his social ethic, and responding specifically to ethicist James Gustafson's charge that his ethical approach is sectarian, Hauerwas reasons in a manner that has typified Protestant thought, namely, by arguing that nature and grace, natural morality and Christ's lordship, creation and Christology, are diametrically opposed: "I certainly have never denied the Christian affirmation of God as Creator; rather, I have refused to use that affirmation to underwrite an autonomous realm of morality separate from Christ's lordship."[121] The issue is *not* creation, Hauerwas vigorously maintains. "What allows us to look expectantly for agreement among those who do not worship God is not that we have a common morality based on autonomous knowledge of autonomous nature, but that God's kingdom is wider than the church."[122] But this widespread presumption of "autonomy" that worries Hauerwas, the assumption that nature and grace stand in opposition, would seem to erect a false dualism that finds no place in historic Christian theology, as Oliver O'Donovan has reminded us.[123] It is a fairly late development, found predominately in Protestant theology.

Ultimately, Hauerwas believes that "Christian ethics theologically does not have a stake in 'natural law.'"[124] In *The Peaceable Kingdom* he identifies a number of "difficulties" that the natural law is thought to present:

- It creates a distorted moral psychology by ignoring the dispositions of the moral agent.
- It fails to offer a sufficient account of community.
- It confuses nature and grace.
- It fails to acknowledge that there is no such thing as a universal morality, only many moralities.

121. Stanley Hauerwas, "Why the 'Sectarian Temptation' Is a Misrepresentation: A Response to James Gustafson (1988)," in *The Hauerwas Reader*, ed. John Berkman and Michael Cartwright (Durham, N.C., and London: Duke University Press, 2001), 107-8. This response to Gustafson is reproduced in the introduction to *Christian Existence Today: Essays on Church, World, and Living In Between* (Grand Rapids: Brazos, 2001), 1-21, here 17.

122. Hauerwas, "Why the 'Sectarian Temptation,'" 108.

123. Oliver O'Donovan, *Resurrection and Moral Order: An Outline for Evangelical Ethics* (Grand Rapids: Eerdmans, 1986), 15.

124. Stanley Hauerwas, *Truthfulness and Tragedy: Further Investigations in Christian Ethics* (South Bend, Ind.: University of Notre Dame Press, 1983), 58.

- It fails to inhibit the inherent violence of this world; in fact, violence and coercion are said to become conceptually intelligible from a natural-law standpoint.
- It ignores the narrative character of Christian ethics.
- It tempts us to coerce those who disagree with us.[125]

Broader difficulties for Hauerwas regarding natural-law thinking present themselves as it applies to the ethical task.[126] These include:

- that reason is insufficient to lead people to basic moral principle.
- that natural-law arguments often take the form of ideological commitments.
- that natural-law thinking is a reflection of the Constantinian era.
- that natural-law thinking well nigh "perverts" the nature of the Christian moral life.
- that natural-law thinking and "natural theology" breed a sort of "primitive metaphysics."

Some of these concerns, the reader will recognize, issue out of Hauerwas's ideological precommitment to pacifism and nonviolent resistance to the state.[127] Like Yoder, Hauerwas worries that affirming the natural-law tradition offers justification for war, violence, or military conflict. And in part he is right when he writes, "For if just war is based on natural law, a law written in the conscience of all men and women by God, then it seems that war must be understood as the outgrowth of legitimate moral commitments."[128] But just use of force and reluctantly going to war for justified purposes are for Hauerwas necessarily (and thus *always*) "the

---

125. Hauerwas, *The Peaceable Kingdom*, 61-64.

126. Hauerwas, *The Peaceable Kingdom*, 51-64.

127. In *Unleashing the Scripture: Freeing the Bible from Captivity to America* (Nashville: Abingdon, 1993), 64, 72, he writes: "[P]ut as contentiously as I can, you cannot rightly read the Sermon on the Mount unless you are a pacifist. . . . The Sermon does not generate an ethic of nonviolence, but rather a community of nonviolence is necessary if the Sermon is to be read rightly." Thus, it would seem that the mainstream of the church — representing the historic Christian tradition — has been unable to properly interpret Jesus' ethical teaching on Matt. 5–7, given the fact that it has not been pacifist.

128. Stanley Hauerwas, "Should War Be Eliminated? A Thought Experiment," in *The Hauerwas Reader*, 404.

compromises we make with sin" and "cooperating with sin" (and therefore always unjust).[129] In this regard, John Courtney Murray's basic distinction between "violence" and "force" is, I think, helpful in making necessary moral discriminations: "Force is the measure of power necessary and sufficient to uphold . . . law and politics. What exceeds this measure is violence, which destroys the order of both law and politics. . . . As an instrument, force is morally neutral in itself."[130] For this reason, as Murray and moral theologians past and present have intuited, the just-war tradition is lodged squarely within the mainstream of the Christian moral tradition, even though it is beyond the scope of our present discussion.

What is relevant in light of Hauerwas's objections to natural law, however, is that, far from preparing society for violence, contra Hauerwas, the natural law *preserves* social bonds and *guards* basic freedoms rather than threatening them.[131] Not only is it the grammar of a common moral discourse that Christians must utilize with unbelievers, it is also part of divine revelation — not antithetical to a genuinely "Christian" social ethics that Hauerwas is so concerned to defend — by which the public square not only *can* but also *must* be preserved. Thus, Hauerwas is mistaken to suggest that "Christian ethics" narrowly construed must be that which all people embrace. *Not all will embrace a Christian ethic,* just as *not all will embrace Christian religion.* But the Christian is *not* "compromising" by seeking to work for justice in the public square based on the natural law and shared humanity.[132]

129. Hauerwas, "Should War Be Eliminated?" 404.

130. John Courtney Murray, *We Hold These Truths: Catholic Reflections on the American Proposition* (New York: Sheed and Ward, 1960), 274.

131. Political ethicist Jean Bethke Elshtain has persuasively argued that the very moral principles and distinctions governing just-war reasoning are those that are requisite for and undergird civil society. See, notably, chapter 4 ("The Attempt to Disarm Civic Virtue") of *Women and War,* rev. ed. (Chicago and London: University of Chicago Press, 1995), 121-59; and the introductory chapters of *Just War against Terror: The American Burden in a Violent World* (New York: Basic Books, 2003).

132. In *Resident Aliens: Life in the Christian Colony* (Nashville: Abingdon, 1989), 38, Hauerwas and William Willimon, wishing to stress the uniqueness of a "Christian" ethics, write: "The church really does not know what these words ['peace' and 'justice'] mean apart from the life and death of Jesus of Nazareth." However, the notion that *justice* is unintelligible apart from the Christian religion is simply not true, and it does not represent mainstream thinking within the Christian moral tradition. This would make the work and message of the prophets, including John the Baptist, all but meaningless, since their calls for *repentance* were predicated on their audiences having prior moral knowledge. And it would render the "cardinal virtues" meaningless for all who are outside the church.

Not only Aristotle but also Christian moral thinkers from Aquinas to Jacques Maritain and C. S. Lewis to John Paul II have argued for the application of natural-law thinking in the realm of public discourse. All were cognizant of the need to argue for moral first principles on the basis of human nature. To do such in a pluralistic environment is *not* to capitulate to the culture as Hauerwas would suggest.

In chapter 2 we observed how noted Christian thinkers of prior generations were known for their affirmation of the "permanent things." One of the most important lessons we can learn from them is that, in contrast to the Yoderian-Hauerwasian approach to ethics, public morality must rest upon public principles — principles rooted in the fabric of creation. For this reason they championed the time-honored idea of the natural law — out of the conviction that basic moral principles, assumed by and standing in agreement with biblical revelation, are accessible to all people by virtue of God-given reason. In this light we gain new appreciation for the ever-relevant argument of C. S. Lewis regarding the Tao in both *Mere Christianity* and *The Abolition of Man.* Not only does the natural law not contravene the ethics of Christ, as an ethical standard it simply cannot be circumvented insofar as it is the source from which all moral judgments spring. Basic virtues such as reliability, faithfulness, justice, mercy, and generosity form the backbone of all "civilized" societies and are intuited as true independent of human or religious experience.[133]

Lewis, of course, was well aware that Christians — and Protestants in particular — object to the natural law precisely because they are convinced that it detracts from Christianity. But Lewis rejected this view. Far from contradicting Christian social ethics, as John West reminds us in his delightful essay "Politics from the Shadowlands,"[134] the natural law is in truth presupposed by it. And Lewis himself leaves little room for misunderstanding, offering the reader further rationale in *Christian Reflections:* "The idea that Christianity brought an entirely new ethical code into the world is a grave error. If it had done so, then we should have to conclude that all who first-preached it wholly misunderstood their own message: for

133. The point needing emphasis is this: it is not our job to make all of society "Christian"; rather, all Christians are to offer up, in myriads of creative ways, a public witness, and a critical element in this public witness is to serve as a preserving agent in society. Such does not *merely* consist of denouncing the "powers" in accordance with radical Anabaptism.

134. John G. West, Jr., "Politics from the Shadowlands: C. S. Lewis on Earthly Government," *Policy Review*, Spring 1994, 68-70.

all of them, its Founder, His precursor, His apostles, came demanding repentance and offering forgiveness, a demand and an offer both meaningless except on the assumption of a moral law *already known* and *already broken.*"[135]

In a certain sense, Lewis continues, "it is no more possible to invent a new ethics than to place a new sun in the sky. Some precept from traditional morality always has to be presumed. We never start from a *tabula rasa:* if we did, we should end, ethically speaking, with a *tabula rasa.*"[136] There is, I think, wisdom in what Lewis is saying — wisdom that counters the autonomy, arrogance, and false dichotomies of much contemporary Protestant ethics.

In his important book *Ethics after Christendom,* ethicist Vigen Guroian offers a helpful assessment of the "radical critique" of the powers that characterize much "Christian ethics." While this perspective is useful in pointing out the dangers inherent in the attempt to "re-Christianize" America (I write in the American context), Guroian finds its ethics insufficient in helping us to construct a responsible public philosophy.[137] Part of the reason for its inadequacy, notwithstanding its partial truth in sensitizing us to the political temptation, is that it tends to be simplistic, even dismissive, of the church's fathers and the church's wider cultural mandate — a mandate that subsists not only in "prophetic" denunciation. In its unrelenting "radical" critique of "Constantinianism,"[138] it is unable to view Ambrose and Augustine as any other than unwitting — or perhaps witting — accomplices to the perversion of the church by the "powers" in the fourth century. Missing is any serious attempt to read patristic works such as Ambrose's *Duties of the Clergy* or Augustine's *City of God* and interpret the two fathers in the light of historic Christian thought; both fathers are

135. C. S. Lewis, "On Ethics," in *Christian Reflections,* ed. Walter Hooper (Grand Rapids: Eerdmans, 1967), 46.

136. Lewis, "On Ethics," 53.

137. See, especially, the first two chapters of Guroian's *Ethics after Christendom: Toward an Ecclesial Christian Ethic* (Grand Rapids: Eerdmans, 1994).

138. To suggest that the "radical critique of Constantinianism" is *generally* misguided as a hermeneutic of church history is not to deny that it contains elements of truth. It is only (a) to recognize its ideological commitment to radical separatism that issues out of Anabaptist beginnings and that results in an extremely biased reading of patristic literature (or literature of any age) and (b) to recognize that all heterodox views (I use "heterodox" in the sense of lying outside the mainstream of the historic Christian tradition) begin with a partial truth while resisting corrective balance.

thought to be irredeemably compromised by the powers that in the fourth century had co-opted the church.

Though not unrelated, a further weakness of natural-law opponents needing some exploration is the inability of a so-called "narrative" approach to ethics to root itself in the broader historic tradition. Given the pride of place accorded personal "narratives," experience and subjective interpretation of texts in postmodern, post-consensus culture, one is justified in raising certain critical questions. *Whose* narrative is authoritative? On what basis? By what measure? And by what hermeneutical prescriptions? Surely, a narrative approach to ethics has something distinctive to offer, but like an unruly child, which downplays or eschews doctrinal moorings, and law in general, it will need chastening — and subordination to the greater "narrative" of historic Christian faith — if it is to remain legitimate. Thus, for example, the assertion that "Christian ethics does not begin by emphasizing rules or principles" and that Christian ethics is foremost *descriptive* and not *prescriptive*[139] needs moderation, since it is impossible to ignore the "rules and principles" that are woven into the Pentateuchal "narrative" virtually from the beginning, not to mention the whole of the Old Testament. And, in the end, the lesson of Israel is not merely "narrative"; it is that she did not *obey*. That is to say, narrative is useful to the extent that it unveils and teaches moral principle, the goal of which is obedience. What's more, not only Jesus but also Paul and James, as well as 1, 2, and 3 John, affirm the "rules and principles" of the Old Testament. For this reason Gilbert Meilaender reminds us that all serious moral theory will require (1) that we judge actions, in terms of right and wrong; (2) that we judge character, i.e., the goodness or badness of the moral agent; and (3) that we evaluate the goals, values, and intentions of actions.[140] Though perhaps inconvenient, and decidedly out of step with postmodern culture, "rules and principles" nonetheless are at the heart of any ethic that purports to be authentically Christian. A "narrative" approach to ethics will be useful — and faithfully "Christian" — to the extent that it takes into consideration all three of these realms.

Voices as diverse as ethicist Gilbert Meilaender,[141] Lutheran theolo-

---

139. Hauerwas, *The Peaceable Kingdom*, 24-25, 50.

140. Gilbert Meilaender, *Faith and Faithfulness: Basic Themes in Christian Ethics* (Notre Dame, Ind., and London: University of Notre Dame Press, 1991), 90-91.

141. Meilaender, *Faith and Faithfulness*, 19-22.

gian Carl Braaten,[142] and Roman Catholic social critics George Weigel[143] and David Schindler[144] join in offering a helpful evaluation of the Anabaptist/sectarian approach to Christian ethics, which in its practice, they worry, wittingly or unwittingly discourages responsible Christian participation in society.[145] Braaten laments, with some justification, I think, that highly visible Christian ethicists, in their rejection of the notion of natural law, are unable, despite their considerable influence, to equip the Christian community effectively in terms of its cultural mandate.[146] I am inclined, at some level, to agree.

H. Richard Niebuhr

A further debilitating factor in the Protestant understanding of natural law might be measured, indirectly, by the influence of theologians and thinkers who do not reject natural-law thinking outright but rather proceed from a faulty understanding of it. The writings of H. Richard Niebuhr are sufficient to illustrate. Extending his discussion in *Christ and Culture* of the five models showing how faith and culture interact, Niebuhr, in a previously unpublished essay, subsumes his treatment of natural law under the rubric of "Christ of Culture; The Accommodationist Type."[147] In this discussion Niebuhr attributes the natural law to what he calls the "cultural type" (i.e., the "Christ of culture" model). His reason for this is his conviction that

142. Braaten, "Protestants and Natural Law," 20-26.

143. George Weigel, *Catholicism and the Renewal of American Democracy* (New York: Paulist, 1989), especially 196-200.

144. David L. Schindler, *Heart of the World, Center of the Church: Communio, Ecclesiology, Liberalism, and Liberation* (Grand Rapids: Eerdmans, 1996).

145. Yoder is quite sensitive to the criticism from the outside that his radical Anabaptist separatism engenders social withdrawal; he counters that, properly understood, it is a principled posture that voluntarily embraces "faithful non-participation." However forceful Yoder's protest, it is a fact that his "radical critique of Constantinianism" and his "radical Anabaptism," in their practice, have tended to engender social withdrawal from precisely those social institutions that need the leavening effect of Christian participation. I offer this assessment as one who grew up in the Anabaptist — and specifically, Mennonite — context, and thus understand it somewhat sympathetically from the inside.

146. Braaten, "Protestants and Natural Law," 20-26.

147. Glen H. Stassen, D. M. Yeager, and John Howard Yoder, *Authentic Transformation: A New Vision of Christ and Culture* (Nashville: Abingdon, 1996), 22-24. Page references to this work have been placed in the text.

"nature is known only through culture." Those Christians who belong to this model "are characterized by the fact that they tend to interpret the revelation of values and imperatives . . . from the standpoint of the common reason of their culture. They assimilate the church to culture, identify cultural good and law with Christian good and law, yet seek also to interpret the cultural ends and imperatives in Christian fashion" (22).

Within the "Christ of culture" model, Niebuhr summarizes his understanding of Christians who affirm natural law:

1. These individuals assimilate the injunctions and values of the gospel to those of the society at large, while the imperatives of Jesus are regarded as the expression of reason or nature. Christian values are religious equivalents of the culture's best values.

2. Those elements that are most intelligible to culture are taken to be primary and understood in the context of culture.

3. Natural-law thinking is characterized by a quest for harmony. The strategy of Christians who affirm the natural law is to ameliorate rather than separate from or alienate the culture. (23)

These baseline assumptions, it should be emphasized, would surprise most natural lawyers. In concluding his discussion of natural law as an expression of the "Christ of culture" model, Niebuhr, in a striking manner, lumps together natural-law advocates with what he calls "Christian liberalism." This association is regrettable, insofar as "Christian liberalism" constitutes in *Christ and Culture* the chief example of the accommodationist model. With its "slurring over the end-terms of the gospel imperative," Christian liberalism, in its method, is noted by Niebuhr "to adopt the value judgment of modern society" (24).

Much might be said in response to Niebuhr's critique of natural law. A sympathetic reader of *Christ and Culture*, I have profited immensely from the typology Niebuhr offers in his classic work. And I disagree sharply with George Marsden, who recently argued that Niebuhr's typology "could be near the end of its usefulness."[148] Such is certainly *not* the

---

148. George Marsden, "Christianity and Cultures: Transforming Niebuhr's Categories," *Christian Ethics Today*, December 2000, 18-24. Niebuhr's typology remains extremely useful because of the perennial nature of the tension between Christian faith and culture. That it needs reformulation in the idiom of the day is *not* to say, with Marsden, that it is insufficient and no longer useful.

case, even though Marsden is correct to suggest that Niebuhr's typology requires translation into the idiom of the day. What does need to be said is that through his conflation of natural law and accommodationism, Niebuhr establishes false premises upon which to proceed. Mainstream Christian moral thinkers through the ages — e.g., Justin, Ambrose, Augustine, Aquinas, the Protestant Reformers, Francisco de Vitoria, Francisco Suárez, Hugo Grotius, not to mention Catholic social ethics down to John Paul II and the present — affirm the natural law as an integral component to divine revelation, and thus do not illustrate, according to Niebuhr's typology, the "Christ of culture" model. Rather, of the five models proposed by Niebuhr in *Christ and Culture,* these Christian moral thinkers illustrate the three mediating positions between faith and culture.[149] The result of Niebuhr's construal of the natural law is that it confuses the necessity of bridge-building between Christians and non-Christians with cultural accommodation and "compromise." Natural lawyers would not recognize themselves in this critique — a critique constructed on a false understanding of the natural law from the start.

Concluding Reflections

It is time to draw our assessment of Protestant ethics, at least for the moment, to a close. The focus of the present chapter has been theologians who reject the natural law chiefly for christocentric reasons, thereby erecting a false dichotomy between nature and grace and rejecting the natural law as purportedly standing autonomous from "Christian social ethics."[150] In this manner they fail to take into consideration the role that our common human nature plays in moral theory and moral discourse. This failure undermines any attempts to enter the public square and engage in eth-

---

149. Even Tertullian, for whom "Athens" has little or nothing to do with "Jerusalem," affirms the natural law.

150. While it is true, as Dean Curry ("Reclaiming Natural Law," *First Things,* November 1997, 56-59) insists, that much of Protestants' reluctance to acknowledge the natural law undoubtedly derives from a virulent strain of anti-Catholic bigotry that has dogged Protestant fundamentalism for the last hundred years, perhaps we should not make too much of this as a factor in the Protestant aversion to the natural law, since in many corners common-cause cooperation can be found between conservative Protestants and Roman Catholics.

ical discourse with non-like-minded people when and where critical ethical and bioethical issues are at stake.[151] At best, we convince ourselves that in our "radical" commitment to the "ethics of Jesus," in our "radical" separation and denunciation of the "powers," in our "radical critique of Constantinianism," or in our apocalypticism, we most faithfully embody Christian discipleship and Christian responsibility in the world. At worst, we delude ourselves by being severed from the mainstream of historic Christian thought, even when we believe we are acting "prophetically." In practice, this posture prevents us — and those falling under our influence — from entering into responsible — and heartfelt — dialogue with unbelievers. There remains for those who are so predisposed no language of ethical "transmission" that is intelligible to the nonbeliever and to which the nonbeliever might respond. In the end, apart from the natural law, we appear to lose any basis upon which to build a moral apologetic and to preserve civil society.

A principal fallacy in the thinking of natural-law opponents is their aversion to — indeed, a seemingly fundamental misunderstanding of — law. For many Protestant theologians "law" can be explained only in terms of Christ and a concept of grace that is confined to a reading of the New Testament presupposing ethical *discontinuity* with the Old Testament.[152] But law is not merely a "Christian" question, though it is indeed that. It is rather a *human* question, as Wolfhart Pannenberg rightly argues.[153] Since law is part of creation, the very order of things as they are, it is a biblical,

---

151. I am not disputing the fact that many who reject the natural law exercise a considerable influence within the Christian community; clearly they do, and for this reason I have placed under examination in this chapter five Christian spokespersons who have exerted an inordinate influence on contemporary Christian thinking. Rather, what I wish to underscore is that, wittingly or unwittingly, opposition to the natural law hamstrings the Christian community in the public square. It does so by denying (1) a moral nature that is common to all people, (2) a common moral standard to which all people, religious or not, are held accountable, and (3) a language of moral engagement to which all people have access. In this way it removes the one instrument that facilitates the development of a robust public philosophy on the part of Christians.

152. It is a supreme irony that many opponents of natural-law thinking — indeed, of law as a concept — view the "Sermon on the Mount" as the crux New Testament text for Christian social ethics yet fail to grasp its context, established in Matt. 5:17-21, where ethical *continuity*, not discontinuity, is painstakingly clarified by Jesus.

153. Wolfhart Pannenberg, *Ethics*, trans. K. Crim (Philadelphia and London: Search Press, 1981), 24-41.

anthropological, and eminently theological question. Law is therefore neither a creative luxury, nor a form of second-tier theological speculation, nor the domain of "grace-denying" Catholics. Rather, it is of the order of necessity and consequently must remain at the heart of theological reflection.[154] Human beings cannot avoid or deny their true nature, which due to the *imago Dei* seeks order. Natural theology, then, properly understood, concerns creation and cosmic reality, not human autonomy. And cosmic reality entails *law*. The structure of law is such that it guides the commandments; it always has had this function in the divine economy and it always will. The new covenant does not abrogate this moral reality. Therefore, religion — indeed, *Christian religion* — and law go hand in hand. While love speaks to the proper motivation to obey, law provides the necessary God-given structure in which obedience is carried out. Paul and James speak with one voice in this regard: love fulfills the law.[155] And short of the eschaton, law will always and everywhere be necessary; for this reason, justice has an abiding character and universal contours.

In response to the mistaken and widespread belief that natural law is "autonomous" and that it serves to undermine grace and a distinctly "Christian" ethics, Aquinas answers that virtue — that is, the good — is rooted in the natural obligations of all human beings to God. There is no dualism in Aquinas's thinking between the natural law and "Christian social ethics." And the argument of Aquinas stands in agreement with the teaching of Jesus: the Ten Commandments, which express the contours of the natural law, are *summed up* in — not abrogated or eclipsed by — the "Christian social ethic." John Courtney Murray expresses it well, observing that the natural law, "which preserves humanity, still exists at the interior of the Gospel."[156] Thus, those Protestants who oppose or reject the natural law, for whatever reason, are burying the wrong corpse.

If we are to accept the moral imperatives of Barth, Niebuhr, Ellul, Yoder, Hauerwas, and others, any attempt at communication with the non-believer incurs serious — indeed, insurmountable — obstacles. But un-

---

154. While the present chapter is not the proper context in which to explore a theology of "law," Protestant understanding of law as a concept is generally limited to Saint Paul's use of "the law." This is problematic, however, since the apostle uses νόμος in assorted ways. For example, the law in Paul can mean works righteousness, Pharisaism, the Decalogue, the ceremonial aspects of the Mosaic code, as well as the Pentateuch as a whole.

155. Rom. 13:8-10 and James 2:8-11.

156. This is the theme of the final chapter in *We Hold These Truths;* see also 298.

avoidable questions arise. How can the Christian community make moral claims that are universally applicable?[157] It cannot. How can it participate in the public square if it disavows any sort of common moral discourse? It cannot. How can Protestants avoid the tendencies toward relativism, situationism, and subjectivism on the one hand, and apocalypticism on the other, if they reject universally binding moral "first things" that predate or transcend the teaching of Jesus and find their origin in creation? They cannot. But why not, at least from the standpoint of being faithful to the teaching of the New Testament, seek to build a case for natural law on the Pauline teaching of Romans 1 and 2, which affirms the "law written on the heart," and on Paul's use of nature and the created order in his address at Mars Hill (Acts 17)? There is no reason, theologically, why we cannot.

An abiding task for the Christian community is to understand natural law in relationship to public discourse. Because of the inherent tension in this relationship between faith and culture, we are naturally prone to multiple errors and thus need to be sensitized to their character. One error is the hope to find some sort of "neutral" common ground. While common ground — based on our shared life — indeed must be exploited in a pluralistic cultural setting, no aspect of the public square is neutral or naked, as we have often been reminded in recent years. Christians, like all others, will need to contend. *How* they do this allows for considerable disagreement and debate. However, *that* they should be involved does not remain in question.[158]

Theocratic visions that issue out of an imperialist Christian vision also need chastening. While not many Christians set out to "Christianize" the culture, such is nonetheless an ever-present temptation. Jean Elshtain rightly speaks of Christian citizens as "chastened patriots." That is, taking our cue from Augustine, we take seriously our earthly citizenship and do not abandon the public square. At the same time, we do this with a certain detachment, ever conscious that we have ultimate allegiances that are not of this world.[159]

---

157. If Christians are prevented from making truth claims that have universal application, why should anyone feel compelled to embrace Christian faith? All that is left is everyone sharing his or her "narrative."

158. Stephen Grabill is surely right to maintain that the privatization of religious belief and the impoverishment of public moral discourse together provide the occasion for renewed interest in the natural law (*Rediscovering the Natural Law*, 7).

159. See, e.g., Elshtain, *Women and War*, 268.

Yet another error is a retreat into pietism. Pietists, largely evangelical in character, tend to focus on worship, evangelism, and the devotional life, in the hopes either that social problems will rectify themselves or that as "faithful" Christians they will be raptured away from responsibility in the world. This vision, while suffering from a bloated eschatology, also fails to take the world — and Christian stewardship — seriously. The existentialist error, whether it is evangelical or more mainline Protestant in character, seems to be ever occurring in Protestant thought life. This tendency makes it supremely difficult for Protestants of all types to acknowledge or develop in a public philosophy universally applicable principles of morality.[160]

Natural-law thinking presupposes both the existence of universal moral norms and a basic awareness of these norms in all humans, Christian and non-Christian. The natural law is an imprint made on nature itself, inscribed by the moral Governor of the universe. Because it remains universal, eradicable, and immutable, the natural law "provides guidance for life in a real world of contingencies."[161] Natural-law thinking assumes that good and evil are discernible through reason, that the good is intelligible and attainable, and that human beings "participate in eternal law" despite the ramifications of sin. While the effects of sin have darkened the human heart, they have not obliterated its ability to recognize basic good and evil. For this reason, all people are morally "without excuse." Living virtuously and doing good are no more refuted by the effects of sin than falsehood is able to eclipse — and render unimportant — truth. And divine grace, while it perfects (i.e., completes) the moral life, no more eliminates the reality of the natural law than the theological virtues — faith, hope, and love — set aside the need for justice, wisdom, temperance, and courage.

Implied in the present argument is the conviction that ecumenical dialogue on the place of the natural law in Christian ethics is both necessary and timely, especially given the wholesale deconstruction of metaphysical foundations going on in our culture — a deconstruction that has moral, social, political, and legal implications.

---

160. Dennis Hollinger's very helpful discussion of negative ethical options for the Christian community identifies three distortions needing our vigilance: privatization of faith, the theocratic stance, and civil religion. See the chapter "Pluralism and Christian Ethics," in *Choosing the Good: Christian Ethics in a Complex World* (Grand Rapids: Baker, 2002), especially 242-52.

161. Cessario, *Introduction to Moral Theology*, 94.

CHAPTER FIVE

Moral Law, Christian Belief, and Social Ethics

The Nature of Law

One of the abiding weaknesses of Protestant theology is its inattention to the role of law and its place in a theology of creation. The subject of law is very much neglected in our day and age. But because the moral law has permanent validity and application to society, not only the natural law but also civil law in general calls us to rethink the nature of the surrounding moral order. For if law and morality are separated, as they have become in modern Protestant thought and in secular society as a whole, then we operate at a severe ethical disadvantage. I say "disadvantage" because law has a foremost *ethical* end. Without law, "laws" become arbitrary. And without law, there is no foundation for ethics, for demarcating human behavior.

But immediately I can hear objections. And understandably so. "Laws," writes one legal scholar, "cannot make men moral. Only men can do that; and they can do it only by freely choosing to do the morally right thing for the right reason. Laws can command outward conformity to moral rules, but cannot compel the internal acts of reason and will which make an act of external conformity to the requirements of morality a moral act."[1] The author of this statement is correct to argue that law has an *external* function. But this is half the truth. As an expression of a moral universe unveiled to human beings by the Creator, law as a moral concept has an ethical end, or telos. It is not merely "external," which is to say, in its

---

1. Robert P. George, *Making Men Moral: Civil Liberties and Public Morality* (London: Clarendon/Oxford University Press, 1994), 3.

negative function, that it is not *only* a safeguard or protection against the obliteration of antecedent human rights or against moral evil. Positively stated, law as divinely intended constitutes the very moral fabric of the universe in which we live, a mirror of the moral perfection of the Creator.[2] Recall the words of the psalmist:

Blessed is the man who fears the LORD,
    who finds great delight in his commands. (Ps. 112:1)

I delight in your decrees. (119:16)

Your statutes are my delight. (119:24)

I delight in your law. (119:70)

For your law is my delight. (119:77)

If your law had not been my delight,
    I would have perished in my affliction. (119:92)

Your law is my delight. (119:174)

Here once more we find refuge in Aquinas, for whom the task of reconciling faith and culture — indeed, a pluralism of cultures, given the ascendancy of Islam in his day — was primary. Law, he writes, "is a rule and measure of acts"; it is the means by which "man is induced to act or is restrained from acting."[3] Consider what is implied in Thomas's assertion. In its essence law is ethical in nature, serving as a "measure." Moreover, law can "induce" or "restrain," which is to say that, behaviorally, it has a positive and negative role. What is hereby inferred is that human beings are morally free agents, exercising their free will. But precisely how, or by what moral standard, do they exercise their freedom and make moral judgments? If there is no content to their decisions, then moral actions — indeed, *all* actions — are meaningless.

An important element in Aquinas's argument is that human beings

---

2. For this reason Aquinas can distinguish between eternal law, divine law, the natural law, and civil (human) law. That human law can subvert justice does not negate the moral framework of the universe, which mirrors divine attributes and divine intention.

3. Aquinas, *Summa Theologiae* (hereafter *ST*) I-II Q. 90.

rationally discern a moral "law." This argument, of course, is not unique to him, for Saint Paul presses this very point: there is a law "written on the heart" of every human being that witnesses to what is right and wrong. All people, therefore, are "without excuse" on the moral day of reckoning. The good and the right, of which law is a mirror (Rom. 7:12) and which are intuited through the natural law (Rom. 2:15), are that for which all people should strive, based on their creation in the image of God. Not only does this have profound implications for individual action, but it also gives meaning to family, the church, society, the state, indeed all of life. Law, then, discerned through reason and the "moral sense," is a moral guide directed toward the common good of all. It is not merely the repository of Moses or Israel of old; it is woven into all of creation, for all of time. Alas, what Christians discover is that the "inner witness of the Holy Spirit" turns out to be none other than the eternal moral law of God. Loving God, loving one's neighbor, desiring God, and obedience to the moral law — these turn out to be both old and new covenant priorities, to the surprise of some who had convinced themselves that "in Christ" there is an end to the law.[4]

While there is an element of truth in the legal scholar's contention that the law cannot "make men moral," Aquinas poses the countertruth: the aim of law is to make men — the law's subjects — good.[5] That is, law is no mere safeguard, though it is that. It is also the object, the goal, the telos, of men's longings, since it is divine in its origin. In this foundational way law educates, guides, corrects, and admonishes. Such, in the end, is the character of law, for it guides, when it also restrains, human moral aspirations.[6] Law, because it is derivative of divine nature, is a universal reality, timeless in its application, whether in relation to Israel, Rome, or the European Union. Whether human laws accurately reflect the divine law varies.

---

4. Of course, where the apostle Paul argues for an "end" to the law, he means an end to "works righteousness." But, as Heb. 11 makes abundantly clear, all saints, at all times, have always lived *by faith* in order to please God.

5. Aquinas, *ST* I-II Q. 92; cf. Rom. 7:12.

6. This is why the conclusion of Spitzer et al. — "Law . . . can never replace ethics. . . . Therefore, ethics, not the law, must be the basis of culture" (Robert J. Spitzer, Robin A. Bernhoft, and Camille E. De Blasi, *Healing the Culture: A Commonsense Philosophy of Happiness, Freedom, and the Life Issues* [San Francisco: Ignatius, 2000], 196) — though well intended, misses the mark; it is a half-truth. While it is accurate to say with Robert George (see n. 1) that humans must be *internally* motivated to do right, the matter does not reduce to *either* ethics *or* law; *both* are necessary to establish and maintain a society.

The degree to which they mirror the natural law grants them legitimacy. As such, the natural law, which as general revelation points to the existence of a Creator and Lawgiver, bears witness to the reality that all people are both aware of its moral obligations and accountable to its moral dictates. In the simplest of terms, it obligates all human creatures, through every action, to live in accordance with the foundational moral axiom "Do good and eschew evil."

Precisely in this light we come to recognize moral law at work in the hearts and minds of human beings. For this reason the *Catechism of the Catholic Church* states, "The moral law is the work of divine Wisdom."[7] As "God's pedagogy," the moral law "prescribes for man the ways, the rules of conduct that lead to the promised beatitude; it proscribes the ways of evil which turn him away from God and his love. It is at once firm in its precepts and, in its promises, worthy of love" (no. 1950). Hereby, man "participates in the wisdom and goodness of the Creator who gives him mastery over his acts and the ability to govern himself with a view to the true and the good. The natural law expresses the original moral sense which enables man to discern by reason the good and the evil, the truth and the lie" (no. 1954). The moral law "presupposes the rational order, established among creatures for their good and to serve their final end." And because all law "finds its first and ultimate truth in the eternal law," the moral law "finds its fullness and its unity in Christ." Hence, law is "declared and established by reason as a participation in the providence of the living God, Creator and Redeemer of all" (nos. 1951-53).

Aquinas reminds us that there are different expressions of the moral law, all of them interrelated. There is the eternal law — the source, in God, of all law — as well as the natural law, which "states the first and essential precepts which govern the moral life" and whose "principal precepts are expressed in the Decalogue." This law, it is important to note, is called "natural," not "in reference to the nature of irrational beings, but because reason which decrees it properly belongs to human nature" (no. 1955). Yet a third category of "revealed" law comprises Old Testament law as well as the "Law of the Gospel." And there are civil and ecclesiastical laws.[8]

---

7. The citations that follow are from the discussion of "The Moral Law" (part 3, chapter 3, article 1) in the *Catechism of the Catholic Church* (Washington, D.C.: U.S. Catholic Conference, 1994) (hereafter *CCC*). We will place the references in the text when possible.

8. Here the *Catechism* (no. 1952) is reiterating what Thomas teaches.

As to the role and place of the natural law, Aquinas asserts that it is "nothing other than the light of understanding placed in us by God; through it we know what we must do and what we must avoid. God has given this light or law at the creation."[9] Present in the heart of every person and established by reason, the natural law "is universal in its precepts and its authority extends to all men"; it is "immutable and permanent throughout the variations of history" (*CCC*, nos. 1956 and 1958). As such, the natural law provides both "the solid foundation on which man can build the structure of moral rules to guide his choices" and "the indispensable moral foundation for building the human community" (no. 1959). Finally, it establishes "the necessary basis for the civil law with which it is connected, whether by a reflection that draws conclusions from its principles, or by additions of a positive and juridical nature" (no. 1959).

Evidence of the abiding significance of law — hence, the emphasis in Aquinas on "the eternal law" — is omnipresent in human society. Where law is undermined, it is inevitable that human dignity and personhood are denied, human rights are violated in egregious ways, and tyranny waxes bold. Thus, the autonomous individual, i.e., the antinomian (literally, the lawless), as well as the autonomous state, with its usurpation of absolute authority, are diametrically — and, we may say, diabolically — opposed to Christian moral truth.

Both the neglect and the rejection of law are a product of a deeply secularizing tendency within our culture, the fruit of which is an amoral society. And yet the Christian community is partly to blame for this development. It is an unfortunate reality that Christian churches, particularly those of a strongly evangelical character that have placed an inordinately strong emphasis on grace, have contributed to the negation — when not the exclusion — of works and social ethics. The result has been an absence of the abiding dimensions of law, spawning not only insincere or superficial "conversions" to the Christian faith and shallow religious experience but also a truncated understanding of the gospel of the kingdom. This ought not to be.

Law, before it is anything, is a *theological* entity. It is a reflection of the moral universe into which we have been birthed. But it is more: law has been ordained as a means of grace for the "sanctification" not only of the "redeemed community" but also of the entire human race, a claim that

---

9. *Collationes de decem praeceptis* 1; *CCC*, no. 1956.

does *not* deny the sole sufficiency of Christ's atonement. One writer has framed it properly: "the bestowal of the power for a holy life needs to be accompanied by instruction in the pattern [thereof]. . . . What is it that pleases God? The doing of His will. Where is His will to be discerned? In His holy Law."[10] Furthermore, there would be "fewer moral tragedies among professing Christians," he writes, "if the salutary instruction of the Law of God were more consciously heeded."[11]

Wise pastoral advice. But on what basis? To insist upon the enduring function of law in the life of the believer is not to succumb to works righteousness or to become legalistic. Rather, legalism is "an abuse of the Law: it is a reliance on Law-keeping for acceptance with God."[12] The joyfully rendered obedience that arises from love toward the Creator is the very essence of the Christian life, and for someone to obey God because he loves to do so is not legalism; it is liberty, as the epistle of James makes clear. Consequently, "law" does not terminate in our delighting in it (cf. Pss. 1:2; 119:16, 24, 47, 70, 77, 92, 174); it has simply been "internalized" through an attitude of trust toward the Lawgiver. Here we must expose the all-too-frequent tendency among religious people to divorce love and truth. There is nothing incompatible between love and obedience.[13]

In those human domains wherein law is denied, darkness and disorder become the "law." It stands to reason, then, that where the origin of law is obscured or denied, either by secularists or religionists, the social order is undermined, and with it any hope of securing peace and stability — the *tranquillitas ordinis* — for which Augustine and saints innumerable past and present prayed.[14]

As John Paul has emphasized in *Evangelium Vitae*, once a society removes all reference to God, the manner in which "law" is understood is radically transmuted: "The eclipse of the sense of God and of man inevitably leads to a practical materialism, which breeds individualism, utilitari-

10. Ernest Kevan, *Moral Law* (Escondido, Calif.: Den Dulk Christian Foundation; Phillipsburg, N.J.: Presbyterian and Reformed, 1991), 1.

11. Kevan, *Moral Law*, 2.

12. Kevan, *Moral Law*, 2.

13. Kevan (*Moral Law*, 3) properly notes: "The obligation of obedience is perpetual and belongs to man's creaturely relation to God, and it is one of the richest fruits of grace." Unhappily, the reason that many Christians would react negatively to this statement is theological.

14. Cf. also 1 Tim. 2:1-5.

anism and hedonism."[15] All of life as a result becomes distorted. "Nature," for example, is no longer understood in relation to human essence, but rather is now reduced to mere "matter." Human laws, rather than being grounded in the unchanging norms of moral wisdom, become subject to every kind of human manipulation. Such a shift in thinking inevitably breeds seismic distortions in the realm of scientific, technological, and biomedical thinking.

Christians, as it turns out, more than any social grouping, have a vested interest in law, given its preserving and restraining character. But we must reiterate what law is *not*. It is not reason or pure intellect, as the ancients had thought. Nor is it pure will, as tyrants old and young have demanded, in order to impose their will. Rather, law is moral truth, which in its application requires both right reason and moral agency, tempered by the fact of its recognition of — and submission to — a higher authority.

Morality and Law

It scarcely needs pointing out that ours is a day in which the relationship between morality and law is hotly contested. We have grown accustomed to the denial of law's objectivity and society's insistence on a strict separation between moral and legal realms. This development, however, did not occur overnight. As not a few legal scholars are prone to do, one might readily point to Oliver Wendell Holmes's argument already a century removed as having laid the foundation for an "enlightened skepticism" that imbibes contemporary legal thought.[16] Can law represent moral objectivity? Are there objective moral standards by which to interpret law? Is law discovered or is it created? Our questioning is not concerned with how cultural values that are negotiable — social, ethnic, or cultural diversity, for example — might be determined. In this realm is plenty of elasticity and room for disagreement. The greater question is whether law might serve as a mirror of the eternal, whether justice is conceived as fluid or nonfluid, and whether in the marketplace we might contend, over against the regnant moral nihilism of our day, for the "permanent things."

15. *Evangelium Vitae* (hereafter *EV*), no. 23.
16. Oliver Wendell Holmes, "The Path of the Law," *Harvard Law Review* 10 (1897): 458-69.

If I am correct in my conviction that the greatest challenge to life — from the embryonic stage to genetic enhancement to euthanasia — lies ahead of us, then Christians of all varieties will need not only to rethink their own position regarding a comprehensive cultural strategy of "life" but also to contend for that conviction — comprehensively — in terms of broader social and public policy. *Someone's* basic assumptions about "life," *someone's morality,* after all, will be imposed on the culture through the social, legal, and political apparatus.[17] But I get ahead of myself.

Morality and law have not always been separated, as they are in our culture. In fact, until relatively recently it was universally assumed that morality informs — which is to say, supersedes and thus transcends — human law. Otherwise, justice would remain fluid and never have any fixed referents, and moral atrocity could not be condemned as universally wrong. Morality in any society is predicated on what that society values as good and acceptable, and every society possesses a hierarchy of "goods" by which to demarcate "acceptable" and "unacceptable."[18]

It stands to reason, then, that human morality consists in preserving those goods. In the democratic tradition, those goods have included commodities such as "inalienable rights" and free speech, based on the memory of diverse forms of political oppression that denied those very entities, and responsible citizenship, without which the very moral-social order is undermined. The upholding of "civil" society requires a proper understanding of the roles of "intermediate" social institutions such as the family, churches, and civic groups, as well as of the state, which performs its

17. An instructive tale is told by Robert P. George, who chronicles dissent and faithfulness among Roman Catholics in the United States over the last three decades as it applies to "pro-life" issues. See his "Bioethics and Public Policy," in George, *The Clash of Orthodoxies: Law, Religion, and Morality in Crisis* (Wilmington, Del.: ISI Books, 2001), 273-302.

18. The argument of John Rawls — see, e.g., his *Political Liberalism* (New York: Columbia University, 1993) — and those who follow a similar line of thinking, namely, that "acceptable" and "unacceptable" behavior is predicated on what is "reasonable," itself is amoral and insufficient to the preservation of the common good. What is deemed "reasonable" in terms of social consensus, per Rawls, can be manipulated, since it is not grounded in what is *permanent.* Similar approaches to the public square are advanced by H. L. A. Hart, *The Concept of Law* (Oxford: Clarendon, 1961), and Kent Greenawalt, *Religious Convictions and Political Choice* (New York: Oxford University Press, 1988). How this line of thinking translates into basic "life" issues is perhaps most graphically on display in Ronald Dworkin, *Life's Dominion: An Argument about Abortion, Euthanasia, and Individual Freedom* (New York: Knopf, 1993).

tasks by means of derivative authority. Realms such as politics, law, economics and commerce, science, and the arts also play a role in "mediating" culture as a whole.

Historically, moral philosophy or ethics has acknowledged three principal spheres of obligation — to the Creator, to oneself, and to one's neighbor. The social character of this division, while representative of Christian social ethics, is by no means limited to it. Even nontheistic ethics, from antiquity, has stressed the relational character of moral obligation. Such forms the basis of Plato's *Republic* and Aristotle's *Nichomachean Ethics*, for whom justice is predicated on horizontal — i.e., relational — duties. It is only in the sense of obligations to others that we may understand the role of "law." When morality and law are severed, which is a relatively recent development, the result is epistemological uncertainty or denial; the very essence of all things becomes unknowable.

Does "law," however, originate in human ingenuity? Does it subsist in "legality"? Expressed otherwise, do human beings create morality or is it discovered? Correlatively, is the state apparatus sovereign in its construction — and requirement — of responsibilities?[19] Or is human government, regardless of its form, derivative in nature? For those who have lived only in democratic societies, such questions may seem trivial. But for those who are intimately acquainted with political tyranny, these questions are momentous. If not only moral philosophy but also legal philosophy is to have a nonfluid foundation, both must be grounded in metaphysical realities. All human creatures, as Aquinas reminds the obstinate postmodern, are subject to divine governance through the "eternal law."[20] That is to say, the teleological structuring of all of creation is impressed upon our human nature to pursue the good and avoid evil. Human beings are thusly wired.

It is reasonable to argue that most people (and most societies) hold to the belief, however vague, that morality — pursuing the good or accept-

---

19. Dictators, wrote German legal theorist Heinrich Rommen, "are masters of legality" (*The State in Catholic Thought: A Treatise in Political Philosophy* [St. Louis: Herder, 1945], 212, cited also in the introduction, written by Russell Hittinger, to Heinrich Rommen, *The Natural Law: A Study in Legal and Social History and Philosophy*, trans. T. R. Hanley [Indianapolis: Liberty Fund, 1998], xi). While this is true, one might reasonably argue that modern democracy itself has the same dubious distinction, to the extent that it does not aim at a revolution in the narrowest sense, but that "legal institutions themselves can be made the object of the non-legal power struggle" (*State in Catholic Thought*, 718).

20. Aquinas, *ST* I-II Q. 91.

able and avoiding evil or the unacceptable — is a higher norm than what we, in the Western cultural context, call "positive law." Thereby society shows a basic concern for the health of the wider community.[21] The presumption among this nation's founders and framers of the "Laws of Nature" and of "Nature's God," regardless of how quaint it may strike contemporary culture, simply mirrors a broader consensus that has withstood the test of time. John Paul II, in *Veritatis Splendor*, speaks of this consensus as "participated theonomy," by which he refers to the natural law with its metaphysical realities, not a theocracy in the narrower sense.[22] Moreover, this consensus, and *only this consensus*, furnished the basis with which to oppose slavery and address egregious human rights violations, and to argue for human rights that are "inalienable." For this reason we are justified in calling the natural law a "first principle." Because of the reality of this "first principle," individuals and societies are inclined to establish a hierarchy of goods and values. Thus, public morality will be a reflection, for better or worse, of this assumed moral hierarchy.[23] Public policy, therefore, will be designed to accord with and mirror these priorities — whether that legislation affects business, commerce, employment, science and technology, family, the arts, or education.

By way of illustration, it would be morally askew if a society were to establish free artistic expression or economic equality as its highest principle. Not that art and economics are insignificant in the life of a culture. Rather, they simply find their place in a society's moral hierarchy, and they derive their meaning not from themselves as ends but from the "first things" that order all of society. Hence, for artistic courage to be a "cardinal virtue" would be to foster anarchy, since art is always and everywhere an expression of one's worldview, i.e., one's ultimate commitments in life. In the same way, to force an equal distribution of economic goods throughout society would be to undermine individual incentive and

21. Aquinas, *ST* I-II Q. 91.

22. John Paul's understanding of a "participated theonomy" finds parallels in the "sphere sovereignty" of Dutch Reformed political thought, notably that of Abraham Kuyper; see his *Lectures on Calvinism* (1931; reprint, Grand Rapids: Eerdmans, 1998).

23. Well has Steven A. Long asserted, "If Kant, Nietzsche, and Foucault share nothing else, they share this common negation of metaphysical objectivity and of the doctrine that human nature is knowably ordered to ends which have the nature of the good, leading to the *finis ultimis*, the final end and supreme good" ("Reproductive Technologies and the Natural Law," *National Catholic Bioethics Quarterly*, Summer 2002, 226).

achievement, thereby creating greater injustice and inequity than had previously existed.

It is out of this preunderstanding of "first things" that our basic notions of fairness, "rights," and justice must proceed. These entities, while "enforced" by the state, nevertheless are derived and not self-evident without a prior commitment to what is permanent (the "first things"). That is, justice and rights are not predicated on the *individual;* they do not originate in private will, preference, or imagination, which are subject in nature. Rather, they have an objective cast, the fruit of collective experience that is tempered by intergenerational wisdom. In this manner they are agreed upon, after being "discovered," as it were, and thus reflect the emergence of a social "consensus" that is the product of right reason. The element of "consensus," while needing strong qualification and passing the test of time, can scarcely be overstated, since an individual's attempts to overturn the consensus have been traditionally viewed as subversive, even tyrannical.

For this reason, law, which is a mirror of moral "first things," is not merely "legality." It serves as a conduit through which justice is executed. Justice, writes Aquinas, "directs man in his relations with other men."[24] This occurs at two levels — in a person's relations with other individuals and in the person's relations with society as a whole. Both give expression to the maxim "To each his due." That to each person something is "due" means that every person incurs a *debt,* a conspicuously *public* debt. But what precisely is "due" each person? What is indeed "owed" to all? That which is owed we call a "right"; rights are owed to every citizen. The character of a right, however, if it is "inalienable," is that it *cannot be removed* — by the state or by other individuals, by decree or by personal whim. The state merely recognizes what is "owed"; it does not create it. Rights do not correspond to an individual's inner, subjective state or feelings; they do not express an individual's private wants and desires. The private realm cannot be adjudicated in the public square or by the state. By nature, the personal realm is open to differing interpretations and differing responses, even sharp public debate, but as such it possesses no intrinsic authority with which to make demands on the public square.[25]

24. Aquinas, *ST* II-II Q. 58.

25. This is not to argue that personal wants and needs are unimportant, only that they remain *personal* and not society's legal concerns.

To illustrate this point, we might consider the much misunderstood statements by Jesus recorded in Matthew 5:39-42: "But I tell you, don't resist an evildoer. On the contrary . . . turn the other cheek as well. As for the one who wants . . . to take away your shirt, let him have your coat as well. And if anyone forces you to go one mile, go with him two. Give to the one who asks you, and don't turn away from the one who wants to borrow from you." While religious pacifists typically cite these statements to support an ideological position that *requires* nonretaliation and nonviolence in the *absolute* sense, this interpretation does injustice to the text itself. Not only does it place itself in conflict with other biblical texts, it also fails to make the critical distinction between public and private accounts of justice.

Let us consider Jesus' words. The slap with the back of the hand constitutes an *insult*, not an *assault*. Very likely the reason for this "slap" of the hand is personal enmity (cf., similarly, Rom. 12:17-21). Moreover, *all* of Scripture calls the faithful person to *resist evil;* therefore, Jesus cannot be requiring, in the absolute sense, nonviolence and nonretaliation, for if he were, criminal justice would be impossible, and governing authorities would be unable to carry out their divinely instituted function in preserving the social order (cf. Rom. 13:1-10; 1 Tim. 2:1-5; 1 Pet. 2:15-17). Furthermore, giving other people particular articles of clothing is not a *public or legal* (in the classical sense of "legal") matter; nor is loaning to those in need. Rather, all these situations point to *personal* matters of "justice" — more accurately, what we call insult, mistreatment, even persecution — that are not to be adjudicated by the state but rather should be met at the personal level with Christian charity and forbearance. Such is the thrust of Jesus' teaching as indicated by the context.[26]

The point is this: the needs expressed in the four examples of Matthew 5:39-42 are not to be understood as "rights," even though they all are legitimate realms of personal experience. Not all human activity, not all personal experience, falls under the category of "law." Only what is morally *required* is prescribed by law. As it applies to the circumstances being mirrored in Matthew 5, not *all* disciples of Jesus will be *morally obligated* to

---

26. I have developed more fully the context and implications of Jesus' imperatives in Matt. 5:38-42 to "turn the other cheek" and "not resist evil" in "Do Not Suppose That I Have Come . . . : The Ethic of the 'Sermon on the Mount' Reconsidered," *Southwestern Journal of Theology* 46, no. 3 (2004): 47-70.

carry a soldier's bag or equipment a second mile; the point of Jesus' admonition is that such an accommodating and charitable response has the effect of opening up relationships, thereby creating a climate in which Christian claims have greater moral authority. Likewise, not *all* disciples will always and everywhere be morally obligated to give away "the shirt off their back." This *may* on occasion be necessary, and it doubtless will engender a response that is remarkable; nevertheless, it is *not* a moral absolute that hence is to be safeguarded by the governing authorities. The same would apply to lending to those in need.

Ethics, therefore, concerns itself with what is morally requisite. That is why, in the realm of law, there is no place either for what is "private" or for what is arbitrary. When laws are arbitrary, or when they are interpreted arbitrarily, the public is inclined to lose confidence in those who establish the laws, and the populace reacts in ways that are immoral and socially unhealthy. For this reason Qoheleth can write, "When the sentence for a criminal is not carried out quickly, the hearts of a people are filled with schemes to do wrong" (Eccles. 8:11). There is much wisdom in this observation. At the very least, it suggests that evenness, consistency, and promptness are essential in criminal justice. And when these elements are absent, the effect is culturally corrosive.[27]

Every generation, writes legal scholar Russell Hittinger, finds a new reason for the study of the natural law.[28] For a generation past, in the mid-twentieth century, totalitarianism provided the occasion. Hittinger cites German legal scholar and émigré to the United States Heinrich Rommen to make his point: "When one of the relativist theories is made the basis for a totalitarian state, man is stirred to free himself from the pessimistic resignation that characterizes these relativist theories and to return to his principles."[29] Hittinger sees parallels between today's mood and the "pessimistic resignation" of Rommen's day, with its "tired agnosticism" regarding the moral bases and ends of law that had left the German legal profession intellectually defenseless in the face of changes in German society in the 1930s. Like Rommen, Hittinger calls us to rediscover the "moral predicates" of law and politics, without which democratic institutions cannot

27. In my view, the implications of these three elements — evenness, consistency, and promptness — for the entire criminal justice system cannot be overstated. Indeed, they constitute the heart and soul of "criminal justice."

28. From the introduction of Rommen, *The Natural Law*, xii.

29. Rommen, *State in Catholic Thought*, 48, cited in Rommen, *The Natural Law*, xii.

long survive. When these "moral predicates," or "first things," are challenged, obscured, or denied, it becomes once again necessary to assert not only their reality but also their place in the culture.[30]

Human Behavior and Moral Accountability[31]

Biology as Destiny

In the last two decades a naturalistic account of morality has been offered by a number of intellectual heavyweights. One thinks, for example, of the work done by evolutionary social biologist E. O. Wilson[32] and philosopher Michael Ruse.[33] And no less than the fabled naturalist himself, Richard Dawkins, has weighed in on matters moral in his celebrated work *The Selfish Gene.*[34]

---

30. Hittinger's recent book, *The First Grace: Rediscovering the Natural Law in a Post-Christian World* (Wilmington, Del.: ISI Books, 2003), is lucidly written and argues for the place of the natural law in the culture.

31. Elsewhere I have explored in a similar manner the relationship between biology as destiny, free will, and the newer general consensus concerning crime. Some of this material originally appeared in J. Daryl Charles, "Blame It on the Beta-Boosters: Genetics, Self-Determination and Moral Accountability," in *Genetic Engineering: A Christian Response,* ed. Timothy J. Demy and Gary P. Stewart (Grand Rapids: Kregel, 1999), 241-60, and is used with permission.

32. See, for example, *Sociobiology: The New Synthesis* (Cambridge: Harvard University Press, [1975] 2000); *Consilience: The Unity of Knowledge* (New York: Knopf, 1998); *On Human Nature* (Cambridge: Harvard University Press, 1978); and *The Diversity of Life* (Cambridge: Harvard University Press, 1976).

33. See, for example, *Darwin and Design: Does Evolution Have a Purpose?* (Cambridge: Harvard University Press, 2003); *The Darwinian Revolution* (Chicago: University of Chicago Press, 1999); *Can a Darwinian Be a Christian? The Relationship between Science and Religion* (Cambridge: Harvard University Press, 2001); and *The Evolution Wars* (Santa Barbara: ABC Clio, 2000).

34. Originally published in 1976 and reissued in 1989, *The Selfish Gene* once again thrusts itself in our faces through the "30th anniversary edition" that Oxford University Press published in 2006. Dawkins is not inattentive to the fact that readers will quite naturally question the book's title. Why the choice of "selfish"? Most of the book's introduction (vii-xiv) is devoted to an explanation. Dawkins's reasoning is this: given their "self-interested" nature insofar as they survive predation, genes affect the behavior of their bearers, and thus we may attribute to them a measure of personification. Dawkins's paean to the gene ends with a notable crescendo: the gene is said to be "an immortal replicator" (266).

It is worth noting that at the very time Dawkins's "30th anniversary edition" of *The*

And this is but the tip of the iceberg.[35] At the same time that Darwinian assumptions, so we were told, were on the defensive, spirited defenders of evolution as a worldview and explanation of ultimate things have stepped forth to reassert Darwin's place in the cosmos.

Evolutionary accounts of ethics proceed on the belief that morality originates with biology. So, for example, Michael Ruse can confidently declare, "The question is not whether biology — specifically, our evolution — is connected with ethics, but how."[36] Sociobiologist E. O. Wilson is equally assertive that "causal explanations of the brain activity and evolution . . . already cover most facts known about behavior we term 'moral.'"[37] If this is not enough certitude with which to convince us, Ruse and Wilson combine in an essay published in the journal *Philosophy* to contend that "the time has come to turn moral philosophy into an applied science because . . . one hundred years without Darwin are enough."[38] Intimidating stuff.

For evolutionists such as Ruse and Wilson, morality is "universal" only to the extent that it has a biological, genetic basis and mirrors our in-

---

Selfish Gene was appearing, one of his colleagues was publishing a very different sort of book, written in a very different sort of tone. Trained as a molecular biophysicist before devoting himself to the study of theology, Alister McGrath came to very different conclusions than Dawkins about the nature of genes, human nature, and the existence of God. With coauthor Joanna C. McGrath, McGrath responds, in *The Dawkins Delusion* (London: SPCK, 2007), to Dawkins's high-profile, ill-tempered dismissal of religious faith in *The God Delusion* (New York: Bantam Books, 2006), which for him is both saddening and troubling (vii-xiii).

35. See Frans de Waal, *Primates and Philosophers: How Morality Evolved* (Princeton: Princeton University Press, 2006); de Waal, *Good Natured: The Origins of Right and Wrong in Humans and Other Animals* (Cambridge: Harvard University Press, 1996); Marc D. Hauser, *Moral Minds: How Nature Designed Our Universal Sense of Right and Wrong* (New York: Ecco, 2006); Richard Joyce, *The Evolution of Morality* (Cambridge: MIT Press, 2006); and Joyce, *The Myth of Morality* (Cambridge, U.K., and New York; Cambridge University Press, 2001). Other representative works of note include Holmes Rolston III, *Genes, Genesis, and God: Values and Their Origins in Natural and Human History* (Cambridge: Cambridge University Press, 1999); Rolston, *Biology, Ethics, and the Origins of Life* (Boston: Jones and Bartlett, 1995); Jane Maienschen and Michael Ruse, eds., *Biology and the Foundation of Ethics* (Cambridge: Cambridge University Press, 1999); and Matthew H. Nitecki and Doris V. Nitecki, *Evolutionary Ethics* (Albany: State University of New York Press, 1993).

36. Michael Ruse, "Evolutionary Ethics: A Defense," in Rolston, *Biology, Ethics, and the Origins of Life*, 93.

37. Edward O. Wilson, *Consilience*, 278.

38. Michael Ruse and Edward O. Wilson, "Moral Philosophy as an Applied Science," *Philosophy*, April 1986, 173-92.

terface with the environment. That is to say, the moral "sense" within the human species is an evolutionary adaptation that is part of the natural selection process. Human morality, on the evolutionist's account, is merely an adaptation to further our reproductive ends. It is a human convention that is in place for survival, to which we are genetically predisposed.[39]

While the likes of Wilson, Ruse, and Dawkins may be daunting to the rest of us who are still working out our natural selection, a rather conspicuous fault line emerges in their work. A primary philosophical vulnerability among secular naturalists, of which they are certainly representative, is their disavowal or abrogation of free will, whether this has been witting or not on their part. This weakness, both at the theoretical and practical level, will need some probing, especially given its implications for ethics, moral agency, self-responsibility, and civil society.

In the ongoing debate over nature versus nurture, nature currently has the upper hand. Biology is destiny — at least the scientific pendulum has been swinging in that direction. The received wisdom of the behavioral sciences regarding the relationship between genetics and environment in explaining human behavior has changed dramatically in the last two decades.[40] In 1992, significantly, the American Psychological Association identified genetics as one of several themes best representing the present and future of psychology.[41]

Given recent advances in genetic research, the gene is becoming — if it has not already become — a cultural icon. This development can be measured by the gene's iconic status not only in scientific and medical journals but also in popular culture and political discourse. In outlining the contours of this cultural phenomenon, one writer observes that "[t]he whole culture is metaphorically awash in genes, which are depicted as pervasive and powerful agents central to understanding both everyday behavior and the secret of life. Foraging through countless specialty periodicals and mass-culture sources, [one uncovers] references to selfish genes,

---

39. For a thoughtful evaluation of the evolutionary account of ethics, see Miguel Endara, "Deficiencies in the 'Selfish Genes' View of Ethics: A Critique of the Evolutionary Account," *National Catholic Bioethics Quarterly,* Autumn 2003, 517-30.

40. Thus, for example, Dorothy Nelkin and Mary S. Lindee, *The DNA Mystique: The Gene as a Cultural Icon* (New York: Freeman, 1995), and Evelyn Fox Keller, *Refiguring Life: Metaphors of Twentieth Century Biology* (New York: Columbia University Press, 1995).

41. See Robert Plomin et al., eds., *Nature, Nurture, and Psychology* (Washington, D.C.: American Psychological Association, 1993).

pleasure-seeking genes, violence genes, gay genes, couch-potato genes, celebrity genes, depression genes. Everything but the kitchen-sink gene."[42]

Increasingly, diverse social commentators maintain that we stand on the threshold of the "biological century." Indeed, it is difficult to argue with this claim. While physics dominated the century just past, advances in other laboratories suggest a noteworthy shift. Writes Gregory Benford, a professor of physics at the University of California, Irvine: "Just as the 1890s hummed with physical gadgetry, our decade [and beyond] bristles with striking biological inventions. Conceptual shifts will surely follow. Beyond 2000, the principal social, moral, and economic issues will probably spring from biology's metaphors and approach, and from its cornucopia of technology. Bio-thinking will inform our world and shape our vision of ourselves."[43] Seven years into the "biological century," Benford's prophecy certainly appears true.

And what shall we make of these vaunted biotechnological advances? What place shall these advances be accorded? And from an ethical standpoint, what do they portend?

With exhilarating speed, ongoing progress in the biomedical and biotechnological fields confronts contemporary society with inherently perplexing ethical dilemmas — dilemmas that will need to be addressed against a prevailing backdrop of scientific materialism and moral skepticism. In the view of the authors of *The DNA Mystique,* the gene has become an explanation for human behavior that is too readily appropriated, too seldom criticized, and too frequently misused in the service of socially destructive ends.[44] In the end, the gene is not merely a cultural metaphor; it holds sway over scientific assumptions and theory, both of which trickle down to drive common culture.

The relationship between biology and free will, fully apart from recent advances in science, has long occupied scientists and philosophers. Are human beings capable of moral reason and free choice and thus responsible for their actions? Is there a dimension of human existence that transcends the gene and biology, thereby allowing humans to define themselves morally and spiritually? Is human behavior determined by one's genetic makeup?

42. Jeffrey Reid, "The DNA-ing of America," *Utne Reader,* September-October 1995, 26.
43. Gregory Benford, "Biology 2001: Understanding Culture, Technology, and Politics in 'The Biological Century,'" *Reason,* November 1995, 23.
44. This is the general concern of Nelkin and Lindee, *The DNA Mystique.*

In light of the more recent progress in genetics, notably the mapping of the human genome, the stakes are raised significantly about whether humans are fully "accountable" for their behavior. While identifying the genetic basis for an ever-growing number of diseases has been a particular focus of medical genetic research, of equal interest among scientists has been the attempt to explain the interplay between genes and behavior. Are human beings truly capable of self-determination, whatever their gene-based psychological and physiological predispositions? Or are humans mere robots programmed by their genes and thus not to be held morally responsible for their actions? Writing in *Ethics and Medics*, Renée Mirkes summarizes the critical issues that stand before us with the new genetic twist to the question of moral self-responsibility: "According to chemical reductionism central to biological determinism, the causal laws of the tightly structured nexus of human biology — a nexus that is becoming ever more refined through the advances of human genetics — dictate human behavior. It is illogical within this view of human behavior to require personal responsibility for the moral quality of one's actions; moral accountability makes sense only if actions . . . [proceed] from a free agent."[45] The biological metaphor, then, which is no mere metaphor, would appear to have the potential of allowing us to reconceive the entire realm of human behavior. What indeed does biology tell us regarding human activity? And, perhaps more importantly, what does it *not* tell us?

For much of the previous century, human behavior was explained by its relationship to humans' environment. And broadly speaking, social science — from social psychology to cultural anthropology to criminology — remains in thrall to the notion that one's identity and behavior are the products of one's environment.[46] Yet, curiously parallel to the "nurture" model has been the accumulation of biogenetic evidence suggesting that human behavior is less socially constructed or manipulated than behavioral theorists have heretofore believed. Molecular biologists, through their mapping, classification, and analysis of the human genome, posit an entirely different model for understanding human actions.[47]

45. Renée Mirkes, "Programmed by Our Genes?" *Ethics and Medics* 16, no. 6 (1991): 1.

46. For a critique of this see Francis Fukuyama, "Is It All in the Genes?" *Commentary,* September 1997, 30-35.

47. Roger Masters, director of an annual seminar at Dartmouth College on biological perspectives in the social sciences, has pointed out that most university departments of social science have relatively few members who stay abreast of research in the life sciences. That gap

Like medical research in general, medical genetics operates on the principles employed in the natural sciences. Modern science will seek to objectify and quantify what is observed, establish causal relationships among those phenomena, and formulate corresponding models. This methodology of abstraction can be observed to guide the investigation of the structure of human hereditary information.[48] Science and technology, like all other disciplines, proceed on the basis of certain assumptions about life, material and nonmaterial reality, and human nature. As such, then, scientists and researchers are not "neutral" in terms of the interpretation of their work. At a presuppositional level, what guiding philosophical assumptions are implicit in their findings? What understanding of the cosmos — material and nonmaterial — is being presupposed? Correlatively, what are the implications of these assumptions for ethics and human behavior? Messrs. Dawkins and Wilson and Ruse, as we saw, certainly have not been "neutral" in this regard.

According to the central dogma of molecular genetics, hereditary information is stored in the DNA, transcribed into RNA, and then translated into specific proteins that specify human traits and characteristics.[49] The

---

prompted the Gruter Institute for Law and Behavioral Research and Dartmouth's Nelson Rockefeller Center for the Social Sciences to begin cosponsoring annual seminars for the purpose of bringing together the two disciplines. Writing on the emerging conversations that began to surface in the mid-1990s between social scientists and evolutionary biologists is Kim A. McDonald, "Biology and Behavior," *Chronicle of Higher Education,* September 1994, A19-21. These conversations continue and are more spirited than ever. One need only peruse sources as diverse as the *Chronicle of Higher Education,* the *American Journal of Bioethics,* as well as numerous scientific and philosophical periodicals and quarterlies to observe the extent to which these debates proceed unabated.

48. See Udo Eibach, *Gentechnik — Der Begriff nach dem Leben* (Wuppertal: Brockhaus, 1986). For a succinct critique not only of the methodology but also of the philosophical presuppositions operating in the biotechnological field, see Henk Jochemsen, "Medical Genetics: Its Presuppositions, Possibilities and Problems," *Ethics and Medics* 8, no. 2 (1992): 18-31; and more recently, Edmund D. Pellegrino, "Biotechnology, Human Enhancement, and the Ends of Medicine," accessible at www.cbhd.org/resources/biotech, posted November 30, 2004, and Nancy L. Jones and John F. Kilner, "Genetics, Biotechnology and the Future," accessible at www.cbhd.org/resources/biotech.

49. Hereon see, for example, Victor A. McKusick, "Mapping and Sequencing the Human Genome," *New England Journal of Medicine* 320 (1989): 910-15; David Suzuki and Peter Knudtson, "Maps and Dreams: Deciphering the Human Genome," in Suzuki and Knudtson, *Genethics: The Clash between the New Genetics and Human Values* (Cambridge: Harvard University Press, 1989), 316-40; and, from a more philosophical perspective, David

flow of genetic information is understood to occur in one direction — from DNA via RNA and proteins to individual traits. *The gene is thus defined as the determining unit of heredity.* This governing model suggests at the very least a deterministic account of human identity and behavior.[50] One scientist expresses what for many behavioral theorists is axiomatic, namely, that "the assumption that most human behavior is adaptive in neo-Darwinian terms of inclusive fitness . . . has yet to be falsified."[51]

But the character of presuppositions that undergird and guide genetic research invites scrutiny. Those who are critical of an evolutionary explanation for human behavior might point out at least two problems in the "new biology." One is the shaky philosophical ground — reductionism and determinism — on which some science proceeds and by which its findings are being interpreted. The second is more practical, though equally problematic, namely, the fact that *the general public is eager for simplistic explanations that absolve people of personal responsibility* for their actions. What is roundly needed is a robust and nuanced critique of reigning assumptions of scientific models, particularly where both methodology and interpretation tend to make impersonal or depersonalize the individual human for the purposes of investigation.[52]

If, for example, the discovery of genes or gene groups correlates not merely with acknowledged disease conditions[53] but also with normal per-

Heyd, *Genethics: Moral Issues in the Creation of People* (Berkeley: University of California Press, 1992). These are useful resources even when significant advances have occurred since their publication.

50. This forms the basis of author G. J. V. Nossal's statements in the introduction to the volume *Human Genetic Information: Science, Law, and Ethics,* Ciba Foundation Symposium (Chichester, U.K.: Wiley, 1990). States Nossal: "DNA is iconic for the new biology, a biology that seeks to explain phenomena not . . . at the level of the whole organism . . . but at the level of the cell, of the individual protein molecule *with its near-magical powers* as a molecular machine" (2, emphasis added).

51. Mildred Dickeman, "Human Sociobiology: The First Decade," *New Scientist* 147 (1985): 42.

52. An evenhanded and thorough critique, although it needs updating, is L. Foss, "The Challenge to Biomedicine: A Foundation Perspective," *Journal of Medicine and Philosophy* 14 (1989): 165-91. See also Jochemsen, "Medical Genetics," 18-31.

53. Mark J. Daly and David Altshuler, research scientists at the Broad Institute of Harvard and MIT, concede that the genetic "culprits" contributing to many debilitating diseases remain at large and unidentified, despite dedicated "sleuthing" by research laboratories. In their assessment, "only a tiny fraction of the genetic culprits in common disease have been identified" ("Partners in Crime," *Nature Genetics* 37 [2005]: 337).

sonality traits such as shyness, impulsiveness, and aggressiveness, it is not difficult to extrapolate how overzealous or impatient behavioral theorists — and criminologists — might utilize these "findings."[54] Consider for a moment what the effects of one exemplary "finding" — the identification of the genetic roots of *an inability to defer gratification* — on parents or politicians or criminologists or social workers might be. Erik Parens cautions against the mistaken theoretical moves common to both genetic researchers and those behavioral theorists who interpret the data:

> When speaking about the contribution that genetics can make toward understanding . . . complex behaviors, it is enormously important to remember that genes are but one component of fabulously complex biological, and ultimately biopsychosocial, systems. Even if there are strong correlations between single-gene defects and certain dispositions to some complex behaviors, such correlations will never provide anything approximating a full account of those behaviors. . . . And as genetics always will be only one important part of biology, biology always will be only one important part of any richer human behavior.[55]

Inasmuch as the starting point for much current science tends toward reductionistic and deterministic models, these methods show themselves to be utilitarian and instrumental in nature. Questions such as the origin and meaning of life or moral obligations to others, which are eminently philosophical and theological issues, are transmuted into questions of functionality and material cause, and often as well, economics.

A further danger lies in the potential wedding of biomedical technology and political power. French political and moral philosopher Michel Schooyans warns against the markedly undemocratic character of the considerable achievements of reproductive technology and biomedical sci-

---

54. A prime example in the realm of criminal justice is the volume edited by Roger D. Masters and Michael T. McGuire, *The Neurotransmitter Revolution: Serotonin, Social Behavior, and the Law* (Carbondale and Edwardsville: Southern Illinois University Press, 1994), which contains proposals and calls for the elimination of the traditional system of criminal justice, based on retributive justice, and the implementation of a system that is based on medical genetics. Thus, people whose genetic makeup "predisposes" them toward violence would undergo, early in life, "preventative" therapy.

55. Erik Parens, "Taking Behavioral Genetics Seriously," *Hastings Center Report*, July-August 1996, 13.

ence. In *Maîtrise de la vie — domination des hommes*,[56] he raises a caution regarding the ambiguous relationship between science and political power — what he calls "biopolitics" — which in his view does not bode well for the Western democratic context. Our present commitment to scientific and biomedical *technique*, coupled with our recourse to political power rather than ethical reflection to promote and monitor these commitments, has had the effect of nurturing a de facto control over both the "quality" and existence of human life.

The method of ethical reflection on bioethical and biotechnological matters that in our day does emerge prevents the application of universally binding moral principles. Laws defining the parameters within which acceptable biotechnological and genetic research is done typically mirror not the broader multigenerational wisdom of consensual human values but the preferences of particular social or economic interest groups and wider secular Western cultural values. When moral decisions are based on ethics-by-committee, however, particular social interests are negotiated away at the expense of lesser interests based on a utilitarian calculus. Without binding moral principles, eventually anything and everything becomes negotiable — from abortion and fetal tissue research to mechanical reproduction and eugenics to euthanasia. All forms of bioethical discrimination and manipulation can be justified, not merely *for the sake* of quality of life but *against* life itself.

Crime and the New Consensus

While most people would not see an organic connection between bioethical developments and crime, evidence strongly suggests that developments in the one arena *inevitably correlate* to developments in the other. Consider society's response to violent crime. With a significant number of policy analysts, politicians, and pundits having cited crime as the issue of the 1990s, it is guaranteed a preeminent place in our national discourse well into the present decade and beyond. In the midnineties, thoughtful social commentators such as James Q. Wilson, John J. DiIu-

---

56. The title literally renders "The Matrix of Life — Human Domination." An English translation of this volume appeared in 1996 and was published by the Catholic Central Verein of America.

lio, Jr., and Daniel Polsby were warning that American society, within the next two decades, was headed for a deluge of violent crime perpetrated chiefly by young predatory males, the likes of which this culture has not known. The prognosis of DiIulio in particular was rather bleak: "What [is] really frightening to everyone from D.A.'s to demographers, old cops to old convicts, is not what's happening now but what's just around the corner — namely, a sharp increase in the number of super-prone young males."[57]

Reader beware: this forecast by DiIulio transcends political labels of "liberal" and "conservative." At a different location on the political and ideological spectrum, compared to Wilson and DiIulio, stands James Alan Fox, dean of the College of Criminal Justice at Northeastern University. Fox's studies of homicide led him to conclude as well that the United States is headed for a crime wave, despite an overall drop in crime — a drop that, as it turns out, is largely due to policies implemented at both the federal and local level. The surge predicted by Fox can be seen in the murder rate among fourteen-to-seventeen-year-olds. At the time, he noted, roughly 40 million people, the result of the most recent baby boomlet, were under the age of ten. Through the first decade of the twenty-first century, by his calculations, this "baby boomerang," as he called it in 1996, would enter the most crime-prone years. The next crime wave would get "so bad that it will make 1995 look like the good old days."[58] In 2007, as I write, some elements of Fox's dire forecast are present, although adjustments in policing policy suggest otherwise.

As American society becomes increasingly violent and loses patience with the criminal justice system in its present form, behavioral scientists are coming to a "consensus" that deviant behavior has a foremost *biological* explanation. It may well be that we are currently witnessing what historian Christopher Dawson observed with prophetic insight two generations ago. In a small but important volume titled *Progress and Religion*, Dawson wrote tellingly about the contradiction of the secular mind-set. He observed that the most enthusiastic supporters of the doctrine of human progress in Western culture have been the very people who were most im-

57. John J. DiIulio, Jr., "The Coming of the Super-Predators," *Weekly Standard*, November 27, 1995, 23.

58. Fox is cited in Peter Yam, "Catching a Coming Crime Wave," *Scientific American*, June 1996, 40-44.

patient with the purported injustices of existing social institutions.[59] Fulfillment of Dawson's "prediction," inter alia, can be found in the growing chorus of behavioral theorists and criminologists who propose an end to criminal justice theory as we have traditionally known it — based on moral agency — and a "medicalized," genetic basis not only to understand human behavior with but also to prevent crime in the future.

Robert M. Sade, very matter-of-factly, writes that because violent behavior "seems to be omnipresent in human societies," this "suggests that such behavior may somehow be *determined*, arising from hormones, neural connections, or other chemical, physiological, or anatomical substrates, which in turn may arise from our common genetic heritage."[60] Writing in the journal *Psychiatric Services*, Paul S. Appelbaum acknowledges that this view of human behavior is not marginal among behavioral theorists, emphasizing that behavioral genetics will be "the next frontier for the world of criminal justice, and mental health professionals are likely to play a critical role in helping the courts make sense of the new data."[61] Even if genetic predispositions are not exculpatory, Appelbaum believes that they might be seen as a mitigating factor and be taken into account at sentencing.[62]

---

59. Christopher Dawson, *Religion and Progress* (Garden City, N.Y.: Doubleday, 1960). A telling illustration hereof is the fact that James Q. Wilson's *The Moral Sense* set off a veritable firestorm of criticism among criminologists, social scientists, and behavioral theorists following its publication in 1993, though not because of a failure to interact with interpretive paradigms in philosophy, biology, and the social sciences — indeed, the book is an ambitious synthesis of social-scientific insight. Wilson takes the position that moral judgment begins with intuitions about what one *ought* to do (hence, *the* moral sense in the title). And this was the unforgivable sin, as it turns out, given the assumption among academics that it is impossible to arrive at a valid moral judgment about any given act. For a representative reaction to Wilson's thesis, see the Summer-Fall 1994 issue (vol. 13) of *Criminal Justice Ethics*, in which is published a symposium designed to evaluate Wilson's book. In supreme irony, the one panel member who reacts most vehemently to Wilson's argument of a universal "moral sense" is a criminologist. Reacting to Wilson's rejection of cannibalism on moral grounds, the criminologist asserts that the consumption of flesh in some cultures also can be "a physical channel for communicating social value," since it "ties together one generation to the other by virtue of sharing certain substances." In the end, he laments, "Christianity spoils our feasts."

60. Robert M. Sade, "Evolution, Prevention, and Responses to Aggressive Behavior and Violence," *Journal of Law, Medicine and Ethics* 32 (2004): 9, emphasis added.

61. Paul S. Appelbaum, "Law and Psychiatry: Behavioral Genetics and the Punishment of Crime," *Psychiatric Services* 56 (2005): 25.

62. Appelbaum, "Law and Psychiatry," 27.

Nita A. Farahany and William Bernet agree, making the rather sobering observation that outpacing even the rapid advances in science are the applications of human behavioral genetics in the criminal justice system.[63] Farahany and Bernet predict that in the future genetic testing will play an increasingly central role in criminal trials, particularly in attempts to show that one's genotype predisposes one to schizophrenia, bipolar disorder or sexual disorders, for example, and to psychiatric disorders more generally.[64]

Already a decade ago, the *Scientific American* reported on the optimism among a growing number of social and behavioral theorists that science would identify markers of maleficence that, within fifteen years, could revolutionize our criminal justice system. One of those interviewed, psychologist and author Adrian Raine, confessed that after his seventeen years of biological research on crime,[65] he envisioned that the following scenario could easily be with us in the near future. Given the breadth and accuracy of available statistical measurements, we would be able to predict with 80 percent certainty that someone's son will become seriously violent within twenty years. Therefore, as a society we are under obligation to offer a series of biological, social, and cognitive intervention programs on his behalf.[66] Similarly, Nicolas Rose, of the University of London, urges "a new 'public health'" conception of crime control. Related strategies, which are legitimated not in the light of law, justice, and rights but in terms of protecting "normal people" against risks that threaten them, call for therapy as a form of control. Such requires, in Rose's view, "the pre-emptive identification and management of 'risky individuals,' and risk-generating environments," and it demands "interventions upon . . . actual and potential offenders to reduce their riskiness where possible, and, where not, their in-

---

63. Nita A. Farahany and William Bernet, "Behavioral Genetics in Criminal Cases: Past, Present and Future," *Genomics, Society and Policy* 2, no. 1 (2006): 72-79.

64. Farahany and Bernet, "Behavioral Genetics," 77.

65. Representative of Raine's work are *The Psychopathology of Crime: Criminal Behavior as a Clinical Disorder* (San Diego: Academic Press, 1993); "Brain Abnormalities in Murderers Indicated by Positron Emission Tomography," *Biological Psychiatry* 42 (1997): 495-508; and more recently, with Yaling Yang, "Neural Foundations to Moral Reasoning and Antisocial Behavior," *Social, Cognitive and Affective Neuroscience* 1 (2006): 203-13.

66. Cited in W. Wayt Gibbs, "Seeking the Criminal Element," *Scientific American*, March 1995, 101. See also Raine, *The Psychopathology of Crime*; Raine and José Sanmartin, *Violence and Psychopathy* (New York: Kluwer Academic/Plenum, 2001); and J. A. Tehrani, "Genetic Factors and Criminal Behavior," *Federal Probation* 64, no. 2 (2000): 24-26.

definite containment in the name of public safety."[67] And more recently, Richard E. Redding has pressed the argument that the law must develop a "neurojurisprudence" that comports with modern neuroscience research on the role of brain dysfunction in compulsive criminal behavior.[68]

Do Raine, Rose, and Redding represent an isolated minority in holding this view? Stuart Yudofsky, chairman of the department of psychiatry and behavioral sciences at Baylor College of Medicine, is one who welcomes this development: "[W]e're going to be able to diagnose many people who are biologically brain-prone to violence."[69] Yodofsky seems less worried about the dangers intrinsic to prediction models than he is encouraged by the opportunities for prevention. And Redding's enthusiasm for a biological explanation and "solution" to crime is by no means subtle. He applauds the fact that "we are closer to realizing the early criminologist's dream of identifying the biological roots of criminality," citing "many neuroscientists and mental health professionals" who speak in terms of "crime as a disease," "the psychopathololgy of crime," and "the neurobiology of violence."[70] To this we may add Nicolas Rose's category "the biology of culpability." Rose uses this phrase while proposing new crime-control measures that draw upon human genetics and neurobiology to account for violent and antisocial conduct.[71]

What we are observing here is noteworthy: we are witnesses to the emergence of a new "problem," the person who is genetically "at risk." The implications hereof for "civil society" as we know it should give us pause. While a growing chorus of behavioral scientists contends that American society should trade its traditional system of criminal justice based on guilt and punishment for a medical or biological model based on prevention diagnosis and treatment, some have grave reservations. Ronald Akers, former director of the Center for Studies in Criminology and Law at the University of Florida, points out the dangers in this approach to social pathologies. Out of desperation, Akers warns, we can readily succumb to the

67. Nicolas Rose, "The Biology of Culpability: Pathological Identity and Crime Control in a Biological Culture," *Theoretical Criminology* 4, no. 1 (2000): 7.

68. Richard E. Redding, "The Brain-Disordered Defendant: Neuroscience and Legal Insanity in the Twenty-First Century," *American University Law Review* 56, no. 1 (2006): 51-127.

69. Cited in Gibbs, "Seeking the Criminal Element," 101.

70. Redding, "The Brain-Disordered Defendant," 56.

71. Rose, "The Biology of Culpability," 5-34. For a fascinating look at the "new brain science" and the trajectories of rapidly progressing neurobiology and neurochemistry, see Adam Keiper, "The Age of Neuroelectronics," *New Atlantis*, Winter 2006, 4-41.

temptation of premature or inappropriate use of knowledge. Such a precedent is found in the eugenics movement of the 1930s, when criminality and mental illness were considered to be inherited. By 1931, Akers notes, twenty-seven states had passed laws allowing compulsory sterilization of the feebleminded and the habitually criminal.[72]

In his 1993 book *The Psychopathology of Crime,* Raine stated that "a future generation *will* reconceptualize nontrivial recidivistic [i.e., repeated] crime as a 'disorder.'"[73] A frightening eventuality presents itself. When the "disease" reaches a socially intolerable level, will "treatment" become compulsory even for those who are innocent? Ray Jeffrey, professor emeritus at Florida State University, one of several criminologists interviewed by *Scientific American,* is indicative of many who are looking to psychiatrists, neurologists, and geneticists to provide answers to nagging questions, ready or not: "Science must tell us what individuals will or will not become criminals . . . and what law enforcement strategies will or will not work."[74]

Human behavioral theorists and geneticists, since the late 1990s, have increasingly moved away from the twins and adoption studies that were undertaken during the 1990s to embrace newer methodologies that are based on direct correlations between DNA sequence variation and deviant behavior.[75] Part of the reason for this, as research scientist Jay Joseph points out in his exhaustive rehearsal of research from the late 1980s to the late 1990s, is that the twin and adoption studies on which so much extrapolation was founded did not in the end produce substantial evidence of a genetic basis for any type of criminal or antisocial behavior.[76] Answering

72. Cited in Gibbs, "Seeking the Criminal Element," 101.

73. Adrian Raine, *The Psychopathology of Crime: Criminal Behavior as a Clinical Disorder* (San Diego: Academic Press, 1993), 319, emphasis Raine's. Chapter 12 poses the central question in its title: "Is Crime a Disorder?" Raine's answer is yes, based on sociobiological and psychosocial factors.

74. Gibbs, "Seeking the Criminal Element," 104. In *The Neurotransmitter Revolution,* Ray Jeffrey has this to say: "We must shift the emphasis from punishment to treatment and prevention. Crime prevention must replace the police-courts-prison system" (174).

75. Dean Hamer, "Rethinking Behavioral Genetics," *Science* 298 (October 4, 2002): 71-72; Appelbaum, "Law and Psychiatry," 25-27; and Sade, "Evolution, Prevention, and Responses," 8-17.

76. Jay Joseph, "Is Crime in the Genes? A Critical Review of Twin and Adoption Studies of Criminality and Antisocial Behavior," *Journal of Mind and Behavior* 22, no. 2 (2001): 179-218. Other critical reviews of the literature concur. A meta-analysis of the literature found only a "low-moderate correlation" between heredity and crime (G. D. Walters, "A Meta-Analysis of

the question of what it was, bad genes or bad research, Joseph is emphatic that it was the latter.[77]

While most scientists and theorists are willing to acknowledge that there is no "crime gene" that causes crime, many do believe that genes are responsible for aggressiveness and impulsiveness, and research in this area will surely increase exponentially.[78] Evan Balaban and Richard Lewontin concede that modern molecular and behavioral genetics research remains as tentative and inconclusive as its historical, nonmolecular counterpart, even though its proponents have become much more sophisticated about discussing the complexity of the link between genes, brains and behavior.[79] We may very well see a shift in criminal defense and alibis, from "Blame it on the knife" during the 1980s and 1990s to "Blame it on my criminal brain," if we may extrapolate from the direction of current biogenetic and behavioral research as well as evidence of public policy considerations as reported in the scientific press.[80] Research scientist Richard E. Redding would seem to be instructing us all when he intones that there is a difference between *being* immoral and *acting* immoral.[81]

Untangling the mystery of the genetic code creates for many scientists a "moral imperative" to use that knowledge; to ignore it would be indefensible. Yet to replace the justice in "criminal justice" with forced biomedical therapy based on the evaluations of scientific "experts" surely is to invite greater — indeed catastrophic — injustice. If science is being pressed to provide sociological and biological answers to pathological behavior,[82]

---

the Gene-Crime Relationship," *Criminology* 30 [1992]: 595-613), and a similar review found the same: taken together, "the data do not suggest a strong role for heredity in violence" (G. Carey, "Genetics and Violence," in *Understanding and Preventing Violence,* vol. 2, *Biobehavioral Influences,* ed. A. J. Reiss, Jr., et al. [Washington, D.C.: National Academy Press, 1994], 21-58).

77. Joseph, "Is Crime?" 213.

78. So L. F. Lowenstein, "The Genetic Aspects of Criminality," *Journal of Human Behavior in the Social Environment* 8, no. 1 (April 6, 2004): 63-78.

79. Evan Balaban and Richard Lewontin, "Brief on Crime and Genetics" (paper prepared on February 28, 2007, and accessible at www.gene-watch.org/DNADatabases/GeneCrimeBrief).

80. See, e.g., Apoorva Mandavilli, "Actions Speaker Louder than Images," *Nature* 444 (2006): 664-65.

81. Redding, "The Brain-Disordered Defendant," 118.

82. Of course, the absurd length to which some will go to obviate moral responsibility is illustrated in the hilarious headline that appeared on page 8 of the February 1998 issue (vol. 29, no. 2) of the *APA Monitor,* published by the American Psychological Association, which

whence will come the necessary moral restraints to hold bad science in check?[83] And if a consensus regarding crime in the public mind is not molded by a view that sees human beings personally responsible for their actions, what prevents the reign of social anarchy?[84]

Given the demographic realities of the present and future crime dilemma, it is not premature to be thinking about responses to the tide of violence that is with us and that lies ahead.[85] On a theoretical level, are we indeed willing to accept the conclusion that science "must tell us what individuals will or will not become criminals"? Is biology in fact destiny? Are individuals genetically predisposed to crime and deviant behavior?[86]

---

read: "Will Global Warming Inflame Our Tempers?" The reader learns from this piece that "Over the last 10 years, research has shown that uncomfortably hot temperatures directly cause increases in aggressive and violent behavior, including violent crime." The conclusion: "If global warming progresses as now seems likely, we can expect the recent reductions in the U.S. violent crime rate to disappear, only to be replaced by a steadily climbing rate of violence, along with all the grief, anguish, costs and waste associated with it."

83. If violence is best understood as a biological condition that is to be "prevented" by therapy or, more radically, for example, through selective implantation of embryos in women who have a history of being susceptible to abusive parenting, what shall we say of societies that have a history of violence — for example, Bosnia, Rwanda, Northern Ireland, or Liberia?

84. Arriving at a basic definition of "crime" or "criminal" is not easy for scientists, as acknowledged by Patwain and Sammons, who write: "It is a matter of some debate which people should be studied by criminal psychologists" (David Patwain and Aidan Sammons, *Psychology and Crime* [East Sussex, U.K., and New York: Routledge, 2002], 13-14). Significantly, crime is rarely understood as a moral concept; rather, as Cassel and Bernstein point out, it is conceived by scientists in either legal or sociological terms (Elaine Cassel and Douglas A. Bernstein, *Criminal Behavior*, 2nd ed. [Mahwah, N.J.: Lawrence Erlbaum Associates, 2007], 2-6). Consequently, measures of preventing crime all tend to be antiseptic and cosmetic: education, individual and family intervention, policing, community action, and gun reduction (280-85).

85. It needs saying that sociologists will continue to view social institutions and wider social forces as responsible for individual conduct, psychologists will continue to search for personal trauma in the criminal's past, and biologists will continue to find the "root cause" of crime and antisocial behavior in one's genotype. Those paradigms will continue to hold sway over research in their respective disciplines. And academic research will continue to oppose any theoretical position that recognizes moral agency and emphasizes the human capacity for self-control, notwithstanding valiant attempts by people like T. Hirschi and M. R. Gottfredson, "In Defense of Self-Control," *Theoretical Criminology* 4, no. 1 (2000): 55-69, to challenge prevailing assumptions.

86. Responding to research being done on genetically influenced deficiencies in the brain, Case Western Reserve bioethicist Stephen Post wisely warns against developing new drugs to treat violent and antisocial behavior. "Many people will have the genetic susceptibility and yet show remarkable resiliency" in overcoming unfortunate family situations that

Free Will in the Christian Moral Tradition

When Richard Berendzen resigned amid uproar the presidency of American University in 1990, after admitting that he made obscene phone calls from his presidential office, a physician by the name of Kenneth M. Grundfast argued in the *Washington Post* that Berendzen deserved public sympathy. The reason? Berendzen was the "victim" of "an obsessive-compulsive disorder" that frequently was "caused more by abnormal DNA sequences within an individual's chromosomes than by the moral lapses commonly described as wickedness, hostility or turpitude."[87] In breathtaking fashion Grundfast shifted the locus of scrutiny with these words: "I feel that the tragedy does not lie in what the man did or is accused of doing. Rather the tragedy is *ours more than his.* We may be the weak and misguided, not Berendzen."[88] So there you have it. A 180-degree twist with scarcely a bat of the eye.

Multiple forms of mischief abound in Grundfast's op-ed piece.[89] Not only does Grundfast remove Berendzen's guilt and place it squarely on all of us, he also engages in a bit of Orwellian obfuscation by writing that the president of the university "*allegedly* has made obscene phone calls." This despite Berendzen's pleading guilty to charges and also offering "anguished" accounts of how he felt after making pornographic phone calls to a Fairfax County (Virginia) woman who ran a day-care service. (Police had traced the calls to the university president's office. Berendzen then entered the sexual disorders clinic at Johns Hopkins Hospital in Baltimore and later pleaded guilty to two misdemeanor counts. He received two thirty-day prison sentences, both of which were suspended on the condition that he remain in outpatient psychological treatment.)

---

might encourage negative behavior. If violence is encouraged in the family, Post contends, let us help families and not "add to the problem by layering in a new generation of so-called violence preventing drugs"; cited in "Bad Behavior Linked to Gene," *BBCNews World Edition,* August 2, 2002, accessible at news.bc.co.uk/2/hi/health/2165719.

87. Kenneth M. Grundfast, "Bring Back Berendzen," *Washington Post,* May 4, 1990, A27. Berendzen is one of countless examples in a hit parade of extraordinary "victims" critiqued by John Taylor that is simultaneously hilarious and saddening. See John Taylor, "Don't Blame Me! The New Culture of Victimhood," *New York,* June 3, 1991, 27-34.

88. Grundfast, "Bring Back Berendzen," A27.

89. At the time he wrote the *Post* op-ed piece, Grundfast was chairman of the Department of Otolaryngology at Children's Hospital and studying molecular biology at the National Institutes of Health.

Not long after the Berendzen episode, a Georgia jury sentenced to death a young man named Stephen Mobley for his role in the murder of a Domino's Pizza store manager. Following the sentence, Mobley had tattooed on his back the word "Domino" and hung a pizza box on the wall of his prison cell. At the very time Mobley was celebrating in prison, his lawyers set in motion an appeal of his case to the state supreme court, submitting a controversial defense that argued that Mobley's genes may have predisposed him to commit crimes.[90]

Roughly concurrent with the Mobley case, a team of five scientists at Harvard Medical School, led by neuroscientist Xandra Breakefield, released a study that purported to identify a genetic mutation in a middle-class family prone to violence. According to Breakefield, a female member of the family had approached one of the researchers out of concern about incidents of aggression, arson, attempted rape, and exhibitionism occurring among her male relatives.[91]

What are we to make of cases such as these? Are they aberrations? What do they suggest, both in legal culture and in civil society? And what might they portend for the future? Not a few social critics are concerned that advances in genetic research, coupled with the "triumph" of therapeutic culture, have the sum effect of creating a social climate in which people cannot be held accountable for their actions since people do not act out of their own volition. When behavioral deviancy reaches pandemic proportions, will society respond by therapeutically defining away the moral "disease" on the one hand and biologically negating free will on the other?

The Judeo-Christian moral tradition, which arises from the natural law discerned through reason working in concert with revealed truth operating by faith, historically has affirmed what pre-Christian philosophers previously and Christian philosophers since have acknowledged in common: human beings are significantly "free" and therefore morally accountable for their actions. Even when Friedrich Nietzsche trumpeted in 1878 that "the history of moral feelings is the history of an error, an error called 'responsibility,' which in turn rests on an error called 'freedom of the will,'"[92] few people lived out that Nietzschean perspective. Only in the late

90. Edward Felsenthal, "Man's Genes Made Him Kill, His Lawyers Claim," *Wall Street Journal*, November 15, 1994, B1.

91. Reported in Felsenthal, "Man's Genes," B1.

92. Friedrich Nietzsche, *Human, All Too Human: A Book for Free Spirits*, trans. M. Faber (Lincoln: University of Nebraska Press, 1984), 4-5.

twentieth and early twenty-first century has the notion entered civilization that people are not morally self-responsible. Irenaeus is representative of consensual early Christian thinking on the matter: "God made man free from the beginning, so that he possessed his own power just as his own soul . . . to follow God's will freely, not being compelled by God. For with God, there is no coercion, but a good will is present with him always. He, therefore, gives good counsel to all. In man as well as in angels — for angels are rational — he has placed a power of choice, so that those who obeyed might just possess the good things which, indeed, God gives but which they themselves must preserve."[93] Similarly, Thomas Aquinas, in developing the implications of our moral freedom and our rational intuition of the natural law, identifies five natural inclinations through which the moral life expresses itself. These realms include a desire for the good, the instinct of preservation, procreation and the rearing of children, seeking the truth, and cultivating the social life with its attendant social obligations.[94] Aquinas insists that as a shadow of divine law, the natural law serves as a foundation for civil law, giving human beings the naturally discerned moral parameters within which to identify and do justice.[95]

Recall the crucial link between freedom and truth that was the focus of John Paul II in *Veritatis Splendor.* This link, elucidated by reason, allows human beings to discern between good and evil both for themselves and for those around them. As with Aquinas, *Veritatis* locates the natural human inclinations foremost in the realm of the spiritual-moral and not mere biological order, insisting on the profound oneness of body and soul, material and immaterial, in a "unified totality" of the human person.[96] Biology is *not* destiny for John Paul, even while it is an important part of our being. Accomplishing what is good and virtuous, therefore, is *the product of discernment through reason and conscience,* rendering human beings moral agents. Thus, humans have the capacity for free choice. When an action is freely undertaken, i.e., when it is performed with sufficient knowledge yet with no coercion, the agent is accountable for the good or evil that is generated as a result of the act.

But let us suppose that strong evidence of a link between biological

93. Irenaeus, *Adversus haereses* 4.37.1.
94. Aquinas, *ST* I-II Q. 90.
95. Aquinas, *ST* I-II Q. 90; also II-II Q. 58.
96. *Veritatis Splendor,* nos. 48-50.

predispositions and certain behaviors does exist. Can one truly be held responsible for one's actions? To understand human behavior in accordance with our inherited moral-philosophical tradition, of which Irenaeus, Aquinas, and John Paul are representative, is to reject a view of human nature as purely biological raw material. Judeo-Christian anthropology acknowledges the primacy not only of the person as a physical-biological endowment but also of *the person as a moral agent with a soul,* created in the image — i.e., the likeness — of God. There is therefore more to humanness than mere genes. The human being has capacities that are rooted in the spiritual-soulish nature. Thus, from the very point of fertilization, a human being cannot be reduced to patterns or tendencies mirrored in the genome, whatever those predilections might be. Human dignity transcends human biology. This understanding establishes — or perhaps, in our time, reestablishes — the preeminence of ethics over technology[97] as well as ethics over biology, even when evidence of a link between genetic predisposition and behavior might exist.[98]

On Working for a Consensus: Moral Insanity or Moral Sagacity?

While a biophysical and biochemical relationship can be said to exist between particular sequences of DNA and the structure of particular pro-

---

97. This point has been persuasively argued by Servais Pinckaers, "*Veritatis Splendor:* Human Freedom and the Natural Law," *Ethics and Medics,* February 1995, 3-4.

98. We have learned recently from scientists at the Scripps Research Institute in La Jolla, California, that researchers have developed an anti-obesity vaccine that significantly slowed weight gain and reduced body fat in animal models. See Eric P. Zorilla et al., "Vaccination against Weight Gain," *Proceedings of the National Academy of Sciences* 103, no. 35 (August 29, 2006): 13226-31. The new vaccine developed in this study is directed at the hormone ghrelin, which helps regulate energy balance in the body, and has shown the potential, at least in animal subjects, to put an end to that annoying — and often futile — struggle to lose weight. Given the estimate by the World Health Organization that roughly 1 billion people worldwide are overweight or obese (most of whom are located in developed nations), being overweight would seem to have reached epidemic proportions worldwide. Perhaps the solution to a controlled diet is indeed immunopharmacotherapy. But that some people appear to be genetically inclined toward obesity, or alcoholism, for example, is *not* to say that they have no willpower, or that they cannot resist abuse of alcohol or food. It is only to acknowledge that they struggle more than others with controlling their appetites and habits and *not* to posit that they lose their ability to choose and be rational, moral agents.

teins, the precise relationship between specific proteins, the expression of particular traits of an organism, and an explanation of *how* this occurs all remain a mystery. Genetic information can be described, quite properly, as an essential precondition for biological life. This information, however, neither describes nor determines *the life of the organism as a whole*. Although biophysics and biochemistry assist us in explaining the level of molecular interaction, they do not explain the identity of the moral subject at the level of consciousness, reflection, and action, all of which are dependent to a certain extent on the presence and activity of the central nervous system. Neither do they account for the mental, social, and spiritual development of the human beings that are constitutive of human identity. Nor do they account for the role that emotional well-being plays psychosomatically in the total healing process of human beings. Questions that belong to the domain of science, narrowly speaking, must be distinguished from those that do not or cannot. To fail to acknowledge these limits, or to fail to maintain them, is to fall prey to a kind of scientific imperialism.

While the relationship between biology and moral agency has long been studied by scientists, philosophers, and ethicists, with the current breakdown of civil norms in common culture this question takes on new urgency. Given society's relative paralysis in terms of dealing with deviant behavior, calls for biological "solutions" will be taken much more seriously as we progress into the twenty-first century. As a result, genetic research will be endowed with new authority to assist us with our social pathologies. The question remaining open is the degree to which Christians and people of goodwill everywhere will help shape a moral consensus. The cultivation — or the *absence* — of a moral consensus in society fundamentally depends on two criteria: (1) the correspondence of moral theory and practice to reality, and (2) the integrity and resilience of those advocating such moral standards.

Presupposed in all moral theory and practice is a particular view of human nature. Nowhere are the implications of competing anthropologies more critical than in the realm of bioethics, since anthropological assumptions will inform ethical responses to the questions of human life's origin, its dignity, the unity and totality of human existence, human suffering, and death. If human beings bear the divine image, and if there exists a divinely ordered moral structure to the universe through the natural law, as we have argued, then it is incumbent upon all who bear such convictions to work toward the shaping of a moral consensus in culture.[99]

Return for a moment to the Berendzen case, for it has much to teach us. In the aftermath of his resignation Richard Berendzen was to receive a $1 million settlement from American University, authorized by the board of trustees, for giving up his tenure as a professor. (His salary, which reflected both administrative and teaching duties, had been $140,000.) As a result of an uproar among both faculty and students following the announcement of this agreement, the settlement was rescinded by the board.[100] Following the whole episode Berendzen was in a reflective mood. While 1990, the year of his exposure, "was for me just hell," he noted, the following year was "very restorative" and "healing," indeed "quite an exceptional year."[101] Adding to the "restoration" and "healing" process in this sordid state of moral affairs was an invitation to appear on ABC's *Nightline*, where Berendzen proceeded before a national television audience to recount the abuse of his childhood.[102] He said the abuse, inflicted by a "woman very close to me," started when he was eight years of age. Asked by Ted Koppel why, during the two years of obscene phone calls, he never reached out for help, Berendzen replied that a Ph.D. who was a university president should not have needed help.[103]

But let us consider the moral madness of the other key player in the Berendzen case, Kenneth Grundfast. Assessing the role of biology in the initiation of obscene phone calls, our researcher-doctor friend informed us in

99. How "successful" we are is beside the point. What is called for is our *faithfulness* to moral reality, not our "success" in convincing others. We simply commit our cause to the Judge of the whole earth, who is just.

100. Berendzen, as it turned out, was restored to the faculty two years later and assigned to teach two sections of Astronomy 220, an elective course for freshmen and sophomores, and Physics 370, an introduction to quantum mechanics required for physics majors. In 1992 Berendzen addressed a national conference on child victimization, at which he lectured on "survival techniques." In 1993 he published *Come Here: A Man Overcomes the Tragic Aftermath of Childhood Sexual Abuse* (New York: Villard Books), an autobiographical account of his discovery that he was the true victim, given the sexual abuse he had experienced as a child. Significantly, in the book he describes his obscene phone calls as a form of involuntary "data gathering."

101. Cited in Ari L. Goldstein, "Berendzen Set to Teach at AU," *Washington Post*, December 9, 1991, C3.

102. He appeared on *Nightline* on May 23, 1990.

103. See also Daniel L. Brown, "I Thought I Had It under Control," *Washington Post*, May 24, 1990, A40.

the *Washington Post* that "[s]tress plays a role in causing individuals with a genetic predisposition to actually behave abnormally. When a certain stress level is reached, then some biological and molecular systems that control behavior break down, and people can be *forced* to do things that they ordinarily would not want to do. . . . Recent research on obsessive-compulsive disorders is revealing that genetic factors and biochemical imbalances can predispose certain individuals to behave in abnormal ways."[104] Note the backbone of the good doctor's apologetic: genetic predisposition not only *causes* us to act, it does so *against our wills*, transforming *all* of us into occasional victims of deviant behavior. And on this level, Grundfast clearly wishes to instruct us. Moreover, subsequent news accounts worked in concert with Grundfast's propaganda and were perfectly willing to describe Berendzen's problem in terms of an "addiction."

Science itself has been quite willing along the way to provide necessary justification for this tale of moral exculpation. The medicalization of vice,[105] for example, is amply on display in the October 1997 issue of *Science* magazine, where the author of the article "Addiction Is a Brain Disease, and It Matters"[106] and researcher at the National Institutes of Health also wishes to instruct us. In fact, he is upset. Upset because many, perhaps most, people see drug abuse and addiction as "social problems" rather than as "brain problems." Listen to the essence of his argument: "Research has begun . . . to reveal major differences between the brains of addicted and nonaddicted individuals and to indicate some common elements of addiction, regardless of the substance. . . . That is the good news. The bad news is the dramatic lag between these advances in science and their appreciation by the general public or their application in either practice or public policy settings."

But this is not the only bad news. The author is further troubled by

104. Grundfast, "Bring Back Berendzen," A27, emphasis added.

105. On the medicalizing of morality in broadly therapeutic terms, see Christina Hoff Sommers and Sally Satel, *One Nation under Therapy: How the Helping Culture Is Eroding Self-Reliance* (New York: St. Martin's Press, 2005). Clearly, whether via therapy or genetics, there is abundant room in the present cultural climate for the "medicalization" of vice. In this regard, one is reminded of Victor Hugo's observation that crime eventually would be viewed as a disease, physicians would replace judges, and hospitals galleys. The cultural context of this remark, of course, was very different from our own. Nonetheless, there is unpleasant truth in his prediction. See Victor Hugo, *The Last Days of a Condemned*, collected with *Bug-Jargal* and *Claude Gueux*, trans. unknown (Boston: Little, Brown, 1894), 331.

106. Alan I. Leshner, "Addiction Is a Brain Disease, and It Matters," *Science* 278 (October 1997): 45-47. The quotations in the following text have been taken from this article.

the "tremendous stigma" attached to being an addict: "For example, many, perhaps most, people see drug abuse and addiction as social problems, to be handled only with social solutions, particularly through the criminal justice system." "The most beneficent public view" of addicts is to view them "as victims of their societal situation" rather than see them as "weak or bad people, unwilling to lead moral lives and to control their behavior and gratifications." But this is moralistic and wrongheaded; rather, we are instructed, "addiction is actually a chronic, relapsing illness."

With "science" as his backing, the author authoritatively concludes: "It is time to replace ideology with science. . . . Not only must the underlying brain disease be treated, but the behavioral and social cue components must also be addressed, just as they are with many other brain diseases," a category that includes "stroke, schizophrenia, and Alzheimer's disease." Understanding addiction as a "brain disease," he notes, "explains in part why historic policy strategies focusing solely on the social or criminal justice aspects of drug abuse or addiction have been unsuccessful. . . . If the brain is the core of the problem, attending to the brain needs to be a core part of the solution." The author does not tell us what sort of treatment is most highly recommended. Perhaps mandatory shock therapy is just around the corner.

"Addiction Is a Brain Disease" well could have been written by Kenneth Grundfast. What its author and Grundfast share in common, not insignificantly, is that both at the time were conducting research at the National Institutes of Health. But let us return to the Berendzen episode, for Mr. Grundfast wishes to instruct us further. In arguing that the American University president is to be exonerated, he argues that *we all are exonerated from the consequences of the evil that we perpetrate*. Recall his twisted line of reasoning: "I feel that the tragedy does not lie in what the man did or is accused of doing. Rather the tragedy is ours more than his. We may be the weak and misguided, not Berendzen."[107]

Based on this line of reasoning, the October 1997 *Science* article could just as easily have been titled "Making Obscene Phone Calls Is a Brain Disease." The argument employed, based on "science," is precisely the same as that advanced by Kenneth Grundfast. In response to this biomedical nonsense, syndicated columnist Charles Krauthammer offers a most useful assessment. Trained as a psychiatrist, Krauthammer summarizes the way in

---

107. Grundfast, "Bring Back Berendzen," A27.

which a shift is occurring, whereby genetic exculpation, rooted in moral and intellectual promiscuity, is transplanting sociological "root causes" to explain deviant behavior: "Not very long ago, when someone did something awful, a loud liberal chorus would explain that because of childhood deprivation, poverty or racism, the criminal was not truly responsible for his actions. Society — a sick society — made him do it. This environmental exculpation, popular in the guilt-ridden 60's and 70's, is now in decline." But now we have a new model of exoneration, Krauthammer points out, one that is "shiny, scientific and designed for the guilt-free" of today. The new root cause? "Nature made me do it." The beauty of this excuse is that "it is adaptable to middle-class malefactors whose white-collar crimes cannot be blamed on a wretched environment. They are blamed instead on disease. . . . By this logic, when a pedophile rapes a child, it is the disease raping. The rapist, like the child, is a victim. It takes little effort to relate almost any punishable misbehavior to some . . . syndrome."[108]

Presently, despite the appearance of "genetic tendencies" in some individuals or families that seemingly "predispose" them toward aggressive responses, we are not yet letting convicted murderers off the hook and go scot-free because they were dealt a bad hand genetically. But this may change. Because genes seem to provide a more powerful explanation than mere "childhood abuse," it is safe to assume that the day is not far off when murderers and pedophiles *will* be exonerated. Already they have *excellent* chances of reduced sentences, parole, and a return to society.

The opposition between determinism and responsibility raises critical questions about the nature of justice, and justice in its essence requires that people be held accountable for their actions — accountable, that is, *if* human behavior is at all predictable and human beings are moral agents. If, on the other hand, human behavior is unpredictable and unaffected by what behavioral scientists call "reinforcement contingencies," then *there is no point to punishment or any other form of behavioral control* — whether incentives, rewards, pay raises, academic grades, speeding tickets, you name it. For no positive or negative reinforcement would ever under any conditions have any predictable effect. Correlatively, there would be no such thing as "civil" society — or human and civil rights, for that matter. If we wish to be intellectually honest, we simply cannot have our cake and eat

---

108. Charles Krauthammer, "Illness Made Me Do It? The Excuse Is Criminal," *St. Louis Post-Dispatch*, May 15, 1990, 3B.

it too, morally speaking. Either people are *always* morally accountable for their actions or they are *never* so. There is no middle position.

Today I can claim, with the backing of science, that "society made me do it." Tomorrow a new vista spreads itself before me with new potentialities, anointing my claim that "my genes made me do it" and bolstering my case with stubborn biological evidence. And in the end, who will prevent me from relinquishing my moral self-responsibility?[109]

109. While the purported role that biology plays in homosexuality takes us too far afield of the present discussion, natural-law thinking will need to inform intelligent and reasoned responses to claims of genetically induced same-sex orientation. Helpful resources in this regard include works by the following authors, who have thoroughly and thoughtfully examined the scientific evidence: Gerard J. M. van den Aardweg, *On the Origins and Treatment of Homosexuality: A Psychoanalytic Reinterpretation* (New York: Praeger, 1986); van den Aardweg, *The Battle for Normality: A Guide for (Self-)Therapy for Homosexuality* (San Francisco: Ignatius, 1997), especially chapter 2 ("Development of Homosexuality"); John F. Harvey, *The Homosexual Person* (San Francisco: Ignatius, 1987); Harvey, *The Truth about Homosexuality* (San Francisco: Ignatius, 1997); Joseph Nicolosi, *Reparative Therapy of Male Homosexuality* (Northvale, N.J., and London: Jason Aronson, 1991); Stanton L. Jones and Mark A. Yarhouse, *Homosexuality: The Use of Scientific Research in the Church's Moral Debate* (Downers Grove, Ill.: InterVarsity, 2000), especially chapter 3 ("What Causes Homosexuality?"); and Peter Sprigg and Timothy Dailey, eds., *Getting It Straight: What the Research Shows about Homosexuality* (Washington, D.C.: Family Research Council, 2004), especially chapter 1 ("What Causes Homosexuality").

CHAPTER SIX

Contending for Moral First Things in Ethical and Bioethical Debates: Critical Categories — Part 1

Rethinking Personhood: Sanctity or Quality?

Personhood and the Human Consensus

It has become increasingly evident in recent years that most — if not all — of our culture's critical ethical and bioethical issues hinge in some way on the question of personhood.[1] For this reason, in the view of Gilbert

---

1. For the sake of clarity, I am distinguishing bioethics not as ethics per se, nor as "medical ethics." Rather, as practiced today and as mirrored in governmental "advisory" groups, in committees, and in regulations, bioethics may be best understood as an academic theory of ethics that was formally articulated in 1979 by the *Belmont Report: Ethical Principles and Guidelines for the Protection of Human Subjects of Research*, produced by the Congressionally mandated National Commission for the Protection of Human Subjects of Biomedical and Behavioral Research. The *Report* identified three guiding bioethical principles that up to the present have formed the core of bioethical discourse. These three principles — autonomy or respect for the individual, justice, and beneficence — need severe qualification, particularly from the standpoint of a distinctly Christian social ethics, since they are not morally "neutral" categories but rather represent secular, "preference"-utilitarian thinking about bioethics as a field. Moreover, biomedicine has increasingly been preoccupied with patient autonomy and utility, a development that requires a morally compelling counterbalance, given its tendency to trump all other ethical concerns. As evidence that biotechnology is not morally neutral, one only need compare the National Conference of Catholic Bishops' *Ethical and Religious Directives for Catholic Health Care Services* (Washington, D.C.:

Meilaender, because bioethical reflection has lost the moral significance of the body, it has in truth lost its very "soul."[2] Recall, for a moment, the pronouncements set forth by esteemed bioethicists at the outset of chapter 1. John Harris informs us, "We all know lots of people; we all know lots of persons . . . [and] we are also familiar with the idea that there are nonhuman persons," that is, "humans who are not, or may not be[,] persons or full persons." These "human nonpersons," or humans "who are not fully fledged persons," were said to include zygotes and embryos, individuals who are "brain-dead," anencephalic infants, and individuals persisting in a vegetative state.

Bioethicist Tom Beauchamp shares Harris's assumptions about personhood, arguing that "many humans lack properties of personhood or are less than full persons" and are consequently "rendered equal or inferior in moral standing to some nonhumans." And Peter Singer, it will be recalled, states categorically that "membership of the human species is not morally relevant." It follows, therefore, for Singer, that there are "some nonhuman animals whose lives, by any standard, are more valuable than the lives of some humans." In consequence, "[a] chimpanzee, a dog, or pig, for instance, will have a higher degree of self-awareness and a greater ca-

---

USCC, 1995), as well as the *Catechism of the Catholic Church,* which represents authoritative teaching of the Roman Catholic Church on all matters of faith and ethics, with mainstream bioethical literature — e.g., the *Hastings Center Report,* the *Journal of Medicine and Philosophy,* the *American Journal of Law and Medicine,* the *Kennedy Institute of Ethics Journal,* and *Bioethics* — in their treatment of issues ranging from abortion to euthanasia. These two contrasting "systems" or approaches to bioethical issues lead to diametrically opposing conclusions, at the center of which lies the issue of personhood. Nigel Cameron observes that the move away from medical ethics to "bioethics" in effect "has undermined the professional character of medicine" and also "helped cut loose the ethics discussion itself from the constraints of its . . . tradition" ("The Christian Stake in Bioethics: The State of the Question," in *Bioethics and the Future of Medicine: A Christian Appraisal,* ed. John F. Kilner, Nigel M. de S. Cameron, and David L. Schiedermayer [Grand Rapids: Eerdmans; Carlisle, U.K.: Paternoster, 2005], 3). Moreover, it is instructive that the first president and cofounder of the International Association of Bioethics, founded in 1997, was none other than Peter Singer. While such definition and qualification of "bioethics" remain outside the scope of the present discussion, a useful — and very thorough — resource in this regard is Dianne N. Irving, "What Is Bioethics?" in *Life and Learning X: Proceedings of the Tenth University Faculty for Life Conference,* ed. Joseph W. Koterski (Washington, D.C.: University Faculty for Life, 2002), 1-84.

2. Gilbert C. Meilaender, *Body, Soul, and Bioethics* (Notre Dame, Ind., and London: University of Notre Dame Press, 1995), 37.

pacity for meaningful relations with others than a severely retarded infant or someone in a state of advanced senility."

Whether Singer genuinely is convinced that "membership of the human species is not morally relevant" is debatable. Nonetheless, Singer performs a valuable service in framing the relevant moral issue: Is human personhood, with its criteria for "membership," morally relevant?

But if human personhood *is* a morally relevant question, then our initial aim in this discussion will be to identify the *nature* of what a person is. To identify and amplify human "nature" is to identify and underscore an *abiding consensus* about personhood. That some bioethicists, theorists, and social activists in our day call into question the very notion of personhood is not to grant them any particular authoritative status on the matter. Indeed, one of the strikingly salient features of contemporary culture — and the "postmodern" moment — is the hubris and sheer arrogance with which it asserts itself. Intractably severed from the past, cut off from intergenerational wisdom, and unaccountable to any cultural authority, the "postmodern turn" sets itself up as autonomous.[3] Thus, we must see contemporary pronouncements about human beings and personhood for what they are: in and of themselves they possess no more authority than rival pronouncements. And if they are found outside of the human and cultural consensus that has endured, they are to be rejected in the interest of intellectual and moral honesty. This conclusion should be beyond debate and noncontroversial.

Authentic understanding of personhood lays hold of the *nature* of what is "human." When philosophers and scientists are accustomed to speak of the human being as a "rational animal," they invite qualification. At a rudimentary level, rationality is understood to convey sentience, self-conscious awareness, and the ability to reflect. Hereby humans distinguish themselves from other "animals" — in their aspirations, in their creativity, in their moral imagination, in their pursuit of what is good. This "consensual" understanding of human nature did not arrive yesterday. It is af-

---

3. An examination of the contrast and similarities between modernity and postmodernity takes us too far afield and requires another context for discussion. However, I proceed on the assumption that what we have come to call "postmodern" is a child of — indeed an extension of — conclusions reached by modernity. Autonomy characterizes *both* ways of thinking, and hubris is lodged in both even when the epistemological rationale differs.

firmed by both ancients and moderns, and as a consensus it exists irrespective of culture and social location.

Illustrative of this abiding "consensus" is Aristotle's oft-used example of the oak. Resident within the acorn is all the potential that distinguishes the genus oak. This potential furnishes a sufficient explanation of both the diversity and sameness within the genus, and offers an adequate description of the nature of the oak, at whatever stage of the oak's development along the way. This description of "nature" has nothing to do with how the genus oak functions, or how it may be used, or the strength and characteristics of its wood, or how large it may eventually grow, or how it may weather the elements throughout its growth process. Nor does this understanding vary among Asians, Africans, Europeans, or North and South Americans. Rather, it corresponds narrowly yet precisely enough to what the oak is *in its essence.*

Summarily, we are permitted to make several conclusions regarding the existence and interrelation of the oak and acorn:

- Without the oak tree the acorn would not exist.
- The acorn is thus dependent on the oak tree for its existence.
- Conversely, the oak tree is dependent on the acorn for its existence.
- The acorn may or may not grow sufficiently, but this possibility does not bear on its essential nature.
- The oak tree may or may not grow to the size of other oak trees, but this possibility does not bear on its essential nature.

In considering the relationship between the acorn and the oak, we wish to observe only that, whether or not the acorn develops to its fullest or greatest potential and regardless of the extent of its development, lodged within — from its inception — is the genus oak. Our awareness of the essential nature of the genus oak does not vary, nor is it subject to question. It corresponds to reality as humans experience it universally and perennially.

Or, using another analogy, we might attempt to make the same point about "nature" through computers and computer processing. While a central processing unit, random-access memory, various drives, computer chips, and electromagnetic circuitry all constitute elements within each computer system and describe the functions of what a computer *does,* without the software the computer is not operational. The computer software may be said, albeit crudely, to have intrinsic value.[4]

Thomas Aquinas offers a definition of personhood that simultaneously accords with the consensus of classical philosophy and is distinctly Christian. "Person" signifies the individual substance of a rational nature. "Personhood" thus signifies what is distinct about the being who is in the process of being perfected. In Thomistic thought, personhood may even be applied to God to the extent that it is relational, even when the Persons within the Godhead are not three isolated individuals.[5] For Thomas, dignity is what distinguishes human beings through the act of creation, which bestows on them a status that is unique within all of the cosmos.

Humans possess an intrinsic dignity by virtue of their being human. Were this not the case, then their value would rise or fall according to the development or deterioration of their functions. Such valuation, based on functionality, is extremely subjective and relative to the interests of the valuer. Human sanctity and human rights are meaningless apart from the notion of inherent dignity and what we *are*.[6] Not for nothing did Bernard Lonergan observe that when nonhuman animals run out of biological opportunities and activities — e.g., seeking food and shelter, mating and reproducing, playing, avoiding pain and predators — they fall asleep. When humans, however, run out of biological opportunities and activities, they ask questions.[7] The nature of this questioning always and again returns to what it means to be human. Who am I? Whence do I come? Where am I headed? Is there a knowable truth? Is there an ultimate good? Is love authentically possible? Why do I suffer? What are the consequences of my actions? To what or whom am I morally accountable?

But precisely *why* do humans ask questions in the first place? Considering this very question, Robert Spitzer frames the matter pointedly: "It is not simply the ability to ask questions" in the generic sense. It is rather

---

4. Robert J. Spitzer, Robin A. Bernhoft, and Camille E. De Blasi, *Healing the Culture: A Commonsense Philosophy of Happiness, Freedom, and the Life Issues* (San Francisco: Ignatius, 2000), 43-44, helpfully make use of precisely this sort of logic.

5. Aquinas, *Summa Theologiae* I-II Q. 29, art. 1, 3, and 4.

6. This is effectively argued by Anthony McCarthy in his philosophical discussion of cloning. See his *Cloning and Stem Cell Research* (London: Catholic Truth Society, 2003), 22-26 and 60-61.

7. Bernard Lonergan, *Insight: A Study of Human Understanding*, ed. F. E. Crowe and R. M. Doran (Toronto: University of Toronto Press, 1992), 34.

the ability "to ask questions about what is ultimate, unconditional, perfect, infinite, absolute, and eternal with respect to love, goodness, truth, beauty, and being. This is what humans seem to do uniquely by comparison with the other members of the animal kingdom. It is reasonable to believe that these powers are unique to beings of human origin."[8] And if this is reasonably the case, then these powers constitute, in an objective sense, part of human *nature*.[9] Moreover, we can speak in this vein of a certain "objectivity" to the extent that we operate within a consensus of what human beings, broadly speaking, collectively know, believe, and affirm. That is to say, this knowing and believing based on a set of convictions is not dependent on subjective, private, or inaccessible data; it is a common fund that is accessible to philosophers, scientists, social scientists, and theologians, to teachers, theorists, clinicians, and laypersons. And it is a consensus around which there has been and remains — even when that consensus has been dissipating of late — fundamental agreement.

Life in the Divine Image: Contending for Human Dignity

But an increasingly regular question regarding personhood is being posed in the marketplace of ideas, and not infrequently in bioethical discussions. What if a particular person has not reached his or her full potential? What if a person's existence seems to lack demonstrable social utility? Or *any* social utility? Let us, for the moment, return to Aristotle. The acorn may or may not reach its full potential, depending on any number of conditions that are present. These conditions include, for example, proper nutrients in the soil, pH level, sunlight, water, and the like. Thus, an acorn may not in time become a towering oak. Nevertheless, this does not negate the fact that the acorn belongs to the genus oak. As such, undeveloped and "fetal" though it may be, it contains the "genetic code" for the oak.

It is fair to apply this way of thinking to human beings. Shall a handicapped neonate, whatever the handicap, not be called "human"? Shall a "preemie," born several months prematurely (and often remarkably so),

---

8. Spitzer, Bernhoft, and De Blasi, *Healing the Culture*, 47.

9. Geneticists, of course, may object that this propensity for asking *why* is owing to biological conditioning, that it lies in the genetic apparatus. The question of what within the human accounts for this propensity removes us too far afield of the question at hand. That this propensity resides uniquely within humans is the immediate concern.

not be considered "human," even though wanted and loved by the parents? Shall the anencephalic or the hydrocephalic baby be refused the classification "human"? Shall the elderly, because of decreased social "utility" and capacities, be rendered "nonhuman"? For those who believe that "personhood" is accorded only at particular points along the life spectrum — three months, six months, eight months, or for some handicapped children, a year or several years, or for other handicapped children, never in the present lifetime — and for those who argue that "personhood" is determined by external quality, social utility, or functionality and as such can be removed, it stands to reason that less-than-perfectly-functioning humans are *not* true persons. Having denied personhood, then, they will need to determine *at what point* — i.e., precisely when and where along the life spectrum — "personhood" is achieved. This line, of course, will be drawn in a wholly arbitrary fashion. Complicating matters for them is that every less-than-perfectly-functioning human differs only by a matter of *degrees*. Establishing or denying personhood, it goes without saying, will thus become a wholly subjective endeavor, since there is no consensus, only personal "choice," as to what version of human life is "desired" or "undesired" at a particular stage of life growth. But what is *intrinsically* valuable does not derive its value from mere experience, utility, or perceived quality.

What are the consequences or repercussions of viewing personhood merely in terms of its external "quality"? Several things occur. One is that people are inclined toward a foremost sensory and "temporal" existence. They will seek to avoid pain — at virtually any cost — and they will increasingly pursue material-physical pleasures. If self-worth and personal identity subsist in pleasure and possession, one will have little tolerance for pain, material deprivation, weakness, and illness. Further, one will judge others on the same basis of externality and sensorial pleasure, adopting a mistaken value system that is in full denial of the reason for which they were created, namely, to express life in the context of human community. One's ethics will be reduced to egoistic utilitarianism, while "freedom" will be interpreted as an escape from the mundane affairs of life.

Robert Spitzer wisely suggests a moral principle that would well serve us as a society, whether we are agonizing over the human embryo, the genetic apparatus, handicapped neonates, the unborn, or the infirm: *when in doubt, we should err on the side of personhood rather than denying it.* The reasoning behind this is not indecipherable: "If we will not budge on either our definition of personhood or in our assumption of personhood in the most ambiguous cases, then we will not allow ourselves to compromise or undermine our awareness of personhood in the less ambiguous ones. . . . We can see this with respect to slavery in ancient and recent times, genocide, and totalitarian political persecutions of every kind."[10] This method of moral reasoning, after all, is one that everyone — religious or not — can embrace.

In historic Christian theology, the significance of the doctrine of the *imago Dei* is that every human creature points toward a Creator. The image is a reflection of its origin. It follows then that our full imaging of the Creator expresses itself through our fundamental *nature* and not merely our functionality, social utility, or qualitative development. That is, we live as knowing, loving, reasoning, serving beings, always mirroring the image of the Creator in our humanness, whether in our birthing, in our dying, or in between. Furthermore, because the image of God is an endowment, personhood is neither developmental nor incremental; nor is it the product of performance.[11] The true image of God in us is never removed from the human creature. The human person is a body-soul composite, with the soulish dimension continuing to exist beyond physical death.[12] Viewed differently, in the words of William May, God cannot incarnate himself in a pig or cow or ape because those creatures are incapable of reflecting the divine image. God has, however, incarnated himself in a human, mysteriously choosing as the eternal uncreated Logos to become one of us.[13]

---

10. Spitzer, Bernhoft, and De Blasi, *Healing the Culture*, 51-52. The authors demonstrate great insight into the human condition in their discussion of pain and pleasure.

11. This is not to deny that an infant progresses through developmental stages, only that it has the natural capacity to do so because of human *nature*.

12. The implications of human personhood and dignity for contemporary bioethical debates are developed with unusual sensitivity by Patrick Lee in "Personhood, Dignity, Suicide, and Euthanasia," *National Catholic Bioethics Quarterly*, Autumn 2001, 329-43.

13. William E. May, "The Sanctity of Human Life," in *In Search of a National Morality: A Manifesto for Evangelicals and Catholics*, ed. William Bentley Ball (Grand Rapids: Baker; San Francisco: Ignatius, 1992), 105. I am rejecting a dualism that permeates Western thought and *separates the person from his or her body*. If the body does not in truth constitute part of personhood, as most of our culture believes, then human existence becomes subhuman or subpersonal, and therefore the destruction of life is not perceived as an attack on the person. Accordingly, such lives — whether unborn, handicapped, diseased, or dying — possess no inherent value because they cannot engage in socially meaningful activities or capacities. For a fuller treatment of current debates over contrasting conceptions

An important implication for human beings' mirroring of the divine image is that human moral action will transcend mere impulse and desire. It will conform to what is true, what is good, what is virtuous, and what is in harmony with our intrinsic nature, as Aquinas wishes to make clear. Intrinsic human nature, issuing out of the *imago Dei,* allows human beings to flourish, for they can distinguish between ultimate and less-than-ultimate ends. Human actions are morally good when humans use their moral freedom in ways that correspond with their created nature. Therefore, deep within the interior life human beings discover a "law" — the natural moral law — that they themselves do not create yet that they feel obliged to obey. The Ten Commandments merely describe the broader contours of this law, which through faith and virtue are obeyed from the heart.

At the core of Judeo-Christian moral tradition is the proscription against taking innocent life (Gen. 9:5-6; Exod. 20:13; Deut. 5:17; Matt. 5:21; Rom. 13:9; James 2:11)[14] — a proscription that undergirds civilized society. The reason for this is that life is inherently sacred (Gen. 1:26-27; 9:5-6). The scope of this "innocence" is spelled out in a remarkably prescient statement to a group of physicians several generations removed: "As long as a man is not guilty, his life is untouchable, and therefore any act directly tending to destroy it is illicit, whether such an act is intended as an end in itself or only as a means to an end, whether it is a question of life in the embryonic stage or in a stage of full development or already in its final stages."[15] The contours of sacred life are further reiterated by one Vatican II document, with almost prophetic insight: "All offenses against life itself, such as murder, genocide, abortion, euthanasia, and willful self-destruction," are to be understood as "criminal," since they "poison civilization," "debase" both perpetrators and victims, and "militate against the honor of the Creator."[16]

---

of personhood, see J. P. Moreland and Scott B. Rae, *Body and Soul: Human Nature and the Crisis in Ethics* (Downers Grove, Ill.: InterVarsity, 2000).

14. As borne out by Hebrew grammar, the sixth commandment is an absolute proscription not against all killing but against the taking of innocent life. Excluded from the command are the killing of animals, war that is justified, the execution of criminals, and killing in self-defense.

15. Pope Pius XII, "Address to the St. Luke Union of Italian Physicians" (November 12, 1944), recorded in *Acta Apostolicae Sedis* 66 (1974): 735, and reproduced, with English translation, in *Vatican Council II: More Post-Conciliar Documents* (Northport, N.Y.: Costello, 1982), 452.

16. *Gaudium et Spes,* no. 27.

Affirming objective moral truth — as witnessed to by the natural moral law — yields the common moral judgment to protect and dignify human life, and particularly vulnerable human life. Given our commitment to the intrinsic dignity of the human person, we are forbidden categorically from eliminating it. There is a moral line that connects the human embryo, fetal destruction, euthanasia, slavery, genocide, and totalitarian rule. If it is agreed that we never take the life of an innocent human, at any developmental stage and regardless of its functionality, then intentionally taking life at *any* point along the life spectrum for *any* reason will *always* be wrong. It is wrong not merely because the Christian church or the Bible teaches that it is wrong but because the moral law, "written on the heart" of every human, witnesses to its wrongness.

Protecting Personhood

Among those events that forced Christian reflection on the moral status of human life, including embryos, was the birth of Louise Brown, the first baby born through in vitro fertilization in 1978. The first official Christian response came in the form of the document *Donum Vitae*, published in 1987 by the Catholic Church's Congregation for the Doctrine of the Faith. In this document it was argued, unreservedly, that human life begins at conception, which was understood as the time of fertilization. This position was reaffirmed by John Paul II in his 1995 encyclical *Evangelium Vitae:*

> Some people try to justify abortion by claiming that the result of conception, at least up to a certain number of days, cannot yet be considered a personal human life. But in fact, "from the time that the ovum is fertilized, a life is begun which is neither that of the father nor the mother; it is rather the life of a new human being with his own growth. It would never be made human if it were not human already. This has always been clear, and . . . modern genetic science offers clear confirmation. It has demonstrated that from the first instant there is established the program of what this living being will be: a person, this individual person with his characteristic aspects already well determined. Right from fertilization the adventure of a human life begins. . . ."[17]

17. *Evangelium Vitae* (hereafter *EV*), no. 60. Here John Paul is citing *Donum Vitae* 1.1. The section numbers to *EV* in the following paragraphs are placed in the text.

Elsewhere in the encyclical John Paul reiterates the nature of this attack on human life at its earliest stages:

The various techniques of artificial reproduction . . . actually open the door to new threats against life. Apart from the fact that they are morally unacceptable, since they separate procreation from the fully human context of the conjugal act, these techniques have a high rate of failure: not just failure in relation to fertilization but with regard to the subsequent development of the embryo, which is exposed to the risk of death. . . . Furthermore, the number of embryos produced is often greater than that needed for implantation in the woman's womb, and these so-called "spare embryos" are then destroyed or used for research which, under the pretext of scientific or medical progress, in fact reduces human life to the level of simple "biological material" to be freely disposed of. (*EV*, no. 14)

Even if "the presence of a spiritual soul cannot be ascertained by empirical data," John Paul cautions, the very results of scientific research on the human embryo provide a strong indication of the presence of a person "at the moment of the first appearance of a human life." The conclusion is difficult to avoid: "How could a human individual not be a human person?" (no. 14).

What John Paul is developing in *Evangelium Vitae* is a consistent "life" ethic, one that offers a moral rationale for *why* there is *a continuum from embryo to the grave*. For this reason he speaks in the encyclical of "the entire unified process of human existence" (no. 2). Developing a moral rationale, in John Paul's view, is critically urgent in our day: "With the new prospects opened up by scientific and technological progress there arise new forms of attacks on the dignity of the human being. . . . Broad sectors of public opinion justify certain crimes against life in the name of the rights of individual freedom" (no. 4). Some might object that John Paul's reference to "crimes against life" is surely hyperbole. However, he rejects this claim, arguing that "we are in fact faced by an objective 'conspiracy against life,' involving even international institutions engaged in encouraging and carrying out actual campaigns to make contraception, sterilization and abortion widely available" (no. 17). This "conspiracy," moreover, is finding support among the culture's gatekeepers: "Nor can it be denied that the mass media are often implicated . . . by lending credit to that culture which presents recourse to contraception, sterilization, abortion and even euthanasia as a mark of progress and a victory of freedom, while depicting as enemies of freedom and progress those positions which are unreservedly pro-life." Furthermore, from the standpoint of moral obligation, what is at stake is so important that

> the mere probability that a human person is involved would suffice to justify an absolutely clear prohibition of any intervention aimed at killing a human embryo. Precisely for this reason, over and above all the scientific debates and those philosophical affirmations to which the magisterium has not expressly committed itself, the church has always taught and continues to teach that the result of human procreation, from the first moment of its existence, must be guaranteed that unconditional respect which is morally due to the human being in his or her totality and unity as body and spirit.

The result is that the human being is to be "respected and treated as a person from the moment of conception, and therefore from that same moment his rights as a person must be recognized, among which in the first place is the inviolable right of every innocent human being to life" (no. 17).

Before we bring to a close our consideration of the sacredness and dignity of human personhood, the above thoughts from *Evangelium Vitae* on the beginning of the life spectrum raise an important question. Can the Christian affirm a "delayed personhood"? Is "delayed personhood" theologically and morally plausible?

The standard position of broader culture — at least, secular naturalists — is that personhood is acquired, that it develops progressively. The progressive view has important ramifications for both ends of the life continuum. Writes John Harris: "The life cycle of a given individual passes through a number of stages of different moral significance. . . . This individual will gradually move from being a potential or a pre-person into an actual person when she becomes capable of valuing her own existence. And if, eventually, she permanently loses this capacity prior to death, she will have ceased to be a person."[18] In moral terms this stance is necessary to get around the ethical problem of killing. The position consistent with Christian moral teaching — even when Christians differ on the status of the embryo — is grounded in the moral imperative to protect human

---

18. John Harris, "The Concept of the Person and the Value of Life," *Kennedy Institute of Ethics Journal* 9, no. 4 (1999): 308.

personhood, to dignify what is intrinsically human, to view all of life as sacred. This does not mean that the church turns a blind eye to scientific research; it does mean, however, that science does not — cannot — determine "personhood," which is a theological-philosophical construct. There are good — indeed, even scientific — reasons for believing that personhood begins at conception. For this reason Christian moral teaching has the obligation to protect the "margins" of life. Norman Ford puts the matter this way: "From conception, the ongoing unity of the embryo is demonstrated by its unidirectional development and growth as one and the same living human being. According to this account the zygote is an actual human person and not simply a potential human person *in much the same way as an infant is an actual human person with potential to develop to maturity.* This view is simple, easy to grasp, and is supported by eminent scientists and philosophers."[19]

By this rationale the fertilized egg, which is the product of conception, and the developing fetus and the developing infant all are accorded "human" status.[20] All are in the process of developing; all demonstrate at various stages potential for growth and maturity. Accordingly, it is arbitrary to decide, as secularists do, at what point these "developing persons" actually *become* "full-fledged persons." That the genetic code of the zygote, "programmed" to develop into a human being, is resident therein must be considered as we reflect theologically and philosophically about human life, even when the church resists the temptation to pronounce *precisely at what genetic or cellular stage* personhood "begins." Recall the Christian position on personhood stressed by John Paul: we endorse the "entire unified process of human existence."[21]

We must recapitulate. Our intrinsic human *nature* can be understood to account for what all people hold in common, while human *personhood* gives expression to that which makes the human species utterly unique and separate from the rest of the created order. The reality of a shared nature fosters a kind of communicability within the human species,

---

19. Norman Ford, "The Human Embryo as Person in Catholic Teaching," *National Catholic Bioethics Quarterly,* Summer 2001, 159.

20. In a fascinating essay, Richard M. Lebovitz, "Embryonic Rights: Self-Interest and the Thirteenth Amendment," *National Catholic Bioethics Quarterly,* Winter 2003, 681-87, has even gone to the extent of arguing for embryos' "rights" over against parents or an authority wishing to take away their life.

21. *EV,* no. 2.

whereas personhood implies an incommunicability with the rest of creation.[22] Nature and personhood together, however, bequeath human dignity[23] and life's sanctity. Both elements exist *irrespective* of the degree to which nonperfected human beings function and the extent to which they are thought to be socially useful. In the words of Karol Wojtyla, before he became John Paul II, a human being represents "the kind of good that does not admit of use and cannot be treated as an object of use and as such a means to an end." Human dignity and sanctity are such that a human being is "a good toward which the only adequate response is love."[24]

Rethinking Suffering: From Elimination to Transformation

Society and Suffering

Few would deny that, at the start of the third millennium, our culture faces enormous ethical and bioethical challenges. It should not, then, come as a surprise that the very idea of personhood — and human nature — is challenged at the most rudimentary level. Tempestuous cultural currents, threatening the very notion of human sanctity, force us to rethink basic notions of compassion, justice, and the good. Ultimately, how we construe personhood will dictate how we express neighbor-love, and at the most practical level, how we extend morally responsible health care to those in need.

The ethical challenges that mirror the stormy nature of our present cultural life seem to have coagulated on three principal fronts: beginning-of-life issues, life-enhancement issues, and end-of-life issues. How we as a soci-

22. Romanus Cessario, *Introduction to Moral Theology* (Washington, D.C.: Catholic University of America Press, 2001), 83, develops this point quite effectively.

23. Perhaps we should qualify the word "dignity," since humans use this term in several ways. By "dignity" we do not signify how one feels, such as when one's "sense of dignity" — i.e., one's sense of self-worth or self-esteem — is threatened. Nor is dignity a property or quality that we know through intuition. It is rather a possession, an endowment, an essence that merits respect and consideration from other persons. Comparatively, it can be appreciated by the fact that it distinguishes us from animals, since we are by nature rational, moral agents. Most importantly, it follows that dignity cannot be lost or diminished because of the reasons just stated.

24. Karol Wojtyla, *Love and Responsibility,* trans. H. Willetts (New York: Farrar, Straus and Giroux, 1981), 41.

ety view suffering plays a critical role in how we approach each of these three domains. But it will foremost govern how we approach aging and dying.

Given the increasing openness to euthanasia in the Western cultural context,[25] it is proper to ask what attitudes in the culture currently push us in the direction of assisted suicide. It is fair to say that a common denominator unites many of our contemporaries as they reflect on death and dying. That common denominator is *fear*. As a society we fear prolonged disability, we fear becoming a burden to our families, we fear economic burden, we fear being trapped by sterile technology and not dying in peace, we fear losing control, and most fundamentally, we fear pain and suffering. Because of the pervasiveness of these fears, we can predict, along with Sidney Callahan,[26] the appearance of more campaigns and referenda to compel state legislatures to approve physician-assisted death. This development is compounded by the fact that respected secular ethicists and physicians defend the morality of euthanasia.[27]

Because our attitudes toward death and aging are shaped by our fundamental beliefs about personhood and the meaning of life, the challenge before us, it should be emphasized, is foremost one of *moral persuasion* and not political protest. Sadly, the religious tradition of which I am a part, in its more recent history, has tended to opt for the latter, the short-term strategy, rather than the former, the long-term strategy, which (truth be told) is hard work. It is hard work because it requires (1) moral education and (2) engaging culture in socially relevant ways rather than merely shouting from the sidelines. A significant element in the moral argument that we will need to make against suicide, physician-assisted suicide, and euthanasia concerns the ethics of suffering. This will be no easy task.

Suffering, in the eyes of contemporary culture, is meaningless and

25. Few have described the euthanasic impulse of Western culture with such prescience as Arthur J. Dyck, *Life's Worth: The Case against Assisted Suicide* (Grand Rapids and Cambridge, U.K.: Eerdmans, 2002).

26. Sidney Callahan, "The Moral Case against Euthanasia," *Health Progress*, February 1995, 38-39.

27. In the view of Dyck, *Life's Worth*, 11-25, the euthanasic impulse in the United States was greatly facilitated in the late 1980s and early 1990s by a distorted understanding of freedom — so, for example, Alan Gewirth, *Human Rights: Essays on Justification and Application* (Chicago: University of Chicago, 1982) — coupled with medical recommendations that appeared in the *New England Journal of Medicine*. See, in particular, S. H. Wanzer et al., "The Physician's Resonsibility toward Hopelessly Ill Patients: A Second Look," *New England Journal of Medicine* 320 (1989): 844-49.

hence to be avoided at all costs and by all means. For this reason abortion and euthanasia — and to a lesser extent infanticide — receive substantial popular support. They are perceived as necessary to end present — or to prevent future — suffering. Each measure, therefore, becomes a "compassionate choice."[28] As it relates to end-of-life issues, the reality of suffering is thought to imbue a person with both a moral and a legal "right" to die.[29]

The argument that the Christian community will need to advance has both a negative and a positive component. Negatively, we must make a public case in exposing euthanasia and physician-assisted death for what it is — an evil that destroys both individual integrity and the common good in society, thereby rending asunder the fabric of civil society.[30] We in the West must be convinced of "the interconnectedness of [all spheres of] life and the limits of a cult of privacy, autonomy, and private property."[31] Posi-

---

28. This mind-set is described with utmost clarity by N. C. Lund-Molfese in "The Gift of Suffering versus Euthanasia," *Social Justice Review,* November-December 1999, 170-73, and Lund-Molfese, "SALVIFICI DOLORIS: A Challenge to Catholic Social Scientists," *Social Justice Review,* July-August 2000, 108-11.

29. Thus, on October 27, 1997, Oregon became the first state to legalize physician-assisted suicide. Initiated in 1994 as Measure 16 ("The Oregon Death with Dignity Act"), the initiative was voted into law by a margin of 51 percent to 49 percent. Oregon Health Division's second annual report, published in the *New England Journal of Medicine* 342, no. 8 (2000): 598-604, is noteworthy for what it does *not* report. For example, according to the report, only 37 percent of the patients killing themselves in 1999 received a psychiatric evaluation. For a helpful assessment of the report, see K. Foley and H. Hendin, "The Oregon Report: Don't Ask, Don't Tell," *Hastings Center Report,* May-June 1999, 37-42. What is exceedingly alarming in Oregon is that those who are sanctioned by the state government to assess its operation are *advocates* of physician-assisted death. What's more, the very same issue of the *New England Journal of Medicine* contained results of a Dutch study showing that 18 percent of the physician-assisted suicides in the Netherlands are botched (pp. 551-56).

30. A forceful, and timely, response to the social consequences of euthanasia is the declaration "Always to Care, Never to Kill: A Declaration on Euthanasia," which was produced by the Ramsey Colloquium of the Institute on Religion and Public Life in New York City in 1991 and published in the February 1992 issue of the journal *First Things* (pp. 45-47).

31. Thus Callahan, "Moral Case," 40. The interconnectedness of all life can be graphically illustrated on two levels by one very tragic suicide. Just over a decade ago the Navy — as well as the whole nation — was rocked by news that Admiral Jeremy ("Mike") Boorda, the U.S. Navy's Chief of Naval Operations, had taken his life. Because of the social stigma attached to self-inflicted death as a result of a shotgun wound to the head, most people in the media, shell-shocked, were extremely reticent to use the "s" word in reporting Boorda's death. The press made no mention of the hellish nightmare and lifelong emotional scars that Boorda's suicide had inflicted upon a wife and four children. What's more, no one dared

tively, we must make a compelling case for the alternative — namely, caring for the aged and dying in a way that preserves both individual integrity and the common good. An important "plank" in that campaign is to re-educate society regarding the "redemptive" side of suffering.[32] This task, it must be stressed, is both conceptual and pragmatic; it will need confronting at both the theoretical and existential levels.

Arthur Dyck and Edmund Pellegrino are among those who caution us to distinguish between pain and suffering, for indeed the two are not the same. Most people will acknowledge that suffering itself is a subjective entity, and that reasons other than pain contribute to human suffering — among them guilt, depression, fear of dying, spiritual confusion, lack of purpose, alienated relationships, even the desire to escape life's realities.[33] From the standpoint of technology and research, the elimination of suffering is typically extolled as a primary goal in debates over genetics and end-of-life issues. The drive to eliminate suffering, however, does not *necessarily* spring from authentic compassion for people who are in pain or suffering. Let the reader beware. Its motivation may issue out of a utopian desire to rid society of its imperfections by means of technology. Not surprisingly, this unfettered optimism in technological advancement inevitably carries with it a deep-seated bias against traditional religion and moral codes. In a culture in which scientific and biomedical technology flourishes, disconcerting questions will need to be raised by *someone*. For exam-

conjecture the immensely demoralizing effect the suicide had on the millions of our nation's servicemen, irrespective of rank. Was it now preferable for officers or nonofficers alike, following Boorda's lead, to take their own lives, given the demands associated with serving national interests? For this reason, because of the impact of suicide on communal bonds, Sidney Callahan writes: "Maintaining an absolute prohibition against actively taking a human life — self or other, with or without consent, dying or not — is necessary to protect human communal bonds. All human living, loving, declining, and dying is full of stress that must be endured and overcome by communal support. What humans need most is an unconditional commitment to steadfastly care for one another through any illness or impairment until the end comes" (40).

32. Although suicide is a personal response to the pressures of a life deemed not worth living, its thought germinates in a social climate in which a collapse both of the intellect *and* of faith has already taken place. For a cultural analysis of our own time, see J. Daryl Charles, "Suicidal Thought in a Culture of Death," in *Suicide: A Christian Response*, ed. T. J. Demy and G. P. Stewart (Grand Rapids: Kregel, 1997), 209-20.

33. Dyck, *Life's Worth*, 27, and Edmund D. Pellegrino, "Euthanasia and Assisted Suicide," in *Dignity and Dying: A Christian Appraisal*, ed. John F. Kilner, Arlene B. Miller, and Edmund D. Pellegrino (Grand Rapids: Eerdmans, 1996), 114.

ple, is the desire to eliminate suffering in some cases misguided? Is it possible to find any meaning in suffering? What if the desire to eliminate suffering bleaches society of its "humanizing" dimensions such as service of love, sacrifice, compassionate care-giving, community, and personal character growth and development, in the end rendering these elements nonsensical and illusory to people?[34]

Salvifici Doloris: John Paul II on Redemptive Suffering

In his 1995 encyclical *Evangelium Vitae (The Gospel of Life)*, John Paul II challenged his audience to embody a culture of life in the face of what he called a "culture of death." While this encyclical was primarily a philosophical reflection on contemporary culture and an exhortation toward authentic Christian witness, part of its theological groundwork was laid eleven years earlier in a significant though relatively unknown apostolic letter titled *Salvifici Doloris (The Christian Meaning of Human Suffering)*.[35] In this letter John Paul examines the meaning of personal suffering as well as the Christian responsibility to the suffering of others. Because much in this letter commends itself to all people of faith, we offer a brief summary of its contents.[36] As a tool it should greatly encourage the wider Christian community as we seek to embody a redemptive presence in the current cultural context.

Though much shorter than an encyclical, *Salvifici Doloris* is divided into eight progressively developing parts.[37] John Paul's basic thesis is that meaning can be found in suffering only as a result of revelation, and specifically the revelation of Christ's suffering on the cross and redemption of humankind that ensued. This, however, does not simply remain a religious *ideal;* it becomes incarnated in meaningful and relevant ways.

34. Such a grim scenario has been thoughtfully critiqued by D. A. du Toit in "Anthropology and Bioethics," *Ethics and Medicine* 10, no. 2 (1994): 35-42, especially 39-40.

35. *Salvifici Doloris* is literally rendered "redemptive suffering."

36. Elsewhere I have examined the contents of *Salvifici Doloris* in "John Paul II and the Meaning of Suffering: Protestant Reflections on *Salvifici Doloris*," *National Catholic Bioethics Quarterly* 2, no. 1 (Summer 2002): 211-20. Portions of that discussion are used with permission.

37. Between introduction and conclusion are found the following sections: "The World of Human Suffering," "The Quest for an Answer to the Question of the Meaning of Suffering," "Jesus Christ: Suffering Conquered by Love," "Sharers in the Suffering of Christ," "The Gospel of Suffering," and "The Good Samaritan."

Suffering, observes John Paul, is "a universal theme that accompanies man at every point on earth," and therefore demands to be constantly reconsidered.[38] In fact, Saint Paul's words to the Roman Christians, that "the whole creation has been groaning in travail together until now" (Rom. 8:22), are a poignant reminder of the universality of the problem, even when suffering "seems to be particularly essential to the nature of man" (*SD*, no. 2). Suffering, then, is "almost inseparable from man's earthly existence" (no. 3). Early on in the letter, John Paul reminds his audience that pain and suffering have something of an *apologetic* function; that is, the church must "try to meet man in a special way on the path of his suffering" (no. 3). Effective apologetics, after all, wrestles seriously with building bridges to surrounding pagan culture; it will not suffice merely to cite Scripture or affirm scriptural authority, as Protestant evangelicals frequently have been willing to do.

The former pontiff points to the limits of medicine, insofar as the science of healing is unidimensional.[39] Humans suffer in a variety of ways. Their anguish can be moral, psychological, and spiritual as well as physical. So it is inevitable that human beings are occupied by one perplexing question: Why do we suffer? Although physical pain is widespread and measurable in the animal kingdom, only humans reflect on the *why* question. This anguish is intensified by the fact that no satisfactory answer is forthcoming (*SD*, no. 9).

For John Paul, as for most Christians, no resource expresses so vividly the emotion, anxiety, and dissonance of human suffering as does the book of Job. And what is particularly striking to the reader is the amount of the story devoted to the dialogue between Job and his acquaintances. Their task, as they understand it, is to convince him that he must have done something seriously wrong, for "suffering — they say — always strikes a man as punishment for a crime" (no. 10). In this "theology of retribution" (see Job 2:11–31:40), suffering has meaning only in the context of moral justice, whereby evil is repaid for evil.

While much of the Old Testament in fact corroborates the retribu-

---

38. *Salvifici Doloris* (hereafter *SD*), no. 2. References to *SD* have been placed in the text. The letter is reprinted in *Origins* 13, no. 37 (1984): 609-24.

39. At the same time, it is legitimate to argue that the task of medicine is to cure and care even when it cannot heal. A basic ingredient in that caring process is palliative. Thus, David Beauregard, "The Mystery of Suffering," *Ethics and Medics*, August 1995, 1-2, and J. F. Bresnahan, "Palliative Care or Assisted Suicide?" *America*, March 14, 1998, 16-21.

tive truth that suffering is the direct result of evil, this explanation is incomplete and is challenged by Job. That is, *not* the moral law of reaping and sowing is to be rejected, but rather his friends' application of this law to *his own situation*. Hence, "it is not true that all suffering is a consequence of a fault," for Job is not being punished (no. 11). Rather, as the context of the story immediately establishes, suffering in Job has the character of a test — a test to *demonstrate Job's righteousness*.

But there are problems. Although such a "stock Christian" answer has validity, "at the same time it is seen to be not only unsatisfactory . . . but it even seems to trivialize and impoverish" the notion of divine justice (no. 11). For John Paul, a satisfactory "answer" to the problem of suffering can only be grasped when it is tethered to "the entire revelation of the Old and above all the New Covenant." Suffering, thus viewed, "must serve for conversion, that is, for the rebuilding of goodness in the subject" (no. 12).

To perceive the true answer to the *why* of suffering, "we must look to the revelation of divine love, to what God has done for man in the cross of Jesus Christ" (no. 13).

Because the very essence of Christian soteriology is liberation from evil, herein we behold *salvific love*. The mission of the only-begotten Son consists in conquering sin and death, by which "we have in mind not only evil and definitive, eschatological suffering . . . but also . . . evil and suffering in their *temporal and historical* dimension" (no. 15).[40] Evil remains bound to sin and death. Hence it is necessary that in his messianic ministry "Christ drew increasingly closer to the world of human suffering. 'He went about doing good' [Acts 10:38], and his actions were directed primarily to those who were suffering and seeking help" (*SD*, no. 16). Moreover, because of his full awareness that his mission was to *suffer and die*, Christ therefore severely rebuked Peter when the latter wished him to abandon the thought of suffering and death (no. 16).

Thus, as innocent sufferer, Christ takes upon himself the sufferings of the world. And this we call "substitutionary" — and above all, redemptive — suffering. Christ has accomplished the world's redemption through his suffering (no. 17).

---

40. Here evangelical Protestants would do well to pay attention. In our recent history we have stressed the eschatological over the temporal, with a deficient "theology of creation"; hence, we have not always been responsible in the cultural mandate.

John Paul wishes his audience to ponder the fact that "with the passion of Christ all human suffering has found itself in a *new situation*. In the cross of Christ not only is the redemption accomplished through suffering, but also human suffering itself has been redeemed" (no. 19).[41] To suffer, writes John Paul, "means to become particularly susceptible, particularly open, to the working of the salvific powers of God offered to humanity through Christ" (no. 23).

Despite its relative absence in our pulpits, our classrooms, our bookstores, and our study groups, the question of suffering nevertheless has "a special value in the eyes of the church. It is something good, before which the church bows down in reverence with all the depth of her faith in the redemption" (no. 24). As the individual embraces suffering through the grace of the crucified Redeemer, gradually, notes John Paul, the salvific meaning of suffering is revealed (no. 26).

Finally, and most significantly, in the thinking of John Paul the question of suffering is inextricably linked to the parable of the Good Samaritan (Luke 10:25-37), for it is precisely the Samaritan who shows himself to be the real "neighbor" to the victim. If the parable teaches anything, it teaches that we may not "pass by on the other side" indifferently, thereby underscoring the redemptive character of suffering by its condemnation of passivity. The Good Samaritan is "good" because he has compassion and is sensitive to the sufferings of others (*SD*, nos. 28-30). In this concrete expression of the Samaritan's love, John Paul is convinced, "the salvific meaning of suffering is completely accomplished and reaches its definitive dimension." Namely, suffering is present in the world "in order to release love, in order to give birth to works of love toward neighbor, in order to transform the whole of human civilization" (no. 30).[42]

"Compassion" and the Culture of Death

Someone has observed that when a revolutionary group wishes to wage war on human decency, the first — and most effective — strategy is to co-

---

41. For this reason Paul can write to the Corinthians, "For this slight momentary affliction is preparing for us an eternal weight of glory beyond all comparison" (2 Cor. 4:17-18).

42. Although John Paul is sensitive to the isolation that suffering forces upon the individual, the emphasis of his letter is conspicuously communal and ecclesial.

opt language in the service of the cause. It is therefore not surprising that proponents of physician-assisted death routinely speak in terms of "mercy," "compassion," and human "dignity."[43] As they seek to expand their agenda both on a popular level and in the context of policy debates, the rhetoric of compassion allows them to capture the moral high ground. It is precisely this sort of verbal sleight of hand that George Orwell had in mind as he penned in 1947 a brief but highly important essay titled "Politics and the English Language." What Orwell found in his own day can be applied to our own: "One ought to recognize that the present political chaos is connected with the decay of language. . . . Political language — and this is true of all political parties, from Conservatives to Anarchists — is designed to make lies sound truthful, and murder respectable, and to give an appearance of solidity to pure wind."[44]

Orwell rightly saw the connection between our moral vocabulary and social-political tyranny, which is reality control.[45] If "the Party" — indeed, any cultural authority — could inject itself into the past and make related pronouncements about it in order to falsify or eliminate it, then one is truly powerless to say that anything is right or wrong. Nothing is certain, and nothing lasts; nothing can be maintained as good and true, and nothing can be denied as false and evil. Such a political-moral climate leaves us amputated. In the words of Jean Elshtain, "Cut off from the bonds that help us to hold our 'selves' intact, we are more readily ground down to become the generic mulch of the order."[46] Surely, Orwell would

43. The "linguistic turn" in preparing the social climate for ethical shifts is examined in greater length later in this chapter. The perversion of language in ethical debates is conveniently illustrated by relativist Joseph Fletcher: "Christian Europe started moving from *pagan Rome's compassionate regard* for the dignity of free persons to the *savagery* of an indiscriminating condemnation of all suicide in the Middle Ages" ("In Defense of Suicide," in *Suizid und Euthanasie,* ed. Albin Eser [Stuttgart: Ferdinand Enke Verlag, 1976], 237-38, emphasis added).

44. *The Collected Essays, Journalism, and Letters of George Orwell,* ed. Sonia Orwell and Ian Angus, 4 vols. (New York: Harcourt, Brace and World, 1968), 4:136.

45. While the essay "Politics" gives theoretical explanation to this linkage, the novel *1984* serves as a graphic illustration of it.

46. Jean Bethke Elshtain, *Real Politics: At the Center of Everyday Life* (Baltimore and London: Johns Hopkins University Press, 1997), 52. In a very sensitive manner Elshtain is atuned to the terrifying nature of Orwell's vision, without being alarmist. She notes that Orwell worried over the fact that totalitarian ideas had "taken root in the minds of intellectuals everywhere," i.e., that modern intellectual culture tends toward oppressive orthodoxies;

have much to say about current debates over bioethical and health-care issues, which, to a large extent, are strikingly battles over words and their meanings and not discussions about morality.

Consider, for the moment, contemporary usage of the words "dignity" and "compassion." If "dignity," as we have sought to demonstrate, is inherent in every human being, then it must have a source outside of human beings' heroic or noble deeds and accomplishments. That is, it must be an entity that is *bestowed and not achieved.*[47] More problematic, however, is the word "compassion," given contemporary parlance. Denoting a literal "suffering with," "compassion" occurs with utmost frequency in the moral lexicon of both the Christian community and secular naturalists. Both groups will invoke the term in articulating their response to human suffering, as is particularly evident in debates over sustaining and ending life. On the one hand, naturalists will claim to operate in the name of compassion. To the extent that suffering constitutes the ultimate evil, the relief of suffering is seen as the greatest good.[48] Thus, terminating life, due to the threat of suffering, is invested with moral meaning.

On the other hand, there pleads for our consideration the classic Christian understanding of compassion, eloquently articulated by John Paul in *Salvifici Doloris,* and more recently in *Evangelium Vitae.* The for-

---

herein Elshtain seems to stand in broad agreement with Orwell. For this reason Orwell's target audience consisted of "friends of totalitarianism," whether politically leftist or rightist. Why was Orwell so concerned to target the intellectual? In offering an explanation, Elshtain states a truism: "Fearful of offending the public opinion within his own group, the intellectual lives in dread of being tagged with a label . . . and trims his thought and words energetically in order to conform and stay in good graces with the group" (52). This condition, I think, is continually validated in the academy. In a certain sense, much of the professoriate — politically and ideologically — remains "friends of totalitarianism," in Elshtain's terms.

47. Gen. 1:26; Eph. 1:10; 1 Tim 2:4-6; and 1 Cor. 15:42-57. For a clear statement of the implications of human dignity in the classic Christian sense for health-care issues, see J. M. Haas, "Human Dignity and Health Care," *Ethics and Medics,* February 1997, 1-2.

48. Christian ethics, it should be stated, seeks to alleviate all human suffering, both present and future, as far as is reasonably possible. Only psychopaths and sadomasochists would deliberately choose to revel in it. In my view, traditional Catholic approaches to health care and alleviation of suffering seem to embody the best method, given the recognized distinction between *ordinary* and *extraordinary, customary* and *unusual,* treatment. As stewards of life, we Christians are under obligation to utilize *proportionate* means of treatment to maintain life. To forgo *disproportionate* means of treatment is not the equivalent of euthanasia or physician-assisted death; rather, it signals our acceptance of the inevitability of dying and death as part of human experience.

mer pontiff notes that while evil can cause forms of suffering, suffering is *not* to be equated with evil in and of itself. Consider how the human body functions. Physical pain is a sensory experience that informs us that some defect has come upon the body. Individuals who lack the sensory ability to detect or feel pain — a condition we traditionally have called leprosy — are prone to constant injury and may die prematurely. Similarly, on a psychospiritual level, "pangs of conscience" inform us that something within the realm of the soul needs attending. At bottom, the basic knowledge of pain itself is something that is good.[49]

Acknowledging that suffering is not the equivalent of evil, Christian compassion calls us to "suffer with" those who are suffering, using Christ — and the Good Samaritan — as our model, ever mindful of the redemptive element in suffering. Authentic compassion does not eliminate the sufferer as the means to alleviating suffering itself. The Christian moral tradition rather has always called us toward compassion for the sick, the unborn, the aged, and the dying. It calls us to strive to alleviate suffering, but always with respect for *the inviolable sanctity of all human life,* irrespective of how fragile.

Edmund Pellegrino, former director of the Center for Clinical Bioethics at Georgetown University Medical Center who presently chairs the President's Council on Bioethics, has pointed out the moral dissonance between (and irreconcilable nature of) Christian and secular understandings of "compassion." "For the secularist, the sentiment of compassion has moral weight of its own. It is, itself, a virtue which entails relief of pain and suffering as a major end of moral life. For the Christian, sentiment cannot function as a reason for moral choice, sentiment is not a virtue unless ordered by reason, and suffering has a distinct meaning in human lives."[50] Although the Christian and the secular naturalist both *feel* compassion as an emotion, they are worlds apart in *how they interpret and order it.* For the Christian, compassion is not self-justifying; i.e., it must be harnessed to and controlled by faith-oriented reason, *if,* that is, it is to be a virtue and not prostituted as a vice. For the naturalist, compassion remains a sentiment; to the extent that something *feels* good, it is viewed as morally good. Outside the Christian ethic, the only life worth living is a life without suffering. Therefore, "compassion" expresses itself in killing or assisting in the

---

49. *SD,* nos. 5 and 6.

50. Edmund D. Pellegrino, "The Moral Status of Compassion in Bioethics: The Sacred and the Secular," *Ethics and Medics,* September 1995, 3.

death of the severely handicapped, the chronically ill, or the comatose. But as John Paul has frequently observed, when compassion is loosed from the moorings of its Christian moral tradition, the result is a "culture of death." And though it may shock, it is not an overstatement to suggest that in time this ethical divorce breeds terror and moral atrocity.[51]

Most people with terminal illnesses die in the sterile environment of a hospital, if not in a nursing home. As people anticipate death, few things create a more dreadful sense of anxiety than the anticipation of unrelieved pain and suffering. The solution, a growing chorus tells us, is physician-assisted death. After all, in the words of Faye Girsh of the Hemlock Society, "The only way to achieve a quick and painless and certain death is through medications that only a physician has access to."[52] What the public frequently does not hear is that there is another way to die, namely, under medical care that stresses adequate pain management while offering the individual spiritual and emotional support.

According to policy analyst Joseph Loconte, every year roughly 450,000 people die this way; they die in hospice.[53] But the vast majority of terminally ill patients can have freedom from pain and clarity of mind, as Edmund Pellegrino[54] and Arthur Dyck[55] contend. Martha Twaddle, medical director at the hospice division of the Palliative Care Center of the North Shore in Evanston, Illinois, agrees. "Hospice care," she emphasizes, "helps liberate patients from their afflictions of their symptoms so that they can truly live until they die."[56] Adds Nicholas Christakis, assistant professor of medicine and sociology at the University of Chicago, "Most people nowadays see two options: a medicalized, depersonalized and painful death in a hospital or a swift death that rejects medical institutions and technology."[57] This is a false choice, he notes; hospice offers a way out of this dilemma.

---

51. Pellegrino ("The Moral Status," 3) clearly sees this eventuality. Moral atrocity, it should be remembered, *does not happen overnight;* it is prepared by social and cultural currents. Therefore, the Christian community *must* be actively engaged in the great ethical debates of the day.

52. Cited in Joseph Loconte, "Hospice, Not Hemlock," *Policy Review,* March-April 1998, 41.

53. Loconte, "Hospice, Not Hemlock," 41.

54. Pellegrino, "Euthanasia and Assisted Suicide," 114.

55. Dyck, *Life's Worth,* 25-28.

56. Cited in Loconte, "Hospice, Not Hemlock," 41.

57. Cited in Loconte, "Hospice, Not Hemlock," 41.

Leon Kass, the respected bioethicist from the Committee on Social Thought at the University of Chicago who chaired the President's Council on Bioethics from 2002 to 2005, lauds the moral vision of the hospice movement that places the movement in diametric opposition to physician-assisted death: "Hospice borrows from a certain Judeo-Christian view of our obligations to suffering humanity. . . . It is the idea that company and care, rather than attempts at cure, are abiding human obligations. Those obligations are put to the severest test when the recipient of care is at his lowest and most unattractive."[58] Citing the unparalleled record of hospice programs and their compassionate end-of-life care for people with incurable diseases, Loconte believes that the hospice movement, with the palliative approach to medicine it represents, could revolutionize America's culture of dying.[59] Indeed, it is exhilarating to ponder what might result from the combined forces of the hospice movement and the Christian community, with its commitment to an enduring moral vision.

As people of faith we have a critical — indeed, an irreplaceable — role to fill in the public discussion of end-of-life matters. If the Christian community does not foster opposition to our "culture of death," no one will. Whence will come the moral argument to counter bioethicist John Harris, of the Institute of Medicine, Law and Bioethics, at the University of Manchester, who argues: "Persons who do not want to live are not . . . harmed by having their wish to die granted, through voluntary euthanasia for example. Nonpersons or potential persons cannot be wronged in this way because death does not deprive them of anything they can value. If they cannot wish to live, they cannot have that wish frustrated by being killed."[60] Opposition to death on demand must be the *corporate* expression of Protestants, Roman Catholics, and Orthodox working together with like-minded individuals in common-cause witness to our culture. We build on the natural-law assumption that human beings exist and persist

58. Cited in Loconte, "Hospice, Not Hemlock," 48.
59. Loconte, "Hospice, Not Hemlock," 42. Unquestionably, Oregon's Measure 16 will challenge hospice's identity and integrity. The roughly fifty individual hospice programs in the state that provide care to four or five thousand terminally ill Oregonians will be hard pressed not to abandon their commitment not to hasten death. The specific contours of these challenges were detailed by C. S. Campbell et al., in "Conflicts of Conscience: Hospice and Assisted Suicide," *Hastings Center Report*, May-June 1995, 36-43, before Measure 16 became official law; the challenges remain in force and serve to warn us.
60. Harris, "Concept of the Person," 308.

through procreation, moral formation, affirming life's sanctity, upholding basic (i.e., inalienable) human rights, and guarding the common good. At the same time, our passionate opposition to a culture of death, in which the redemptive character of suffering is fully denied, must be validated by compassionate action. Only then will there be sufficient reason to choose life, even in the face of present or future suffering.

John Paul's call in *Salvifici Doloris* is a call to learn how to "suffer well," in order that we might then minister to others who suffer.[61] This is, after all, the true nature of "compassion" (literally, "agonizing with") and "empathy" ("sharing in agony"). Pain, frailty, and deprivation need not lead us automatically to the place of depression or despondency. Suffering can be seen in a redemptive light only if it is infused with meaning, and clearly, such is impossible apart from faith in an all-wise, all-loving, all-powerful Creator to reenvision suffering. The conviction that there is a redemptive element in suffering requires a patient trust in God and a committing of ourselves into his merciful care.

Rethinking Freedom:
From Personal "Rights" to Moral Responsibility

Contemporary Rights Talk and Our "Pursuit of Happiness"

Based on the doctrine of creation, historic Christian theology, as we have sought to argue, affirms human personhood and moral agency based on the *imago Dei*. The dignity and sanctity of the human being, as a guiding principle in Christian social teaching, "leads to the full recognition of the dignity of each individual created in God's image. From this dignity flow natural rights and duties. In the light of the image of God, freedom, which is the essential prerogative of the human person, is manifested in all its depth."[62]

One of the hallmarks of contemporary Western culture is its accent on individual rights. While a rights-based political philosophy and jurisprudence is nothing new to Americans, what is relatively new is its extension and application to realms of social life that heretofore have been considered

---

61. On the process of learning how to "suffer well," see also the valuable discussion in Spitzer, Bernhoft, and De Blasi, *Healing the Culture,* 159-92.

62. Congregation for the Doctrine of the Faith, *Instruction on Christian Freedom and Liberation* (1986), no. 73.

merely personal or preferential. Aleksander Solzhenitsyn, in his historic speech at Harvard University in 1978, noted already that the defense of individual rights had reached "such extremes as to make society as a whole defenseless against certain individuals." Solzhenitsyn went on to assert: "It is time, in the West, to defend not so much human rights as human obligations."[63] Solzhenitsyn's prophetic outcry, which was not well received by our cultural gatekeepers, is in desperate need of an audience thirty years later.

Certainly, no one needs to be reminded of Americans' love affair with rights. But contemporary public discourse has become a veritable cacophony of rights claims, in a manner that might even stun Solzhenitsyn. What we currently face is not merely a "love" of rights but a rights "mania," as one social critic put it.[64] Which is to say, we are a people *obsessed* not merely with "rights" but with a particular understanding of "rights" that bears little resemblance to that of this nation's fathers and framers; it is to the exclusion of equal responsibilities. This obsession reflects itself in our chief mode of public discourse, what Mary Ann Glendon has called a "rights talk,"[65] and increasingly in our political debates, which typically in our day have come to be framed as clashes of rights. Unhappily, Americans' aggressive romance with personal rights, which columnist George Will has aptly described as "sharp elbows in an endless jostling for social space,"[66] erodes the language of community and virtue, breeding callousness toward others, civil discord, and ultimately damage to the social order. And as Carl Schneider has painfully observed, the deeply corrosive effect of rights trumping responsibility is *pervasive*, permeating not just our social relations but the realm of law as well as politics.[67] More often than not, this phenomenon manifests itself in the bestowal upon ourselves of *victimhood* status whenever those "rights" are violated. Thus, as Charles Sykes has described it, we are "a nation of victims," or in the words of

63. Ronald Berman, ed., *Solzhenitsyn at Harvard: The Address, Twelve Early Responses, and Six Later Reflections* (Washington, D.C.: Ethics and Public Policy Center, 1980), 8.

64. William A. Donohue, *The New Freedom: Individualism and Collectivism in the Social Lives of Americans* (New Brunswick, N.J.: Rutgers University Press, 1990), 26.

65. Mary Ann Glendon, *Rights Talk: The Impoverishment of Political Discourse* (New York: Free Press, 1991). Glendon's analysis of rights thinking can also be found in a predecessor volume, *Abortion and Divorce in Western Law.*

66. George F. Will, "Too Much of a Good Thing," *Newsweek,* September 23, 1991, 68.

67. Carl Schneider, "Talking about Rights," *Hastings Center Report,* May/June 1992, 43-44.

Christina Hoff Summers and Sally Satel more recently, "one nation under therapy," for whom the vocabulary of duties and moral responsibility is not merely foreign; it would seem nonexistent.[68]

This state of affairs would be utterly laughable were it not so deadly serious. For the maneuvering of rights-rhetoric into spheres well beyond the classical understanding of rights as *protection* or *liberties* carries enormous consequences, both philosophically and practically, insofar as "inalienable rights" as envisaged by this nation's founders and its constitutional framers were conceived of foremost with political tyranny in mind. Alas, the true victim in contemporary culture's obsession with personal "rights" is none other than the common good of our culture, and, a step further, what we want to bequeath to our children (and our children's children).

But what precisely is the genesis of this social development? For some such as Kenneth Grasso, our rights obsession originated in "Enlightenment liberalism," by which Grasso means a particular intellectual tradition that "originated in the seventeenth century and has since come to dominate modern Western political thought."[69] This he understands as the tradition that has been infused with the political theory of Hobbes, Locke, Kant, and others. While Grasso acknowledges that constitutional and limited government also proceed from this tradition, he believes that within the broader tradition are to be found *two distinct developments* calling for our discernment — rights orientation (a liberalism of the "sovereign self") and limited government ("integral liberalism").[70] What inspires the for-

---

68. Charles A. Sykes, *A Nation of Victims* (New York: Free Press, 1991); Christina Hoff Sommers and Sally Satel, *One Nation under Therapy: How the Helping Culture Is Eroding Self-Reliance* (New York: St. Martin's Press, 2005). Reader beware: the latter volume, although only 220 pages in length, nevertheless has 80 pages of notes. In this well-written cultural critique, the authors are highly critical of the "trauma industry" and coin a new word, "therapism," to depict a philosophy or way of life whereby humans are viewed as infinitely fragile and thus needing "experts" to walk them through the vicissitudes of everyday life.

69. Kenneth L. Grasso, "The Triumph of Will: Rights Mania, the Culture of Death, and the Crisis of Enlightenment Liberalism," in *Politics, Reason, and the Human Good: Essays in Honor of Francis Canavan*, ed. Kenneth L. Grasso and Robert P. Hunt (Wilmington, Del.: ISI Books, 2002), 222-23.

70. Grasso, "The Triumph of Will," 222-30. In a similar vein, James W. Skillen, *Recharging the American Experiment: Principled Pluralism for Genuine Civic Community* (Grand Rapids: Baker, 1994), 31, believes that the extent of the current moral-political-legal crisis arises from just this ambiguity of our nation's dual origins — Christian faith and the newer Enlightenment.

mer is liberalism's commitment to individual autonomy.[71] For by insisting that "any subjection to the will of another, to the will of any personal capricious authority" is "incompatible" with human dignity, liberalism, as interpreted by Grasso, "demanded freedom for each individual from other individuals, from the state, from every arbitrary will."[72] In consequence, the "pursuit of happiness," so central to the fathers of the American experiment, has been extended well beyond what is "self-evident" in nature.

But a strong qualification is in order. The "pursuit of happiness," it needs to be stressed, does not merely represent Jeffersonian rhetorical flourish. Rather, the content of the creed "life, liberty and the pursuit of happiness" was a profoundly moral basis by which men were to live and govern society. This reality, despite objections by postmodern theorists and legal-judicial activists in our own day, was for them beyond controversy. To the founders, "happiness" lay at the center of human existence and was rooted not merely in the private domain but also in public virtue and social duty. James Wilson, one of the architects of the Constitution, wrote in 1769 that the only reason men consented to have government was "with a view to ensure and to increase the happiness of the governed." The first law of every government, he insisted, was to preserve "the happiness of the society."[73] John Adams concurred: "Upon this point all . . . politicians will agree, that the happiness of society is the end of government."[74]

As to precisely what the founders meant by "happiness," Jefferson himself could hardly be clearer: "the happy man," he insisted, "must be virtuous: for without virtue, happiness cannot be." The right to the "pursuit of happiness," for Jefferson, ultimately sprang from the minimum right to live, which was the *absence of tyranny.* Jefferson realized that "hap-

71. In terms similar to those of Grasso, Leonard Fortin identifies "political hedonism" as that which characterizes the shift in Western intellectual thought. See his essay "The Natural Wrong in Natural Rights," *Crisis,* May 1994, 20-25.

72. So, John H. Hallowell, *The Doctrine of Liberalism as an Ideology* (reprint, New York: Howard Fertig, 1971), 5-33. Grasso also cites, inter alia, Michael Walzer, "The Communitarian Critique of Liberalism," *Political Theory* 18 (February 1990): 14-15, and Michael Sandel, *Democracy's Discontent: America in Search of a Public Philosophy* (Cambridge: Harvard University Press, 1996), in support of his own construal of liberalism.

73. "Considerations on the Nature and the Extent of Legislative Authority of the British Parliament," cited in Carl L. Becker, *The Declaration of Independence: A Study in the History of Political Ideas* (New York: Vintage, 1958), 108.

74. "Thoughts on Government," cited in Michael White, *Philosophers of the American Revolution* (New York: Oxford University Press, 1978), 233.

piness" as construed by some of the ancient philosophers could be inherently *antisocial.* Epicureans, for example, stressed pleasure as happiness and a concomitant avoidance of pain. But the Epicurean outlook might cause one to withdraw from society. Therefore, happiness must be virtuous and it must involve people, being consciously *social* in its character. One's individual freedoms cannot threaten the minimum rights to life and liberty of another; otherwise, the other's well-being is invaded.

The stress in classical thought placed on reasoned moral judgment as a precondition for "freedom" mirrored the concern to educate and refine the passions so that passion would not dominate and misguide the intellect. As affirmed in the Declaration of Independence, "prudence . . . will dictate" according to what "all experience hath shown." By contrast, the contemporary understanding of "freedom" results in the promotion of an impulse-seeking liberation from cultural "taboos," normative traditions, and societal restraints on the passions.

In the previous three decades American culture has been witness to the extension of rights language by persons and minority social groups to previously unexplored territories. Some of these realms are less innocuous than others; they include: privacy (as in abortion and homosexuality), contraception,[75] free speech (as in pornography), consumer affairs, education, employment, the environment, even the "right" to die. More recently, obesity as a disability and universal health care have been added to this ever-expanding list, thereby introducing some new and intriguing questions into the sphere of public discourse. Does a person have a *right* to employment in spite of poor dietary habits or morbid obesity? To protection against unexpected health crises or even untimely death? Are rights being violated when a child is born with a disability? When kidneys fail? When cancer takes its toll?

Unhappily, if something tragic occurs in our lives, instead of the community rushing to help meet the need, we are increasingly inclined to search in our outrage for a source — *any* source — of identifiable blame.[76] So, for example, when anything unfortunate occurs in the world, it is automatically attributed to someone — someone *else,* that is. Bad moral choices? Blame it on the parents or a traumatic childhood, if not a defec-

---

75. The Supreme Court determined in 1972 that unmarried women had a "right" to birth control.

76. With wit yet sobriety, Wilfred M. McClay has described this disposition in "Mastery's Anger," *Touchstone,* November 2005, 16-18.

tive gene or invasive circumstances. Hurricanes devastating the Gulf Coast? Blame it on the president. And murder? Well, blame it on the knife.

From Freedom to Social-Political Tyranny

But something deeper seems to be at work. The perversion of personal freedoms as "rights," with its twin need to find eternal "blame," is seen by John Paul II as the fruit of a false — i.e., absolute — view of *autonomy* that corrupts society as a whole. If the promotion of the self is understood in terms of absolute autonomy,

> people inevitably reach the point of rejecting one another. Everyone else is considered an enemy from whom one has to defend oneself. Thus society becomes a mass of individuals placed side by side, but without mutual bonds. . . . In this way, any reference to common values and to a truth absolutely binding on everyone is lost and social life ventures onto the shifting sands of complete relativism. At that point, everything is negotiable, everything is open to bargaining: even the first of the fundamental rights, the right to life.[77]

In our cultural tradition, however, until relatively recently rights have been thought of chiefly as an endowment, even when secular Enlightenment thinkers such as Rousseau and Paine attributed such endowments to "Nature" or "Reason." It should be emphasized that the common-law tradition, of which we are beneficiaries, is based on the "reason" not of isolated self-interest but of intergenerational wisdom and experience — recall the framers' language: as "all experience hath shown." This collective human wisdom is reflected not only in the Declaration of Independence but also in the Federalist Papers and the Constitution. A conspicuous feature of these documents is the perspective that is simultaneously aware of a conscious debt owed to the past and yet able to adapt to the changing needs of the present.[78] The "new rights" mentality, by contrast, is markedly "postconstitutional," in the view of Constitutional scholar Harvey Mansfield,[79] for it ignores the

77. *EV,* nos. 19-20.
78. This dual perspective has been argued quite persuasively by Mary Ann Glendon, "Tradition and Creativity in Culture and Law," *First Things,* November 1992, 13-15.
79. Harvey Mansfield, "Responsibility versus Self-Expression," in *Old Rights and New,* ed. Robert A. Licht (Washington, D.C.: American Enterprise Institute, 1993), 108.

fund of collective human wisdom and "what experience hath shown." Natural rights are those abiding endowments — inalienable and thus universal — upon which civil society rests, and civil rights are the procurement of natural rights. Therefore, what is urgently needed in our day, though it is denied or resisted tooth and nail by cultural deconstructionists, is a *recoupling* of "civil rights" to *natural rights,* a theoretical process that will purge society of a prostituted understanding and application of "rights."

As endowments that support basic human liberty, natural rights are universally applicable, and therefore "absolute," furnishing society with the social conditions necessary to carry out its responsibilities to its members. While the emphasis on rights preserves individual autonomy, this autonomy is not absolute; rather, it is limited, for it is not permitted to violate what is fundamentally "human." Moreover, because rights are meaningful only in a *social* context, every right imposes on others some form of obligation.[80] Obligations toward one's neighbor, after all, lie at the heart of the Christian gospel. While the subject of human rights is beyond the scope of our discussion, "human rights" properly construed constitute an important aspect of the Christian church's social witness.[81] Viewed historically, a proper rights perspective lay at the center of the common-law tradition, which was indispensable in preserving English society from various forms of social-political tyranny that had managed to spread across continental Europe.[82]

With the dust of the French Revolution still settling, the Frenchman Alexis de Tocqueville, in his visit to America in the early 1830s, reflected on the *process* of moving from freedom and "rights" to sociopolitical tyranny.

80. See Karol Wojtyla, "The Person: Subject and Community," *Crisis,* May 1994, 39-43, and David Brodeur, "The Rights Debate," *Health Progress,* June 1990, 48-51, both of whom, from differing angles, press this important argument.

81. For a useful, when very concise, statement on the relationship between human rights and the church's witness to the world, see John A. Lapp, "Human Rights: An Agenda for the Church," in *In Search of a National Morality,* 235-45.

82. The student of history will not fail to note the relationship between a bloated doctrine of rights (over against *duties*) and the totalitarian suppression of liberties that can follow. This correlation is evident, notably, both in France, where 1789 marked the publication of *The Rights of Man* as well as the eruption of events leading to the Revolution, and in Russia, where the late-nineteenth- and early-twentieth-century agitation by intellectuals culminated in the Bolshevik uprising. Revolutionaries — be they social, political, or aesthetic — are driven to overturn conventional forms of authority. Hence, always associated with revolutionary causes will be a parallel hostility directed toward the Judeo-Christian tradition and its purported "dehumanizing" strictures placed on human behavior.

He posed what is perhaps the question of the hour for Americans living at the entrance of the twenty-first century: "What now remains of those barriers which formerly arrested the aggression of tyranny?"[83] His answer is worth pondering: "[When] religion has lost its empire over the souls of men, the most prominent boundary which divides good from evil is overthrown; the very elements of the moral world are indeterminate; the princes and the peoples of the earth are guided by chance, and none can define the natural limits of despotism and the bounds of license."[84]

Tocqueville proceeds to trace the features of social despotism where they appear in the world. His initial diagnosis is telling. "The first thing that strikes the observation is an innumerable multitude of men all equal and alike, incessantly endeavoring to procure the petty and paltry pleasures with which they glut their lives. Each of them, living apart, is as a stranger to the fate of all the rest . . . ; as for the rest of his fellow-citizens, he . . . sees them not; he exists but in himself and for himself alone."[85] Tocqueville concludes with a noteworthy observation: "I believe that it is easier to establish an absolute and despotic government among a people in which the conditions of society are equal than among any other; and I think that if such a government were once established among such a people, it would not only oppress men, but would eventually strip each of them of several of the highest qualities of humanity."[86] Why in Tocqueville's thinking might a worse — that is, a more oppressive — social condition arise out of *a former climate of freedom and equality?* This is a striking assertion. Perhaps because unrestrained individualism and radical antinomianism breed a descending form of social chaos that inevitably leads to tyranny, wherein *all vestiges of tradition must be eradicated.* Thus, for Tocqueville, it would seem, any doctrine of "rights" not held in check by an equal or greater counterbalance of responsibilities contains the seeds of self-destruction, inasmuch as it will seek the legitimation of inherently anarchistic and evil demands.

83. We do well to remember that Tocqueville came from a Catholic family that barely survived the terror of the Revolution. He realized that once religious conviction and loyalties are shattered, nothing remains that can stand erect to prevent political tyranny. Whether the tyranny comes from this or that side of the state apparatus is immaterial.

84. Alexis de Tocqueville, *Democracy in America*, trans. H. Reeve (London: Oxford University Press, 1965), 256.

85. Tocqueville, *Democracy in America*, 256.

86. Tocqueville, *Democracy in America*, 583.

Moreover, those who institute and institutionalize tyranny envision their rule as "salvific." Thereby transcendent standards for law are suspended while temporary-arbitrary law is absolutized. As Hannah Arendt pointed out half a century ago in *The Origins of Totalitarianism,* when National Socialists talked about the "law of nature" or the Bolsheviks talked about history, neither nature nor history was in any way a stabilizing or restraining force. "Nature" and "history" effectively become what the *nomenklatura* wish. This pattern, as Arendt saw it, is reoccurring.

While it is true, as Kenneth Grasso argues, that Enlightenment thinking had the effect of eroding the language of moral reasoning because of the place accorded individual rights, Jefferson — along with many of the founders — understood "happiness" in philosophical rather than psychological terms. Utility and personal rights were meaningful to the extent that they were undergirded by public *virtue.* The shift from a philosophical to a psychological understanding of "happiness" begins to emerge in the late 1800s — a shift from "religious man" to "psychological man" that sociologist Philip Rieff, writing in the 1960s, observes to be complete.[87]

It goes without saying that we are presently reaping the full effects of the *radical self* — the autonomous psychologized self — in social and public policy. One only wonders what Philip Rieff might say today, four decades removed from the time at which he declared "the triumph of the therapeutic."

Freedom, in the end, if rooted in autonomy, ends up *establishing the truth* rather than *being governed* by it.[88] This, of course, has profound implications for the epistemological status of moral knowledge. Hereby the naturalists among us make moral judgments not on the basis of metaphysical realities but on the grounds of human achievement and human desires, in the end creating a subjectivity of values and consequent nihilism. Ultimately, this brand of liberalism, owing to a "radical antinomianism,"[89] rejects any notion of a morally binding order.

Against the cultural flow, John Paul counters that "every man *is* his 'brothers' keeper,' because God entrusts us to one another. And it is also in

87. Philip Rieff, *The Triumph of the Therapeutic: Uses of Faith after Freud* (New York: Harper and Row, 1966).

88. Here Grasso is citing Francis Canavan, "The Empiricist Mind," *Human Life Review* 25 (1999): 78-79.

89. This term is owing to Jean Bethke Elshtain, "Democratic Authority at Century's End," *Hedgehog Review,* Spring 2000, 30.

view of this entrusting that God gives everyone freedom, a freedom which possesses an inherently relational dimension."[90] Faithful living, therefore, as John Paul conceives it, consists "not simply in acquiring an abstract knowledge of the truth, but in a dynamic relationship of faithful self-giving with others."[91]

It is in this light, according to law professor Charles Rice, that we are to understand the fallacy of generic "pro-choice" thinking in our day, for its premises inter alia deny that humans are *social* creatures *by nature.* Consequently, the mother is thought to be an autonomous individual without duty owed to her child or others, except as she *chooses* to consent. Marriage, likewise, implies no inherent stability of relationship; rather, it is up to each partner in the arrangement to decide whether the relationship will be monogamous or adulterous, permanent or temporary. The goal is self-fulfillment of the isolated individual, unencumbered by any inherent duties or relations to others. But if human beings *by nature* stand in relationship to one another, the autonomous individual, who has no responsibility or openness to others except by his own unrestricted choice, is not merely unattractive, as Rice insists, but truly *unhuman.*[92]

Rice is simply underscoring the social dimensions of Christian theology: we have been created in the likeness of the Persons of the Trinity, and thus are not isolated, alienated individuals. We are persons who stand in relation and close proximity to other humans. John Paul concurs: "When man does not recognize in himself and in others the value and grandeur of the human person, he effectively deprives himself of the possibility of benefiting from his humanity and of entering into that relationship of solidarity and communion with others for which God created him. . . . A man is alienated if he refuses to transcend himself and to live the experience of self-giving and of formation of an authentic human community."[93]

In the current cultural climate, the distinction between "inalienable" rights and personal wants or "needs" has been virtually obliterated. By its

---

90. Elshtain, "Democratic Authority," 29, emphasis added.

91. *Fides et Ratio*, no. 32. Charles Rice helpfully draws out the practical implications of the Catholic Church's social teaching in terms of solidarity and subsidiarity over against human autonomy. See *50 Questions on the Natural Law: What It Is and Why It Is Needed*, rev. ed. (San Francisco: Ignatius, 1999), 247-83.

92. Rice, *50 Questions*, 266.

93. *Centesimus Annus*, no. 41.

removal of the social stigma often associated with charity or unmerited favor, contemporary rights talk enshrines the self at the center of the moral universe, unencumbered by moral-social obligations. Forgotten is the role of duties, the foundation upon which any culture survives. Duty before pleasure, a familiar proverb to a previous generation, has become a quaint — and doubtless embarrassing — reminder of things past.

This strain of amnesia, however, is far from innocent. It has a darker side that in its purest form calls into question the most elementary assumptions about human life. The volatile mix of moral relativism, advances in medical and scientific technology, and disintegration of the family as a caring and cohesive social unity does not bode well for American society, apart from cultural rejuvenation. Americans are finding themselves confronted with, if they are not themselves appropriating, even the ultimate in rights claims — the "right to die." This invasion of rights rhetoric into the realm of the sacred calls for a profound response, toward which the following chapter is devoted.

A fusion of freedom and responsibility is the only "mix" that will permit a distinctly free society to remain genuinely "free" — and civil — and conduct its political life in a way that respects human freedom.[94] Authentic freedom is a "freedom for," which stands in contradistinction to a "freedom from." That is, human beings are truly *free* when they *choose* to serve and build the capacities of others rather than using their "freedom" as a pretext to ignore or obliterate moral obligations and restraints. Authentic freedom is conspicuously *proactive* rather than *reactive*.[95] Only through the former can any commitment to others arise; only through the former can civil society truly remain "civil." If freedom *from* restraints becomes the dominant mode by which a culture interprets its liberties, the basic social institutions of the culture, in the end, will no longer be tolerated. Gone is *any* understanding of the common good.

---

94. This is the argument advanced by Jean Bethke Elshtain in an essay titled "Politics without Cliché," originally published in *Social Research* 60, no. 3 (Fall 1993) and reproduced in Elshtain, *Real Politics*, 3-11, wherein she reflects on the differences between democracy and totalitarianism.

95. Spitzer, Bernhoft, and De Blasi, *Healing the Culture*, 209-12, develop this distinction most helpfully.

CHAPTER SEVEN

Contending for Moral First Things
in Ethical and Bioethical Debates:
Critical Categories — Part 2

The Common Good:
Reaffirming Our Commitment to Our Neighbor and Civil Society

Christian Social Morality

Moral principle will find its application to society's moral quandaries not in philosophical abstraction, important as "abstracting" at the philosophical level may be. Rather, it will occur relationally, by people working with other people. But how precisely do we as people of faith proceed? What does the Christian propose for society? What principles inform the Christian's view of society, and by what strategies do we attempt moral persuasion? For some, at the most fundamental level, it is unclear, perhaps even dubious, whether Christians have a stake in how society operates. And if we do not propose a "Christian society" per se, how do we leaven culture, bringing moral truth to bear without succumbing to either the theocratic, the isolationist, or the accommodationist distortions?

The supreme principle of Christian social morality is the great commandment of neighbor love.[1] From the Christian standpoint, love proceeds not merely from obedience but also from a high view of personhood.

---

1. One might argue that the different precepts of the Decalogue, which are social in nature, are simply different ways of expressing neighbor love.

Therefore, issuing out of the Christian view of the human person is a proper vision of human society. For this reason, inextricably linked to the presumption of human *dignity* not only in the teaching of John Paul II, highlighted in previous chapters, but also in Catholic social ethics in general are the principles of solidarity and subsidiarity,[2] or in more Protestant language, the idea of covenant.[3] By virtue of the first, "man with his brothers is obliged to contribute to the common good of society at all its levels."[4] The Christian church, consequently, should be opposed to extreme forms of individualism, since they violate the social nature of human beings. By virtue of the second, "neither the state nor any society must ever substitute for the initiative and responsibility of individuals and of intermediate communities at the level on which they can function, nor must they take away the room necessary for their freedom."[5] For this reason, as well, the church should oppose all forms of collectivism.

The common good may be properly defined as the sum total of social conditions that allow people, whether as groups or as individuals, to reach their fulfillment as human beings within society.[6] Thus, it is concerned to protect all people. The *Catechism of the Catholic Church* lists three components to the common good:

1. First, the common good presupposes respect for the person as such. In the name of the common good, public authorities are bound to

---

2. See the *Catechism of the Catholic Church* (Washington, D.C.: U.S. Catholic Conference, 1994) (hereafter *CCC*), nos. 1939-42 and 1894.

3. So, for example, Max L. Stackhouse, "Broken Covenants: A Threat to Society?" in *Judgment at the White House: A Critical Declaration Exploring Moral Issues and the Political Use and Abuse of Religion*, ed. Gabriel Fackre (Grand Rapids and Cambridge, U.K.: Eerdmans, 1999), 18-27, who examines the political and moral implications of public covenants broken at the highest level of politics in the United States during the 1990s. This volume, regardless of one's political orientation, remains extremely useful because of the manner in which it demonstrates how politics expresses our moral commitments. This volume should be required reading for all teachers of religion and ethics.

4. Congregation for the Doctrine of the Faith, *Instruction on Christian Freedom and Liberation*, no. 73.

5. Congregation for the Doctrine of the Faith, *Instruction*, no. 73.

6. So John Finnis, *Natural Law and Natural Rights*, Clarendon Law Series (Oxford: Clarendon, 1980), 155. Human goods identified by Finnis that comprise the common good might include knowledge, gainful employment, recreation, spirituality and worship, security, friendship, and aesthetics (60-90).

respect the fundamental and inalienable rights of the human person. (no. 1907)

2. Second, the common good requires the social well-being and development of the group itself. Development is the epitome of all social duties. Certainly . . . it should make accessible to each what is needed to lead a truly human life: food, clothing, health, work, education and culture, suitable information, the right to establish a family, and so on. (no. 1908)

3. Finally, the common good requires peace, that is, the stability and security of a just order. It presupposes that authority should ensure by morally acceptable means the security of society and its members. It is the basis of the right to legitimate personal and collective defence. (no. 1909)

One notable feature in the writings of John Paul II, particularly of those published during the 1990s, was his ability simultaneously to critique totalitarianism, which he knew intimately in his lifetime, as well as the thinly veiled totalitarian spirit in Western democratic nations that results from the toxic mix of democratic pluralism and moral relativism. Not surprisingly, John Paul gave considerable attention to the natural moral law. Through rational, philosophical reflection, he maintained, humans discern objective moral criteria. This discernment, in accordance with Christian moral understanding, arises from *our very nature* as moral creatures in the image of God, not merely from philosophical abstraction.[7]

Notably in *Veritatis Splendor,* the former pontiff argues for the necessity of objective moral norms. Without such recognition, freedom and a "genuine democracy" are illusory, and in time this tyranny of the majority becomes oppressive. John Paul is adamant that there can be "no freedom apart from or in opposition to the truth,"[8] for "as history demonstrates, a democracy without values easily turns into open or thinly disguised totalitarianism" (no. 101). Only through "obedience to universal moral norms

---

7. Few have demonstrated so lucidly the role that natural revelation and the natural law play as J. Budziszewski, *Written on the Heart: The Case for Natural Law* (Downers Grove, Ill.: InterVarsity, 1997), and Charles E. Rice, *50 Questions on the Natural Law: What It Is and Why It Is Needed,* rev. ed. (San Francisco: Ignatius, 1999).

8. *Veritatis Splendor* (hereafter *VS*), no. 96. References to the encyclical are placed in the text.

does man find full confirmation of his personal uniqueness and the possibility of authentic moral growth" (no. 101).[9]

Because human rights belong to *persons,* any discussions of "rights" are meaningless apart from a nonfluid — i.e., objective — understanding of personhood. And because one's understanding of "the common good" depends on one's view of rights, the common good in a society stands or falls on society's views of personhood and rights. It follows, then, that where universal moral truths are not acknowledged, persons and human rights will suffer. Human "persons," as we have sought to define them, possess inalienable rights due to the fact of their dignity. This conviction, of course, stands at odds with contemporary usage of the term "rights" — First Amendment rights, abortion rights, privacy rights, the right to die — which are vying for public sanction. But can Christians enter into public debate and require that "rights" be not only defined but also substantiated?

Freedom, John Paul warns, does not extend to the toleration of intrinsic evil, and where the denial of universal moral truth is permitted to exist, the result is that "law" is reduced to a function of "raw, totalitarian power" (nos. 96 and 99). It matters not "whether one is the master of the world or the 'poorest of the poor' on the face of the earth. Before the demands of morality, we are all absolutely equal" (no. 96). How, John Paul asks, shall a society govern itself without recourse to universal moral values? And how are government and the state to be conceived? If there is no ultimate truth to guide and direct political activity, he cautions, then ideas and convictions can easily be manipulated for reasons of power (no. 101).

Responsible Citizenship and the Civic Arena

Democratic culture has been a *wager,* not a frozen accomplishment, writes Jean Elshtain in her book *Real Politics.* It has been a wager "[f]rom Jefferson's bold throwing down of the gauntlet to the British Empire, not know-

---

9. Much of chapter 5 was devoted to a proper understanding of law and its importance for human community, regardless of where it is found. In the argument of Thomas Aquinas for preserving the common good (see especially *ST* I-II Q. 90), law is an instrument of reason to measure human acts; it has both *an inducing* and *a restraining* function. Law exists for the community's common good. Hereon see as well Mark C. Murphy, "The Common Good," *Review of Metaphysics* 59, no. 1 (September 2005): 133-37, wherein Thomistic understanding of the common good is applied to the political community.

ing whether the upshot would be 'hanging together or hanged separately,' to Lincoln's 'nation thus conceived and thus dedicated,' to Martin Luther King's dream of an essentially pacific democratic people who judge their fellow citizens by the content of the character [and] not the color of their skins."[10] Hereby Elshtain wishes to underscore the importance of participation. Responsible citizenship, as the reader will discover, is a recurring theme in Elshtain's writings, and as an Augustinian scholar, she is ever conscious of the tension between faith and culture that imbues the work of this church father. Augustine, of course, lived at a time very much like our own, a time of considerable social and ideological upheaval. Indeed, culture was literally crumbling before his eyes while he penned *De civitate Dei*. An important subtheme in much of Augustine's work, not only in *De civitate,* is the tension between our earthly and heavenly citizenship. Where our loyalties are challenged by compromise, where the possibility of idolatry is present, our ultimate allegiance is always to the heavenly city. However, as Christians we retain dual citizenship, a reality implying that we are obligated to balance — rather than eradicate — the tension between our duties in both realms, since duties to both are divinely bequeathed.

The obligation to "occupy" responsibly, of course, is not an easy word for fundamentalist, pietist, or isolationist types to bear. Nor does it soothe cultural accommodationists, i.e., those who yearn for culture's acceptance. To occupy responsibly requires of us spiritual discernment. As Christians we are required by faith to eschew the twin errors of isolation and capitulation as they relate to faith and culture. On the one hand, we reject the outlook that faith and culture or politics or social involvement have little or nothing to do with one another. This is the later-Tertullian error. On the other hand, we are equally attentive to the idolatry that conflates faith and culture, politics, or society. Both stances are idolatrous; both require our constant vigilance.[11]

It is to this Augustinian burden, namely, to avoid both the flight from culture and an absorption into culture, that much of Elshtain's work is devoted. And this to her credit. Hence, we should not be surprised that the

---

10. Jean Bethke Elshtain, *Real Politics: At the Center of Everyday Life* (Baltimore and London: Johns Hopkins University Press, 1997), 363.

11. Elsewhere I have attempted to apply the Augustinian outlook on citizenship to the problem of justice, war, and peace. See J. Daryl Charles, *Between Pacifism and Jihad: Just War and Christian Tradition* (Downers Grove, Ill.: InterVarsity, 2005), 37-45.

strand of responsible citizenship laces its way through much of Elshtain's work.

The robust spiritedness of democratic culture, by its very nature and from its origin, requires our active engagement to distinguish itself — and remain distinguished — from other forms of political organization that tend toward tyranny. While certainly one cannot participate in all aspects of civic life, neither is one permitted to remain aloof and isolated from that civic life in which he or she is embedded. For to do so is to forfeit, over time, the climate that permits — indeed, fosters — those benefits and advantages of a democratic versus dictatorial system.

Correlatively, and importantly, belonging to such a social system requires the balancing of freedoms and responsibilities. Unquestionably, this runs counter to the cultural Zeitgeist, given that rights and freedoms always trump duties in the present social-political climate. Nevertheless, to acknowledge our moral accountability to an authority higher than self, to live in the shadow and circumference of self-evident "truths," is to embrace our responsibility toward our neighbor. This responsibility is not *actualized* in the prayer closet, important as prayer for the neighbor might be. While social responsibility should be second nature to all people espousing Christian faith, many professing Christians remain remarkably disengaged from public service, even when, to be sure, this "service" can take an infinite number of forms.[12] Not only is this service to others the evidence of true religion (cf., e.g., James 1:27), it is also the prerequisite for maintaining the underpinnings of the democratic social order.

For Elshtain, a political ethicist, our willingness to participate in the civic arena and our ability to balance rights with responsibilities are assured only if we are a people who live with hope. But what does it mean to live in hope? While optimism seeks to ensure that everything will turn out right or that all our problems are solvable, hope — a "theological" virtue — urges us to "a different stance, one aware of human sin and shortcoming but aware also of our capacities for stewardship and decency"; it also creates within us an "openness to grace."[13] And because hope alone will "sustain critical and constructive civic projects" in a manner that will

---

12. One readily thinks, for example, of the disengagement of fundamentalists and a rather large sector of Protestant evangelicalism.

13. Jean Bethke Elshtain, *Who Are We? Critical Reflections and Hopeful Possibilities* (Grand Rapids and Cambridge, U.K.: Eerdmans, 2000), 127.

"promote our collective well-being as a people," whether or not one claims to be "Christian," there are indispensable cultural tasks for which Christians in particular are well suited.[14]

Telling the Truth

One of these tasks, Elshtain believes, is to speak truthfully, that is, to *name* things accurately, honestly, and appropriately. This, of course, will require that we go against the deceptive and illusory spirit of our times and its "radical alteration in language, understanding, and meaning."[15] What does it mean to name things correctly? To illustrate, in the ethical realm as it touches personhood it means that we will expose society's attempts to speak of death and dying euphemistically — for example, in terms of "merciful release," "exit preference," or "death with dignity." It will concomitantly reject the language of "compassion" when applied to killing the unborn, the helpless, the handicapped neonate, and other imperfect humans. Furthermore, it will not sanction the language of "choice" for "a nigh-unlimited 'right' to withdraw the boundary of moral concern from unborn children at any stage of fetal development."[16] Nor will it countenance use of the term "liberation" to disguise our selfishly conceived "freedom" from any social or ethical commitments.[17]

With good reason, in my view, Elshtain is particularly exercised to observe — and decry — the role of linguistic prostitution in destabilizing society. In fact, it has played a critical role in preparing the soil for, and supporting, totalitarian regimes in our not-so-distant past. The sort of critical reflection that calls us to contemplate the roots of cultural demise, while it may strike some as unpleasant, unnecessary, or alarmist, is an indispensable part of living in a fallen world and *need not negate our living hope.* Avoiding the opposing tendencies of cultural withdrawal and cultural capitulation, it wrestles with what the present generation would bequeath to future generations.

As the historical record shows, the power to control language and subvert the meaning of words has inevitably presaged the covering of

---

14. Elshtain, *Who Are We?* 127.
15. Elshtain, *Who Are We?* 128.
16. Elshtain, *Who Are We?* 132.
17. Elshtain, *Who Are We?* 132.

moral atrocity and mass murder with the rhetoric of "improvement of the race" and even "mercy and compassion." It could never happen in our society? This is perhaps unbounded optimism. To the extent that we as a society allow truth to be trimmed to suit political-ideological ends, to the extent that we permit falsehood privately and publicly to be enshrined, we open ourselves to the totalitarian tendency. Not only should this be George Orwell's burden, it should be ours as well.[18] But what *was* Orwell's burden?

A basic premise of Orwell set forth both in his essay "Politics and the English Language" and in the novel *1984* was that human nature can be modified and manipulated through external means. While this ulterior manipulation does not reconstitute "being" in its essence, it does dull one's cognitive and moral senses, one's ability to reflect, and therefore one's ability to act "freely" as a moral agent. The moral dimensions of linguistic-ideological manipulation in *1984*, which in no way are intended to reflect any sort of religious commitment in Orwell (who was agnostic), raise profoundly religious questions nonetheless — questions that relate to the sacred character of human nature. On display in *1984* are competing worldviews that vie for the mental habits of the inhabitants of Oceania.

The "sacred principles" of Ingsoc that are devised to meet the ideological needs of the ruling Party are "Newspeak," "Doublethink," and the "mutability of the past." A supremely useful Party slogan — employed repeatedly throughout the novel — expresses the indivisible link between language and how people perceive reality: "Who controls the past controls the future, and who controls the present controls the past." Accordingly, the past is continuously altered, part of the main character Winston Smith's job in Minitrue ("The Ministry of Truth"), with history being rewritten to meet the demands of the regime.

As noted Orwell scholar Richard Bailey has pointed out, nothing is more central to the definition of "Orwellian" than the deliberate manipulation of language to serve the ends of obscurantism, propaganda, and mind control.[19] The enduring value of *1984* lies in its graphic portrayal of a society in which people exchange their freedoms for the enslavement of an unreflective acceptance of politically orthodox thoughts. This enslavement

18. See in this regard J. Daryl Charles, "The New Verbal Order," *Modern Age* 38, no. 4 (Fall 1996): 321-31. Portions of that discussion are used with permission.

19. Richard Bailey, "George Orwell and the English Language," in *The Future of "Nineteen Eighty-Four,"* ed. E. J. Jensen (Ann Arbor: University of Michigan Press, 1984), 30.

is facilitated by a "centralized" language that has been emptied of meaning, nuance, and creativity.

Perhaps the reader, at this point, might object that my accent on language here is exaggerated. Writing already three decades earlier on the "crisis" of language, the meaning of words and truth, one theologian objected to the cultural drift in this way: "Few times in history has revealed religion been forced to contend with such serious problems of truth and word, and never in the past have the role of words and the nature of truth been as misty and undefined as now. Only if we recognize that the truth of truth — indeed, the meaning of meaning — is today in doubt, and that this uncertainty stifles the word as the carrier of God's truth and moral judgment, do we fathom the depth of the present crisis."[20] It stands to follow that when truth and the meaning of words abide as the standard currency of public discourse, then linguistic-ideological aberrations can be met and effectively challenged. When, however, the very nature of truth and discourse is in dispute, as it is today, a collapse in verbal communication ensues, and with it — over time — the social order that is necessary to any free society.

Language — and with it, reflective thought — is what sets apart humans from animals. It is the basis for and vehicle through which human existence is interpreted. The word, as defined by the linguist, becomes the starting point of ontological strategy. In theological terms, the unknowable God chooses, by his creative *dabar*, to make himself known, and does so by employing the highest human faculty. As a reflection of the fact that language mirrors a basic order in creation, it is not surprising that one of the first recorded tasks in the creation account of Genesis is Adam's classifying of the animals. This story underscores both the dignity and separateness of the human and conveys the significance of language. "In the beginning was the *logos*," the NT writer asserts. Correctly viewed, language is a mirror of divinity, a spark of the divine nature residing in the human community. It transcends mere physical phenomena and hence is metaphysical and sacramental in nature.

For this reason the mutilation of language and thought constitutes an important and early lesson in biblical history, represented by the Babel narrative. Note the divine response to the human undertaking: "This is only the beginning of what they will do, and nothing will be impossible for

---

20. Carl F. H. Henry, *God, Revelation, and Authority*, vol. 1, *God Who Speaks and Shows* (Waco: Word, 1976), 24.

them" (Gen. 11:6). The Babel narrative is instructive in that it teaches us that language becomes the tool by which humans strive for autonomy and sovereignty. Is it perhaps possible that no generation since Babel has encountered so ponderous a crisis in communication as ours?[21] Not for nothing has John Paul II commented, "We need now more than ever to have the courage to look the truth in the eye and to call things by their proper name, without yielding to convenient compromises or to the temptation of self-deception."[22]

Given the deconstructive tendencies in both academic culture and culture at large, it is worth considering how the manipulation of language, meaning, and conceptual truth — whether consciously or unconsciously — is a reflection of one's worldview or life view. To dismantle language and the meaning of words, either for political or ideological purposes, is to dismantle personhood and thus alter the *imago Dei*. To alter the creator-creature relationship is to alter the way in which people perceive divine authority, and in the end, *all* authority. Thus, for Walker Percy, linguistic deconstruction represented an attempt to eradicate God by first disposing of grammar.[23] For Jacques Ellul, words stripped of meaning are at the service of propaganda and falsehood.[24] For A.-A. Upinsky, deconstructing language is a precursor to the deconstruction of the entire living being.[25] In its bald essence, linguistic deconstruction represents the attempt — irrespective of its provenance — to eliminate structures of authority and as such is fundamental to the undermining of cultural institutions that prevent social fluidity.[26]

Although most proponents of radical change would stop short of conceding such, social anarchy is a necessary and inevitable consequence of philosophical and cultural deconstruction. In one form or another, deconstruction is inherent in all radical movements, regardless of their polit-

---

21. In "The New Verbal Order," especially 324-27, I endeavor to assess the mutilation of language and thought in the academic context.

22. *EV,* no. 58.

23. Jay Tolson, *Pilgrim in the Ruins: A Life of Walker Percy* (New York: Norton, 1993), 460.

24. Jacques Ellul, *The Humiliation of the Word,* trans. C. Hanks (Grand Rapids: Eerdmans, 1985), 158.

25. Arnaud-Aaron Upinsky, *La Tête Coupée ou la Parole Coupée* (Paris: OEIL, 1991), 12-36.

26. That is to say, society must be able to define, linguistically, its moral limits in order to avoid a state of anarchy and collapse.

ical orientation, for it is critical to the fomenting of revolutionary social change.[27] One need only consider how language today is trimmed and tailored to suit particular ideological needs in contemporary ethical and bioethical debates. For example, indicative of the government's stake in health care or regulating the economy, taxes become "sacrifice" and health care becomes a "universal crisis." The politicization of disease control becomes "AIDS awareness" and "comprehensive sex education." Correlatively, people of principle become "bigots," "extremists," or religious "fundamentalists," while openness to all ideas — including heinous evil — becomes "tolerance" or "progressive thinking." Suicide, increasingly sanitized, becomes "death with dignity," while one's "exit preference" becomes legally protected by the "right to die."

Significantly, much of the terminology being employed by our "culture of death" has a pronounced antiseptic medical quality. Writes William Brennan, "The contemporary medicalization of destruction — killing portrayed as medical treatment designed to eradicate individuals defined as disease entities — has become a deeply entrenched form of discourse dominating scientific conference and leading medical journals."[28] And John Paul II, in commenting that Cain tries to cover up his crime with a lie, observes that his killing of his brother "is a page rewritten daily."[29]

Of course, the possibilities for transmuting language are endless and invite ingenuity. Totalitarian regimes become "oligarchies," while hate-spewing guerrilla terrorists become "freedom fighters" (a generation ago) or "marginalized peoples" (today). Intellectual promiscuity becomes "academic freedom," while cultural apostasy becomes "democratic liberalism." Illegal aliens become "undocumented residents," while slums and projects become "public housing developments." Prostitutes become "sex-care providers," while the killing of unborn humans becomes "terminating a pregnancy." Sodomy becomes an "alternative lifestyle" or "being true to oneself," while debased pornography becomes "provocative" or "adult" or "controversial" entertainment. And indecency becomes "artistic courage," while rape becomes psychological coercion and murderers are only "alleged" to be such.

27. In the realm of family policy and gender roles, this has been argued persuasively by J. Malmude, "The Emerging Mandate Society: Implications for Sex Roles and Family Life," *Social Justice Review*, May/June 1994, 71-74.

28. William Brennan, "John Paul II on Language Empowering the Culture of Death," *National Catholic Bioethics Quarterly*, Winter 2003, 732.

29. *EV*, no. 8.

Indeed, the opportunities for linguistic foreplay are endless, limited only by one's imagination. Strategically viewed, all sorts of notions can be bombarded by cannonades of linguistic artillery. G. K. Chesterton, it turns out, was not far from the mark in saying that when someone intends to wage a social war against conventional notions of decency and order, the initial requisite step is to find some artificial term that sounds relatively decent.[30]

Jean Elshtain suffers neither fools nor ideologues gladly, and thus she is justified when she calls us to reflect on the more recent lessons of history. And like George Orwell, she writes with a view of warning those of us in the Western cultural context, since not infrequently cultural deconstruction has prepared the way for either a soft or hard form of totalitarianism — a process that has been prepared and abetted by social currents as well as by linguistic manipulation and the rhetoric of social change ("solidarity," "liberation," "empowerment," "social justice," "diversity," "compassion," "equality," "transformation").

Properly, in my view, Elshtain worries that the boundaries of respect for multiple institutions of our social life — our churches, our families, our schools, our politics — will dissipate.[31] Significantly, in a post-Christian climate, increased calls for "social transformation" have run parallel to increasing hostility, both within the academy and in culture at large, toward the classical Judeo-Christian tradition in general.[32] The warning of A.-A. Upinsky, while it may shock, may not be overstated: decapitate language and the meaning of words, and its literal physical counterpart may follow.[33] This "decapitation," it needs to be emphasized, begins in smaller, scarcely noticeable increments. To devalue and manipulate language, however, inevitably leads to a tragic defacing of those created in the image of God. The defacing of the *imago Dei* threatens to proceed in frightening proportions in the twenty-first century. For this reason, de-

30. G. K. Chesterton, *A Miscellany of Man* (London: Methuen, 1920), 145-51.

31. Elshtain, *Who Are We?* 128. "Words and their meanings," writes Elshtain, "are connected to debates about truth. The deformation of language characteristic of totalitarian regimes was an integral feature of their playing fast and loose with facts and undermining, thereby, any possibility of shared truth-claims as a feature of political and personal life" (133-34).

32. One is utterly amazed at how "Christian ethicists," wittingly or unwittingly, have played into the hand of cultural deconstructionists, even when they have thought of themselves as donning a "prophetic" mantle.

33. Upinsky, *La Tête Coupée*, 1-15.

spite secularist tirades about Christian ethics being alarmist, the Christian community does well to heed the counsel of Abraham Kuyper as it prays for discernment: "When the principles that run against your deepest convictions begin to win the day, then the battle is your calling, and peace has become sin; you must, at the price of dearest peace, lay your convictions bare before friend and enemy, with all the fire of your faith."[34]

A Reasoned Defense

In addition to the canons of truth, truthfulness, and linguistic integrity, those who possess a living hope, to participate responsibly in civic life, will need to be prepared to offer a reasoned defense of their convictions (cf. 1 Pet. 3:15). The operative word here is "reasoned." Implied herein are two salient features of cultural involvement: (1) a willingness to *engage* one's contemporaries, one's interlocutors, indeed, even one's opponents, irenically, and (2) "an insistence that there is some truth to be found" and conveyed in creative ways.[35] Now more than ever, Christians as citizens must be defenders of human reason, responding to the epistemological and moral vacuity of the postmodern spirit that has insulated our contemporaries from questions of truth, meaning, and order.[36]

And we are not without resources in our attempts to respond to the epistemological and moral malaise that surrounds us. Indeed, Protestants such as I have had the great joy of discovering that the writings of John Paul II, time and again, have addressed significant cultural issues while at the same time calling the Christian community to a higher plane. I have profited immensely from what may well have been John Paul's most important encyclical, *Fides et Ratio*, which was published in 1998 and, as it turns out, was his last major encyclical. Particularly for those in a Christian liberal arts context, at the heart of which stands a commitment toward inculcating a distinctly Christian worldview, few resources are of greater

---

34. Cited in G. C. Berkouwer, *A Half Century of Theology*, trans. L. B. Smedes (Grand Rapids: Eerdmans, 1977), 12.

35. Elshtain, *Who Are We?* 137.

36. While this is not always the case, on occasion we will need to debunk relativism, exposing it for the absurdity it is. By its own assertions it shows itself as self-contradicting. That there are no absolute truths means that all is opinion, including the assertion that there is no objective truth. The very denial of absolutes itself relativizes the relativist's claims. Grotesquely, subjectivism masquerades as an absolute truth.

value than *Fides.* This especially is true for Protestants. But why? Perhaps at work is the reverse side of the "Protestant principle." In our desire, as theological traditionalists, to avoid rationalism and uphold the primacy of grace and faith, we become fideistic, undervaluing the role that reason and philosophy play in the pursuit of truth.

Elshtain is among those who share a high regard for *Fides,* given the encyclical's penetrating cultural critique and its burden to unite, rather than separate, reason and faith. For her as well, John Paul underscores the importance of rational knowledge and philosophical discourse for a proper understanding of faith, and thus calls us to be attentive to the fideist error, while at the same time challenging us to discern the distortions of rationalism, which exalts autonomous reason over — and in opposition to — faith and the theological task. Philosophy, according to John Paul, needs illumination by faith, just as faith needs the rational support of critical reflection.[37]

Let us pause, however, and recall the first point noted above: we must be *willing* to engage our contemporaries. Christians of all stripes and feathers, because they have been taught to "love not the world or the things in the world," find solace in the Tertullian view of culture. Because nothing in the surrounding culture "saves" us, it is thought, we should therefore remove ourselves from the culture in order to preserve our faithfulness. But is *this* faithfulness (cf. John 17:15-16)? Is this the priority to which the Christian is called? It is certainly true that we are not to "love the world," if by that we mean the world system, the realm of cosmic disobedience orchestrated by the "prince of the power of the air" (Eph. 2:2; cf. 1 John 2:15-17). But human culture, and all that is distinctly human, even when marred by the effects of sin, nevertheless refracts the glory of creation and the image of the Creator. And because human beings have been created in the divine image, we are to love — which is to say, esteem — creation.

Here, I confess, I have chiefly in mind those among us who tend toward cultural withdrawal. How can we be effective in our cultural witness if we do not love human beings? If we do not take interest in human institutions? For many Christian believers the words of Jesus' high-priestly

---

37. To argue for the mutual dependence of faith and reason on one another is not to deny that a rightly ordered reason, apart from *salvific* faith, can discern basic moral obligations. John Finnis therefore can argue that as molecular motion, so moral reality does not require "theism" (*Natural Law,* 49).

prayer in John 17, that his disciples are *in the world but not of the world,* have been parsed in such a way as to emphasize only the latter half of the formula. But we are also *in the world.* Which is to say that we are called *to* the world, not away from it. And this calling *to* the world, *to* the society of which we are a part, in no way equates to *compromise with the world.* If we maintain a constant contempt for people — and for the social institutions that comprise human culture — we forfeit any right and authority to speak to the culture.[38] It goes without saying, then, that we relinquish any and all ability to work for the common good.

A Comprehensive Witness

It is in the realm of working for the common good that Christians of all ecclesiastical traditions — and I write as a Protestant — must be willing to learn from — and appropriate — the priorities of Catholic social teaching in working for society's welfare. While Christians of all denominational confessions share the foundation of historic Christian faith, not all share a common commitment to work toward a just social order, to preserve that which is enduring, and to promote the common good. But what does this welfare entail? Inter alia, it entails moral formation and the inculcation of virtue; stewardship over the material and property; family; education; work and vocation; solidarity and fraternity among its citizens; an equilibrium between rights and duties; justice that expresses itself legally, restoratively, distributively, and commutatively; subsidiarity and a proper view of the state; the role of the church in society; and the development of a public philosophy inclusive of a shared public morality.[39] And whether viewed vocationally or avocationally, working for the common good will of necessity be comprehensive in nature; it will entail working through educational institutions, the legal establishment, the media in its varied

---

38. In reading Richard Mouw's *Uncommon Decency: Christian Civility in an Uncivil World* (Downers Grove, Ill.: InterVarsity, 1992), one senses this concern. The first chapter title — "Convicted Civility: Can We Be Faithful and Polite Too?" — seems to express the belief that anger or contempt *might not* be the best method of engaging our contemporaries.

39. See part 3 of the *Catechism of the Catholic Church,* in which the social and ethical implications of Christian doctrine are spelled out. See also the very concise but useful summary of Catholic social teaching that is framed by J. Brian Benestad, "Catholic Social Thought, Virtue and Public Morality," in *The Christian Vision: Man and Morality,* ed. Thomas J. Burke (Hillsdale, Mich.: Hillsdale College Press, 1986), 141-55.

forms, business and commerce, science and technology, as well the political system at diverse levels.[40]

Perhaps the reader will find it surprising that not included in the present discussion of the "common good" is any sort of critique of our political, economic, or social structures based on their fallenness or purported "root causes" of injustice. One way of answering this concern would be to observe that theological liberals, whether Protestant or Catholic, have typically offered a "macro" analysis that focuses and decries these "structures" as evil and unjust per se, while theological conservatives have tended to focus chiefly on personal effects of sin. Joseph Cardinal Ratzinger, before his ascendancy to the pontificate in 2005, offered the following remarks that might serve as a source of political and moral discernment for those concerned about "structures." One cannot "localize" evil, he insisted, "principally or uniquely in bad social, political or economic structures as though all other evils come from them so that the creation of the 'new man' would depend on the establishment of different economic and socio-political structures."

To be sure, Ratzinger grants, "there are structures which are evil and which cause evil and which we must have the courage to change." However, structures, "whether they are good or bad, are the result of man's actions and so are consequences more than causes." Wherein, then, is lodged the root of evil? For Ratzinger, it lies "in free and responsible persons who have to be converted by the grace of Jesus Christ in order to live and act as new creatures in the love of neighbor and in the effective search for justice, self-control and the exercise of virtue."[41]

Working for the common good does not serve as a substitute for evangelism proper, even though in his writings John Paul II has called in the West for a "reevangelization of culture" in the broader sense of seeding all aspects of the culture with redemptive elements. Seeking to develop a moral consensus within culture, to be sure, is tedious work and a long-term project. One cannot change the cultural consensus as one might revise a tax code. And certainly, not everyone has the same obligations in

40. Worthy of note is the discussion in chapter seven ("Person, Rights, and the Common Good," 228-69) of Robert J. Spitzer, Robin A. Bernhoft, and Camille E. De Blasi, *Healing the Culture: A Commonsense Philosophy of Happiness, Freedom, and the Life Issues* (San Francisco: Ignatius, 2000), who examine the relationship between rights and society's welfare.

41. Joseph Cardinal Ratzinger, "Instruction on Certain Aspects of the Theology of Liberation," *Origins* 14, no. 13 (1984): 197.

terms of vocational calling, yet all are required to do what is possible in working for the common good through their gifts, abilities, vocational callings, and spiritual discernment. In faith, individuals must take initiative; sometimes these initiatives are more visible, sometimes less so. But they are initiatives nonetheless.

In the end, will we care about the common good?[42]

Rethinking Tolerance: From Unchaste "Moral Neutrality" to a Chastened and Principled Pluralism[43]

Tolerance Old and New

Along with its siblings "diversity" and "compassion," "tolerance" has achieved remarkable status in our culture's hierarchy of values. It is one of those "thought-killer" words, as someone has remarked, that have come to constitute our cultural lexicon, requiring uncritical acceptance for all seasons and all reasons.[44] In fact, the commandment "Thou shalt not judge" seems to have superseded all revealed commandments — even rationally discovered ones.[45] But how far tolerance? And how is tolerance best understood?

In the English language tolerance in the sense of "bearing" or "indulging" (Latin: *tolerare*) dates from the mid–eighteenth century. Originally "tolerance" denoted a policy of forbearance in the presence of

---

42. While the state is morally (and theologically) obligated to respect the goods that issue from a reasoned reflection on human nature, those goods depend on the individual's own commitment to service. The state, as David F. Forte makes very clear, cannot take the place of nurturing acts between individual persons ("Family, Nurture, and Liberty," in *Natural Law and Contemporary Public Policy* [Washington, D.C.: Georgetown University Press, 1998], 83-97). And although, Aquinas pointed out, it is impossible to do good to everyone everywhere, at the same time we are obligated to do good in particular cases to those our lives touch in daily life (*ST* II-II Q. 31).

43. Portions of this discussion appeared previously in the Winter 2007 issue (vol. 36, no. 2) of *Christian Scholar's Review*, 211-18, which holds copyright, and are used with permission. In that essay, titled "Truth, Tolerance and Christian Conviction — Reflections on a Perennial Question," I review recent literature on pluralism and religious tolerance.

44. So David Warren, "Tolerance/Forgiveness," *Sunday Spectator*, December 4, 2005, accessible at www.davidwarrenonline.com/index.php?artID=546.

45. Adam Wolfson, "What Remains of Toleration?" *Public Interest*, Winter 1999, 40.

something disliked or disapproved. It was foremost a political virtue, demonstrated by a government's readiness to permit a variety of religious beliefs.[46] The notion that government should not enforce a specific religion comes to expression in John Locke's *Letter concerning Tolerance* (1689) and *Two Treatises of Government* (1690). Removed from its political context, tolerance gradually came to be understood as a forbearance, an enduring, of those behaviors or practices that we dislike.[47]

Tolerance in its conception took on the cast of a virtue because of its concern for the common good and its respect for people as persons. We endure particular customs, behaviors, or habits — sometimes even (relatively) bad habits — of people in the interest of preserving a greater unity. In the Lockean context, tolerance was advocated for religious nonconformists. Never was it construed, however, to imply — much less to sanction — *morally questionable behavior*. Consider the devolution of a concept. What was a public virtue in its prior state becomes a vice if and when it ceases to care for truth, ignores the common good, and disdains the values that uphold a community. The culture of "tolerance" in which we presently find ourselves is a culture in which people believe nothing, possess no clear concept of right and wrong, and are remarkably indifferent to this precarious state of affairs.[48] The challenge facing people of faith is learning how to purify tolerance so that it remains a virtue without succumbing to the centripetal forces of relativism.

Any discussion of the notion of tolerance must first presuppose a context of pluralism. But we encounter problems. Pluralism can be understood in multiple ways; therefore, how we define pluralism is critically important. At the most basic level, on the one hand, it can simply signify the

46. By way of strong contrast, one thinks, for example, of sectors within current-day resurgent Islam that demand that the entire political and social order be founded on Sharia.

47. In a volume with the fascinating title *The Long Truce: How Toleration Made the World Safe for Power and Profit* (Dallas: Spence, 2001), A. J. Conyers has traced the modern history of the notion of tolerance in an attempt to answer the question whether tolerance can be considered a virtue. Conyers's answer is that, strictly speaking, it is not a virtue in the classical sense. Rather, in his argument, it is to be viewed as a "strategy" or policy that directs virtues such as patience, humility, moderation, and prudence to a desired end. In the end, the goodness of tolerance is understood as depending entirely on the nature of the goods it serves.

48. David Warren ("Tolerance/Forgiveness") quips that tolerance is one of those ideas "loosely hatched" during the Enlightenment but carried forward today by postmodernists "into the realm of dementia." It is hard to disagree with him.

phenomenological reality of differing cultures, ethnic groups, and traditions, as well as the social structures and mechanisms that order a society. These cultural phenomena and mechanisms are a social fact of life. It is out of this "structured"[49] form of pluralism that the American experience emerged; hence, our nation's motto *E Pluribus Unum* (out of many one).[50] Herein different communities, different identities, different ethnic traditions agree to coexist; they do so because of a commitment to an overarching common cause.

On the other hand, "pluralism" can operate under the assumption — spoken or unspoken — that among competing ideological viewpoints, worldviews, or religious understandings of reality, none has (or is permitted to have) a privileged place as a framework for interpreting reality. On this view all religious or philosophical positions possess an essential unity and all religious viewpoints stand on equal terms. Pluralism thus construed has a leveling effect. Hence, to argue for the authority and supremacy of Christianity, we are told, amounts to religious and cultural imperialism. This allegation, of course, places "pluralism" intrinsically at odds with Christian truth claims, which are uncompromising in their assertion that God has revealed himself uniquely and definitively through Jesus Christ.

For this reason, it is crucial to distinguish between pluralism as a social-cultural fact of life and pluralism as an ideology.[51] And because people use the term "tolerance" indiscriminately and in both aforementioned contexts, preserving this distinction is critically important. In the context of the former, tolerance is a genuine manifestation of virtue. Social, cultural, and ethnic pluralism is to be welcomed and praised; it is the

---

49. "Structured pluralism" is what James W. Skillen, *Recharging the American Experiment: Principled Pluralism for Genuine Civic Community* (Grand Rapids: Baker, 1994), 83-95, uses to describe "the diversity of organizational competencies and social responsibilities" in society.

50. Ethicist Ian Markham, in *Plurality and Christian Ethics*, rev. ed. (New York: Seven Bridges Press, 1999), 5-6, prefers to use the term "plurality," to be distinguished from religious or philosophical pluralism.

51. See Lesslie Newbigin, *The Gospel in a Pluralist Society* (Grand Rapids: Eerdmans, 1989), and *Truth to Tell: The Gospel and Public Truth* (Grand Rapids: Eerdmans, 1991). Very helpful and remarkably concise summaries of this important distinction are found in Alister E. McGrath, *A Passion for Truth* (Downers Grove, Ill.: InterVarsity, 1996), chapter 5, and McGrath, "The Challenge of Pluralism for the Contemporary Christian Church," *Journal of the Evangelical Theological Society* 35, no. 3 (1992): 361-73.

soil in which the gospel exists and furthers itself, since it mirrors the splendor and rich diversity of creation.[52] At stake in this form of pluralism are negotiable issues — e.g., language, cultural customs, ethnic habits, group preferences, etc. In the context of the latter form, however, discernment is necessary, since ideological pluralists demand that we "tolerate" alternative explanations of reality while at the same time pressuring us to negotiate — and abdicate — claims to ultimate truth. In American culture, a shift in understanding "tolerance" has occurred — a shift that calls for vigilance. "Tolerance" has devolved into an indifference toward truth, often belligerently and intolerably so; the result is a baneful permissiveness toward all manner of evil. Thereby a virtue has been transmuted into vice.

Tolerance Rightly Construed

Let us back up for a moment and recall that tolerance, in our cultural tradition, emerged as a political and social virtue. And as such, tolerance has private as well as public or communal dimensions. While we may disagree with another's opinion, vice, or lifestyle, we extend (in principle) that person's "right" to a specific opinion or behavior. Christians and non-Christians of *all* varieties tolerate one another's differences because of what they *all* share in common — the laws of nature, inalienable rights, dignity that inheres in personhood. When, however, a person — in the name of "tolerance" — is making claims on the *public square,* tolerance must then cease, for we tolerate what we dislike *until it affects the wider community in a way that undermines the common good.* Thus, we are compelled to draw a strict distinction between the freedoms of an individual, practiced in private, and the needs of the community, of which we all are contributing parts. This distinction is not necessarily owing to Christian insight, for Locke himself makes the basic observation — an important one for contemporary Americans — that a great deal of difference can be tolerated *provided that it does not endanger social cohesion.*

But, in practical terms, what does this mean? With regard to objectionable behavior, where exactly do we draw the line? How do we as a society determine what behavior is acceptable and what is unacceptable? A

---

52. Of all people, Christians in particular should treasure cultural pluralism, simply because of the enormous opportunities it affords to bear witness to Christ's lordship.

well-worn bit of conventional wisdom among religious folk is that we should "hate the sin while loving the sinner." Granted, there is some truth to this maxim. Nevertheless, as C. S. Lewis pointed out, this nice-sounding piece of piety can easily descend into sloppy sentimentalism. Lewis observes that to love the sinner in fact means that we feel toward him "as we feel about ourselves — to wish that he were not bad, to hope that he may, in this world or another, be cured: in fact, to wish his good. That is what is meant in the Bible by loving him: wishing his good, not feeling fond of him nor saying he is nice when he is not."[53]

Lewis's advice appropriately parallels the New Testament admonition to "speak the truth in love" (Eph. 4:15). To speak the truth in love is to embody a moral honesty that refuses to compromise the consequences of ultimate reality, while it simultaneously is cognizant of the fact that fellow human beings are to be treated as bearers of the image of God. Love and truth are not mutually exclusive, despite the ethical propaganda that emanates from common culture. Those who would call us to "love the sinner" frequently *really* want us to *sympathize nonjudgmentally* with him. By which they mean we should refrain from stigmatizing and expressing disapproval. The person, then, will feel better. But as one social critic has quipped, this attitude only "makes the world safe for moral dereliction."[54]

If "tolerance" and "compassion" are not rooted in moral principle, they end up corrupting both the practitioner *and* the object. Elevating them to the status of cardinal virtues, while disengaging them from unbending moral realities, sends the signal to the unscrupulous that "a good strategy for getting their way is to play on other people's pity, which is dreadfully destructive to character. It encourages malingering, self-pity, and claims of victimhood. It encourages not self-sufficiency, but dependence . . . ; not strength, but weakness; not honesty and integrity, but shameless and vicious exploitation of others; not cheerfulness in adversity, but whining; not acceptance of life's vicissitudes, but a readiness to find fault."[55]

But we return to the nagging question of drawing the line. As to precisely where Christians are to draw the line, our answer is this: we must

53. C. S. Lewis, *Mere Christianity* (New York: Macmillan, 1960), 108.

54. John Attarian, "In Dispraise of Tolerance, Sensitivity and Compassion," *Social Critic*, Spring 1998, 16.

55. Attarian, "Dispraise," 18.

draw the line *where private preferences that undermine the communal good make claims in the public sphere.* Are Christians called to tolerate an individual whose sexual behavior differs? Indeed. Are Christians called to tolerate the theoretical and practical promotion of that behavior in the form of social or public policy? By no means. Whereas sexuality is a private matter, educating on human sexuality (at least through a public, tax-supported institution) ceases to be private; it is very much a public and communal concern.[56]

Therefore, whatever the cost and inconvenience, Christians are not only free to contend, they are *required* to do so, and that *for the purposes of preserving social cohesion and the moral order.*[57] This response, of course, will lead to charges that we are "imposing" our morality on those around us. Christians are reminded ad nauseam by secularists that because we live in a pluralistic democracy, we are *forbidden* from such imposition. But are we?

If morality is indeed a *private* matter as some contend, then critics of Christianity would be justified in excluding the voice of Christian ethics from the public square. But since the square is *public,* that means that all *may* contend — especially those of Christian faith. In the last two decades vigorous debate has transpired between professors of law, political scientists, and philosophers over interlocking questions of justice, the public square, and moral neutrality. The strongest advocates of "tolerance" in our day insist on the idea that the public square is morally neutral. And because it is thought to be neutral, the state must remain "neutral" in adjudicating various claims to "rights." But *is* there such a thing as moral neutrality?

If there are particular goods identified by a society that need protecting, then society cannot be "neutral" about those goods. It has a vested interest in maintaining and preserving them. And those goods, of course, are established on the basis of what a society considers to be ultimate and authoritative. Moral neutrality is neither self-evident nor self-justifying; rather, it must be shown to be true or correct. When its proponents press their argument in the public square for a particular position — for example, on the nature of the family or marriage, same-sex unions, free speech,

---

56. A brief but excellent overview of the limitations of tolerance within the communal context as well as the contours of Christian responsibility is found in Kent Weber, "How Far Is Tolerance a Virtue?" *Regeneration Quarterly,* Winter 1996, 29-31.

57. Adopting *the appropriate language* with which to contend, however, is of vital importance.

or abortion rights — they argue that competing notions are controversial, mistaken, and therefore to be rejected. Thus, "moral neutrality" is very much akin to moral relativism insofar as its proponents demonstrate through arguments *for* or *against* competing moral positions the falsehood of its alleged existence.[58]

Robert George has analyzed contemporary debates regarding same-sex marriage in this light. Up until recently, society's laws affecting marriage have been predicated on the moral assumption that marriage is heterosexual. This is, of course, not the only moral judgment that exists; polygamy and polyandry can be found in other cultures. For those in our culture who would propose that government is unjust to refuse to authorize same-sex marriages, two arguments are possible. One is to deny the soundness, reasonableness, and necessity of heterosexual marriages. The second is to argue that they are inherently unjust. But either argument, as it turns out, becomes an intrinsically *moral* argument. That is, *contrasting visions* of marriage are in competition, not a "moral" and a "morally neutral" vision of marriage. Therefore, sound marriage laws are not those that aspire to "moral neutrality"; rather, they are those that accord with moral truth. And to "tolerate" through public policy the normalizing of those practices that are in defiance of moral truth is to destroy civil society.[59]

It is here that we must stress the symbiosis between tolerance and the common good. Tolerance as an authentic *virtue* is rooted in a commitment to what is true and good for society; correlatively, as a *vice* it is indifferent to these realities. Therefore, tolerance is not — indeed, cannot be — neutral toward what affects society. Even staunchly secular approaches to public and political life themselves are *thoroughly religious* in nature. That is to say, they arise out of deeply held or binding commitments (from the Latin verb *religare*, "to bind") to what they believe to be right and wrong, acceptable and unacceptable. Any comprehensive orientation toward life has an inherently "religious" character, and every political and legal mode of rea-

58. J. Budziszewski, "The Illusion of Moral Neutrality," *First Things,* August/September 1993, 32-37, has pointed out that intolerance — ironically furthered by the "tolerance police" of our day — demonstrates itself in two ways — through a "softheadedness," i.e., through excessive indulgence that is morally spineless, and through the opposite extreme of "narrow-mindedness."

59. Robert P. George, "'Same-Sex Marriage' and 'Moral Neutrality,'" in George, *The Clash of Orthodoxies: Law, Religion, and Morality in Crisis* (Wilmington, Del.: ISI Books, 2001), 75-89.

soning begins and ends with fundamental assumptions, precommitments, and preconceptions about the origin and nature of life.[60]

But what we are prepared to tolerate pivots, as we have sought to emphasize, on what is ultimate — in our personal lives and in the life of culture. There is something ultimate before which every person — indeed, every society — will bow. Modern and postmodern idolatries abound, but there is no escaping the fact that everyone has a hierarchy of values. What society tolerates is predicated on this hierarchy, atop which sits something ultimate. Social consensus is possible where there are overlapping realms of agreed-upon moral-social capital. Where there is no overlapping agreement, consensus is impossible and anarchy is invited.[61]

But let us proceed one step further. By contending that there is *no such thing* as moral neutrality, we are also declaring that *someone's morality will be imposed*. Francis Canavan has expressed it this way: "it is an old half-truth that you cannot legislate morality. The other and more significant half of the truth is that a society's laws inevitably reflect its morals and its religion. As a society's religious and moral beliefs change, then, so will its laws."[62] Therefore, we must expose the falsehood of the philosophical and sociological notion that a pluralistic society can be neutral on moral matters, since this thinking inevitably leads to the establishing of the most secularized, materialistic, and hedonistic elements of the population. In other words, ultimately *someone's* morality will be legislated.[63] Two examples of this moral reasoning may suffice to illustrate. If someone claims the "right to die," society is morally constrained to respond on the basis of the natural law: as an objective "good," human life has intrinsic value that must be protected by the state (if

60. Skillen, *Recharging the American Experiment*, 30-33, argues this point quite succinctly. For a more extensive treatment of "neutrality," see Roy Clouser, *The Myth of Religious Neutrality: An Essay on the Hidden Role of Religious Belief in Theories* (Notre Dame, Ind.: University of Notre Dame Press, 1991).

61. Hence, as James Davison Hunter, in his book *Culture Wars: The Struggle to Define America* (New York: Basic Books, 1990), and J. Budziszewski, in *True Tolerance: Liberalism and the Necessity of Judgment* (New Brunswick, N.J.: Transaction, 1992), have attempted to demonstrate, the metaphor of "culture wars" is no mere metaphor; two competing, all-encompassing visions for humanity and society are clashing.

62. Francis Canavan, "Pluralism and the Limits of Neutrality," in *The Battle for Morality in Pluralistic America*, ed. Carl Horn (Ann Arbor: Servant, 1985), 158.

63. Canavan writes: "If we are a plurality of communities," the right "to maintain and transmit the community's beliefs and values is at least as important as the right of the individual to live as he pleases" ("Pluralism," 160-61).

the state is legitimate). Neutrality is not an option, permitting right-to-die advocates the luxury of finding a constitutional "right to privacy." Likewise, in response to homosexual activists who insist on gay marriage as a "civil right" on par with heterosexual marriages, we might argue that neither government nor the public can seek refuge in a purported "neutrality," since there exist a particular "nature" and function of human activity that are consensually demonstrable throughout human civilization.

The fathers of the American experiment assumed that people will broadly agree on rationally discernible moral norms, a *consensus juris,* that will inform a society's understanding of rights, justice, good, and evil. This consensus, it should be noted, guards against a tyranny of both the minority and the majority, since "tyranny" per se is a fundamental violation of human (i.e., natural) rights that are inalienable. There is, then, no moral "neutrality" as envisioned by the framers of this nation's charter documents; in the interest of all of society, particular "goods" will need to be defended. Otherwise, the cannibal has the "right" to be "different," pedophilia is defensible "self-expression," and one man's mugging is simply another man's good time.[64]

Thus, the public nature of the marketplace (of both ideas and goods), then and now, as well as of social institutions, coupled with the very public nature of requisite Christian witness (then and now), compels people of Christian faith to work for the common good using any and all means, so long as democratic pluralism resists the centripetal slide into a soft form of totalitarian statism.[65] For those of us who tend to shy away from confrontation, the hard truth is this: a society

---

64. Certainly, an examination of how the overt deconstruction of the notion of deviant behavior by academic theorists has proceeded carries us too far afield of the present discussion. Nevertheless, useful studies of this phenomenon include Daniel Patrick Moynihan, *Miles to Go* (Cambridge: Harvard University Press, 1996); Myron Magnet, *The Dream and the Nightmare: The Sixties' Legacy to the Underclass,* 2nd ed. (San Francisco: Encounter Books, 2000); and Anne Hendershott, *The Politics of Deviance* (San Francisco: Encounter Books, 2002). Most readers will recall Moynihan's much-debated essay "Defining Deviancy Down" that appeared in the *American Scholar,* Winter 1993, 17-30.

65. In response to the potential objection that a balance of power — namely, judicial, executive, and legislative — excludes the possibility of political tyranny of various degrees in the United States, I would simply pose the following question: What if all three branches of "democratic" government, mirroring the values of elitist culture, are (more or less) committed to a bleaching of the religious viewpoint and an eradication of Christian participation in the moral, legal, as well as political process?

cannot function well, cannot survive, and cannot protect the innocent
. . . from harm and evil, without a large measure of intolerance. Yes, intolerance — of theft, burglary, cruelty, classroom hooliganism, disre-
spect for parental authority, and violent crime of all sorts; of substance
abuse, infidelity, illegitimacy, perversion, pornography, rape, and child
molestation; of fraud, envy, covetousness, and knavery; of sloth, medi-
ocrity, incompetence, maleducation, improvidence, irresponsibility
and fecklessness. A society tolerant of those things would soon find itself in serious trouble, even facing dissolution, and many people in
that society would be in peril of their lives.[66]

Everyone has claims on the public square — most notably, Christians, whose cultural mandate rests on a firm commitment to the redemption of all things (Col. 1:17-20; cf. Eph. 1:10). While it is not a "given" that
everyone's claim will be "tolerated," tolerance properly understood mirrors a strong and principled commitment to promote moral truth and
work for the common good.[67] For in the words of Yves Simon, nothing
would be right by enactment if some things were not right by nature.[68]

Bioethics and the Permanent — a Test Case:
The Natural Law and Reproductive Technology

There are those who, quite understandably, question whether reason is capable of leading people to metaphysical truth. The natural law, consequently, is viewed — again, quite understandably, as we argued in chapter
4 — as a "minimalist" attempt at developing morals and a common moral
grammar. One way of responding to this challenge — certainly, a typically
Protestant challenge — is to find recourse in Thomas Aquinas, in whom
both Catholics and Protestants find refuge. For Aquinas the natural law is
not merely the effect of practical reason, though it is indeed that. Rather, it

---

66. Attarian, "Dispraise," 22.

67. Two recent and related volumes commend themselves to the reader: Joseph Cardinal Ratzinger (Benedict XVI), *Truth and Tolerance: Christian Belief and World Religions*
(San Francisco: Ignatius, 2004), and Brad Stetson and Joseph G. Conti, *The Truth about Tolerance: Pluralism, Diversity, and the Culture Wars* (Downers Grove, Ill.: InterVarsity, 2005).

68. Yves R. Simon, *The Tradition of Natural Law* (New York: Fordham University
Press, 1965), 118.

is to be viewed as the *precondition* or *preunderstanding* that exists for human moral reasoning. Is it possible, at least on the basis of Christian theological conviction, that through the exercise of our practical moral reason we embody the *imago Dei*? If human nature conforms to creation, and human passions conform to right moral judgments, as Aquinas argued,[69] then prior knowledge of the right end must be assumed of human nature, sin's effects notwithstanding. Otherwise, we might mistakenly assume that humans attempting to make moral judgments are doing so in a moral vacuum. But on this matter Saint Paul could hardly be clearer: all people are "without excuse" (Rom. 1:20).[70]

But is the natural moral law, practically measured, to be reduced to a "lowest common (moral) denominator," as many Christian ethicists worry? After all, moral knowledge is only *partially* known, and acted upon, without God's providential intervention. Again, we find refuge in Aquinas. All of creation — including human beings as moral agents — are subject to, and reflective of, the divine order that characterizes the cosmos. Aquinas speaks of this reality as the "eternal law." This "law" implies that all human beings, as moral agents, are active participants in the moral order. They participate by their ability to engage in moral reasoning, working within the parameters that God as moral governor has set. Even when the means to those moral ends vary and are subject to wisdom and discretion, "the right ends of human life are fixed."[71]

If, according to Aquinas, human moral ends are "fixed," which means that the natural law is known rationally and that human moral reasoning moves in a particular direction, then it is proper to argue that *how we as humans propagate the species* is a matter of Christian concern. Does the technology with which we conceive of the human species accord with what we "know"? Does the means of procreation serve the proper "end" for which humans have been created? What has "nature" ordered, based on prior assumptions of human personhood, dignity, and sanctity? And be-

---

69. Aquinas, *Summa Theologiae* (hereafter *ST*) I-II Q. 1, 19, 79, and 90.

70. On this, all natural law proponents agree, as expressed in the argument of Samuel Pufendorf, that "every Man . . . has so much Natural Light in him, as that, with necessary Care and due Consideration, he may rightly comprehend at least those general Precepts and Principles which are requisite in order to pass our Lives here honestly and quietly; and be able to judge that these are congruous to the Nature of Man" (*The Whole Duty of Man, according to the Law of Nature*, trans. A. Tooke [Indianapolis: Liberty Fund, 2003], 28-29).

71. Aquinas, *ST* II-II Q. 47.

cause human personhood and dignity entail a right use of the human *body*, how might our procreative abilities therefore be rightly directed?

"Choice," Reproductive "Freedom," and the Abolition of Personhood

Books such as Daniel Maguire's *Sacred Choices: The Right to Contraception and Abortion in Ten World Religions*[72] and John Robertson's *Children of Choice: Freedom and the New Reproductive Technologies*[73] stand as a powerful witness to the degree to which personal freedoms have been prostituted in our day. Maguire's long-standing opposition to normative Roman Catholic social ethics and his own church's authority perhaps renders his arguments unpersuasive. The philosophical trajectory of Robertson's argument, by contrast, is more compelling, requiring of us an informed and thoughtful response. With considerable force, Robertson argues that people have the fundamental right both *not* to reproduce and to reproduce *where, when, and how* they so choose.[74] Not only should this right extend to noncoital reproduction, it also encompasses our ability to be selective about the characteristics our children should possess — that is, should we will those children into existence. In a pluralistic context, Robertson believes, this "right" to reproductive liberty cannot be curtailed: to deny procreative choice is to deny or impose a crucial self-defining experience, thus denying persons respect and dignity at the most basic level.[75]

Because Robertson's argument is rights-laden, and because for him the "right" of reproductive liberty is emblematic of human freedom in general, and therefore nigh unto inalienable, his stance must be taken seriously. In Robertson's world there is no biological necessity in the production of offspring, no moral meaning in the biological bond: only the need for what the author calls "quality control."[76] Rather, reproduction is foremost a matter of the *will*, not biological ties. Robertson informs us: "The decision to have or not have children is, at some important level, no longer a matter of God or nature, but has been made subject to human will and

---

72. (Minneapolis: Fortress, 2000).
73. (Princeton: Princeton University Press, 1994).
74. Robertson, *Children of Choice*, 5, 26-34.
75. Robertson, *Children of Choice*, 4.
76. Robertson, *Children of Choice*, 10.

technical expertise."[77] Robertson appears to welcome the future possibilities that will create "a widespread market in paid conception, pregnancies, and adoptions."[78] Falling within these future "possibilities" for him is even having offspring for the purpose of becoming tissue donors.[79] Are there any reproductive restraints, according to Robertson's "modified pro-choice" worldview?[80] Two are cited. Nontherapeutic genetic enhancement and cloning trouble Robertson, although based on his precommitment to "freedom" no moral rationale can be discerned by the reader.[81]

Robertson's argument is significant not solely because it powerfully mirrors contemporary society's "need" for reproductive freedom. It is also noteworthy because, like most secular bioethical debates, it wholly ignores the questions of human personhood, dignity, and "nature" that form the true heart and soul of bioethics.[82] Indeed, *Children of Choice* is utterly bereft of any moral reasoning.[83] And as Gilbert Meilaender rightly points out, the shift from "procreation" to "reproduction" is in part nothing less than "a manifestation of human freedom to master and reshape our world."[84] As one reads and reflects on Robertson's reproductive apologetic, one shutters at the sheer hubris of the claims being advanced: "Religious or moral objections to the separation of sex and reproduction should not override the use of these techniques for forming a family."[85]

77. Robertson, *Children of Choice*, 5.

78. Robertson, *Children of Choice*, 143.

79. Robertson, *Children of Choice*, 192-93, 207-19.

80. Robertson, *Children of Choice*, 45.

81. Robertson, *Children of Choice*, 165-70.

82. To my knowledge, Gilbert Meilaender is the only Christian ethicist who has offered a detailed assessment of Robertson's book. See his *Body, Soul, and Bioethics* (Notre Dame, Ind., and London: University of Notre Dame Press, 1995), chapter 3 ("How Bioethics Lost the Body: Producing Children").

83. At the same time, Robertson describes procreative liberty as "a deeply held moral . . . value" (Robertson, *Children of Choice*, 4). Contrast this with Gilbert Meilaender's profound and delicately handled discussions of personhood, dignity, and moral intuition in *Bioethics: A Primer for Christians* (Grand Rapids: Eerdmans, 1996), chapter 2, and *Body, Soul, and Bioethics,* chapters 2 and 3.

84. Meilaender, *Bioethics,* 12.

85. Robertson, *Children of Choice,* 39. This statement is made in the context of the author's argument that people have a "moral right" to noncoital reproduction, whether or not that "right" is viewed as constitutionally guarded (38-42). Thus, applying the same "moral" logic, Robertson writes, "If a woman has a moral right to end an unwanted pregnancy when the fetus is healthy, she would also have a right to terminate a pregnancy when the fetus has a

At a moment in history increasingly being called "posthuman," scientifically thwarting the procreative act is not a feat that accords with human dignity. Neither do unhuman (inhumane?) attempts at manipulating conception, via abortifacients or reproductive technologies, in any stretch of the human imagination promote the good of the person, the community, or the broader society. Not infrequently these attempts emanate from what one commentator has called "neophiliacs," that is, people infatuated by the new, if they are not intoxicated by a freedom from moral restraints.[86]

As it applies to bioethics and biotechnology in general, calls to eliminate disease and "suffering" *may or may not* be grounded in respect for the image of God.[87] Indeed, the proverbial "cure" may be more dreadful than the actual "disease" itself. So, for example, if fetal tissue might be used to improve the health of others, or embryonic stem cells might be manipulated to produce insulin and cure diabetes, or coagulate into heart tissue and cure heart disease, or replace neurons and heal a damaged spine, what possible argument could be raised to stop "progress" and "further humanity" by way of genetic "enhancement"? But is this perhaps not the Faustian bargain, by which we gain knowledge required to "cure disease" but do so at the price of our very souls?[88] That most "neophiliacs" have a deep-seated contempt for moral reflection at the cutting edge of biotechnology is telling. The fact that reproductive technologies are taking on an increasingly unhuman cast causes Steven Long to use the following analogy: "Suppose it were possible to avoid developing the virtue of temperance by having an electrode placed in the brain to suppress angry emotion: the dehumanization is apparent. This is likewise true of

---

genetic defect. . . . This practice need no more devalue the life of handicapped persons than carrier screening to avoid their birth does, or than aborting a normal fetus devalues children generally. If abortion is accepted generally, then it should be available for genetic selection reasons as well" (158-59).

86. Richard John Neuhaus, "While We're at It," *First Things*, November 2005, 62.

87. Dennis Hollinger rightly notes that it is possible to isolate scientific knowledge from noble and moral purposes, thereby rendering the scientific enterprise a questionable end in itself ("A Theology of Healing and Genetic Engineering," in *Genetic Engineering: A Christian Response*, ed. Timothy J. Demy and Gary P. Stewart [Grand Rapids: Kregel, 1999], 297).

88. For James Tonkowich, the answer is yes. See his commentary "Curing Disease at the Price of Our Souls," accessible at www.prolifenews.blogspot.com/2005/12/christian-pro-life-news-curing-disease.

the negation through in vitro fertilization of the essential importance of the unitive good for procreation in marriage. Both the electrode to suppress anger . . . and the in vitro fertilization in some sense partially achieve the end, but do so deviantly and without regard for the right order of subordinate ends."[89]

While we by no means wish to belittle those couples who desperately wish to have children but cannot, at the same time we must not lose sight of the moral and spiritual significance of the biological bonds by which we enter the world.[90] We must see the rights talk that has engulfed our culture—including the "right to reproduce" — for what it is: the idolatrous aspiration to usurp human freedom and control our destiny.[91] But procreation, as Gilbert Meilaender has wisely written, is "neither the exercise of a right nor a means of self-fulfillment." Rather, it is, "by God's blessing, the internal fruition of the act of love."[92]

Respecting Life at the Margins: A Case for Human Dignity

But what about the more "difficult" categories, such as developing embryos, harvested solely for the purpose of stem-cell research, or prenatal screening of the fetus and abortion of a "defective" fetus? Clearly, for many people the protection of the human embryo is not a "consensus" value. Nevertheless, over the last two decades four major policy advisory groups, *none of which was appointed with any input from pro-life organizations,* have achieved something of a consensus on the matter, as Richard Doerflinger, associate director of the Secretariat for Pro-Life Activities of

89. Steven A. Long, "Reproductive Technologies and the Natural Law," *National Catholic Bioethics Quarterly,* Summer 2002, 227.

90. As I prepare this manuscript, I read in the university's daily newspaper a quarter-page ad that reads as follows: "We are looking for a special egg donor. Compensation $100,000. This ad is being placed for a particular client and is not soliciting eggs for a donor bank or registry. We provide a unique program that only undertakes one match at a time. . . ."

91. Thus, in response to the question "Do we all have a *right* to a child *at any cost?*" ethicist Dennis Hollinger replies no. Given our God-given place in the moral order, our ultimate purpose is to pursue the good. There are then ethical limitations to our attempts at reproduction. See his essay "The Right to Have a Child: Are There Ethical Considerations?" accessible at www.cbhd.org/resources/reproductive/hollinger_2003-05-07.

92. Meilaender, *Bioethics,* 25.

the U.S. Catholic Conference of Bishops, has recently chronicled.[93] The findings of these advisory panels can be summarized as follows:

- The Ethics Advisory Board to the Department of Health, Education and Welfare (1979) concluded that the early human embryo deserves "profound respect" as a form of developing life.[94]
- The National Institutes of Health (NIH) Human Embryo Research Panel in 1994 concluded that "the preimplantation human embryo warrants serious moral consideration as a developing form of human life."[95]
- The National Bioethics Advisory Commission stated in 1999 that "human embryos deserve respect as a form of human life."[96]
- The National Academy of Sciences acknowledged in 2002 that the embryo "from fertilization" is "a developing human."[97]

Although Doerflinger is quick to point out that policy initiatives, when it came time to decide on funding, have frequently deviated or conflicted with the above pronouncements, what is nevertheless significant is that all these bodies, *without religious justification,* have conceded that the embryo is "a developing human life." That is, the embryo is not merely "capable of life"; it *is,* in germinal form, human life. Every person at one time had embryo status, and even when we stop short of explicitly ascribing to the embryo "personhood," the issue of moral obligation remains intact. Any other standard, by which we as a culture assign dignity or personhood based on functionality, social utility, appearance, or capacities, "will exclude many more people from personhood than just the embryo."[98] Has the burden of proof needed to justify human embryo research to the National Bioethics Advisory Commission been set aside yet?

---

93. See Richard M. Doerflinger, "Testimony on Embryo Research and Related Issues," *National Catholic Bioethics Quarterly,* Winter 2003, 772-78.

94. "Report of the Ethics Advisory Board," *Federal Register* 44 (June 18, 1979): 350-56.

95. *Transcript of the NIH Human Embryo Research Panel* (Rockville, Md.: National Institutes of Health, 1994), 2.

96. *Ethical Issues in Human Stem Cell Research* (Rockville, Md.: National Bioethics Advisory Commission, 1999), 1.2.

97. *Scientific and Medical Aspects of Human Reproductive Cloning* (Washington, D.C.: National Academy Press, 2002), E5.

98. Doerflinger, "Testimony," 773.

Doerflinger thinks not, based on statements made by the board itself.[99] Therefore, as the NIH acknowledged in 2001, the burden of proof remains.

Human life finds itself most vulnerable when it enters the world and when it leaves the temporal order. For this reason moral constraints to protect vulnerable human life will need the benefit of the doubt. Recently, Nathan Adams IV has attempted to apply natural-law moral reasoning to biotechnological research. Adams cites four rudimentary facts verified by science that accord with a Christian view of human personhood and help guide us toward a moral biotechnological policy:

- The subject of biotechnological research is *living and genetically unique.*
- The embryo is *human* and *capable of developing into an adult.*
- Every adult passes through the embryonic stage of development.
- Deprivation of an embryo's stem cells and various other components necessarily kills the embryo.[100]

Adams wishes to argue that embryos are living human beings because they possess the single defining characteristic of human life that is lost at death. That is, they are "totipotent," capable of developing into every organ of the human body; they are thus a "coordinated organism" and not merely living cells.

Where precision regarding a biological definition of personhood eludes our grasp, the Christian is morally bound to "err" on the side of creational theology, which calls us to "respect" life absolutely. So, for example, we soberly consider the implications of the psalmist's declaration,

> For you created my inmost being;
> you knit me together in my mother's womb.

99. The NIH's review of stem cell research concluded that therapeutic research involving embryonic stem cells was "hypothetical and highly experimental," failing to demonstrate any advantage that might offset morally problematic alternatives. See *Stem Cells: Scientific Progress and Future Research Directions* (Bethesda, Md.: Department of Health and Human Services, 2001), 17, also cited in Doerflinger, "Testimony," 774.

100. Nathan A. Adams IV, "An Unnatural Assault on Natural Law: Regulating Biotechnology Using a Just Research Theory," in *Human Dignity in the Biotech Century: A Christian Vision for Public Policy,* ed. Nigel M. de S. Cameron and Charles W. Colson (Downers Grove, Ill.: InterVarsity, 2004), 162-64, emphasis added.

I praise you because I am fearfully and wonderfully made. . . .
Your eyes beheld my unformed substance,

(Ps. 139:13-14a, 16a)

or the word of the Lord to Jeremiah:

Before I formed you in the womb I knew you,
before you were born I set you apart.

(Jer. 1:5)

If human life is sacred and inviolable at every moment of existence, *this is true at the initial phase of life* as we know it. Therefore, we cannot be morally "neutral" with regard to any phase of human life, even human embryos.[101]

A sense of the Christian understanding of personhood is mirrored by Tertullian in the second century: "It is anticipated murder to prevent someone from being born; it makes little difference whether one kills a soul already born or puts it to death at birth. He who will one day be a man is a man already."[102] Even scientific research and theological-philosophical speculation about the presence or infusion of a "soul" in no way call into question human personhood at the *earliest* stages. For this reason, from the moment of conception life must be guarded with the greatest of care and respect.[103] It follows then that biotechnological research, which potentially affords enormous promise in the humane service of mankind, "must always reject experimentation, research or applications which disregard the inviolable dignity of the human being and thus cease to be at the service of people and become instead means which, under the guise of helping people, actually harm them."[104]

101. The same moral logic would apply to cloning as well. Thus far, attempts at animal cloning have yielded far more "failures" than "successes." The sheep Dolly, it will be remembered, was conceived only after 176 unsuccessful attempts. As of this writing, Dolly is dead. Apart from that, scientists have questioned the morality of cloning because of the high degree of genetic mutation. As it concerns the use of human embryos, see, more recently, Nancy L. Jones and William P. Cheshire, "Can Artificial Techniques Supply Morally Neutral Human Embryos for Research?" *Ethics and Medicine* 12, no. 1 (2005): 29-40, and Roger Hoedemaeckers, "Human Embryos, Human Ingenuity, and Government Policy," *Ethics and Medicine* 19, no. 2 (2003): 75-84.

102. Tertullian, *Apology* 9.8 (English translation from Corpus scriptorum ecclesiasticorum latinorum 69.24).

103. If this is not the case, then abortion cannot be condemned.

104. *EV*, no. 89.

But Christian moral teaching, in accordance with the natural law, calls us to take other factors into consideration than the mere technical possibilities and probabilities of scientific experimentation. These remain constant, even when tomorrow researchers announce that the precise nature of cell division of the embryo removes our moral angst. In what ways do "reproductive freedom" and the new technologies mirror, or undermine, the integrity of our families, our kinships, our biological and social commitments? The integrity of the family erodes when the bonds between husband and wife and between parents and children are blurred by reproductive procedures.[105] What does the injection of outside third parties do in the familial context? How is love expressed? What do the technologies say about the way we treat our children? In what manner do these procedures reflect our dominion as stewards of creation? This, of course, is not particularly owing to Christian insight; it is embedded in our nature. Such are questions that will not "evolve" in the laboratory.[106] Even when the human person is more than the human body, the human body is integral to human being. Such a presupposition rejects the view, therefore, that the body is merely an instrumental good. In the words of William May, "The good of life to which we are directed by first principles of natural law includes human bodily life, and the personal life protected by the moral norms generated by natural law principles includes bodily human life. That truth is the bedrock principle in all bioethical issues."[107]

The natural law, part of the Creator's revelation of moral reality, witnesses to the fact that we have no "original and rightful jurisdiction" over the gift of life. In this light *we possess no moral claim* to develop partial or "subhuman" beings, in the end "mutating the species at the expense of

---

105. John Paul II in *Evangelium Vitae* concurs: "Thus the original import of human sexuality is distorted and falsified, and the two meanings, unitive and procreative, inherent in the very nature of the conjugal act are artificially separated: In this way the marriage union is betrayed and its fruitfulness is subjected to the caprice of the couple. Procreation then becomes the 'enemy' to be avoided in sexual activity" (no. 23).

106. Doerflinger's discussion of these and related issues ("Testimony," 778-82) is particularly thoughtful. In his discussion, Doerflinger develops the implications of Christian moral teaching for the following bioethical concerns: (1) human cloning, (2) patenting human beings, (3) federal funding of embryo research, (4) federal funding of embryonic stem-cell research, (5) federal funding of in vitro fertilization, and (6) regulating in vitro fertilization.

107. William E. May, "Bioethics and Human Life," in *Natural Law and Contemporary Public Policy*, ed. David F. Forte (Washington, D.C.: Georgetown University Press, 1998), 48.

some and for the convenience of others."[108] Our mandate, therefore, as people of faith, is not to "shrink the truth to the point that even a postmodernist can bear it."[109] Rather, it is to contend for moral "first things" in a manner that accords with our inherent dignity as human beings — beings who mirror the image of God. "Man has been given a sublime dignity based on the intimate bond which unites him to his Creator," John Paul II has argued with considerable force. In the human person, "there shines forth a reflection of God himself. . . . The sacredness of life gives rise to its inviolability, written from the beginning in man's heart, in his conscience."[110] It is in this light that we may understand the divine warning recorded in Genesis 9:5: "And from each man, too, I will demand an accounting for human life." Moreover, the negative proscription by the Creator, "Thou shalt not kill," mirrors the *absolute* boundaries that may *never* be breached with regard to innocent human life.[111] Nevertheless, the implicit meaning of this declaration is *positive* insofar as it *safeguards* human life; that is, life is *absolutely* to be respected. One cannot "overrespect" human life; life can, however, for selfish and utilitarian reasons, be *under*valued. And this precisely is the crisis of our time.[112]

108. Long, "Reproductive Technologies," 228.

109. Long, "Reproductive Technologies," 228.

110. *EV,* no. 34.

111. One of those who has argued forcefully in this vein is Robert P. George. See his afterword "We Should Not Kill Human Embryos — for Any Reason: The Ethics of Embryonic Stem Cell Research and Human Cloning," in *The Clash of Orthodoxies,* 317-36. It is unfortunate that this essay is without any footnotes, since George, having served during the Bush administration on the President's Council on Bioethics, relates valuable anecdotal material and cites numerous sources for which there is no bibliographical data available to the reader.

112. What *is* the moral status of the human conceptus? As Christopher Tollefsen properly argues, in "Embryos, Individuals, and Persons: An Argument against Embryo Creation and Research," *Journal of Applied Philosophy* 18, no. 1 (2001): 65-77, this question remains very much the essence of reproductive ethics, notwithstanding the concerted attempts to redirect the central question. Indeed, the question of the moral status of the conceptus *must* be addressed before any informed judgment can be made as to whether, for example, it is permissible to experiment on the embryo or even to cultivate embryonic tissue for medical treatment (66). This is particularly the case insofar as much research and technology entails destroying embryos. Tollefsen perceptively observes that even research that is conducted in the laboratory is a public and not private affair, existing for the social good, and therefore must be held accountable (68). To destroy embryos that we acknowledge might be persons and that are genetically continuous with a recognizable future individual is to be willing to kill persons (69, 74).

From the standpoint of faith, the truth about nature and natural revelation therefore matters. And while government cannot impose by decree moral truth, this truth should nevertheless be debated in the public square, if, for no other reason, it is intuited by all human beings. The alternative is an unhuman — and inhumane — consensus of "choice."

Moral atrocity and self-sacrificing charity, after all, are both "choices." Both are reminders that moral neutrality is an utter myth, even when it masquerades as enlightened sensibility. Therefore, to be "pro-choice" with respect to *any* health and bioethical issue will require severe moral qualification.

CHAPTER EIGHT

Ethics, Bioethics, and the Natural Law — a Test Case: Euthanasia Yesterday and Today

In an increasingly secularized Western world, euthanasia — rivaled per-haps only by genetic enhancement — may be *the* life issue of the early twenty-first century. Thus, it behooves the Christian community — in-deed, all people of good will — both to discern the roots of euthanasic thinking and to develop compassionate strategies for helping those who are terminally ill or dying.

Our task is made more difficult, or perhaps easier, depending on how one views it, with the visibility and outspoken nature of people like philosopher-activist Peter Singer. Because Singer has been a forthright ad-vocate of infanticide and euthanasia,[1] as well as animal rights — and since 2001 bestiality — his views not only invite but also *demand* a morally in-formed response. Indeed, as an apostle of the "culture of death," he seems the perfect counter to John Paul II, who has articulated with considerable eloquence a "culture of life."[2]

1. In his writings, Singer waxes acerbic, at times acrimonious, in his criticisms of Christianity. For him society finds itself in a great struggle between an outmoded sanctity-of-life ethic that needs banishing and a new quality-of-life ethic.

2. See especially John Paul's encyclical *Evangelium Vitae* (1995), although the theme of

This chapter is an expansion of a discussion that first appeared in the epilogue of *The Un-formed Conscience of Evangelism: Recovering the Church's Moral Vision* (Downers Grove, Ill.: InterVarsity, 2002) and subsequently was reprinted with permission as *"Lebensunwertes Leben: The Devolution of Personhood in the Weimar and Pre-Weimar Era," Ethics and Med-icine* 21, no. 1 (Spring 2005): 41-54. Material is used with permission.

While Singer's appointment in 2000 to an endowed chair in ethics at Princeton perhaps startled those who endorse a "pro-life" ethic, such developments may in fact be the logical, "natural" progression of a culture in which secular activists occupy gatekeeping positions, becoming in fact that culture's "knowledge elite." After all, as one cultural commentator quite astutely points out: "Having once believed ourselves to be made in the image of God, we now learn — from the human genome project, the speculations of evolutionary psychologists, and numerous other sources — that humankind, too, is determined by genetic predispositions and the drive to reproduce. We are cleverer than other animals, to be sure, but the difference is one of degree, not of kind."[3]

The sheer irony, and logic, at work in Singer's worldview is placed in a democratic pluralism that is bleached of any moral intuitions. It is a curious fact that "in virtually all of human history, only in liberal democracies — societies founded on the recognition of the innate dignity of all members of the human race — have animals enjoyed certain minimum protections." And it is a no less curious fact that "these same liberal democracies have been infected with a corrosive self-doubt, giving rise in some educated circles to . . . antihuman enthusiasm."

But an inevitability confronts us: Can anyone really doubt that, "were the misanthropic agenda of the animal rights movement actually to succeed, the result would be an *increase* in man's inhumanity, to man and animal alike"? And until the day "when a single animal stands up and, led by a love of justice and a sense of self-worth, insists that the world recognize and respect its dignity, all the philosophical gyrations of the activists will remain so much sophistry."[4] Indeed, only a culture that attributes to

---

building a "culture of life" in response to the prevailing "culture of death" has surfaced in several of his encyclicals during the 1990s. Among Singer's works are *Practical Ethics*, 2nd ed. (Cambridge: Cambridge University Press, [1979] 1993); *How Are We to Live? Ethics in an Age of Self-Interest* (Melbourne: Text, 1993); and *Rethinking Life and Death* (Melbourne: Text, 1994).

3. Damon Linker, "Rights for Rodents," *Commentary*, April 2001, 41-44, here 43. The quotations in the next two paragraphs come from this article.

4. Of course, if the experience of pain is our central concern in esteeming animals in the broader context of creation, animal-rights activists such as Singer and other utilitarians are guilty of failing to (1) distinguish between various categories of pleasure and pain, (2) offer an account of why human beings choose *not* to mate and procreate, and (3) explain the virtue of sacrifice, even sacrifice unto death, for higher purposes. For animals, once their basic physical/biological needs are satisfied, fall asleep rather than reflecting on the problem of evil.

human nature an *intrinsic dignity* will in the end seek to safeguard human beings from a slide into inhumanity.

But the concept of "dignity" surely needs qualification. A telling example thereof: we have grown accustomed to hear the commonly used mantra of euthanasia advocates, "death with dignity." This slogan, with its cognates, well illustrates the great linguistic promiscuity that attends important ethical debates of our day. Yet, at bottom, "dignity" is a mirror of — and is grounded in — our fundamental *nature*. Are we princes or are we swine? Crowned with glory a little lower than the angels or on par with undignified worms? One Christian ethicist has framed it thusly: "When people say, 'I wouldn't treat an animal like that — put them [or me] out of their [my] misery,' they imply that it is undignified to die in great, uncontrolled pain. With palliative care they should not have to. But humans are more than animals; they are kings and queens of creation and have an 'alien dignity' bestowed on them from outside by God's grace. As such they should not be killed."[5]

The push to normalize euthanasia has occurred in societies that have been most deeply committed to the process of secularization — for example, Holland, Belgium, parts of Australia, increasingly in the United Kingdom and the United States. But the issue, we may safely say, will *not* go away, for like abortion it represents, in the words of Gordon Preece, director of the Centre for Applied Ethics at Ridley College (Australia), "a place where the ethical tectonic plates underpinning Western societies are shifting."[6] And as we wish to argue in the present chapter 7, this shift does not occur overnight.

Thus far in this volume we have returned several times to what is a recurring theme in the encyclicals of John Paul II, namely, the necessity of freedom's harnessing to truth. Speaking from the vantage point of one who formerly had intimate acquaintance with political tyranny, John Paul was well placed to address "free" societies of the West, reminding us that the wedding of democratic pluralism and moral relativism constitutes a thinly veiled totalitarianism.[7] Indeed, the historical record would seem to

---

5. Gordon Preece, "Rethinking Singer on Life and Death," in *Rethinking Peter Singer: A Christian Critique*, ed. Gordon Preece (Downers Grove, Ill.: InterVarsity, 2002), 125.

6. Preece, "Rethinking Singer," 22.

7. Hence, the "end of democracy" debate that surfaced several years ago among some political and legal theorists, while controversial and offensive to some, raised questions nevertheless that demand our consideration. There *is* a form of tyranny that democratic pluralism is capable of engendering, precisely when it is wed to the ethical relativism against which John Paul warns.

vindicate the former pontiff: the century immediately behind us constitutes a sobering reminder that freedom is capable of annihilating itself; this occurs when human freedom is no longer tethered to a universal moral law.

Only a half-century removed, we in the West — and we Americans, in particular — seem to have forgotten a most disturbing fact of recent history: *moral atrocity, couched in medical and scientific justification, is the end result of the encroachment on ethics that implants itself in the realm of medical science.* Consequently, we are increasingly comfortable with speaking of "death with dignity," "compassionate release," and "merciful exit preference" for those we deem "no longer worthy of life itself." This utilitarian strain of thinking, perhaps dormant for several brief decades, would appear to have emerged once more in full force.

Perhaps because I married into a German family and spent the early years of marriage living and studying in (former West) Germany, where the first of our children was born, I am all the more interested in exploring the history of ideas as they mirror contemporary ethical debates. This has caused me to be much more sensitive to the character of moral atrocities that lie in the not-too-distant past. What's more, the older I become, the more aware I am of the well-worn truism that ideas indeed have consequences. For example, radical developments in any cultural realm, whether in science and technology, politics, or ethics, require *preparation;* that is, society is conditioned to accept *incrementally over time* radical shifts in attitudes and values. These shifts, it must be reiterated, do not occur overnight, nor do they occur in a vacuum; rather, they evolve. In the sphere of bioethics, the implications of cultural "shifts" and evolving attitudes are enormous.

In what follows I wish to consider the evolution of the notion of *lebensunwertes Leben* ("life unworthy of living") in German academic thought that occurred in the forty-year period roughly between 1890 and 1933, when National Socialism officially took power. Thereby I hope to illustrate that "revolutionary" and totalitarian tendencies require *preparation.* This ideological preparation is particularly significant as we undergo shifts in our social understanding of the notion of human *personhood* — a shift that informs every significant bioethical issue.

Legal theorist Russell Hittinger has written that every generation must discover afresh the necessity of the natural law.[8] And so it does. Whether in

---

8. Hittinger contributes the introduction to the English translation of Heinrich Rom-

the context of totalitarian experiments run amok or amidst the insipid relativism and moral torpor characteristic of our own times, each generation is indeed pressed to discover — or rediscover — the moral predicates of law. For without these predicates, law can be manipulated to justify the inhumane.

Lebensunwertes Leben: Biological and Economic Factors[9]

One of the tragic legacies of social Darwinism is that it assisted in justifying the elimination of *lebensunwertes Leben,* life that is unworthy of living, or, in the language of Darwinists, life that is simply unfit.[10] While it is commonly assumed that the moral atrocities associated with the Holocaust were the exclusive domain of Adolf Hitler and those loyal to him (people such as Joseph Goebbels, Hermann Göring, Heinrich Himmler, and Albert Speer), this was only the final act.[11] Indeed, it would appear, as authors with such diverse backgrounds as Alexander Mitscherlich,[12] Robert Jay Lifton,[13] Robert Proctor,[14] Michael Burleigh,[15]

men's important work, *The Natural Law: A Study of Legal and Social History and Philosophy,* trans. T. R. Hanley (Indianapolis: Liberty Fund, 1998).

9. See also Charles, *"Lebensunwertes Leben,"* 42-44.

10. What writer Hugh Gregory Gallagher rather succinctly states as the essence of Darwinian thinking a century ago could very easily be applied to our own day: "The eugenicists and Darwinists, for all their pretensions, made no distinctions within the fitness category. Crooks and prostitutes, the blind, the paralyzed, the retarded, all were degenerate, all were unfit. These were people with weak genes. The degeneracy of their character, as well as the flawed nature of their bodies, was seen to be inherited" (*By Trust Betrayed: Patients, Physicians, and the License to Kill in the Third Reich,* rev. ed. [Arlington, Va.: Vandamere Press, 1995], 50).

11. Perhaps the best resource for understanding not only the indispensable role that Hitler's assistants played in propping up the Third Reich but also the psychology of totalitarianism as it was played out ethically in their individual lives is Guido Knopp's *Hitlers Helfer* (Munich: Wilhelm Goldmann Verlag, 1996). Unfortunately, this book remains untranslated from the German.

12. Alexander Mitscherlich (with Fred Mielke), *Doctors of Infamy: The Story of the Nazi Medical Crimes* (New York: Henry Schuman, 1949).

13. Robert Jay Lifton, *The Nazi Doctors: Medical Killing and the Psychology of Genocide* (New York: Basic Books, 1986).

14. Robert N. Proctor, *Racial Hygiene: Medicine under the Nazis* (Cambridge, Mass., and London: Harvard University Press, 1988).

15. Michael Burleigh, *Death and Deliverance: "Euthanasia" in Germany ca. 1900-1945* (Cambridge: Cambridge University Press, 1994).

and Wesley Smith[16] have documented, that the path to medical evil was prepared long before Nazism was even a cloud on the German horizon. In addition to the ascendancy of biological determinism,[17] an important step in legitimizing the killing of the weak, the infirm, the terminally ill, and the incompetent was the shift in ethos among medical doctors and psychiatrists several decades prior to WWII. Historian Robert Proctor has argued persuasively that the Nazi experiment was rooted in *pre-1933 thinking* about the essence of personhood, racial hygienics, and survival economics, and that physicians were instrumental both in pioneering research and in carrying out this program.[18] In fact, Proctor is adamant that scientists and physicians were *pioneers* and not pawns in this process. By 1933, however, when political power was consolidated by National Socialists, it was already too late for resistance within the medical community. Proctor notes, for example, that most of the fifteen-odd journals devoted to racial hygienics were established long before the rise of National Socialism.[19]

Few accounts of this period are more thoroughly researched than Michael Burleigh's *Death and Deliverance: "Euthanasia" in Germany ca. 1900-1945*. Particularly important is Burleigh's discussion of psychiatric reform and medical utilitarianism during the Weimar period.[20] During the years of WWI, it is estimated that over 140,000 people died in German psychiatric asylums.[21] This would suggest that about 30 percent of the entire

16. Wesley J. Smith, *Forced Exit: The Slippery Slope from Assisted Suicide to Legalized Murder* (New York: Times Books, 1997), and more recently, *Culture of Death: The Assault on Medical Ethics in America* (San Francisco: Encounter Books, 2000).

17. It is telling that National Socialist leaders commonly referred to the phenomenon of National Socialism as "applied biology." An example of this in the literature is Fritz Lenz, *Menschliche Auslese und Rassenhygiene* (Munich: Beck, 1931), which remains untranslated from the German. (The title translates: "Human Selection and Race-Based Health.") Significantly, the 1931 version of Lenz's book was the *third* edition already.

18. Robert N. Proctor, "Nazi Doctors, Racial Medicine, and Human Experimentation," in *The Nazi Doctors and the Nuremberg Code: Human Rights in Human Experimentation*, ed. George J. Annas and Michael A. Grodin (New York and Oxford: Oxford University Press, 1992), 19-31.

19. Proctor, "Nazi Doctors," 20.

20. The Weimar Republic corresponds to the period extending from 1919, the year of a German constitutional assembly at Weimar, to 1933, when the republic was dissolved with Hitler becoming chancellor.

21. Hans-Ludwig Siemen, *Menschen bleiben auf der Strecke. Psychiatrie zwischen Reform und Nationalsozialismus* (Gütersloh: Gütersloher Verlag, 1987), 29-30.

prewar asylum population died as a result of hunger, disease, or neglect.[22] Following the war, evidence indicates that a shift in the moral climate was in progress. In the spring of 1920 the chairman of the German Psychiatric Association (GPA), Karl Bonhoeffer, told the GPA annual meeting that "we have witnessed a change in the concept of humanity"; moreover, "in emphasizing the right of the healthy to stay alive, which is an inevitable result of periods of necessity, there is also a danger of going too far: a danger that the self-sacrificing subordination of the strong to the needs of the helpless and ill, which lies at the heart of any true concern for the sick, will give ground to the demand of the healthy to live."[23] According to Burleigh, Bonhoeffer went on in the 1930s to offer courses that trained those who in time would be authorized with implementing sterilization policies introduced by the National Socialists.[24]

Already in the 1890s, the traditional view of medicine that physicians are not to harm and only to cure was being questioned in some corners by a "right-to-die" ethos. Voluntary euthanasia was supported by a concept of negative human worth — i.e., the combined notion that suffering negates human worth and the incurably ill and mentally defective place an enormous burden on families and surrounding communities. It is at this time that the expression "life unworthy of being lived" seems to have emerged; it was to become the subject of heated debate by the time WWI had ended.[25]

One notable "early" proponent of involuntary euthanasia was influential biologist and Darwinian social theorist Ernst Haeckel. In 1899 Haeckel published *The Riddle of the Universe*, which achieved enormous success and became one of the most widely read science books of the era.[26]

22. This is Burleigh's calculation (*Death and Deliverance*, 11).

23. Bonhoeffer's address was published in the *Allgemeine Zeitschrift für Psychiatrie* 76 (1920/21); the citation is from p. 600 (an English translation of which appears in Burleigh, *Death and Deliverance*, 11-12).

24. Burleigh, *Death and Deliverance*, 12. What Burleigh does *not* mention — nor, significantly, do other historians of this era of German history — is that Karl Bonhoeffer was the father of Dietrich Bonhoeffer.

25. This is the view of historians Burleigh, *Death and Deliverance*, 12-13, and Proctor, *Racial Hygiene*, 177-222 ("The Destruction of 'Lives Not Worth Living,'" which is chapter 7 of Proctor's book).

26. According to historian Daniel Gasman, *The Scientific Origins of National Socialism: Social Darwinism in Ernst Haeckel and the German Monist League* (New York: American Elsevier, 1971), 14, *Riddle* sold more than 100,000 copies in its first year, went through ten

One of several influential voices contending for the utility of euthanasia, Haeckel combined the notion of euthanasia as an act of mercy with economic concerns that considerable money might be thereby saved.[27]

Further justification for euthanasia in the pre-WWI era was provided by people such as social theorist Adolf Jost and Nobel Prize–winning chemist Wilhelm Ostwald. According to Ostwald, "in all circumstances suffering represents a restriction upon, and diminution of, the individual and capacity to perform in society of the person suffering."[28] In his 1895 book *Das Recht auf den Tod (The Right to Death)*,[29] Jost set forth the argument — almost forty years in advance of Nazi prescriptions — that the "right" to kill existed in the context of the higher rights possessed by the state, since all individuals belonged to the social organism of the state. Furthermore, this was couched in terms of "compassion" and "relief" from one's suffering. Finally, and not least importantly, the right to kill compassionately was predicated on biology, in accordance with the spirit of the age: the state must ensure that the social organism remains fit and healthy.[30]

Lebensunwertes Leben: Medical and Legal Factors[31]

Well before the outbreak of WWI, multiple influential voices appear in the literature agitating for a legalization of assisted death. One such legal proposal is spelled out in the following protocol:

---

editions by 1919, had sold over 500,000 copies by 1933, and in time was translated into twenty-five languages. Gasman has called Haeckel "Germany's major prophet of political biology" (150).

27. See Walter Schmuhl, *Rassenhygiene, Nationalsozialismus, Euthanasie. Von der Verhütung zur Vernichtung 'lebensunwerten Lebens' 1890-1945* (Göttingen: Vandenhoeck & Ruprecht, 1987), especially 109.

28. This was part of an exchange published in Wilhelm Börner, "Euthanasie," *Das monistische Jahrhundert* 2 (1913): 251-54. An English translation of this text appears in Burleigh, *Death and Deliverance,* 14.

29. Adolf Jost, *Das Recht auf den Tod: Sociale Studie* (Göttingen: Dietrich'sche Verlagsbuchhandlung, 1895).

30. English-language assessments of Jost can be found in Lifton (*The Nazi Doctors,* 46) and Burleigh (*Death and Deliverance,* 12-15), with a more thorough untranslated examination in Klaus Dörner, "Nationalsozialismus und Lebensvernichtung," *Vierteljahrshefte für Zeitgeschichte* 15 (1967): 121-52.

31. See also Charles, *"Lebensunwertes Leben,"* 44-46.

1. Whoever is incurably ill has the right to assisted death.
2. The right to assisted death will be established by the patient's petition to the relevant judicial authorities.
3. On the basis of the petition, the court will instigate an examination of the patient by the court physician in association with two qualified specialists.
4. The record of the examination must show whether the examining doctors were scientifically convinced that the illness was more likely to follow a terminal course than that the patient would recover permanent ability to work.
5. If the examination finds that a terminal outcome is the most probable one, then the court should accord the patient the right to die. In contrary cases, the patient's request will be firmly denied.
6. Whoever painlessly kills the patient as a result of the latter's express and unambiguous request is not to be punished, provided that the patient has been accorded the right to die under clause 5 of the law, or if posthumous examination reveals that he was incurably ill.
7. Whoever kills the patient without his express and unambiguous request will be punished with hard labour.
8. Clauses 1 to 7 are equally applicable to the elderly and crippled.[32]

In many respects the most significant contribution to the debate over euthanasia was the publication in 1920 of *Die Freigabe der Vernichtung lebensunwerten Lebens: Ihr Mass und ihre Form*,[33] by esteemed law profes-

---

32. This "draft" was originally published in volume 2 of *Das monistische Jahrhundert*, 1913, 170-71. A translation from the German appears in Burleigh, *Death and Deliverance*, 13-14.

33. Karl Binding and Alfred Hoche, *Die Freigabe der Vernichtung lebensunwerten Lebens: Ihr Mass und ihre Form* (Leipzig: Felix Meiner Verlag, 1920); the title is typically rendered *The Permission to Destroy Life Unworthy of Life*. This translation, cited in most historical accounts of this period (see, for example, those listed in the following footnote), does not adequately capture the nuance and the euphemism that inhere in the German original. A better rendering would be "Release for the Extermination of Life Unworthy of Being Lived." The German verb *freigeben*, from which the noun *Freigabe* is derived, can mean "permit," but more often than not it carries the sense of "release" or "set free." (In my research I came across only one historical source that rendered *Freigabe* as "Release": Proctor, *Racial Hygiene*, p. 178.) Hence, in the title of Binding and Hoche's volume, it is probably intended to convey a *therapeutic* nuance and not merely descriptive or prescriptive function; significantly, from the standpoint of euthanasia advocates, people are "released" or "set free" by the act of "mercy killing." *Freigabe* in this context is a partner-term standing alongside another

sor Karl Binding and psychiatrist Alfred Hoche.[34] By 1920 the subject of euthanasia was no longer merely a matter of academic debate. Binding and Hoche argued with considerable precision that the medical profession had the responsibility not only of promoting health but, where necessary, also of facilitating death *(Sterbehilfe)*. The Binding-Hoche book is significant for several reasons. One is the way in which the authors seek to mainstream the distinction between *lebenswertes Leben* ("life worth living") and *lebensunwertes Leben* ("life not worth living").[35] Binding attempts to extrapolate from what he believes to be a "weakness" in the German criminal code by suggesting that certain life, e.g., that of someone "deathly ill or fatally wounded,"[36] "no longer merits full legal protection."[37] He laments that this distinguishing between worthwhile and unworthwhile life "has made no progress"[38] in the actual practice of German criminal law, although in the academic literature it has "gained a lively reception."[39]

What's more, they stressed that ending "life unworthy of living" had a *therapeutic* goal. But in what instances was the facilitation of death necessary? Binding and Hoche carefully reasoned that certain categories of persons were living "unworthy" lives but also that assisting in their death was ethically, medically, and economically justifiable. These categories included the retarded, the deformed, the mentally ill, and the severely disabled.[40] In a remarkable comment confined to a footnote, Binding insinuates that death would prevent the "mentally dead" person or "idiot" from having to endure the shame of being a public spectacle and mistreatment

German euphemism, *Gnadentod* (mercy death). This language, it should be emphasized, comports perfectly with the ethos of contemporary euthanasia proponents.

34. This view is shared by American Holocaust historian Robert Jay Lifton, *The Nazi Doctors*, 46-48; German historian Christian Pross, "Nazi Doctors, German Medicine, and Historical Truth," in *The Nazi Doctors and the Nuremberg Code*, 40; American historian Robert Proctor, *Racial Hygiene*, 177-80; British historian Michael Burleigh, *Death and Deliverance*, 15-21; writer Hugh Gregory Gallagher, *By Trust Betrayed*, 60; and writer/legal expert Wesley Smith, *Forced Exit*, 73-75.

35. The expression "life unworthy of living" occurs regularly throughout *Freigabe* and is never qualified or questioned. Examples of this are found on 24, 51, and 53.

36. German translation: *einer Todkranker oder tödlich Verwundete* (*Freigabe*, 24).

37. *Freigabe*, 24-25.

38. *Freigabe*, 25.

39. *Freigabe*, 25.

40. These individuals Binding calls *die unrettbar Kranken*, "the hopelessly ill" (e.g., on p. 34 of *Freigabe*).

that results from other people's verbal abuse. He claims: "The life of such poor people is an unending invitation to die."[41]

Freigabe consists of two essays, the first being a "legal explanation" by Binding, whose reflections followed forty years of teaching law at the university level, and the second a "medical explanation" by Hoche. What follows is a summary of their twofold argument — an argument remarkably similar to the one being advocated by present-day proponents of assisted death.[42]

Binding, one of Germany's leading constitutional scholars, restates a question that has "much occupied" his thinking for many years, "but which most people timidly avoid because it is seen as delicate and hard to answer" (231-32). His question is this: "Should permissible taking of life be restricted, except in emergency situations, to an individual's act of suicide as it is in current law, or should it be legally extended to the killing of fellow human beings, and under what conditions?" (232). Binding is a passionate and deeply committed secularist. Foreclosing any debate, he asserts unequivocally: "Religious reasons have no probative force in law for two reasons. First, in this instance, they rest on a wholly unworthy concept of God. Second, law is thoroughly secular and is focused on the regulation of our external common life. Additionally, the New Testament says nothing about the problem of suicide" (233). Binding's prejudice against religion allows him to recast traditional Christian morality as the true villain, thereby paving the way for a universal "right to die":

> After an extended, deeply unchristian, interruption in the recognition
> of this right [the right to end one's life] (an interruption demanded by
> the church and supported by the obscene idea that the God of love

41. This is my translation of *Das Leben solcher Armen isst ein ewiges Spiessrutenlaufen*.

42. My commentary on the Binding-Hoche book is based on the German original, but for the benefit of the reader I locate most of the citations in the English translation of *Freigabe* ("The Permission to Destroy Life Unworthy of Life") that appeared in the journal *Issues in Law and Medicine* 5, no. 2 (1992): 231-65. The citations of this article have been placed in the text. Where the *Law and Medicine* translation is weak or misses particular nuances of the authors' language, I allude in the footnotes directly to the pages of the German original. (In addition, it is mildly distracting that the translators' enumeration of footnotes does not follow that of the authors.) The team of translators who prepared the text of *Freigabe* ("Permission") for *Law and Medicine* consisted of three individuals, one of whom received his medical degree from the Johann Wolfgang von Goethe University of Frankfurt in 1925, where he attended lectures in neurology and psychiatry by coauthor Hoche. Reprints of the English translation of *Freigabe* are available from: The Editor, *Issues in Law & Medicine*, P.O. Box 1586, Terre Haute, IN 47808.

could wish that human beings not die until they undergo endless physical and spiritual suffering) . . . , it has now been fully reestablished (except in a few backward countries) as an inalienable possession for all time. Natural law would have grounds for calling this freedom the primary "human right." . . . For the law, nothing else remains except to regard the living person as the sovereign of his own existence and manner of life. (233, 237)[43]

Notice how Binding's argument proceeds. "Natural law," having been bleached of its metaphysical basis, becomes the grounds for a "right" to kill those who suffer. What's more, the right of persons to kill themselves is to be protected legally.[44] Moreover, this "right" is "transferable" to "all so-called accomplices who act with the suicide's express consent" ("Permission," 236-37).[45] The practical rationale for euthanasia is that it "replaces a death which is painful . . . with a less painful death" (240). To reassure his audience, Binding adds: "This is not 'an act of killing in the legal sense' but is rather the modification of an irrevocably present cause of a death which can no longer be evaded. *In truth it is a purely healing act*" (240, emphasis Binding's). Such "healing intervention" must extend even to "unconscious patients," since, according to Binding, "the permission of the suffering patient is not required" (241).

"Compassion" as Release: The Function of Linguistic Prostitution in Justifying Moral-Social Evil[46]

Anticipating objection among his readers, Binding assures them that "in truth it [the euthanasic impulse] arises from nothing but the deepest sympathy" ("Permission," 246). "The act of euthanasia," he intones, "must be a

43. This statement is staggering not only for its hubris but also in its distortion of language, its distortion of Christian belief, and its distortion of natural-law thinking.

44. Binding acknowledges that in 1885 he had written from the opposite viewpoint, arguing that assisted death should remain illegal or *verboten* (*Freigabe*, 19 n. 32). Binding's sole objection to the legality of suicide is the possible loss of potentially valuable members of society.

45. In fact, Binding asserts that "this act must be considered as not legally forbidden even when the law does not explicitly recognize it" (241).

46. See also Charles, *"Lebensunwertes Leben,"* 46-48.

consequence of free sympathy" (252). Thus, given the combination of his illustrious career teaching law and his thinking about "the hopelessly ill" that is motivated by this "deepest sympathy," Binding seems well positioned to pose questions that "raise an uneasy feeling in anyone who is accustomed to assessing the value of individual life" (246). One such question is this: "Are there human lives which have so completely lost the attribute of legal status . . . that their continuation has permanently lost all value, both for the bearer of that life and for society?" Binding's own response has the ring of authority as well as common sense: "It is impossible to doubt that there are living people to whom death would be a release, and whose death would simultaneously free society and the state from carrying a burden which serves no conceivable purpose, except that of providing an example of the greatest unselfishness" (246).

Binding's reflections compel him to tread — and agitate — where German society heretofore had not legally trod: "Is it our duty actively to advocate for this life's asocial continuance . . . , or to permit its destruction under specific conditions? One could also state the question legislatively, like this: Does the energetic preservation of such life deserve preference . . . ? Or does permitting its termination, which frees everyone involved, seem the lesser evil?" (246-47). Because his logic appears to be airtight, Binding is resolute: "I cannot find the least reason — legally, socially, ethically, or religiously — not to permit those requested to do so to kill such hopeless cases who urgently demand death; indeed I consider this permission to be simply a duty of legal mercy (a mercy which also asserts itself in many other forms)" (248).

Binding proceeds to discuss "the necessary means" of carrying out this "duty of legal mercy." "With good reason," he observes, "permission always presupposes a clinical diagnosis." This diagnosis, moreover, "requires competent objective verification, which cannot possibly be placed in the agent's own hands" (251).[47] He recommends (1) that the initiative takes "the form of an application for permission from a qualified applicant"[48] and (2) that "this application goes to a government board, whose primary task is limited to investigating whether the presuppositions for permission

---

47. Note, as well, that this diagnosis cannot be placed in the hands of family members or spiritual leaders.

48. Instigation of the request, however, may originate with relatives or the person's doctor.

are met" (252). According to the Binding prescription, each case was to be evaluated by a three-person panel consisting of a physician, a psychiatrist, and a lawyer, who "alone have the right to vote." This "Permission Board" shall decree that "after thorough investigation on the basis of current scientific opinion, the patient seems beyond help; that there is no reason to doubt the sincerity of his consent; that accordingly no impediment stands in the way of killing the patient; and that the petitioner is entrusted with bringing about the patient's release from his evil situation in the most expedient way" (252). Death, according to this process, was to be "expertly" administered by a physician, in whom the right to grant death was a "natural extension of the responsibilities of the attending physician"; the "final release must be completely painless, and only qualified persons are justified in applying the means" (252).[49]

And what about the possibility of error? While Binding is confident that scientific consensus broadly operates beyond the realm of error, he realizes, of course, that objections to "mercy killing" will be many. Proof of "alleged error by the Permission Board would be very difficult to come by," he assures the potential Permission Board member; nonetheless, he does not deny the *possibility* of error by the board. Indeed, "Error is possible in all human actions, and no one would draw the foolish conclusion that, considering this possible defect, we must forego all useful and wholesome activities. Even the physician in private practice can make errors which have serious consequences, but no one would bar him from practice because he is capable of erring. *What is good and reasonable must be done despite the risk of error*" (254). Ultimately, even the possibility of fatal mistakes should not stand in the way of carrying out the "good and reasonable" prescription of Prof. Binding, which is the elimination of "life unworthy of living." Prof. Binding's self-proclaimed "deepest sympathy" for "valueless lives" comes to full expression at the conclusion of his essay: "But humanity loses so many members through error that one more or one less really scarcely matters" (254).

In the second essay of *Freigabe*, Alfred Hoche examines the medical relationship of physicians to their patients and physicians' relationship to killing. Hoche opens the essay by observing that a "code of medical ethics

---

49. The authors use several German words in the text therapeutically and euphemistically to speak of the patient's "release." The term here is *Erlösung*, which can be translated "solution" or "salvation" as well as "release."

is nowhere explicitly established": "There is no medical moral law set out in paragraphs, no *Moral Service Regulations*. The young physician enters practice without any legal delineation of his rights and duties — especially regarding the most important points. Not even the Hippocratic Oath . . . , with its generalities, is operative today" ("Permission," 255). In practice, what physicians "may do, or ought to do, emanates from peer opinion." Indeed, in some instances physicians "are compelled to destroy life" — for example, in "killing a living child during delivery for the purpose of saving the mother, terminating a pregnancy for the same reason." This is done "in the interest of serving a higher good." Furthermore, "in all surgical procedures, one tacitly counts on a certain percentage of fatal outcomes," and these "can never be wholly avoided. Our moral sensibility is completely reconciled to this" (256).

One recurring "inner dilemma" that "not infrequently touches the physician" is whether or not, through "passive acquiescence," to yield to the "temptation to let nature run its course" in matters of dying. Hoche is convinced that in certain cases such "passive acquiescence" to natural death is to be resisted. For example, "when the patient is incurably mentally ill," then "death is at all events preferable." Hoche emphasizes how "immensely complicated it has already become for doctors to balance, in daily life, the rigid basic principles of medical ethics and the demands of a higher conception of life's value," and when these two stand in conflict, the physician must recognize that "he has no absolute relation to this [latter] obligation in all circumstances" (257). Rather, "this relation is merely relative, alterable under new conditions, and always open to question"; medical ethics, as Hoche understands it, "cannot be viewed as an eternally fixed pattern" (257-58). For example, "If killing incurables or eliminating those who are mentally dead should come to be recognized (and generally acknowledged) as not only unpunishable, but as desirable for the general welfare, then, from that very moment, no opposing grounds for excluding this could be found in medical ethics" (258).

Hoche is not unmindful of practical concerns as he ponders the ethical duties of the medical profession. Extreme cases of "hopeless illness" that require the continuation of life, in his view, render "nonsensical" the need for lifesaving measures. "Is there human life which has utterly forfeited its claim to worth . . . that its continuation has forever lost all value both for the bearer of that life and society?" Hoche answers this question, "with certainty: Yes." One particular example of this sort of "valueless life" is what Hoche calls "mental death," i.e., the condition of people who are deemed "complete idiots," those "whose existence weighs most heavily on the community" (260).

When All Else Fails: Economics as Trump Card[50]

As the reader of Binding and Hoche's work will discover, the economic "burdens" that are "alleviated" by euthanizing people constitute perhaps the most compelling argument for assisted death. Wrestling with the "burden to the community" is what causes Hoche instinctively to return to the economic dimensions of caring for those who have severe physical or mental needs. Hoche calculates, based on the number of "complete idiots" cared for in German institutions in his day, the amount of money and resources that would be saved. His calculations: were the recommendations of his friend Prof. Binding acted upon, "it is easy to estimate what *incredible capital* is withdrawn from the nation's wealth for food, clothing, and heating — for an unproductive purpose" ("Permission," 260-61). This great loss due to "such dead weight" of "valueless lives" calls for "the liberation of every available power for productive ends" (261, 262).[51]

Consider the following dilemma, "Problem 97," found in a German mathematics textbook published in 1935:

> A mental patient costs about 4 RMS [*Reichmarks*] a day to keep, a cripple 5.50 RMS, a Criminal 3.50 RMS. In many cases a civil servant only has about 4 RMS, a salaried employee scarcely 3.50 RMS, an unskilled worker barely 2 RMS for his family. (a) Illustrate these figures with the aid of pictures. According to conservative estimates, there are about 300,000 mental patients, epileptics, etc. in asylums in Germany. (b) What do they cost together per annum at a rate of 4 RMS per per-

---

50. See also Charles, *"Lebensunwertes Leben,"* 48-49.

51. The sheer arrogance and inhumanity of Hoche's statements are breathtaking. Hoche writes: "Naturally no doctor would conclude with certainty that a two- or three-year-old was suffering permanent mental death. But, *even in childhood,* the moment comes when this prediction can be made without doubt" (Binding and Hoche, "Permission," 265, emphasis Hoche's).

son? . . . How many marriage loans at 1,000 RMS each could be awarded per annum with this money, disregarding later repayment?[52]

The solution to "Problem 97" follows:

Assuming an average daily outlay of 3.50 RMS there hereby results:

1. a daily savings of RM 245.955
2. an annual saving of RM 88,543.98
3. assuming a life expectancy of ten years.

After the math is done, it is established that by September of 1951, i.e., sixteen years after the calculation, a savings of 885,439,800 RMS (Reichmarks) would be had based on the 70,273 persons who had been "disinfected."[53]

Historian Robert Proctor has argued that the primary impetus for forcible euthanasia in the 1930s was economic, with assisted death being justified as a kind of "preemptive triage" to free up beds.[54] Persons considered a burden on German society included handicapped infants, the mentally ill, the terminally ill, the comatose, and criminals. By 1941, Proctor writes, euthanasia had become part of normal hospital routine.[55] This "disposal," or "disinfection," of human lives, of course, was to be done "humanely" but at the same time "economically." Lest we think, however, that the euthanasic impulse was narrowly confined to totalitarian regimes, Proctor writes that until reports of wholesale Nazi exterminations began to appear in American newspapers in 1942, the merits of forced euthanasia were being vigorously debated in various American scholarly journals.

Hoche is by no means naive in realizing that overturning conventional thinking, especially at the popular level, takes time and conditioning. Legislative as well as religious roadblocks serve as additional imped-

---

52. Adolf Dörner, ed., *Mathematik im Dienste der nationalpolitischen Erziehung mit Anwendungsbeispielen aus Volkswissenschaft, Geländekunde und Naturwissenschaft* (Frankfurt am Main: Fischer, 1935), 42. (An English translation of the title would be "Mathematics in the Service of National Political Education with Examples Drawn from Social Science, Folk Art, and Natural Science." An English translation of the above citation, with the title untranslated, appears in Burleigh, *Death and Deliverance*, ix.)

53. Dörner, *Mathematik*, 42.

54. Proctor, "Nazi Doctors," 24.

55. Proctor, "Nazi Doctors," 24.

iments to the advancement of scientific thinking. Hoche waxes realistic: "The enormous difficulty of trying to address these problems legislatively will continue for a long time. Likewise, the ideas of gaining relief from our national burden by permitting the destruction of wholly worthless mentally dead persons will (from the start and for a long time) encounter lively, strident, and passionately stated opposition. This opposition will draw its strength from many different sources: resistance to the new and unfamiliar, religious ideas, sentimental feelings, and so on."[56] Up to now, he laments, when "the individual's subjective right to exist" has clashed with "objective expediency and necessity," the former has typically won. This "difficult" problem has been a result of "the essential participation of Christian ideas." But "alien perspectives" should not prevent us from realizing — and acting on the conviction — that "valueless lives" and "dead weight existences" are a drain to society as a "civil organism."[57]

Putting Euthanasia in Perspective: The Preparation of an Idea[58]

With the accession of the National Socialists to power in 1933, two developments that had reached their critical mass were promptly codified into law. One was the long-discussed sterilization program, which had been debated but had not achieved majority support. The second was authorized euthanasia. The proposal, issued by the German Ministry of Justice, was reported on the front page of the *New York Times* and stated: "It shall be made possible for physicians to end the tortures of incurable patients, upon request, in the interests of true humanity." Moreover, the ministry ensured, "no life still valuable to the state will be wantonly destroyed."[59]

Andrew C. Ivy, M.D., asked in 1946 by the board of trustees of the American Medical Association to serve as a consultant at the Nuremberg trial of Nazi physicians who had been indicted for "crimes against humanity," reflected on his difficult experience: "It was inconceivable that a group

56. Binding and Hoche, "Permission," 261.

57. Binding and Hoche, "Permission," 262.

58. See Charles, *"Lebensunwertes Leben,"* 49-51.

59. This was printed on page 1 of the *New York Times,* October 8, 1933, and is cited in Gallagher, *By Trust Betrayed,* 62.

of men trained in medicine and in official positions of power in German governmental circles could ignore the ethical principles of medicine and the unwritten law that a doctor should be nearer humanity than other men. . . . [W]e had assumed that the sacred aspects of medicine and its ethics would certainly remain inviolate."[60] Although "fewer than two hundred German physicians participated directly in the medical war crimes," it became clear to Ivy that these atrocities were only "the end result" of the "complete encroachment on the ethics and freedom of medicine" by those in positions of influence.[61]

Only a half-century removed, we in the West — including we in North America — seem to have forgotten a most disturbing fact of recent history: *moral atrocity, couched in medical and scientific justification, is the "end result" of the "encroachment on ethics" in the realm of medical science.* Consequently, we are increasingly comfortable with speaking of "death with dignity," "compassionate release," and "merciful exit preference" for those we deem "no longer worthy of life itself."[62]

This utilitarian strain of thinking, perhaps dormant for several brief decades, would appear to have emerged once more in full force. Unquestionably, it dominates current bioethical debates, where we find it most conspicuously on display in contemporary discussions of what constitutes personhood. Moreover, utilitarian thinking about ethics is ubiquitous; it is the air we breathe, surfacing among and propagated by ethicists, healthcare practitioners, social theorists, and sundry consultants, all of whom weigh the value of personhood against the economics of health care and the cumulative "burden" on society.[63] Lacking any strong commitment to the sanctity of life, utilitarian ethicists and practitioners adopt a "quality-of-life" ethic. The inevitable question that follows is this: At what point does an individual no longer have a "quality of life" that is "worthy of life" itself? Rightly bioethicist Leon Kass has warned: "There is the very real danger that what constitutes a 'meaningful life' among the intellectual elite

---

60. Cited in the foreword to Mitscherlich, *Doctors of Infamy*, ix-x.

61. Mitscherlich, *Doctors of Infamy*, x-xi.

62. Recall the attempts to redefine personhood by ethicists as noted in the beginning of chapter 6.

63. See, for example, Daniel Callahan's book *Setting Limits: Medical Goals in an Aging Society* (New York: Simon and Schuster, 1987), as well as the rather breathtaking essay by John Hardwig titled "Is There a Duty to Die?" that appeared in the journal edited by Callahan, *Hastings Center Report*, March-April 1997, 37-38.

will be imposed on the people as the only standard by which the value of human life is measured."[64]

Natural Rights and the "Right" to Die

In previous discussion we considered the nature of rights, properly and improperly construed. We argued that because natural rights are universally valid and applicable, they should be protected equally for *all* persons in *all* situations, regardless of an individual's social utility or functionality. Beyond brute medical-technological issues, the remarkable claim of a "right to die" mirrors in its simplest form the "right" to *control one's own destiny.* University of Utah philosopher Margaret Battin illustrates the centrality of control for proponents of euthanasia as she poses the question that has become increasingly commonplace: "Doesn't a person have the right to determine the manner of his or her own death and to avoid suffering and pain?"[65] Already by 1990 Hastings Center director Daniel Callahan could declare that the issue of control was now out in the open.[66]

Without question, the reasons the initiatives for assisted suicide and euthanasia garner support in society is the value that is ascribed to individual freedom and personal autonomy. Yet, the "right" to be able to choose the manner, timing, and circumstances surrounding one's death — and the "right" to impose this obligation in some way on *others* — wholly perverts and vastly exceeds the substance and scope of common-law "rights" as traditionally understood. And it violates the natural law. Every right, we must remember, imposes some obligations — which is to say, moral demands — on others. And should such a "right" be granted, what is to prevent the *right* to kill from being followed by the *duty* to kill?[67]

64. Leon Kass, in a personal interview with author Wesley Smith, cited in Smith, *Culture of Death,* 9.

65. Cited in James Horgan, "Death with Dignity," *Scientific American,* March 1991, 17.

66. Daniel Callahan, *What Kind of Life? The Limits of Medical Progress* (New York and Toronto: Simon and Schuster, 1990), 242.

67. That the language and concept of "rights" and personal "autonomy" are extremely fluid can be seen in the noticeable shift that has occurred within the last two decades. In 1984 James Childress argued passionately for the necessity of autonomy as an ethical principle ("Ensuring Care, Respect, and Fairness for the Elderly," *Hastings Center Report* 14, no. 5 [1984]: 27-31). Today the locus has shifted so that "autonomy" is typically used to *justify euthanasia as a right,* not a call for "respect, care and fairness for the elderly."

Implicit in the freedom being demanded by one individual is the obligation of others to permit, and facilitate, that freedom. Once society decides that euthanasia is acceptable, there is nothing to prevent the next step, which is to place pressure on others to actualize this duty.[68] The most vulnerable people, for example, those who suffer from clinical depression or who suffer from acute anxiety or who are marginalized or economically deprived, could readily be pressured — through fear of being a burden to their family, to their doctor, or to society as a whole — to submit to an "option" of suicide that heretofore had not existed.

Rights, in their purest form, go beyond charity, which is to be understood as *voluntary* aid to others. A "right to die" would obligate others, *involuntarily,* to aid or in some way support acts that are deemed morally repugnant. A "right to die" surely is not a right if its entails the sacrifice of virtues such as charity, kindness, and generosity; after all, the highest human virtue of all is to *give*. Rights language, as it metastasizes, removes a social stigma that is indispensable for a free, civil, and self-regulating society. It lends the air of legitimacy to the illegitimate. In the end, the "right to die" represents the ultimate perversion of public discourse — by transforming questions of what is right, good, noble, and virtuous into questions of individual preference and deep-rooted selfishness.

From both a legal and a moral standpoint, does an individual have a "right" to suicide? If not, the case for euthanasia collapses. Logically, if a constitutional right to becoming dead in fact were to exist, anyone could bring suit to force government or social structures to comply. Hence, the right to self-destruction in our day is a most extraordinary claim. Normally, the "right" to die is based on three claims: (1) personal sovereignty over one's life, (2) the involvement of consent (namely, oneself), and (3) the purported lack of harm inflicted on others. These claims qua claims are certainly dubious at best. If their insufficiency can be demonstrated, the legal-moral case for euthanasia is undermined.

At the more basic level, however, the moral argument against the "right to die," based on our intrinsic nature,[69] can be made by both reli-

---

68. Robert J. Spitzer, Robin A. Bernhoft, and Camille E. De Blasi, *Healing the Culture: A Commonsense Philosophy of Happiness, Freedom, and the Life Issues* (San Francisco: Ignatius, 2000), 325-31, have developed the implications of this line of thinking quite effectively.

69. In maintaining that humans have an intrinsic "nature," I am not meaning "natural inclinations" or "natural impulses." Virtue, i.e., moral excellence as evidenced by self-discipline, is "virtuous" to the extent that it masters and controls our impulses and inclina-

gious and nonreligious people. If I stop shoveling my driveway in a heavy snowstorm because, in truth, I am unable to keep up with the increasing amount of snowfall, I am not thereby *intending* a driveway full of snow. I merely acquiesce to nature and what is inevitable. Since death is biologically inevitable, sooner or later, and not the consequence of human actions per se, we can hardly be said to intend death when we admit that we can no longer stop it.[70] Thus, *establishing the clear moral distinction between assisting death and letting die* is basic to a morally responsible approach toward death and dying.

---

tions. Rather, the natural law corresponds with those goods, based on our created nature, to which we "naturally" are oriented and of which we have a basic knowledge. See in this regard Thomas Aquinas's discussion of the first precepts of the natural law in *ST* I-II 94 and 100.

70. This line of reasoning has been set forth by Daniel Callahan, *The Troubled Dream of Life: Living with Mortality* (New York and Toronto: Simon and Schuster, 1993), 112.

CHAPTER NINE

The Natural Law and Public Morality:
Second Thoughts on What Is at Stake

Many have doubtless heard the wonderfully prescient anecdote illustrating the consequences of the moral obtuseness that intimidates — and dominates — contemporary culture. Robert George retells the incident — perhaps belonging to academic legend — of the student in an ethics class who submitted a passionately argued paper titled "There Is No Such Thing as Justice." Without so much as a single marginal comment or concluding evaluation, the professor returned the paper to the student with a failing grade. Outraged, given the effort that went into the paper, the student went to see the professor — the requisite step, of course, before lodging an academic protest *against injustice* with the dean — and proceeded to plead his case, seeking to convince the professor of how hard he had worked on the paper.

Not only did the professor proffer no counterargument, he readily conceded that this was one of the better papers he had received in his many years of teaching. As a matter of fact, he stated, so powerful was the student's argument that the professor in the end was forced to agree. In which case, the professor announced, "there *is* no such thing as justice, so quit your whining!"[1]

Our culture, like the student, will need to make up its mind. For as G. K. Chesterton put the matter, people differ less about what things they call evil (although they indeed disagree) than about *what evils they are*

---

1. Here I take the liberty to paraphrase. See Robert P. George, *The Clash of Orthodoxies: Law, Religion, and Morality in Crisis* (Wilmington, Del.: ISI Books, 2001), ix.

willing to excuse. Chesterton, I think, is on to something. Nevertheless, we must force the baseline issue that post-consensus culture stubbornly refuses to confront: *Are there or are there not moral first principles — the "permanent" things — to which the natural law and human moral discernment point us?* If there are, then we shall have the means by which to find our bearings amidst a morally obtuse and radically skeptical generation. If there are not, then we shall need to be perfectly honest: "justice" and "law" and "good" and "evil" are but cloudy wisps that appear and vanish, a mere figment of the imagination, only mental constructs to be denied at will *or* to be asserted by brute willpower. But we *cannot* have it both ways: we are simply not permitted to live as if justice and truth really matter and yet deny that justice and truth are fixed universal referents.

Alas, there comes a time of moral reckoning both for the student and for the culture. To dissolve or undermine the time-honored moral consensus that has guided human affairs, to deny moral realities that furnish the social, political, and legal foundations of a civil and humane society, in the end is not only self-defeating but indeed downright dangerous for all of society.[2] Without the natural law, without the moral "first principles" that help us maintain our moral equilibrium, we become, in C. S. Lewis's words, "men without chests" who, wittingly or unwittingly, facilitate the degradation of all that is humane, what he called "the abolition of man."

My intent in this book has not been to assuage secular fundamentalists, who have little or no interest in dialogue with other perspectives on life and for whom spirited public debate on issues of religion, law, and moral philosophy is utterly threatening, when not impermissible. Neither has it been to convince religious isolationists, who await the forty-seventh installment of the Left Behind series and in so doing have helped build the most remarkable religious publishing empire imaginable. Both brands of fundamentalism are toxic to the public square.

The burden of this volume, rather, is to argue afresh for the acknowledgment of moral "first things," particularly as they affect "life issues," whether these be beginning-of-life, life-enhancement, or end-of-life in nature. Because the debates that rage today concern the very meaning and essence of life, they point us back to the natural law. For this reason the present volume is aimed not only at those who are religiously inclined but also

2. Few have pressed this argument more persuasively than J. Budziszewski, *What We Can't Not Know: A Guide* (Dallas: Spence, 2003).

at those who seek to affirm moral truth. In no way do I wish to give the impression of being morally neutral myself; I am part of a long-standing moral tradition that is rooted in historic Christian convictions. But because there is no such thing as moral neutrality, it is incumbent upon people of good will everywhere to contend in the marketplace for their fundamental convictions.

Democracy, as Russell Hittinger reminds us in his splendid work aptly titled *The First Grace,* is beneficial only to the extent that it holds in check human despotism — a despotism that begins in the recesses of the human heart but ends with the subjection of all things to its inhumane excesses. This means that the democratic process is legitimate only insofar as it resists and checks the idea of absolute human autonomy; of necessity it will affirm simultaneously human dignity *and* human depravity, the twin poles of human anthropology. A pluralism of private associations, for this reason, is necessary in a liberal democratic order because these associations "let off the steam," as it were, of illiberal and inhuman tendencies.[3] Democracy must therefore resist the tendency of many in culture to view it as a *substitute for morality.* This is because democracy is a *means* to an end — the maintenance of a civil society — rather than an end in itself. Morality in a democratic order, consequently, "depends on the morality of the ends which it pursues and of the means which it employs."[4] In the words of Don Eberly, "the lawmaking process can at best suppress the symptoms of cultural disorder. It can do very little about the underlying causes. . . . The vast majority of moral problems that trouble us cannot be eradicated by law."[5]

The value of democracy hence stands or falls with the values it embodies and promotes — values such as the fundamental respect for human personhood, the dignity of every individual, inalienable human rights that are basic to every individual, a high regard for one's neighbor, and the adoption of the common good in society. These values, if they are nonfluid and constant, must be grounded in moral "first things"; they cannot be provisional or "majoritarian" opinions. They must be the reflection of ob-

3. Russell Hittinger, *The First Grace: Rediscovering the Natural Law in a Post-Christian World* (Wilmington, Del.: ISI Books, 2003), 269.

4. John Paul II, *Evangelium Vitae* (hereafter *EV*), no. 70.

5. Don Eberly, "The Place of Law and Politics in a Civil Society," in *Politics and Policy: A Christian Response,* ed. Timothy J. Demy and Gary P. Stewart (Grand Rapids: Kregel, 2000), 208.

jective moral law, in accordance with the natural law "written on the heart," thereby serving as a nonfluid, stable, and obligatory point of reference for civil and positive law itself. Without an objective moral grounding, not even democracy itself is capable of ensuring a stable social peace. This, then, is the flaw of John Rawls's argument from "the fact of reasonable pluralism."[6] Per Rawls, "reasonable" people deliberate in a "liberal" democracy. They render as "legitimate" those decisions in the realm of social and public policy that are most "reasonable," and they do so in a reciprocal fashion for the benefit of "reasonable" people. What is unclear from Rawls is how the influence of people such as Martin Luther King, Jr., who disrupt the consensus of "reasonable" people, is to be justified, particularly when religious language enters the public forum. Whence derives King's moral authority? Indeed, whence derives the moral authority to denounce slavery—anywhere in human existence that it might occur?[7] Because Rawls does not presuppose metaphysical or moral "first things," and thus cannot ground human "reason" in anything other than majoritarian thinking, it is difficult — indeed, arbitrary — to determine "reasonability" and its moral basis, especially when markedly different positions on hotly contested ethical issues such as sexuality and abortion and euthanasia characterize public discourse.[8] In notable contrast to Rawls's vision of a stable social peace is that of John Paul II, for whom a "sound democracy" shall need to "rediscover those essential and innate human and moral values which flow from the very truth of the human being and express and safeguard the dignity of the person: values which no individual, no majority and no state can ever create, modify or destroy, but must only acknowledge, respect and promote. . . . Consequently, there is a need to *recover the basic elements of a vision of the relationship between civil law and moral law,*

---

6. John Rawls, *Political Liberalism* (New York: Columbia University Press, 1993). See as well Rawls's earlier but influential work, *A Theory of Justice* (Cambridge: Harvard University Press, Belknap Press, 1971).

7. An important volume that forces us to reflect on the moral nature of the public forum, demonstrating the flaws of presuming a "reasoned" consensus, is Robert P. George and Christopher Wolfe, eds., *Natural Law and Public Reason* (Washington, D.C.: Georgetown University Press, 2000), especially the essays by George and Wolfe ("Natural Law and Public Reason," 51-74) and Paul J. Weithman ("Citizenship and Public Reason," 125-70).

8. Rawls is strangely and particularly "reasonable" — indeed, *adamant* — about permitting abortion, although abortion itself is a very symptom of a corrupt (and dying?) liberalism.

which are . . . part of the patrimony of the great juridical traditions of humanity."[9] It is neither exaggerated nor alarmist to contend that, at present, the future of the democratic process and free society, at least as we have understood it in Western culture, fundamentally depends on whether Rawls's vision or John Paul's vision is embraced.[10]

Reaffirming the Moral Order

But what precisely is the nature of the relationship between civil law and moral law? In no sphere of life is civil law able to be a substitute for conscience; nor is it per se permitted to dictate matters of conscience. Rather, civil law functions — and has legitimacy — to the extent that it serves as a means to an ordered society operating on principles of justice. Civil law is not the *source* of inalienable rights that belong to persons qua persons, even when, *instrumentally,* it must *guard* those rights for all persons.

Chief among those rights is the inviolable right to life for every innocent human being. Correlatively, this means bestowing upon those located on the margins of the life spectrum the protection and dignity due them as part of human creation. Therefore, society can "never presume to legitimize as a right of individuals — even if they are the majority of the members of society — an offense against other persons caused by the disregard of so fundamental a right as the right to life."[11] It follows necessarily from this that the *legal* toleration and justification of any "right" to denigrate or eliminate life, from embryonic and fetal development and abortion to euthanasia, may not rest upon so-called "respect for the conscience" of others or personal "freedom," insofar as society is morally obligated to safe-

9. *EV,* no. 71, emphasis added.

10. It bears repeating that law measures human conduct (necessarily so) and that reason and law work together to furnish and preserve the common good of society, even when these two assumptions run counter to the prevailing views of our day. Therefore, natural-law thinking is essential to building the common good, and natural-law advocates have a major claim in what is deemed "reasonable." Natural-law theory stands irreconcilably opposed to legal positivism, which rejects a moral understanding of the cosmos and of law, a moral understanding of human nature, and a moral understanding of the social common good. See in this regard the important volume by Mark C. Murphy, *Natural Law in Jurisprudence and Politics* (Cambridge, U.K., and New York: Cambridge University Press, 2006), especially 8-24.

11. *EV,* no. 71.

guard life from actual or potential abuses. Lodged squarely within the mainstream of the Christian moral tradition is the conviction that authority — whether political or legal in nature — is a consequence of the moral order and thus is derivative in nature. Because the principal obligation of governing authorities is to create the social environment in which these rights are ensured, government is legitimate or illegitimate to the extent that it recognizes or undermines this duty.

The presence of morally unjustified laws, whether in a more dictatorial or democratic context, unquestionably raises profoundly difficult issues for people of faith, since these individuals are morally bound, by their religious faith and by the natural law, not to participate in intrinsically wrong actions. Therefore, for the sake of conscience they must refuse participation using respectful, creative, and appropriate means. That we not cooperate with evil is not merely a moral duty, though it is truly that; it is also a human right and thus itself must be protected by civil law.[12]

Contributing toward Cultural Renewal — Baseline Recommendations

One instinctively hesitates to suggest specific ways in which we might work toward the renewal of culture around us. This reticence is not merely because of fear. All too frequently such attempts are simplistic and mirror their own brand of cultural captivity. And yet, at the risk of being labeled simplistic, or of appearing to have some sort of "political agenda," we must commit ourselves in concrete ways to priorities both in our lives and in our professions that foster the common good of the society to which we belong. Implicitly suggested thus far in this volume have been a number of priorities that need accentuation.

Moral Formation and Education

A commitment to moral formation and moral education is absolutely imperative in our day. Within our religious communities there exists a critical need to address and remedy the ethical disconnect that privatizes faith and separates it from its ethical obligations. This divorce can manifest it-

---

12. A strong argument for this is developed by John Paul in *EV,* especially nos. 73-74.

self in several ways. On the one hand it can help spawn or reinforce, often unwittingly, a moral relativism that is already culturally so pervasive; on the other hand it can espouse a brand of social-political activism that not infrequently is uncritical of its own secular assumptions — assumptions that have been imported and perhaps even baptized in the name of religion. Anyone who takes the time to examine a representative cross section of catalogues from Protestant colleges or seminaries — whether mainline or evangelical — will discover precious little attention devoted to the moral life, to the acquisition of virtue, and to civic responsibility. Where ethics courses are offered, they tend to be devoted to controversial issues or hot topics without any exploration of the foundations of moral theory or interaction with the historic Christian moral tradition.[13] Compounding this rather unfortunate state of affairs is the fact that, not infrequently, high-profile "Christian ethicists" tend to be political activists before they are students of the Christian moral tradition.

Developing a "Culture of Life"

No one has been more articulate about building a "culture of life" than John Paul II. The inculcation of the values John Paul has set before the Christian community transcends our political, social, ethnic, and sociodemographic differences. Negatively, this priority demands that we resolve to be a "culture-forming counter-culture."[14] To be "counter-cultural" is not enough, even when articulate spokespersons — even articulate Christian ethicists — call us away from the culture and into "authentic Christian community." While "community" is essential, as well as the inculcation of virtue in the communal context, the call *away* from involvement in the social institutions that undergird culture is naive at best and wrongheaded at worst. Positively, our commitment will require both

13. In chapter 8 of *The Unformed Conscience of Evangelicalism: Recovering the Church's Moral Vision* (Downers Grove, Ill.: InterVarsity, 2002), I probe the lack of moral education at the collegiate and seminary level while offering several recommendations.

14. This is what George Weigel has in mind when he considers the role that Catholic social teaching has in helping to "reseed" culture along the lines of John Paul II's thinking. See George Weigel and Kenneth L. Woodward, "New Century, New Story Line: Catholics in America," in *Religion and Politics in America: A Conversation,* ed. Michael Cromartie (Lanham, Md.: Rowman and Littlefield; Washington, D.C.: Ethics and Public Policy Center, 2005), 27-41.

moral education *and* promoting a deep cultural exchange regarding basic issues of human life.[15] This exchange will need to be extended and promoted in various social and professional spheres — among laypeople, professionals, academics, and nonacademics. And it will necessitate our participation in — rather than withdrawal from — the social institutions that form the backbone of culture.

Contributing to Moral Discourse and Moral Consensus Building

Part of the difficulty we encounter in our post-consensus society is that we are scarcely able, in a civil manner, to carry on any sort of moral discourse. We find it supremely difficult, when not downright impossible, to debate public morality as well as contentious ethical and bioethical issues. How might necessary public discussion proceed? How might we go about debating? And what moral vocabulary, what moral reference points, might we utilize? Because of the considerable obstacles before us, works such as John Courtney Murray's *We Hold These Truths* may be of great benefit to us as we struggle with the formidable task of consensus building.[16] Even when the challenges confronting him lay a half-century removed, Murray, it should be remembered, wrestled with the very issue of moral consensus building that plagues us in our own day. He did so, however, on the basis of timeless moral truth and the natural law.

Classic American "doctrine," according to Murray, was asserted by the founders, the framers, and statesmen through Lincoln and beyond, until fairly recently, that this nation was dedicated to a basic "proposition." And what was this proposition? In a word, it was an "experiment," an experiment that needed "working out," and one that was never wholly "finished" (vii). This experiment, moreover, was predicated on certain assumptions, certain "first principles," such as "liberty," "equality," and "inalienable rights," all of which accorded with "Nature" and "Nature's God." To the fathers of our political and social life, Murray reminded us, human existence "did not rest upon such tentative hypotheses as the positivist might cast up," nor was our society's dynamism "furnished as in

15. John Paul's recommendations for the emergence of a "culture of life" have been set forth most eloquently in *Evangelium Vitae*.

16. John Courtney Murray, *We Hold These Truths: Catholic Reflections on the American Proposition* (New York: Sheed and Ward, 1960). Citations from this work have been placed in the text.

Marxist theory, by certain ideological projections of economic facts and interests" (viii-ix). Neither was the structure of the state "ultimately defined in terms of a pragmatic calculus." Furthermore, the rules of politics "were not a set of operational tools wherewith to further at any given juncture the dialectic process of history."

Rather, according to the "American proposition," the life of society under government "is founded on truths, on a certain body of objective truth, universal in its import, accessible to the reason of man, definable, defensible" (ix). But if this assertion and these foundational assumptions, abiding in character as they are, are denied for any pragmatic reasons, then the American experiment, Murray concluded, is "eviscerated at one stroke." For the pragmatist, "there are, properly speaking, no truths; there are only results." But the American experiment, in its founding *and* in its maintenance, "rests on the more traditional conviction," however quaint in a post-consensus culture, "that there are truths; that they can be known; that they must be held." And if these "truths" are not held, if they are not "assented to, consented to, worked into the texture of institutions, there can be no hope of founding a true City," in which people may "dwell in dignity, peace, unity, justice, well-being, freedom" (ix).[17] The alternative, as he saw it, is a descent into moral barbarism.

There is something in Murray's argument that is timeless, ever applicable. Democracy, wherever found, as a form of government cannot maintain itself effectively over the long term merely through its political and procedural resources; it is dependent on the larger web of human culture, of which religious faith and moral first principles are key elements that provide the enduring basis for a normative ethical code. The formal structures of democracy alone cannot furnish this ethical normativity.[18]

---

17. In addition, speaking as a Christian, Murray argues for an incarnational — over against an eschatological or apocalyptic — humanism that draws from the natural-law tradition. See especially chapters 12 and 13 of *We Hold These Truths*. In this way, he believes, and only in this way, can Americans preserve civil society as they presently understand it.

18. This is argued succinctly by W. Norris Clarke, "Democracy, Ethics, Religion: An Intrinsic Connection," in *A Moral Enterprise: Politics, Reason, and the Human Good: Essays in Honor of Francis Canavan*, ed. Kenneth L. Grasso and Robert P. Hunt (Wilmington, Del.: ISI Books, 2002), 265-75.

Education

The broader educational task that is set before us, given the surrounding social climate, requires — *but is by no means limited to* — the development and articulation of the wider contours of the Christian worldview, including the study of the human person, human origins, human sexuality, marriage, family and fatherhood as socially stabilizing units, suffering and death, and the complex relationship between faith and culture. In addition, moral philosophy, philosophy of science and of the social sciences, and the humane use of the sciences and technology are critically important to the educational mandate. John Henry Newman believed that the university exists first and foremost to form the mind and intellectual culture.[19] This is true, yet Newman assumed the sine qua non of this education to be grounded in the broader presuppositions of a robust Christian worldview and life view. And while the program of building a "culture of life" is comprehensive and must involve the efforts of all, in keeping with the program of John Paul II "teachers and educators have a particularly valuable contribution to make. Much will depend on them if young people, trained in true freedom, are to be able to preserve for themselves and make known to others new, authentic ideals of life and if they are to grow in respect for and service to every other person in the family and in society."[20]

Those with academic and intellectual callings, furthermore, play a strategic role in helping to build a new awareness of — and respect for — human life. A special task falls to Christian intellectuals, "who are called to be present and active in the leading centers where culture is formed, in schools and universities, in places of scientific and technological research, of artistic creativity and of the study of man. Allowing their talents and activity to be nourished by the living force of the Gospel, they ought to place themselves at the service of a new culture of life by offering serious and well-documented contributions capable of commanding general respect and interest by reason of their merit."[21]

---

19. Newman's *The Idea of a University* retains an important place in the classic understanding of the university proper, as evidenced by its republication in 1982 by University of Notre Dame Press (ed. M. J. Svaglic) and in 1996 by Yale University Press (ed. Frank M. Turner). The latter volume contains six supplementary essays by contemporary scholars in response to issues Newman raises.

20. *EV,* no. 98.

21. *EV,* no. 98.

Cultural Gatekeeping

A full-orbed vision of both education and Christian permeation of society will recognize the critical importance of penetrating "gatekeeping" vocations, i.e., those vocations inhabited by what one cultural critic calls the "knowledge elite." The very strategic nature of these positions, because they control and dispense information, is addressed in the encyclical *Evangelium Vitae*:

> An important and serious responsibility belongs to those involved in the mass media, who are called to ensure that the messages which they so effectively transmit will support the culture of life. They need to present noble models of life and make room for instances of people's positive and sometimes heroic love for others. With great respect they should also present the positive values of sexuality and human love, and not insist on what defiles and cheapens human dignity. . . . With scrupulous concern for factual truth, they are called to combine freedom of information with respect for every person and a profound sense of humanity.[22]

While civic involvement becomes increasingly difficult due to the saturation and hegemony of the media in our culture, not to mention the impoverished public theology of much of Christendom, it is nevertheless critical that people of faith commit themselves to the service of society. Otherwise, grace and charity are withheld from a wounded and decaying society.[23] The work of the church, a work of which we need constant reminding and affirmation, is to incarnate love, working for the transformation of that culture to which we are called. There is a notable tendency for religious social critics to despise American culture (and I write from the American standpoint). Indeed, there is no shortage of cultural despisers these days, whether religious or secular. But to fail to work for the transformation of *all that can be redeemed* — which is everything material and immaterial — is to fail to realize the context in which, and the extent to

---

22. *EV*, no. 98.

23. This is the flaw both of isolationist pietism and of a "Christian social ethics" that prefers to focus solely on "community." It is pharisaical to denounce the culture from the sidelines (i.e., from the "community"), even under the banner of being "prophetic," when we do not attempt to serve society in tangible and relevant social ways.

which, faithfulness to the Sovereign Lord of creation is required. If we cannot love the world enough to identify and work with it, we will be little more than "clanging cymbals."

Addressing False Cultural Dichotomies

In our efforts to help foster cultural renewal, we shall also need to discern — and resist — several corrosive tendencies in our cultural life. These deficiencies are both theoretical and practical in nature. One is the rigid separation between political realities and religious-ethical conviction. This divide, severing political theory from theology and philosophy, is most unfortunate and closely akin to the supposed "wall" that exists between church and state advanced by one dominant strand of American legal thought. This regnant line of thinking is to be distinguished from the political thought of framers such as Jefferson and Madison, who believed that the state, which "enforces" society's values, is forbidden from dictating the nature of one's religious beliefs and the expression of those beliefs, in contrast to the tyranny of the European context. Jeffersonian and Madisonian thinking opposes the dominant strain of contemporary political and legal thought, developed over the last hundred years, which insists on a *wholesale bleaching of religious commitments of any kind from the public square*. A divide so conceived grotesquely misconstrues the wishes of this nation's founders and ensures that law and politics always trump any and all moral considerations. The result, in the words of Jean Elshtain, is that "thinkers who ought not to have been set apart were sundered and . . . fruitful and important engagements did not occur."[24]

Such a separation is by no means innocuous; it breeds enormous consequences that are "totalitarian" in character. Most of us, from our high school civics classes to legal theory that is taught in our law schools, have been reminded ad infinitum of the tyranny of religion that has surfaced throughout human history. Standard procedure is to trot out the Crusades, the Inquisition, and the worst of religious fundamentalism past and present — *Christian* fundamentalism, that is. Moreover, we are told that faith commitments are to be relegated to the *private* domain. After all, the public square is to remain "neutral," not tainted by the sordid claims and influ-

---

24. Jean Bethke Elshtain, *Who Are We? Critical Reflections and Hopeful Possibilities* (Grand Rapids and Cambridge, U.K.: Eerdmans, 2000), x.

ences of sectarian religion (read: evangelical Protestantism and Roman Catholicism). And because religion is viewed as a potential danger to the political and civic arena, we therefore need — by blithely dismissing or ignoring the original intent of the Constitution's framers — a wall that separates (and "safeguards") politics from religion. But as we have learned time and again, this only makes the world safe for anarchy and moral barbarism.

We shall need, therefore, to remind culture that no descriptions or evaluations or theories are ever or at any point morally neutral. All theoretical assessments of the polis, the *civitas,* or the state are freighted with preunderstandings of what constitutes ultimate reality.[25] These philosophical precommitments are on display in every human sphere — from economics, law, and politics to science, medicine, and bioethics.

Personal and Civic Responsibilities

A further corrosive tendency in our cultural life that will need prophetic adjustment is the contemporary distortion of human freedom that has resulted in a fixation with rights to the exclusion of personal responsibility. Acts of authentic freedom are acts that recognize a limit, whereas freedom perverted refuses to recognize these limits, in time becoming a destroyer of human community. Such disregard for the community ultimately cannot but end in nihilism.[26] True freedom, by contrast, operates within the constraints of truth. From the Christian standpoint, human freedom and autonomy measure themselves against the backdrop of stewardship. The steward has free range of action, yet this freedom is not unlimited. Stewards are stewards to the extent that they operate in relation to others and, most importantly, to an authority higher than the self. Not surprisingly, therefore, a primary motif running throughout the Christian narrative is that of dominion.

Properly understood, dominion entails the idea of limited autonomy, which acknowledges both divine sovereignty and human stewardship

---

25. This forms a notable subtheme in much of Jean Elshtain's work. See, e.g., *Real Politics: At the Center of Everyday Life* (Baltimore and London: Johns Hopkins University Press, 1997), and *Women and War,* rev. ed. (Chicago and London: University of Chicago Press, 1995), especially part 1 ("Armed Civic Virtue").

26. See, in this regard, John Paul II's encyclical *Evangelium Vitae* and Jean Bethke Elshtain, *Augustine and the Limits of Politics* (Notre Dame, Ind.: University of Notre Dame Press, 1996), especially chapter 3.

(Gen. 1:28–2:20). How far does this dominion extend? And to what extent is creative dominion a "shared" realm? Simply put, the Creator never ceases being Creator, and human beings never cease being stewards. Dominion must never be confused with complete autonomy. Such tragic conflation is central to the story line of the biblical narrative; it is this inversion that results in moral evil and the need for redemption. "Dignity" that is blissfully unaware of its depravity is a dignity that descends into inhumanity. Therefore, we must confront the Promethean attitude of our age, an attitude that seeks to control life and death by placing sovereignty into our own hands. Given the place of "freedom" among contemporary idolatries, as politically responsible citizens we will continually need to qualify our cultural understanding of what it means to be "free."[27]

Moral Discrimination

Because of its reign as our culture's "cardinal virtue," not infrequently "tolerance" will create — explicitly or implicitly — social pressure to accept even forms of heinous moral evil. Such is the fruit of living in a "post-Christian," post-consensus cultural climate. The need of the hour is therefore a willingness to make moral judgments. Politics reflects society's capacity to make moral discriminations, for better or for worse. Evil is not an abstract "discursive experience" that we may somehow treat as some hermetically sealed entity. Moral soundness, therefore, will muster the ethical and political will to "look evil in the eye and not to deflect our gaze."[28]

Unquestionably, this will be hard work for American culture at the present time, consumed as we are by "nonjudgmentalism" instead of a resolve to do justly. Consider the events of September 11, 2001. John Paul II referred to the sum total of this day as "unspeakable horror," while Osama bin Laden called it a "glorious deed." Who is right? And why are we reticent, if not resistant, to determine the difference? By conventional moral

---

27. None have argued for civic responsibility with greater cultural fluency and moral persuasion than Jean Elshtain (see nn. 24-26), who, in her own words, "freely mingles theological, ethical, philosophical, and political categories" in her writings (*Who Are We?* ix). I have attempted to assess her broader contribution, both to the academy and to public discourse, in "War, Women and Political Wisdom: Jean Bethke Elshtain on the Contours of Justice," *Journal of Religious Ethics* 34, no. 2 (June 2006): 341-69.

28. Jean Bethke Elshtain, *Just War against Terror: The Burden of American Power in a Violent World* (New York: Basic Books, 2003), 12.

reasoning, both are equally valid positions. After all, who is to say that one is right and one is wrong (that is, until evil visits us *personally*)? Such would presuppose an objective good and objective evil, reflecting in the eyes of our contemporaries an odious moral imperialism.

Notwithstanding the arrogance of moral relativists in our day, the ability to make basic moral discriminations is foundational to any just and decent society. To lose this ability is to lose *any and all* basis for a civil order. In the end, "civil society," if we wish to preserve her, reduces to a quite simple — though not simplistic — acknowledgment of baseline moral reality.

Distinguishing between Retribution and Revenge: A Hallmark of Civil Society

We might illustrate the importance of moral discrimination in the maintenance of civil society by observing the fundamental distinction between justice and revenge, between retribution and "retributivism."[29] A common objection, whether in foreign policy or in criminal justice, is the following: *Isn't justice as retribution merely a pretext for vengeance?* Clearly, revenge is not rooted in love of one's neighbor.

The Christian moral tradition distinguishes the retributive act from revenge, vindication from vindictiveness, in important and unmistakable ways.[30] At the most fundamental level, it understands punishment or retribution to be established by divine agency, manifesting itself both in this life and after death, "often visibly, always invisibly."[31] A letter written by Augustine to his friend Marcellinus, a Roman official in Carthage, is instructive in the way it addresses the subject of punishment. Marcellinus had previously written Augustine to ask for help in answering common objections to Christian faith raised by influential pagans. One of their charges was that Christianity is incompatible with sound political rule and civic responsibility. "You added that they say that the preaching and teach-

29. Oliver O'Donovan, "Payback: Thinking about Retribution," *Books and Culture*, July-August 2000, 16-21, uses the term "retributivism" in contradistinction to "retribution" as a moral good.

30. Elsewhere I develop the distinction between retribution and revenge in *Between Pacifism and Jihad: Just War and Christian Tradition* (Downers Grove, Ill.: InterVarsity, 2005), 143-47.

31. So Augustine, *City of God* 20.1.

ing of Christ are not at all suitable for the morals of a republic. They have in mind the precept that we should not return evil for evil to anyone, but turn the other cheek to anyone who strikes us, give our tunic to anyone who takes our coat, and walk a double journey with anyone who would force us to go with him (Mt. 5:39-41). They assert that all of these things are contrary to the morals of a republic."[32]

Augustine begins his response by asking a rhetorical question. The reasoning goes something like this: "How is it that those who supposedly overlook evil rather than punishing it are able to govern the republic? Is this the way a republic is really maintained? What is a republic if it is not a *public* affair? Is it not a multitude of people who have joined together and made mutual commitments to one another?"

Augustine initially attacks the popular distortion that is widespread. He explains that Jesus' teaching in the "sermon on the mount" is intended to address *personal attitudes:* "these precepts refer to a disposition of the heart." The effect of Christ's teaching is that "a man is freed from an evil that is *not external and foreign* but *inner and personal.*" At the private level, Augustine reminds his friend, overcoming evil with good may be quite effective in changing human behavior. A godly person, therefore, "ought to be prepared to endure patiently the malice of those whom he seeks to make good."[33]

So far, so good. However, "with respect to those who, contrary to their own will, need to be set straight" (in other words, with *those who are a public menace*), we take up *very different* measures, even though these measures are rooted in the same right intention. And how do we respond? Augustine has this to say: "[M]any things must be done with a certain *benevolent harshness.*" And his rationale? "*Their welfare rather than their wishes* must be considered. . . . He whose license for wrongdoing is wrested away is usefully conquered, for nothing is less prosperous than the prosperity of sinners, which nourishes . . . and strengthens the evil will."[34] Thus, charity — if it has moral backbone and is not sloppy sentimentalism — will want what is best for the criminal and for the public at large.

At its base, the moral outrage expressed through retributive justice is

---

32. Augustine, *Epistle to Marcellinus* 138. I am relying on the English translation in Michael W. Tkacz and Douglas Kries, eds., *Augustine: Political Writings* (Indianapolis and Cambridge: Hackett, 1994), 205.

33. Augustine, *Epistle to Marcellinus*, in Tkacz and Kries, 206-7.

34. Augustine, *Epistle to Marcellinus*, in Tkacz and Kries, 208-9, emphasis added.

first and foremost rooted in moral principle, not mere emotional outrage and hatred. Recall Augustine's words to Marcellinus: retribution is a form of "benevolent harshness." The governing authorities, by punishing criminal behavior, mirror a concern for the welfare of the population and for those doing the wrong. Any parent knows the truth of this principle. Indeed, *not to act against the will of a wrongdoer,* in the words of Augustine, is to "nourish and strengthen the will toward evil." It needs reemphasis, especially in our cultural climate, that it is *virtuous and not vicious* to feel anger at moral evil. In truth, something is *very* wrong with us *if we don't* express anger and moral outrage at evil. And yet, moral outrage alone is not enough.

But in what specific ways are retribution and revenge different? There are several critical distinctions. Whereas revenge strikes out at real or perceived injury, retribution speaks to an objective wrong. Whereas revenge is wild, "insatiable," and not subject to limitations, retribution has both upper and lower limits, acknowledging the moral repugnance of assigning both draconian punishment to petty crimes and light punishment to heinous crimes. Vengeance, by its nature, has a *thirst* for injury and delights in bringing further evil upon the offending party. The avenger will not only kill but also rape, torture, plunder, and burn what is left, deriving satisfaction from the victim's direct or indirect suffering. Augustine described this inclination, rooted in the flesh, as a "lust for revenge."[35]

Also, retribution has as its goal a greater social good and takes no pleasure in punishment. The good subsists in the fact that an injury or wrong is amended, that it is presented in the future from occurring, that through example potential wrongdoers are deterred, and that the wrongdoer is forced to reflect on the wrongness of his actions.[36] Finally, whereas revenge, because of its retaliatory mode, will target both the offending party and those perceived to be akin, retribution is both targeted yet impersonal and impartial, not subject to personal bias. For this reason Lady Justice is depicted as blindfolded. The difference between retribution and

---

35. Augustine, *City of God* 14.14.

36. The moral rationale behind punishment is developed with care by the natural lawyer Samuel Pufendorf in *The Whole Duty of Man, according to the Law of Nature,* trans. A. Tooke (Indianapolis: Liberty Fund, 2003), 225-32. Pufendorf's premise is that "so far as the Civil Laws do not openly contradict the Law of GOD, the Subjects stand obliged to obey them, not merely out of Fear of Punishment, but by an internal Obligation confirm'd by the Precepts of the Law of Nature it self" (224).

revenge is the difference between Romans 13 and the end of Romans 12. In the latter the apostle describes and prohibits what renders "justice" illicit: the private sphere. "Vigilante justice" is justice enacted apart from the governing authorities. In another context, the public sphere, justice becomes legitimate, since for this very reason it has been divinely instituted. The authorities are commissioned to "bear the sword," and they do so "not in vain" (Rom. 13:4; cf. 1 Pet. 2:14-17).

Understood properly, retributive justice serves a civilized culture, whether in domestic or international context. It isolates individuals, parties, or people groups who endanger the community — locally, nationally, or internationally — for their wanton disregard for the common good and a just peace. It controls the extent to which a citizenry is victimized by criminal acts. It rewards the perpetrator proportionately with consequences befitting the crime. And it forces both the offender(s) and potential offenders to reflect on the grievous nature of the crime. Each of these elements is critical in preserving the social order.[37]

Augustine is not naive about political realities. He doesn't turn a blind eye toward the injustices of the empire. And he acknowledges the "cruel" nature of much of the Pax Romana. But at the same time, he has little patience for the notion that Christianity will passively tolerate evil based on a particularly distorted understanding of Jesus' teaching. Even pagans, he notes, are capable of displaying extraordinary civic virtue without religious faith. How much more will Christian faith make *us* good citizens?

Some, such as the ideological pacifist, will instinctively argue that retribution constitutes an "uncivilized" or "barbaric" response by society to crime or moral evil. But is this the case? Our answer depends fundamentally on how a society perceives the moral difference between the criminal and the punitive act. If society refuses to make this moral distinction, which the cardinal virtue of justice is committed to do, then it is *impossible* to denounce moral evil — anywhere, in any form, at any time. Those of us who have worked in the criminal justice system, despite its deep flaws, are not yet ready to give up on justice. And justice inheres in the "permanent things," at the heart of which stands natural moral law.

If there is no distinction between the criminal and the punitive act,

---

37. Justice can be said to have three components: other-centeredness, duty (i.e., that which is owed), and equality or proportionality. Thus John Finnis, *Natural Law and Natural Rights*, Clarendon Law Series (Oxford: Clarendon, 1980), 161-97.

then, the Nuremberg Trials, to cite but one instance, were wrongheaded, since Nazi war crimes — indeed, *any crimes against humanity* — cannot in principle be denounced, much less can mass murderers be put on trial and sentenced. In the end, one man's torture is simply another man's good time.

Our society's deeply entrenched moral evasiveness can be seen, for example, with its relative indifference to the marker "Thou shalt not murder." The Torah, it must be remembered, does not forbid taking the life of a human being; rather, it forbids premeditated murder. Indeed, Jewish and Christian moral traditions concur in acknowledging justifiable forms of homicide such as self-defense, protecting civilians, resisting insurrection, and justified war. Where retribution and revenge are viewed as the equivalent, these aforementioned categories become meaningless.

The impulse toward retribution is innate in human beings, not because it is a "lower" or primitive impulse; rather, it is because of the divine image within us. To treat men or nations, however severely, in accordance with the belief that they should have known better — and they *do* know better — is to treat them as responsible human beings, endowed with human dignity and moral agency. A society *unwilling* to direct retributive justice toward those who murder in cold blood or commit morally outrageous acts is a society that has deserted its responsibility to uphold the sanctity of human life. Civilized society will not tolerate murder — at *any* level; an uncivilized one, however, will.

To affirm retribution, which is integral to the history of Judeo-Christian moral thinking and foundational to any self-governing society, is not to abandon one's belief in mercy and forgiveness. Rather it is to acknowledge the difference between the criminal and the punitive act as well as between private and public recourse. Doubtless the reader will take note that in the Christian tradition, forgiveness has a prominent place, particularly in the teaching of Jesus. Are we not commanded to forgive our enemies? Is forgiveness not the hallmark of Christian faith?

Initially, however, we encounter a problem, given the manner in which contemporary society conceives of "forgiveness." Thus, perhaps the first order of business in coming to terms with the notion of forgiveness is cleansing it of its cultural captivity. Modern and postmodern culture have foisted upon us a sentimental understanding of forgiveness by which mercy always trumps justice, by which consequences for wrongdoing are denied and moral self-responsibility is absent.

Complicating matters is the failure — even among religiously inclined people — to distinguish between (a) "forgiveness" as psychological or emotional release of a party who has committed wrong and (b) forgiveness as a declared, formal "release" of a party who has acknowledged guilt and personally and directly requests to be forgiven by the aggrieved party. Authors Avis Clendenen and Troy Martin speak of the former as an *intrapsychic* understanding of forgiveness and the latter as *interpersonal*;[38] the former requires no repentance and confrontation between offender and the offended, while the latter is predicated on repentance and a social exchange between involved parties and corresponds most closely to biblical norms.[39]

Yet another obstacle in the path of our understanding is the mode by which we have come to know retribution and "punishment" in our own experience. Few of us, after all, have grown up in ideal homes; most of us have known less than ideal attempts by our parents or guardians to "discipline" us. Some of us, it goes without saying, are still carrying around those bruises.[40]

38. Avis Clendenen and Troy Martin, *Forgiveness: Finding Freedom through Reconciliation* (New York: Crossroad, 2002), chapters 1 and 2. This volume is the best resource I have found to articulate a proper understanding of forgiveness. Written in a sensitive manner that interprets human experience holistically, it seriously interacts with a variety of therapeutic models advanced by influential practitioners and sets forth a model that is at once biblically faithful and clinically astute.

39. While a fuller treatment of the biblical concept of forgiveness takes us too far afield of our present concern, several basic principles may be culled from Scripture in our attempts to remain theologically faithful: (1) forgiveness is preceded by contrition and repentance; (2) contrition is evidenced when the offender returns to the victim to confess his or her guilt; (3) forgiveness as the result of direct dealings between the offended and the victim is imparted by the victim; (4) forgiveness may not be granted by a third party, in proxy, since only the offended party may grant forgiveness; (5) should the offender refuse to acknowledge guilt and contrition leading to repentance, forgiveness is not granted, and judgment remains on the offender; (6) eschatological judgment does not remove the responsibility of temporal judgment on the offender; (7) while individuals, based on the aforementioned requirements, are required to forgive, nations and states are not, given the primary function that providence has bestowed upon governing authorities.

40. Punishment, properly understood, is not mere coercion, even when it possesses a coercive element. Punishment, rather, is coercion by the authority for the sake of both the common good and the offender. Utilitarian thinking on the subject misses the mark insofar as it is primarily concerned with consequences; therefore, it is unable to morally ground punishment or a rejection of punishment. By contrast, natural-law based retribution, with its moral realism and high view of personhood, argues that there are good reasons for the community, represented by political authority, to set a criminal outside the community based on the common good, since the criminal refuses to honor the community.

But if we insist on driving a wedge between justice and retribution/ punishment, we thereby empty justice of its content; justice, in the end, must be normative and possess universal contours. Doing what is right, or committing evil acts, must be the same for all people, everywhere and at all times. Justice itself is what makes retribution a moral entity. Certain things are wrong because they are wrong universally, which means that to rectify a "wrong" is to affirm the notion of moral desert. People do not get — that is, they *should not* get — different deserts for committing the same moral wrong; such a phenomenon we call a "travesty of justice." Without this sort of baseline moral reckoning, there is no such thing as "criminal justice" or "civil society." Standards themselves become impossible; society disintegrates and becomes ungovernable.

In the end, mercy does not release the public demands that justice imposes; hence, the observations of Oliver O'Donovan: "In Christian thought retribution is one pole of a dialectic with forgiveness. One reason, indeed, that Christians have insisted on retributive justice [historically] is that if one pole is lost, the opposite pole will be lost, too. The theological doctrines for forgiven sin, redemption from punishment, reconciliation of the offender with the offended God, those and nothing else are what have held the philosophical notions of desert and retribution firmly in place."[41]

Retributive justice, then, is a moral necessity for a civilized culture. In responding retributively to moral evil, we channel our energies in several directions. We respond to victims who have been wronged; we respond to wider society, which has been scandalized by the wrong done in its midst; we respond to the actual offending party by declaring that moral evil will not be tolerated; and we respond to future offenders who might be tempted to engage in the same evil. Understood correctly, retributive justice performs a multifaceted moral good. The difference between retribution and revenge, hence, is foundational to making moral judgments.[42]

---

41. O'Donovan, "Payback," 19.
42. In chapter 5 ("Christian Ethics and the Use of Force") of *Between Pacifism and Jihad* I develop the implications of this moral distinction as it applies to issues of war and peace.

Demarcating the Moral Order

We must begin drawing our reflections to a close. Questions of a perplexing nature have set themselves before us. What happens to a society when freedom is not tethered to the true and the permanent? When personal autonomy is absolutized rather than placed at the service of the greater common good? What happens to a society that is unable to distinguish between innocence and guilt, between victim and offender, between those who oppress and those who suffer oppression? And what happens to a society when it fails or refuses to speak truthfully? When it is unable or unwilling to name evil?

The broader task of the Christian community, given the vast cultural confusion that envelops us, is to *demarcate rather than re-create* the moral order. Human autonomy and self-determination are to be understood as relative and not absolute. As issues of personal autonomy surface foremost in the context of pressing bioethical issues, will one's body, one's personhood, one's very being be perceived as subject to the Creator's sovereignty — a sovereignty over life and death? Over the germinal as well as the terminal stages of human life? Any claims over human life that represent human sovereignty place themselves irrevocably at odds with human nature, with divine revelation, and with the Christian church as the vessel through which the parameters of human stewardship are best interpreted.

More recently, the matter of sovereignty as it concerns bioethics in general and life-enhancement issues in particular has been put in perspective quite lucidly by Leon Kass. Kass argues *against* the human project to "perfect" humans at both the *physical and psychological* levels. For him, "a flourishing human life is not a life lived with an ageless body or untroubled soul. . . . It is a life not of better genes and enhancing chemicals but of love and friendship, song and dance, speech and deed, working and learning, revering and worshipping." Kass believes it unwise, indeed foolish, to aspire to "the attitude of mastery," through "unnatural means" and for the purpose of "dubious ends."[43] There is much wisdom, I think, in this viewpoint.

43. The issue of human versus divine sovereignty is put in proper perspective by Kass in "Beyond Therapy: Biotechnology and the Pursuit of Human Improvement," a paper delivered to the President's Council on Bioethics in January of 2003, subsequently published in book form as *Beyond Therapy: Biotechnology and the Pursuit of Happiness* (New York: HarperCollins, 2003). These comments are taken from chapters 5 and 6, which mirror sustained philosophical reflection on what it means to have a human *nature*. To remake human

While the benefits and blessings of bioethical and biotechnological advance are readily identified and lauded, the ethical and social concerns that accompany this advance are not so easily articulated, as Kass makes abundantly clear, for they go beyond the familiar bioethical issues. That is, they go "beyond therapy" and the healing art, as traditionally practiced by medical science, and fade into perfection-seeking and social control, heralding a "posthuman" future.[44] At bottom, they suggest that there is no such thing as "human nature," or that its alteration is not morally problematic. What is at stake is not merely the issue of "killing the creatures" as made in the image of God, but a more attractive possibility: using biotechnological knowledge and power to *refashion* ourselves in *our own* image. Hence, these developments give "unexpected practical urgency" to ancient philosophical questions: What is a good life? What does it mean to have a human nature?[45] As Michael Sandel well noted, when science moves faster than moral understanding, as it does today, people struggle to articulate their unease. In liberal societies, they have tended over the last four decades to reach for the language of autonomy, fairness, and individual rights. But this part of our moral vocabulary, alas, is ill equipped to address the hard question posed by reproductive apologists and genetic engineers.[46] Surely, Sandel is right to contend that a Gattaca-like world in which parents specify the sex and genetic traits of their children would be a world inhospitable to the unbidden, a gated community in the worst sense.[47] Thus we shall need to raise questions that have been largely lost from view—questions that probe the moral status of nature. It is not for science on its own to determine the morality of technological advance; indeed, this it cannot do. Science can only place in bold relief what moral questions need to be raised — questions that require the input of theology and moral philosophy.

---

nature is both cognitively and morally deficient, for in its hubris it fails to appreciate—and embrace—the "giftedness" of life. An appreciation of life's giftedness is essential to "constrain the Promethean project" and to "conduce to a much-needed humility" (*Beyond Therapy*, 288). Such is precisely the meaning of parenthood. To appreciate children for the great gifts that they are is not to view them as extensions or expressions of our own ambition but to receive them as they enter our lives and to accept them unconditionally *as they are*.

44. Kass, *Beyond Therapy*, 6-7.

45. Kass, *Beyond Therapy*, 11.

46. Sandel, "The Case against Perfection," *Atlantic Monthly* 293, no. 3 (April 2004): 51-52.

47. Sandel, "The Case against Perfection," 60.

As it touches the wider Christian community, the church's cultural task is threefold in nature. It has a theological, an apologetic, and an ethical component. Theologically, the Christian community must reaffirm a biblical anthropology, one that stresses human dignity as well as depravity. Both poles of this mystery must be held in tension and not eradicated. Implicit in this tension is the Christian's responsibility to hold the culture morally accountable, for if "the salt has lost its savor," it is fit for nothing, to be "thrown out and trampled by men." Therefore, without becoming self-righteous and pharisaical, we will need to consider the cost necessary to judge between good and evil. Such will require considerable moral backbone.

Apologetically, the church must learn to discern the philosophical underpinnings of culture. In so doing, it can address with credibility the false values upon which modern culture and postconsensus society are built. Responsible and thorough cultural engagement may need emphasis for those believers who, by virtue of their religious heritage, have tended toward isolationism. The equal and opposite heresy, however, capitulating to the culture and its values, must be avoided as well. So often, in our anxiousness to overcome our inferiority complex vis-à-vis the world, we end up worshiping at the altar of "social relevance." For this reason, faithfulness to the biblical mandate requires that we avoid both errors — isolation and capitulation. We are called to engage culture without compromise. And given the importance of language, amplified earlier, Christians who commit themselves to responsible participation in culture must of necessity purify language and redefine terms. When words have lost their meaning, truth and substance must be raised up as a banner against falsehood and image. Slogans, despite their convenience, will not be enough; they are no substitute for thoughtful moral-philosophical reflection.[48]

Ethically, the Christian community should seek to inform ongoing moral discourse wherever it is found. Of all people, it is the great company of Christians, "redeemed" in their values and life priorities, who should be helping shape the contours of the great ethical debates of the day. If the church does *not* do this shaping, it is guaranteed that someone else, some

---

48. Pluralism and post-consensus cultural conditions present not only peril but promise as well. Moreover, they are *not* unique to us, even when they present unique challenges, for they characterize the social environment in which genuine faith has always lived — whether of ancient Israel as the covenant community or the first-century Christians.

other cultural influence, will. People of faith should *both* register vigorous protest when the situation calls for it *and* encourage alternative social remedies — for example, in caring for human need (such as widows, the fatherless, and the destitute; cf. James 1:27), in helping the unborn, or in providing health-care options (such as hospice).

Finally, Christians must see as their fundamental task the imperative — by God's grace — of contributing to a moral consensus in culture. Nothing could be more central to their witness. Solutions to social pathologies are not political; rather, they are profoundly moral. The history of social reform indicates that wherever moral rejuvenation of a society has occurred, social and political reform followed. We must not mistakenly reverse this pattern, as both "conservatives" and "liberals" have been inclined to do.

In the years to come, however many or few opportunities we are granted for redemptive cultural engagement, we will doubtless be confronted with further dehumanizing tendencies that issue from "freedoms" of a contraceptive society, demands for human autonomy, and cries for the "perfection" — both bodily and therapeutically — of the human race. What will serve as our moral resource? What will be our ethical starting point? How will we engage pagan culture that is seemingly hell-bent on reconfiguring human beings?

In the end, heaven and earth cry out against grandiose visions of unbridled autonomy and human lawlessness. Notwithstanding all that changes, the natural law will remain.

Bibliography

Adams, Nathan A., IV. "An Unnatural Assault on Natural Law: Regulating Biotechnology Using a Just Research Theory." In *Human Dignity in the Biotech Century: A Christian Vision for Public Policy,* edited by Nigel M. de S. Cameron and Charles W. Colson, 162-64. Downers Grove, Ill.: InterVarsity, 2004.

Aquinas, Thomas. *Summa Theologica.* 5 vols. New York: Benziger Brothers, 1948.

Aristotle. *Nicomachean Ethics.* Translated by T. Irwin. Indianapolis: Hackett, 1985.

Attarian, John. "In Dispraise of Tolerance, Sensitivity and Compassion." *Social Critic,* Spring 1998, 14-23.

Backus, Irena. "Calvin's Concept of Natural and Roman Law." *Calvin Theological Studies* 38, no. 1 (April 2003): 7-26.

Barrett, C. K., ed. *The New Testament Background: Selected Documents.* New York and Evanston: Harper and Row, 1961.

Barth, Karl. *The Church and the War.* New York: Macmillan, 1944.

————. *Church Dogmatics.* Vol. II/1, *The Doctrine of God.* Translated by G. W. Bromiley et al. Edinburgh: T. & T. Clark, 1957.

————. *Church Dogmatics.* Vol. II/2, *The Doctrine of God.* Translated by G. W. Bromiley et al. Edinburgh: T. & T. Clark, 1957.

————. *Church Dogmatics.* Vol. III/4, *The Doctrine of Creation.* Translated by A. T. Mackay et al. Edinburgh: T. & T. Clark, 1961.

————. *Community, State, and Church: Three Essays.* Garden City: Doubleday, 1960.

————. *Protestant Theology in the Nineteenth Century: Its Background and History.* Rev. ed. London: SCM, 2001.

Beauchamp, Tom L. "The Failure of Theories of Personhood." *Kennedy Institute of Ethics Journal* 9, no. 4 (1999): 309-24.

Beauchamp, Tom L., and James F. Childress. *Principles of Biomedical Ethics.* 4th ed. New York: Oxford University Press, 1994.

Bibliography

Beauregard, David. "The Mystery of Suffering." *Ethics and Medics*, August 1995, 1-2.

Beckwith, Francis J. "Bioethics, the Christian Citizen, and the Pluralist Game." *Christian Bioethics* 13 (2007): 159-70.

————. "Gimme That Ol' Time Separation: A Review Essay." *Chapman Law Review* 8, no. 1 (2005): 309-27.

Beckwith, Francis J., and Gregory Koukl. *Relativism: Feet Firmly Planted in Mid-Air.* Grand Rapids: Baker, 1998.

Benestad, J. Brian. "Catholic Social Thought, Virtue and Public Morality." In *The Christian Vision: Man and Morality,* edited by Thomas J. Burke, 141-55. Hillsdale, Mich.: Hillsdale College Press, 1986.

Berkouwer, G. C. *The Triumph of Grace in the Theology of Karl Barth.* Translated by H. R. Boer. Grand Rapids: Eerdmans, 1956.

Berman, Morris. *The Twilight of American Culture.* New York: Norton, 2000.

Biggar, Nigel, and Rufus Black, eds. *The Revival of Natural Law: Philosophical, Theological, and Ethical Responses to the Finnis-Grisez School.* Aldershot, England, and Burlington, Vt.: Ashgate, 2000.

Binding, Karl, and Alfred Hoche. *Die Freigabe der Vernichtung lebensunwerten Lebens: Ihr Mass und ihre Form.* Leipzig: Felix Meiner Verlag, 1920.

Braaten, Carl E. "God in Public Life: Rehabilitating the 'Orders of Creation.'" *First Things*, December 1990, 32-38.

————. "The Gospel for a Neopagan Culture." In *Either/Or: The Gospel or Neopaganism,* edited by Carl E. Braaten and Robert W. Jenson, 7-21. Grand Rapids: Eerdmans, 1995.

————. "Natural Law in Theology and Ethics." In *The Two Cities of God: The Church's Responsibility for the Earthly City,* edited by Carl E. Braaten and Robert W. Jenson, 42-58. Grand Rapids and Cambridge, U.K.: Eerdmans, 1997.

————. "Protestants and Natural Law." *First Things*, September 1992, 20-26.

Brennan, William. "John Paul II on Language Empowering the Culture of Death." *National Catholic Bioethics Quarterly,* Winter 2003, 731-46.

Brodeur, David. "The Rights Debate." *Health Progress,* June 1990, 48-51.

Brunner, Emil. *Justice and the Social Order.* New York: Harper and Row, 1945.

————. *Revelation and Reason: The Christian Doctrine of Faith and Knowledge.* Translated by O. Wyon. Philadelphia: Westminster, 1946.

Brunner, Emil, and Karl Barth. *Natural Theology.* Translated by P. Fraenkel. London: Geoffrey Bles and Centenary Press, 1946.

Budziszewski, J. "The Illusion of Moral Neutrality." *First Things*, August/September 1993, 32-37.

————. "The Second Tablet Project." *First Things*, June-July 2002, 23-31.

————. *True Tolerance: Liberalism and the Necessity of Judgment.* New Brunswick, N.J.: Transaction, 1992.

———. *What We Can't Not Know: A Guide.* Dallas: Spence, 2003.

———. *Written on the Heart: The Case for Natural Law.* Downers Grove, Ill.: InterVarsity, 1997.

Burleigh, Michael. *Death and Deliverance: "Euthanasia" in Germany ca. 1900-1945.* Cambridge: Cambridge University Press, 1994.

Callahan, Daniel. *The Troubled Dream of Life: Living with Mortality.* New York and Toronto: Simon and Schuster, 1993.

———. *What Kind of Life? The Limits of Medical Progress.* New York and Toronto: Simon and Schuster, 1990.

Callahan, Sidney. "The Moral Case against Euthanasia." *Health Progress,* February 1995, 38-39.

Calvin John. *Institutes of the Christian Religion.* Edited by John T. McNeill. Translated by F. L. Battles. Louisville: Westminster John Knox, 2006.

Cameron, Nigel M. de S., and David L. Schiedermayer, eds. *Bioethics and the Future of Medicine: A Christian Appraisal.* Grand Rapids: Eerdmans; Carlisle, U.K.: Paternoster, 2005.

Canavan, Francis A. "Pluralism and the Limits of Neutrality." In *The Battle for Morality in Pluralistic America,* edited by C. Horn, 153-65. Ann Arbor: Servant, 1985.

———. *The Pluralist Game: Pluralism, Liberalism, and the Moral Conscience.* Lanham, Md.: Rowman and Littlefield, 1995.

Caplan, Arthur. "An Improved Future?" *Scientific American,* September 1995, 142-43.

———. *Moral Matters: Ethical Issues in Medicine and the Life Sciences.* New York: Wiley, 1995.

Cassell, Eric. *The Nature of Suffering.* New York: Oxford University Press, 1991.

Catechism of the Catholic Church. Washington, D.C.: U.S. Catholic Conference, 1994.

Cauchy, Vincent, and Michel Spanneut. "Stoicism." In *The New Catholic Encyclopedia,* 13:534-39. 2nd ed. Detroit: Gale, 2003.

Cessario, Romanus. *Introduction to Moral Theology.* Washington, D.C.: Catholic University of America Press, 2001.

Chang, Curtis. *Engaging Unbelief: A Captivating Strategy from Augustine and Aquinas.* Downers Grove, Ill.: InterVarsity, 2000.

Charles, J. Daryl. "'Do Not Suppose That I Have Come . . .': The Ethic of the 'Sermon on the Mount' Reconsidered." *Southwestern Journal of Theology* 46, no. 3 (2004): 47-70.

———. "Engaging the (Neo)Pagan Mind." *Trinity Journal,* n.s., 16 (1995): 47-62.

———. "*Lebensunwertes Leben:* The Devolution of Personhood in the Weimar and Pre-Weimar Era." *Ethics and Medicine* 21, no. 1 (Spring 2005): 41-54.

———. "The New Verbal Order." *Modern Age* 38, no. 4 (Fall 1996): 321-31.

Bibliography

———. "Paul before the Areopagus: Reflections on the Apostle's Encounter with Cultured Paganism." *Philosophia Christi* 7, no. 1 (2005): 123-38.

———. "Protestant Reflections on *Salvifici Doloris.*" *National Catholic Bioethics Quarterly* 2, no. 2 (Summer 2002): 211-20.

———. "Suicidal Thought in a Culture of Death." In *Suicide: A Christian Response,* edited by Timothy J. Demy and Gary P. Stewart, 209-20. Grand Rapids: Kregel, 1997.

———. *The Unformed Conscience of Evangelicalism: Recovering the Church's Moral Vision.* Downers Grove, Ill.: InterVarsity, 2002.

———. "Vice and Virtue Lists." In *Dictionary of New Testament Background,* edited by Craig A. Evans and Stanley E. Porter, 1252-57. Downers Grove, Ill.: InterVarsity, 2000.

———. *Virtue Amidst Vice.* Journal for the Study of the New Testament Supplemental Series 150. Sheffield: Sheffield Academic Press, 1997.

Clarke, W. Norris. "Democracy, Ethics, Religion: An Intrinsic Connection." In *A Moral Enterprise: Politics, Reason, and the Human Good; Essays in Honor of Francis Canavan,* edited by Kenneth L. Grasso and Robert P. Hunt, 265-75. Wilmington, Del.: ISI Books, 2002.

Clouser, Roy. *The Myth of Religious Neutrality: An Essay on the Hidden Role of Religious Belief in Theories.* Notre Dame: University of Notre Dame Press, 1991.

Cochrane, Arthur C. "Natural Law in Calvin." In *Church State Relations in Ecumenical Perspective,* edited by Elwyn A. Smith, 176-217. Louvain: Duquesne University Press, 1966.

Conyers, A. J. *The Long Truce: How Toleration Made the World Safe for Power and Profit.* Dallas: Spence, 2001.

Cromartie, Michael, ed. *A Preserving Grace: Protestants, Catholics, and Natural Law.* Washington, D.C.: Ethics and Public Policy Center; Grand Rapids: Eerdmans, 1997.

———, ed. *Religion and Politics in America: A Conversation.* Lanham, Md.: Rowman and Littlefield; Washington, D.C.: Ethics and Public Policy Center, 2005.

Curry, Dean. "Reclaiming Natural Law." *First Things,* November 1997, 56-59.

Daly, Bernard M. "Transhumanism: Toward a Brave New World?" *America,* October 25, 2004, 18-20.

Daly, Mark J., and David Altshuler. "Partners in Crime." *Nature Genetics* 37 (2005): 337-38.

Dawkins, Richard. *The Selfish Gene.* New York and Oxford: Oxford University Press, 2006.

Dawson, Christopher. *Religion and Progress.* Garden City, N.Y.: Doubleday, 1960.

Demy, Timothy J., and Gary P. Stewart, eds. *Genetic Engineering: A Christian Response.* Grand Rapids: Kregel, 1999.

————, eds. *Politics and Public Policy: A Christian Response*. Grand Rapids: Kregel, 2000.

————, eds. *Suicide: A Christian Response*. Grand Rapids: Kregel, 1997.

DiIulio, John J., Jr. *Deregulating the Public Service: Can Government Be Improved?* Washington, D.C.: Brookings Institution, 1994.

————. *Performance Measures for the Criminal Justice System*. Washington, D.C.: U.S. Department of Justice/Bureau of Justice Statistics, 1993.

————. *Rethinking the Criminal Justice System: Toward a New Paradigm*. Washington, D.C.: U.S. Department of Justice/Bureau of Justice Statistics, 1992.

Doerflinger, Richard M. "Confronting Technology at the Beginning of Life." In *Human Dignity in the Biotech Century: A Christian Vision for Public Policy*, edited by Charles W. Colson and Nigel M. de S. Cameron, 221-39. Downers Grove, Ill.: InterVarsity, 2004.

————. "Testimony on Embryo Research and Related Issues." *National Catholic Bioethics Quarterly*, Winter 2003, 772-78.

Dworkin, Ronald. "The Illusive Morality of Law." *Villanova Law Review* 10 (1965): 631-39.

————. *Life's Dominion: An Argument about Abortion, Euthanasia, and Individual Freedom*. New York: Knopf, 1993.

————. "Philosophy, Morality, and Laws." *University of Pennsylvania Law Review*, 1965, 668-90.

Dyck, Arthur J. *Life's Worth: The Case against Assisted Suicide*. Critical Issues in Bioethics. Grand Rapids and Cambridge, U.K.: Eerdmans, 2002.

————. *Rethinking Rights and Responsibilities: The Moral Bonds of Community*. Rev. ed. Washington, D.C.: Georgetown University Press, 2005.

Eberly, Don. "The Place of Law and Politics in a Civil Society." In *Politics and Policy: A Christian Response*, edited by Timothy J. Demy and Gary P. Stewart, 203-12. Grand Rapids: Kregel, 2000.

Echeverria, Eduardo J. "FIDES ET RATIO — the Catholic and the Calvinist: Prospects for Rapprochement." *Philosophia Reformata* 65 (2000): 72-104.

————. "The Splendor of Truth in *Fides et Ratio*: Alethic Realism and Dominus Jesus." *Revista Portuguesa de Filosofia* 58 (2002): 17-42.

Eliot, T. S. *After Strange Gods*. London: Faber and Faber, 1933.

Ellul, Jacques. *The Humiliation of the Word*. Translated by C. Hanks. Grand Rapids: Eerdmans, 1985.

————. *The Theological Foundation of Law*. Translated by M. Wieser. New York: Seabury Press, 1969.

————. *To Will and to Do*. Translated by C. E. Hopkin. Philadelphia and Boston: Pilgrim Press, 1969.

Elshtain, Jean Bethke. "Democratic Authority at Century's End." *Hedgehog Review*, Spring 2000, 24-39.

Bibliography

———. "Judge Not?" *First Things*, October 1994, 36-40. Reprinted in *The Moral Life: An Introductory Reader in Ethics and Literature*, edited by Louis J. Pojman, 194-98. New York and Oxford: Oxford University Press, 2004.

———. *Real Politics: At the Center of Everyday Life*. Baltimore and London: Johns Hopkins University Press, 1997.

———. *Who Are We? Critical Reflections and Hopeful Possibilities*. Grand Rapids and Cambridge, U.K.: Eerdmans, 2000.

Endara, Miguel. "Deficiencies in the 'Selfish Genes' View of Ethics: A Critique of the Evolutionary Account." *National Catholic Bioethics Quarterly*, Autumn 2003, 517-30.

Finnis, John. *Aquinas: Moral, Political, and Legal Theory*. Oxford: Oxford University Press, 1998.

———. *Natural Law and Natural Rights*. Oxford: Clarendon, 1980.

Ford, Norman. "The Human Embryo as Person in Catholic Teaching." *National Catholic Bioethics Quarterly*, Summer 2001, 155-60.

Forte, David F., ed. *Natural Law and Contemporary Public Policy*. Washington, D.C.: Georgetown University Press, 1998.

Fortin, Leonard. "The Natural Wrong in Natural Rights." *Crisis*, May 1994, 20-25.

Foss, Laurence. "The Challenge to Biomedicine: A Foundation Perspective." *Journal of Medicine and Philosophy* 14 (1989): 165-91.

Fukuyama, Francis. *The Great Disruption: Human Nature and the Reconstitution of Social Order*. New York: Free Press, 1999.

———. "Is It All in the Genes?" *Commentary*, September 1997, 30-35.

Fuller, Lon. *The Morality of Law*. Rev. ed. New Haven, Conn., and London: Yale University Press, 1969.

Garcia, Jorge. "A Public Prophet?" *First Things*, February 1999, 49-53.

George, Robert P. *The Clash of Orthodoxies: Law, Religion, and Morality in Crisis*. Wilmington, Del.: ISI Books, 2001.

———. *In Defense of Natural Law*. Oxford: Clarendon, 1999.

———. *Making Men Moral: Civil Liberties and Public Morality*. Oxford: Clarendon, 1993.

———. *Natural Law Theory: Contemporary Essays*. Oxford: Clarendon, 1992.

———. "Positivism: Fidelity to Law." *Harvard Law Review* 71 (1958): 630-72.

George, Robert P., and Christopher Wolfe, eds. *Natural Law and Public Reason*. Washington, D.C.: Georgetown University Press, 2000.

Gibbs, W. Wayt. "Seeking the Criminal Element." *Scientific American* 272 (March 1995): 100-109.

Glendon, Mary Ann. *Rights Talk: The Impoverishment of Political Discourse*. New York: Free Press, 1991.

———. "Tradition and Creativity in Culture and Law." *First Things*, November 1992, 13-19.

Glöde, Günter. *Theologia Naturalis bei Calvin*. Stuttgart: Kohlhammer, 1935.

Grabill, Stephen J. *Rediscovering the Natural Law in Reformed Theological Ethics.* Emory University Studies in Law and Religion. Grand Rapids and Cambridge, U.K.: Eerdmans, 2006.

Grasso, Kenneth L. "The Triumph of Will: Rights Mania, the Culture of Death, and the Crisis of Enlightenment Liberalism." In *Politics, Reason, and the Human Good: Essays in Honor of Francis Canavan,* edited by Kenneth L. Grasso and Robert P. Hunt, 203-20. Wilmington, Del.: ISI Books, 2002.

―――. "We Hold These Truths: The Transformation of American Pluralism and the Future of American Democracy." In *John Courtney Murray and the American Civil Conversation,* edited by Robert P. Hunt and Kenneth L. Grasso, 100-115. Grand Rapids: Eerdmans, 1992.

Greenawalt, Kent. *Religious Convictions and Political Choice*. New York: Oxford University Press, 1988.

Grisez, Germain. "The First Principle of Practical Reason: A Commentary on the *Summa Theologiae* 94.2." *Natural Law Forum* 10 (1965): 168-201.

―――. *The Way of the Lord Jesus*. Vol. 1, *Christian Moral Principles*. Chicago: Franciscan Herald, 1983.

Grotius, Hugo. *The Law of War and Peace*. Translated by F. W. Kelsey. Oxford: Oxford University Press, 1925.

Guroian, Vigen. *Ethics after Christendom: Toward an Ecclesial Christian Ethics*. Grand Rapids: Eerdmans, 1994.

Gustafson, James M. *Protestant and Roman Catholic Ethics*. Chicago and London: University of Chicago Press, 1978.

Haas, Guenter H. *The Concept of Equity in Calvin's Ethics*. Waterloo, Ont.: Wilfrid Laurier University Press, 1997.

Harris, John. "The Concept of the Person and the Value of Life." *Kennedy Institute of Ethics Journal* 9, no. 4 (1999): 293-308.

Hart, H. L. A. *The Concept of Law*. Oxford: Clarendon, 1961.

―――. "Positivism and the Separation of Law and Morals." *Harvard Law Review* 71 (1958): 593-629.

Hauerwas, Stanley. "Natural Law, Tragedy, and Theological Ethics." *American Journal of Jurisprudence* 20 (1975): 1-19.

―――. *The Peaceable Kingdom: A Primer in Christian Ethics*. Notre Dame and London: University of Notre Dame Press, 1983.

―――. *Truthfulness and Tragedy: Further Investigations in Christian Ethics*. South Bend, Ind.: University of Notre Dame Press, 1983.

―――. "Why the 'Sectarian Temptation' Is a Misrepresentation: A Response to James Gustafson (1988)." In *The Hauerwas Reader,* edited by John Berman and Michael Cartwright, 90-110. Durham, N.C., and London: Duke University Press, 2001.

Bibliography

Hauerwas, Stanley, and William Willimon. *Resident Aliens: Life in the Christian Colony.* Nashville: Abingdon, 1989.

Helms, Paul. "Calvin and Natural Law." *Scottish Bulletin of Evangelical Theology* 2 (1984): 5-22.

Hendershott, Anne. *The Politics of Deviance.* San Francisco: Encounter Books, 2002.

Henry, Carl F. H. "Natural Law and a Nihilistic Culture." *First Things,* January 1995, 54-60.

Hibbs, Thomas, and John O'Callaghan, eds. *Recovering Nature: Essays in Natural Philosophy, Ethics, and Metaphysics in Honor of Ralph McInerny.* Notre Dame: University of Notre Dame Press, 1999.

Hittinger, Russell. *A Critique of the New Natural Law Theory.* Notre Dame: University of Notre Dame, 1987.

————. *The First Grace: Rediscovering the Natural Law in a Post-Christian World.* Wilmington, Del.: ISI Books, 2003.

————. *Natural and Divine Law: Reclaiming the Tradition for Christian Ethics.* Grand Rapids and Cambridge, U.K.: Eerdmans, 1999.

————. "Natural Law and Catholic Moral Theology." In *A Preserving Grace: Protestants, Catholics, and Natural Law,* edited by Michael Cromartie, 1-30. Washington, D.C.: Ethics and Public Policy Center; Grand Rapids: Eerdmans, 1997.

Hoedemaeckers, Roger. "Human Embryos, Human Ingenuity, and Government Policy." *Ethics and Medicine* 19, no. 2 (2003): 75-84.

Hollinger, Dennis. *Choosing the Good: Christian Ethics in a Complex World.* Grand Rapids: Baker, 2002.

Holmes, Oliver Wendell. "The Path of the Law." *Harvard Law Review* 10 (1897): 359-469.

Hooper, Walter, ed. *Present Concerns: Essays by C. S. Lewis.* New York: Harcourt, Brace, Jovanovich, 1986.

Huldane, John H. "Natural Law and Ethical Pluralism." In *The Many and the One: Religious and Secular Perspectives on Ethical Pluralism in the Modern World,* edited by Richard Madsen and Tracy B. Strong, 89-114. Princeton: Princeton University Press, 2003.

Hunter, James Davison. *The Death of Character.* New York: Basic Books, 2000.

Irving, Dianne N. "What Is Bioethics?" In *Life and Learning X: Proceedings of the Tenth University Faculty for Life Conference,* edited by Joseph W. Koterski, 1-84. Washington, D.C.: University Faculty for Life, 2002.

Jenson, Robert W. "The Church's Responsibility for the World." In *The Two Cities of God: The Church's Responsibility for the Earthly City,* edited by Carl E. Braaten and Robert W. Jenson, 1-11. Grand Rapids and Cambridge, U.K.: Eerdmans, 1997.

―――. "Is There an Ordering Principle?" In *Essays in Theology of Culture*, 67-75. Grand Rapids: Eerdmans, 1995.

―――. "On the Renewing of the Mind." In *Essays in Theology of Culture*, 163-74. Grand Rapids: Eerdmans, 1995.

John Paul II. *Centesimus Annus*. Accessible at www.vatican.va/holy_father/ john_paul_ii/encyclicals/documents/hf_jp-ii_enc_01051991_centesimus-annus_en.

―――. *Evangelium Vitae*. Accessible at www.vatican.va/holy_father/john_ paul_ii/encyclicals/documents/hf_jp-ii_enc_25031995_evangelium-vitae_en.

―――. *Fides et Ratio*. Accessible at www.vatican.va/holy_father/john_paul_ii/en-cyclicals/documents/hf_jp-ii_enc_15101998_fides-et-ratio_en.

―――. *Salvifici Doloris*. Accessible at www.vatican.va/holy_father/john_paul_ii/ apost_letters/documents/hf_jp-ii_apl_11021984_salvifici-doloris_en.

―――. *Veritatis Splendor*. Accessible at www.vatican.va/holy_father/john_ paul_ii/encyclicals/documents/hf_jp-ii_enc_06081993_veritatis-splendor_ en.

Jones, Nancy L., and William P. Cheshire. "Can Artificial Techniques Supply Morally Neutral Human Embryos for Research?" *Ethics and Medicine* 12, no. 1 (2005): 29-40.

Kass, Leon R. *Beyond Therapy: Biotechnology and the Pursuit of Happiness*. New York: HarperCollins, 2003.

―――. *The Hungry Soul: Eating and the Perfecting of Our Nature*. New York: Free Press, 1994.

Kevan, Ernest. *Moral Law*. Escondido, Calif.: Den Dulk Christian Foundation; Phillipsburg, N.J.: Presbyterian and Reformed, 1991.

Kilner, John F. "Hurdles for Natural-Law Ethics: Lessons from Grotius." *American Journal of Jurisprudence* 28 (1983): 149-68.

Kilner, John F., Nigel M. de S. Cameron, and David L. Schiedermayer, eds. *Bioethics and the Future of Medicine: A Christian Appraisal*. Grand Rapids: Eerdmans; Carlisle, U.K.: Paternoster, 1995.

Kilner, John F., C. Christopher Hook, and Diane B. Uustal, eds. *Cutting-Edge Bioethics: A Christian Exploration of Technologies and Trends*. Grand Rapids: Eerdmans, 2002.

Kilner, John F., Arlene B. Miller, and Edmund D. Pellegrino, eds. *Dignity and Dying: A Christian Appraisal*. Grand Rapids: Eerdmans, 1996.

Klempa, William. "Calvin on Natural Law." In *John Calvin and the Church: A Prism of Reform*, edited by Timothy George, 72-95. Louisville: Westminster John Knox, 1990.

Knepper, Paul. *Explaining Criminal Conduct: Theories and Systems in Criminology*. Durham, N.C.: Carolina Academic Press, 2001.

Krauthammer, Charles. "Defining Deviancy Up." *New Republic* 209, no. 21 (November 22, 1993): 20-25.

Kuyper, Abraham. "Common Grace." In *Abraham Kuyper: A Centennial Reader,* edited by James D. Bratt, 165-201. Grand Rapids: Eerdmans, 1998.

Lapp, John A. "Human Rights: An Agenda for the Church." In *In Search of a National Morality: A Manifesto for Evangelicals and Catholics,* edited by William Bentley Ball, 235-45. Grand Rapids: Baker; San Francisco: Ignatius, 1992.

Lebovitz, Richard M. "Embryonic Rights: Self-Interest and the Thirteenth Amendment." *National Catholic Bioethics Quarterly,* Winter 2003, 681-87.

Lee, Patrick. "Personhood, Dignity, Suicide, and Euthanasia." *National Catholic Bioethics Quarterly,* Autumn 2001, 329-43.

———. "The Prolife Argument from Substantial Identity: A Defense." *Bioethics* 18, no. 3 (2004): 249-63.

Lewis, C. S. *The Abolition of Man.* New York: Macmillan, 1947.

———. *The Discarded Image: An Introduction to Medieval and Renaissance Literature.* New York: Cambridge University Press, 1964.

———. *Mere Christianity.* Rev. ed. New York: Macmillan, 1960.

———. "On Ethics." In *Christian Reflections,* edited by Walter Hooper, 44-56. Grand Rapids: Eerdmans, 1967.

Little, David. "Calvin and the Prospects for a Christian Theory of Natural Law." In *Norm and Context in Christian Ethics,* edited by Gene H. Outka and Paul Ramsey, 175-97. New York: Scribner, 1968.

Loconte, Joseph. "Hospice, Not Hemlock." *Policy Review,* March-April 1998, 40-48.

Long, Steven A. "Reproductive Technologies and the Natural Law." *National Catholic Bioethics Quarterly* 2, no. 2 (Summer 2002): 193-208.

Lund-Molfese, N. C. "The Gift of Suffering versus Euthanasia." *Social Justice Review,* November-December 1999, 170-73.

———. "SALVIFICI DOLORIS: A Challenge to Catholic Social Scientists." *Social Justice Review,* July-August 2000, 108-11.

Luther, Martin. "Against the Antinomians." In *Luther's Works,* 47:107-20. Edited by Franklin Sherman. Philadelphia: Fortress, 1971.

———. "Against the Heavenly Prophets in the Matter of Images and Sacraments." In *Luther's Works,* 40:79-223. Edited by Conrad Bergendorff. Philadelphia: Fortress, 1958.

———. "Against the Sabbatarians." In *Luther's Works,* 47:65-98. Edited by Franklin Sherman. Philadelphia: Fortress, 1971.

———. "How Christians Should Regard Moses." In *Luther's Works,* 35:161-74. Edited by E. Theodore Bachmann. Philadelphia: Muhlenberg, 1960.

———. "Temporal Authority: To What Extent It Should Be Obeyed." In *Luther's Works,* 45:81-129. Edited by Walther I. Brandt. Philadelphia: Muhlenberg, 1962.

MacIntyre, Alasdair. *After Virtue: A Study in Moral Theory.* 2nd ed. Notre Dame: University of Notre Dame Press, 1984.

Madison, James. "Memorial and Remonstrance against Religious Assessments." In *Church and State in the Modern Age: A Documentary History,* edited by J. F. MacLear, 59-62. New York and Oxford: Oxford University Press, 1995.

Mansfield, Harvey. "Responsibility versus Self-Expression." In *Old Rights and New,* edited by Robert A. Licht, 96-111. Washington, D.C.: American Enterprise Institute, 1993.

Maritain, Jacques. *The Person and the Common Good.* Translated by J. J. Fitzgerald. New York: Scribner, 1947.

―――. *The Rights of Man and the Natural Law.* San Francisco: Ignatius, 1986.

Markham, Ian. *Plurality and Christian Ethics.* Rev. ed. New York: Seven Bridges Press, 1999.

Marsden, George. "Christianity and Cultures: Transforming Niebuhr's Categories." *Christian Ethics Today,* December 2000, 18-24.

Masters, Roger D., and Michael T. McGuire, *The Neurotransmitter Revolution: Serotonin, Social Behavior, and the Law.* Carbondale and Edwardsville: Southern Illinois University Press, 1994.

May, William E. "The Sanctity of Human Life." In *In Search of a National Morality: A Manifesto for Evangelicals and Catholics,* edited by William Bentley Ball, 103-11. Grand Rapids: Baker; San Francisco: Ignatius, 1992.

McCarthy, Anthony. *Cloning and Stem Cell Research.* London: Catholic Truth Society, 2003.

McClay, Wilfred M. "Mastery's Anger." *Touchstone,* November 2005, 16-18.

McGrath, Alister E. "The Challenge of Pluralism for the Contemporary Christian Church." *Journal of the Evangelical Theological Society* 35, no. 3 (1992): 361-73.

―――. *A Passion for Truth.* Downers Grove, Ill.: InterVarsity, 1996.

McInerny, Ralph. "Are There Moral Truths That Everyone Knows?" In *Common Truths: New Perspectives on Natural Law,* edited by Edward B. McLean, 1-15. Wilmington, Del.: ISI Books, 2000.

―――. "The Case for Natural Law." *Modern Age,* Spring 1982, 168-74.

―――. "Commonsense Ethics." Accessible at www.claremont.org/writings/crb/ spring2004/mcinerny.

―――. *Ethica Thomistica.* Notre Dame: University of Notre Dame Press, 1997.

―――. "The Golden Rule and Natural Law." *Modern Schoolman* 69 (1992): 421-30.

McLean, Edward B., ed. *Common Truths: New Perspectives on Natural Law.* Wilmington, Del.: Intercollegiate Studies Institute, 2000.

McNeill, John T. "Natural Law in the Teaching of the Reformers." *Journal of Religion* 26 (1946): 168-82.

―――. "Natural Law in the Thought of Luther." *Church History* 10 (1941): 211-27.

Meilaender, Gilbert C. *Bioethics: A Primer for Christians.* Grand Rapids: Eerdmans, 1996.

————. *Body, Soul, and Bioethics.* Notre Dame and London: University of Notre Dame Press, 1995.

————. *Faith and Faithfulness: Basic Themes in Christian Ethics.* Notre Dame and London: University of Notre Dame Press, 1991.

————. *The Taste for the Other: The Social and Ethical Thought of C. S. Lewis.* Grand Rapids and Cambridge, U.K.: Eerdmans, 1998.

————. *Things That Count: Essays Moral and Theological.* Wilmington, Del.: Intercollegiate Studies Institute, 2000.

Moreland, J. P., and Scott B. Rae. *Body and Soul: Human Nature and the Crisis in Ethics.* Downers Grove, Ill.: InterVarsity, 2000.

Mouw, Richard. *Uncommon Decency: Christian Civility in an Uncivil World.* Downers Grove, Ill.: InterVarsity, 1992.

Mouw, Richard, and Sander Griffioen, *Pluralisms and Horizons: An Essay in Public Philosophy.* Grand Rapids: Eerdmans, 1993.

Moynihan, Daniel Patrick. "Defining Deviancy Down." *American Scholar,* Winter 1993, 17-30.

Muller, Richard A. "'*Duplex Cognitio Dei*' in the Theology of Early Reformed Orthodoxy." *Sixteenth Century Journal* 10, no. 2 (Summer 1979): 51-62.

Murray, John, *Principles of Conduct: Aspects of Biblical Ethics.* 1957. Reprint, Grand Rapids: Eerdmans, 1991.

Murray, John Courtney. *Freedom and Man.* New York: P. J. Kenedy and Sons, 1965.

————. *We Hold These Truths: Catholic Reflections on the American Proposition.* New York: Sheed and Ward, 1960.

Neuhaus, Richard John. *Time toward Home: The American Experiment as Revelation.* New York: Seabury Press, 1975.

Newbigin, Lesslie. *The Gospel in a Pluralist Society.* Grand Rapids: Eerdmans, 1989.

————. *Truth to Tell: The Gospel and Public Truth.* Grand Rapids: Eerdmans, 1991.

Niebuhr, Reinhold. "Christian Faith and Natural Law." In *Love and Justice: Selections from the Shorter Writings of Reinhold Niebuhr,* edited by D. B. Robertson, 46-54. Louisville: Westminster John Knox, 1957.

Novak, David. "John Courtney Murray, S.J.: A Jewish Appraisal." In *John Courtney Murray and the American Civil Conversation,* edited by Robert P. Hunt and Kenneth L. Grasso, 44-63. Grand Rapids: Eerdmans, 1992.

————. *Natural Law in Judaism.* New York and Cambridge: Cambridge University Press, 1998.

Novak, Michael. "Awakening from Nihilism." *First Things,* August-September 1994, 18-22.

Oakley, Francis. "Locke, Natural Law, and God: Again." In Oakley, *Politics and Eter-*

nity: Studies in the History of Medieval and Early-Modern Political Thought, 217-48. Leiden: Brill, 1999.

O'Donovan, Oliver. *The Desire of the Nations: Rediscovering the Roots of Political Theology*. Cambridge, U.K., and New York: Cambridge University Press, 1996.

————. *Principles in the Public Realm: The Dilemma of Christian Moral Witness*. Oxford: Clarendon, 1984.

————. *Resurrection and Moral Order: An Outline for Evangelical Ethics*. Grand Rapids: Eerdmans, 1986.

O'Donovan, Oliver, and Joan Lockwood O'Donovan, eds. *From Irenaeus to Grotius: A Sourcebook in Christian Political Thought*. Grand Rapids: Eerdmans, 1999.

Owen, H. P. "The Scope of Natural Revelation in Romans 1 and Acts xvii." *New Testament Studies* 5 (1958/59): 133-43.

Pannenberg, Wolfhart. *Ethics*. Translated by K. Crim. Philadelphia and London: Search Press, 1981.

Pavlischek, Keith. "Questioning the New Natural Law Theory: The Case of Religious Liberty as Defended by Robert P. George in *Making Men Moral.*" In *A Moral Enterprise: Politics, Reason, and the Human Good*, edited by Kenneth L. Grasso and Robert P. Hunt, 127-42. Wilmington, Del.: ISI Books, 2002.

Pellegrino, Edmund D. "Euthanasia and Assisted Suicide." In *Dignity and Dying: A Christian Appraisal*, edited by John F. Kilner, Arlene B. Miller, and Edmund D. Pellegrino, 105-18. Grand Rapids: Eerdmans, 1996.

————. "The Moral Status of Compassion in Bioethics: The Sacred and the Secular." *Ethics and Medics*, September 1995, 3-4.

Pellegrino, Edmund D., and David C. Thomasma. *The Christian Virtues in Medical Practice*. Washington, D.C.: Georgetown University Press, 1996.

Pinckaers, Servais. "*Veritatis Splendor:* Human Freedom and the Natural Law." *Ethics and Medics*, February 1995, 3-4.

Pope, Stephen J. "Natural Law and Christian Ethics." In *The Cambridge Companion to Christian Ethics*, edited by Robin Gill, 77-95. Cambridge: Cambridge University Press, 2001.

Porter, Jean. *Natural and Divine Law: Reclaiming the Tradition for Christian Ethics*. Grand Rapids and Cambridge, U.K.: Eerdmans, 1999.

————. *Nature as Reason: A Thomistic Theory of the Natural Law*. Grand Rapids and Cambridge, U.K.: Eerdmans, 2005.

Postman, Neil. *Amusing Ourselves to Death*. New York: Viking Press, 1985.

Prager, Dennis. "Why Aren't People Preoccupied with Good and Evil?" *Ultimate Issues* 7, no. 2 (1991): 6-9.

Preece, Gordon. *Rethinking Peter Singer: A Christian Critique.* Downers Grove, Ill.: InterVarsity, 2002.

Raath, Andries W. G., and Simon de Freitas. "Calling and Resistance: Huldrych Zwingli's Political Theology and His Legacy of Resistance to Tyranny." Unpublished manuscript, University of the Free State, 2001.

Raine, Adrian. *The Psychopathology of Crime: Criminal Behavior as a Clinical Disorder.* San Diego: Academic Press, 1993.

Raine, Adrian, and Yaling Yang. "Neural Foundations to Moral Reasoning and Antisocial Behavior." *Social, Cognitive and Affective Neuroscience* 1 (2006): 203-13.

Ramsey, Paul. "The Indignity of 'Death with Dignity.'" *Hasting Center Studies* 2 (May 1974): 47-62.

Ratzinger, Joseph Cardinal (Benedict XVI). *Truth and Tolerance: Christian Belief and World Religions.* San Francisco: Ignatius, 2004.

Rawls, John. *Political Liberalism.* New York: Columbia University Press, 1993.

———. *A Theory of Justice.* Cambridge: Harvard University Press, Belknap Press, 1971.

Rice, Charles E. *50 Questions on the Natural Law: What It Is and Why We Need It.* Rev. ed. San Francisco: Ignatius, 1999.

———. "Natural Law in the Twenty-First Century." In *Common Truths: New Perspectives on Natural Law,* edited by Edward B. McClean, 293-318. Wilmington, Del.: ISI Books, 2000.

Rieff, Philip. *The Triumph of the Therapeutic: Uses of Faith after Freud.* New York: Harper and Row, 1966.

Robertson, D. B., ed. *Love and Justice: Selections from the Shorter Writings of Reinhold Niebuhr.* Philadelphia: Westminster, 1957.

Robertson, John. *Children of Choice: Freedom and the New Reproductive Technologies.* Princeton: Princeton University Press, 1994.

Rommen, Heinrich A. *The Natural Law: A Study in Legal and Social History and Philosophy.* Translated by T. R. Hanley. Indianapolis: Liberty Fund, 1998; original Eng.: St. Louis: Herder, 1947.

———. *The State in Catholic Thought: A Treatise in Political Philosophy.* St. Louis: Herder, 1945.

Schindler, David L. *Heart of the World, Center of the Church: Communio, Ecclesiology, Liberalism, and Liberation.* Grand Rapids: Eerdmans, 1996.

Schlossberg, Herbert. *Idols for Destruction: The Conflict of Christian Faith and American Culture.* Rev. ed. Wheaton, Ill.: Crossway, 1990.

Schooyans, Michel. *Maitrise de la vie — domination des hommes.* Paris: Lethielleux, 1986; Eng.: *Power over Life.* Translated by J. H. Miller. St. Louis: Catholic Central Union of America, 1996.

Schreiner, Susan. "Calvin's Use of Natural Law." In *A Preserving Grace: Protestants,*

Catholics, and Natural Law, edited by Michael Cromartie, 51-76. Washington, D.C.: Ethics and Public Policy Center; Grand Rapids: Eerdmans, 1997.

————. *The Theater of His Glory: Nature and the Natural Order in the Thought of John Calvin.* Durham, N.C.: Labyrinth Press, 1991.

Sigmund, Paul E. *Natural Law in Political Thought.* Cambridge: Winthrop, 1971.

Simon, Yves R. *The Tradition of Natural Law: A Philosopher's Reflections.* Edited by Vukan Kuic. Rev. ed. New York: Fordham University Press, 1992.

Singer, Peter. *Practical Ethics.* London: Cambridge University Press, 1981.

Skillen, James W. "From Covenant of Grace to Equitable Public Pluralism: The Dutch Calvinist Contribution." *Calvin Theological Journal* 31, no. 1 (April 1996): 72-79.

————. "Natural Law and the Foundations of Government." *Public Justice Report,* November 1991. Accessible at www.cpjustice.org/stories/storyReader$1012.

————. "Natural Law before and after Sovereignty: A Response to Daniel Philpott." In *Sovereignty at the Crossroads: Morality and International Politics in the Post–Cold War Era,* edited by Luis E. Lugo, 63-69. Lanham, Md.: Rowman and Littlefield, 1996.

————. "Pluralism as a Matter of Principle." In *The Many and the One: Religious and Secular Perspectives on Ethical Pluralism in the Modern World,* edited by Richard Madsen and Tracy B. Strong, 257-70. Princeton: Princeton University Press, 2003.

————. *Recharging the American Experiment: Principled Pluralism for Genuine Civic Community.* Grand Rapids: Baker, 1994.

Skillen, James W., and Rockne M. McCarthy, eds. *Political Order and the Plural Structure of Society.* Emory University Studies in Law and Religion. Atlanta: Scholars, 1991.

Skinner, B. F. *Walden Two.* New York: Macmillan, 1948.

Smith, Wesley J. *Culture of Death: The Assault on Medical Ethics in America.* San Francisco: Encounter Books, 2000.

Sommers, Christina Hoff, and Sally Satel. *One Nation under Therapy: How the Helping Culture Is Eroding Self-Reliance.* New York: St. Martin's Press, 2005.

Spitzer, Robert J., Robin A. Bernhoft, and Camille E. De Blasi. *Healing the Culture: A Commonsense Philosophy of Happiness, Freedom, and the Life Issues.* San Francisco: Ignatius, 2000.

Stackhouse, Max L. "Broken Covenants: A Threat to Society?" In *Judgment at the White House: A Critical Declaration Exploring Moral Issues and the Political Use and Abuse of Religion,* edited by Gabriel Fackre, 18-27. Grand Rapids and Cambridge, U.K.: Eerdmans, 1999.

————. *Creeds, Society, and Human Rights: A Study in Three Cultures.* Grand Rapids: Eerdmans, 1984.

Steinfels, Peter. "Natural Law Collides with the Laws of Politics in the Squabble over a Supreme Court Nominee." *New York Times,* August 17, 1991, A8.

Stetson, Brad, and Joseph G. Conti. *The Truth about Tolerance: Pluralism, Diversity, and the Culture Wars.* Downers Grove, Ill.: InterVarsity, 2005.

Suzuki, David, and Peter Knudtson. *Genethics: Moral Issues in the Creation of People.* Berkeley: University of California Press, 1992.

Sweetman, Brendan. *Why Politics Needs Religion: The Place of Religious Arguments in the Public Square.* Downers Grove, Ill.: InterVarsity, 2006.

Sykes, Charles A. *A Nation of Victims.* New York: Free Press, 1991.

Tadie, Andrew A., and Michael H. Macdonald, eds. *Permanent Things: Toward the Recovery of a More Human Scale at the End of the Twentieth Century.* Grand Rapids and Cambridge, U.K.: Eerdmans, 1995.

Taylor, John. "Don't Blame Me! The New Culture of Victimhood." *New York,* June 3, 1991, 27-34.

Thomas, Clarence. "The Higher Law Background of the Privileges or Immunities Clause of the Fourteenth Amendment." *Harvard Journal of Law and Public Policy* 63 (1989): 63-70.

Toit, D. A. du. "Anthropology and Bioethics." *Ethics and Medicine* 10, no. 2 (1994): 35-42.

Upinsky, Arnaud-Aaron. *La Tête Coupée ou la Parole Coupée.* Paris: O.E.I.L., 1991.

Visser 't Hooft, Willem A. "Evangelism in the Neo-Pagan Situation." *International Review of Mission* 65 (1976): 81-86.

Vitz, Paul C. *Psychology as Religion: The Cult of Self-Worship.* Rev. ed. Grand Rapids: Eerdmans, 1995.

Wannenwetsch, Bernd. "Luther's Moral Theology." In *The Cambridge Companion to Martin Luther,* edited by Donald K. McKim, 12-35. Cambridge: Cambridge University Press, 2003.

Weber, Kent. "How Far Is Tolerance a Virtue?" *Regeneration Quarterly,* Winter 1996, 29-31.

Weigel, George. *Catholicism and the Renewal of American Democracy.* New York: Paulist, 1989.

West, John G., Jr. "Politics in the Shadowlands: C. S. Lewis on Earthly Government." *Policy Review,* Spring 1994, 68-70.

Westberg, Daniel. "The Reformed Tradition and Natural Law." In *A Preserving Grace: Protestants, Catholics, and Natural Law,* edited by Michael Cromartie, 103-17. Washington, D.C.: Ethics and Public Policy Center; Grand Rapids: Eerdmans, 1997.

————. "The Relation between Positive and Natural Law in Aquinas." *Journal of Law and Religion* 11, no. 1 (1994/95): 1-22.

Westermann, Claus. *Roots of Wisdom: The Oldest Proverbs of Israel and Other Peoples.* Translated by J. D. Charles. Louisville: Westminster John Knox, 1995.

Wiker, Benjamin D. "The Repaganization of the West." *New Oxford Review,* May 1996, 19-22.

Williams, David. "The Immutability of Natural Law according to Suárez." *Thomist* 62, no. 1 (January 1998): 97-115.

Wilson, Edward O. *Consilience: The Unity of Knowledge.* New York: Knopf, 1998.

———. *The Diversity of Life.* Cambridge: Harvard University Press, 1976.

———. *On Human Nature.* Cambridge: Harvard University Press, 1978.

———. *Sociobiology: The New Synthesis.* Cambridge: Harvard University Press, 2000.

Wilson, James Q. *The Moral Sense.* New York: Free Press, 1993.

———. *On Character.* Washington, D.C.: American Enterprise Institute Press, 1991.

Wilson, James Q., and Richard Herrnstein. *Crime and Human Nature.* New York: Simon and Schuster, 1985.

Wojtyla, Karol. *Love and Responsibility.* Translated by H. Willetts. New York: Farrar, Straus and Giroux, 1981.

———. "The Person: Subject and Community." *Crisis,* May 1994, 39-43.

Wolfson, Adam. "What Remains of Toleration?" *Public Interest,* Winter 1999, 37-51.

Yeago, David. "Martin Luther on Grace, Law and Moral Life: Prolegomena to an Ecumenical Discussion of *Veritatis Splendor.*" *Thomist* 62 (1998): 163-91.

Yoder, John Howard. *Discipleship as Political Responsibility.* Scottdale, Pa., and Waterloo, Ont.: Herald, 2003.

———. *For the Nations: Essays Public and Evangelical.* Grand Rapids and Cambridge, U.K.: Eerdmans, 1997.

———. *Karl Barth and the Problem of War.* Nashville and New York: Abingdon, 1970.

———. *The Politics of Jesus.* Rev. ed. Grand Rapids: Eerdmans, 1994.

Zeller, Eduard. *The Stoics, Epicureans, and Skeptics.* New York: Russell and Russell, 1962.

Index

abolition of man, 19, 35n., 36, 37, 38, 44n., 66-73, 146, 292
abortion, 2, 15n., 17n., 24, 30, 72n., 163n., 177, 196n., 203, 204, 205, 206, 210, 222n., 225, 235, 253-54, 258, 261n., 262, 265n., 271, 294, 295
Abraham, William, 54n.
accommodation, cultural, 151, 236
Acts 17, 45-54, 83, 85n., 86, 106, 154
Adams, John, 224
Adams, Nathan A., IV, 264
addiction, 191-92
Adversus haereses (Irenaeus), 88-89, 187n.
Adversus Judaeos (Tertullian), 87, 88
Adversus Praxean (Tertullian), 87n.
Aeschylus, 51n.
Akers, Ronald, 181
Altschuler, David, 175n.
Ambrose, 89-90, 137, 147, 151
"American proposition," 299
Anabaptism/Anabaptists, 60n., 64, 137-41, 146n., 147, 149
anarchy, moral or social, 16, 103, 122-23, 165, 183-84, 241-42, 255, 303
antinomianism, 228, 229-30
Appelbaum, Paul S., 179, 182n.
Arendt, Hannah, 229
Areopagus Council, 46-54, 83-85

Aristides, Aelius, 48, 49n.
Aristotle, 38-39, 47n., 79-81, 92n., 93, 146, 164, 198, 200
Arkes, Hadley, 23n., 83
assimilation, cultural, 89-90, 142
Athens, 45-54, 79, 82, 83, 86, 87n., 106, 151n.
Attarian, John, 252n., 257n.
Augustine, 26n., 89, 90, 91, 96, 103, 125n., 137, 147, 150, 154, 161, 236, 303n., 305-7, 308
authority: denial of, 241; divine, 128, 162, 241, 303; legitimacy of, 96; moral, 102, 160, 162, 168, 237, 294, 296; political, 116-17, 163-64, 166, 234, 310n.; scriptural, 96, 213; theological, 102
autonomy, 17, 22, 27, 41, 97, 107, 124n., 133, 143, 147, 153, 195, 197n., 210, 226-31, 241, 288, 293, 303, 304, 312, 313, 315

Babel, 240-41
Backus, Irena, 119n.
Bailey, Richard, 239
Balaban, Evan, 183
Barmen Declaration, 126, 129
Barrett, C. K., 52n.
Barth, Karl, 22, 113n., 114n., 126-32, 134, 136n., 137n., 139, 153
Battin, Margaret, 288

333